People Get Ready!
A New History of Black Gospel Music

Gwen Ansell:

Soweto Blues: Jazz, Popular Music, and Politics in South Africa

Donald Bogle:

Toms, Coons, Mulattoes, Mammies, and Bucks:
An Interpretive History of Blacks in American Films

Isabelle Leymarie:

Cuban Fire: The Story of Salsa and Latin Jazz

Richard Palmer:

Sonny Rollins

Oscar Peterson with Richard Palmer:

A Jazz Odyssey: My Life in Jazz

George Shearing with Alyn Shipton:

Lullaby of Birdland: An Autobiography

Alyn Shipton:

A New History of Jazz

John White:

Artie Shaw: His Life and Music

Douglas Wolk:

James Brown's Live at the Apollo

PEOPLE GET READY!

A New History of Black Gospel Music

Robert Darden

continuum

NEW YORK • LONDON

2010

The Continuum International Publishing Group Inc
80 Maiden Lane, New York, NY 10038

The Continuum International Publishing Group Ltd
The Tower Building, 11 York Road, London SE1 7NX

www.continuumbooks.com

Printed in the United States of America

Library of Congress Cataloging-in-Publication Data

Darden, Robert, 1954–
People get ready : a new history of black gospel music / Robert Darden.
   p. cm.
 Includes bibliographical references and index.
 ISBN 0-8264-1436-2 (hardcover : alk. paper)
 ISBN 978-0-8264-1752-7 (paperback : alk. paper)
  1. Gospel music—History and criticism. I. Title.
ML3187.D37 2004
782.25409—dc22

                       2004012677

People Get Ready!
A New History of Black Gospel Music
is dedicated to my highly musical son,
Robert Van Darden,
who has always been interested
in the roots of rock and roll.
I hope this helps,
Van.
—Dad

When I hear music, I fear no danger. I am invulnerable. I see no foe. I am related to the earliest times and to the latest.

—Henry David Thoreau

Special thanks . . .

- To my preternaturally patient wife, Mary.
- To my parents, Robert and Joann Darden, who introduced me to Mahalia Jackson.
- To Baylor University, for two summer sabbaticals, and much more.
- To the English Department at Baylor University.
- To the Baylor Institute for Faith and Learning.
- To the staff of the libraries at Baylor University, especially the invaluable folks at Interlibrary Loan, who brought the world to Waco.
- To Suzanne Flandreau, Librarian and Archivist at the Center for Black Music Research at Columbia College, Chicago.
- To the staff of the various libraries in the University of North Carolina at Chapel Hill.
- To the staff at the Library of Congress and the National Archives.
- To Stephanie Smith at the Smithsonian Institution's Folklife Center.
- To the staff at the Hogan Jazz Archive at Tulane University.
- To Katie Buchanan, RA extraordinaire.
- To Petra Carey, Justin Jones, Crystal Carter, Meg Kirkendall, Casie Beasley, Justin Raab, Holly Vargo, and Jayne Lawrence.
- To D.A. Johnson (Malaco Records), Tracy Milton at AIR Gospel, and Dalia Glickman at Verity for the great photographs.
- To my long-suffering friends and family members.
- To the kind and supportive folks at Seventh & James Baptist Church.
- And to you . . .

Contents

Preface

A few years after my parents were first married, they finally splurged and purchased a high-fidelity record player. First lieutenants' salaries didn't stretch far, even in the mid-1950s, so they bought their albums carefully. One of the very first LPs they bought was by Mahalia Jackson. I'm pretty sure it was one of her Apollo releases rather than one of the early Columbia albums because it's the Apollo stuff that still gets me, forty-five years later.

The Air Force is a great life for a kid. The U.S. military was integrated long before the rest of the country, and I never saw or heard any prejudice, save for the years we didn't live in military housing. As kids, we were in and out of one another's houses, and I remember hearing black gospel music in the homes of my friends Brian Wertz and Joe Davis. When I became a drummer, soul music was big, and I recognized the sound behind the songs of my heroes, Wilson Pickett, Sam and Dave, the Staple Singers, and Solomon Burke. The first time I got to play the drums on our church choir's mangled version of "Oh Happy Day," I was hooked. And when I finally heard Andrae Crouch and the Disciples in concert, I thought, "This is what heaven must sound like."

When I became the gospel music editor of *Billboard* magazine, one of the perks was that I got to talk to my heroes—Andrae, Pops Staples, Shirley Caesar, Kirk Franklin, Twinkie Clark, the Reverend James Cleveland, Vickie Winans, Tramaine Hawkins, Albertina Walker, and the rest. I'm sure I came across like a blithering fan rather than a serious reporter.

People Get Ready! A New History of Black Gospel Music is an attempt to combine fan and reporter.

Even as someone who had loved this music all his life, there was still so much I didn't know. I wanted to find out how it got from western Africa to the South Side of Chicago. What happened to the great quartets of the 1950s and 1960s? How did we get from the spirituals to gospel? And what was this minstrel thing all about?

Fortunately, I was able to stand on the backs of several generations of extraordinary researchers, people like Dena Epstein, Eileen Southern, Horace Boyer, Anthony Heilbut, Ray Funk, Kip Lornell, Alan Lomax, Doug Seroff, Bernice Johnson Reagon, Portia Maultsby, Paul Oliver, Kerill Leslie Rubman, and many more. God bless you all for your tireless work. On the other hand, whenever I'd follow a particularly promising rabbit trail, hot on the scent of a new connection, I'd usually find one of those names at trail's end. If I was going to try and cover the entire history of gospel music, I knew I'd never be able to give the detail that Boyer gives the Golden Age or Lornell gives Memphis or Epstein gives the colonial American South.

Nor was I much interested in writing an encyclopedia of gospel music. Unless you had several volumes to work with (or one very big volume), the end result would be little more than a laundry list of names, album titles, and record labels.

What I really wanted to do was somehow put it all in order, find the connections, and tell the stories of some of the most fascinating people on the planet. *People Get Ready!* is an attempt to learn a little more about some of the most influential people in gospel music, why they did what they did—and how they got over. To do that, I felt like I had to start at the beginning, in Africa. From there, I followed the connections, sound to sound, movement to movement, trend to trend.

What I found thrilled me. I found a people so extraordinary that they could make something out of nothing. When denied a spoken language, they created a language of song of such complexity that researchers are still trying to tease out its meanings. When denied access to religion, they assembled snippets and bits and molded them into a religion that sustained them through America's darkest hours, slavery, and Jim Crow (and, in my opinion, created a theology closer to first-century Christianity).

This is not a musicological study, though there is a little music theory. This is not a straight chronological narrative, though there is some of that, too. What I went searching for were the stories behind the people. I followed every lead looking for personal information on seminal figures like Arizona Dranes, Blind Willie Johnson, and Sister Rosetta Tharpe. I wanted to know where the ferocious, roaring voices of June Cheeks and Archie Brownlee came from. I was interested in the *who, what, where,* and *when.* I was fascinated by the *why* and *how* of gospel.

I don't think I fully answered any of my questions.

But I had a wonderful time trying.

—Robert Darden
Waco, Texas
February 2004

Chapter One

Why Gospel Music?

Black music is unity music. It unites the joy and the sorrow, the love
and the hate, the hope and the despair of black people; and it moves
the people toward the direction of total liberation. It shapes and de-
fines black being and creates cultural structures for black expression.
Black music is unifying because it confronts the individual with the
truth of black existence and affirms that black being is possible only
in a communal context.

> —James H. Cone, *The Spirituals and the Blues: An Interpretation*[1]

Among the richest of the lavish gifts Africa has given to the world is
rhythm. The beat. The sound of wood on wood, hand on hand. That
indefinable pulse that sets blood to racing and toes to tapping.

It is rhythm that drives the great American musical exports, the spiritual
(and, by extension, gospel), the blues, jazz, and rock and roll.

But first you *must* have the spirituals—religion with rhythm.

In the course of these pages, I will attempt to show the evolution of a musical
style that only occasionally slows down its evolution long enough to be classified
before it evolves yet again. In historical terms, spirituals emerged from African
rhythm, work songs, and field hollers in a remarkably short time—years, perhaps
days—after the first African slaves landed on American shores. From the spirituals sprang not just their spiritual heir jubilee, but jazz and blues. And gospel
music in its modern forms morphed from the spirituals, the blues, jubilee,
and—of course—African rhythm.

What today's gospel music *is* and what it is *becoming* is part of the continuing
evolution of African-American music. Religion with rhythm.

Still, why bother with ancient history?

Why study the superstitious chants from the darkest period of American
history? Why read about a genre of music that now includes less than ten percent

of all recorded music? Why invest in a chronology of spirituals and gospel music at all? What do they matter?

At the end of my research, this is what I discovered. Or, more accurately, this is what I *am* discovering, because assembling a comprehensive overview of spirituals and gospel has been a heady journey of gradual revelations and delayed insights.

1. For those of us living 150 years after slavery (but only fifty years after the end of the equally heinous Jim Crow laws), the spirituals are an uncensored, unedited glimpse into the hearts and minds of slaves.

Composer James Weldon Johnson writes that only in the spirituals was the illiterate slave given the freedom to dream his (and her) dreams:

> . . . [H]e uttered his despair and prophesied his victories; he also spoke the group wisdom and expressed the group philosophy of life. Indeed, the Spirituals taken as a whole contain a record and a revelation of the deeper thoughts and experiences of the Negro in this country for a period beginning three hundred years ago and covering two and a half centuries. If you wish to know what they are you will find them written more plainly in these songs than in any pages of history.[2]

John Wesley once called the institution of slavery "the vilest that ever saw the sun," but notes that slavery did not destroy the slave. In fact, John Lovell, Jr., argues that it provided the impetus for unparalleled poetic expression:

> In a sense, the cruelty, malice and bitterness of American slavery; its frenzied effort to shut out all hope of freedom from the black man in a land of the free; its vast and vain expenditure of energy to block every channel by which chattels could become men and spiritual personalities, all these helped to make the black spiritual more colorful and intense.[3]

And they did it under the very noses and in the most repressive "Big Houses" of their masters.

We have only the vaguest inklings of what most spirituals actually meant. In a land where literacy for slaves was forbidden and even the most oblique talk of freedom was punishable by death, slaves developed an extraordinary secret language, a language so rich with meaning and so complex in composition that the lyrics defy explanation today.

Slaves used the spirituals to convey not just religious truth but information vital for survival in the face of ferocious oppression. While W. E. B. Du Bois and Harriet Tubman hint at the meanings of certain spirituals in their writings, few spirituals have been explicitly deciphered. And why should slaves and ex-slaves share that coded information? Betrayed by whites from their arrival in the colonies, through the Civil War, and into the 1960s, an inadvertent slip of the tongue to even a sympathetic white person could ultimately mean the closing of a stop on the Underground Railroad or the lynching of a friend in Selma.

Even Lydia Parrish, whose *Slave Songs of the Georgia Sea Islands* was the last great collection of uncollected spirituals, found penetrating that unwritten code of silence difficult at best:

> There are survivals of African songs on the coast of Georgia. But let no outsider imagine they can be heard for the asking. From experience I know this to be true. It took me three winters on St. Simon's to hear a single slave song, three times as many winters to see the religious dance called the ring-shout, still more winters to unearth the Buzzard Lope, and similar solo dances, and the game songs known as ring-play.[4]

But there is one song where—perhaps, just perhaps—the *omerta* has been broken. The survival of even one such revelation is profoundly instructional even today.

It is found in *Follow de Drinkin' Gou'd*, a publication of the Texas Folk-Lore Society, from 1928. Editor J. Frank Dobie, a much-lauded historian himself, called H. B. Parks's article in that issue "the most original contribution ever printed by the Society."[5]

Parks writes that he first heard "Foller the Drinkin' Gou'd" in 1912 from a small African-American boy gathering sticks in the Big Rich Mountains, near the Tennessee/North Carolina border. The boy sang,

> *Foller the drinkin' gou'd*
> *Foller the drinkin' gou'd*
> *No one know, the wise man say,*
> *Foller the drinkin' gou'd*[6]

"It is very doubtful if this part of the song would have attracted anyone's attention," Parks writes, "had not the old grandfather, who had been sitting on a block of wood in front of the cabin, slowly got up and, taking his cane, given the boy a sound lick across the back with the admonition not to sing that song again."

The old man refused to tell Parks why he had silenced the little boy.

A year later, Parks was in Louisville and heard the same refrain again from an African-American fisherman sitting on the Louisville docks. The fisherman, too, refused to discuss the song.[7]

In 1918, Parks heard the tune yet again from two teenage African-American boys in Waller, Texas, who claimed they'd heard it from a traveling evangelist. They knew nothing of the song's origins.[8]

Finally, Parks befriended an old African-American gentleman in College Station, Texas, a man who had known many freed slaves in his youth.

"He said that just before the Civil War, somewhere in the South, he was not just sure where, there came a sailor who had lost one leg and had the missing member replaced by a peg-leg," Parks writes. "He would appear very suddenly at some plantation and ask for work as a painter or carpenter." The peg-legged man was welcomed everywhere by the slave owners for his skills. He'd quickly make friends with the slaves and soon all were singing "Foller the Drinkin' Gou'd." After a week or two, the sailor would leave as mysteriously as he'd arrived.

"The following spring nearly all the young men among the slaves disappeared and made their way to the north and finally to Canada by following a trail that had been made by the peg-leg sailor and was held in memory by the Negroes in this peculiar song," Parks concludes.[9]

This is all of the song Parks's new friend was able to recall:

1. *When the sun come back*
   When the firs' quail call
   Then the time is come
   Foller the drinkin' gou'd

Chorus:

   Foller the drinkin' gou'd
   Foller the drinkin' gou'd
   No one know, the wise man say,
   Foller the drinkin' gou'd

2. *The riva's bank am a very good road*
   The dead trees show the way
   Lef' foot, peg foot goin' on
   Foller the drinkin' gou'd

Chorus

3. *The riva ends a-tween two hills*
   Foller the drinkin' gou'd
   'Nuther riva on the other side
   Follers the drinkin' gou'd

Chorus

4. *Wha the little riva*
   Meet the grea' big un
   The ole man waits—
   Foller the drinkin' gou'd[10]

Parks's family had been connected with the Underground Railroad, and a great-uncle remembered a story from the annals of the Anti-Slavery Society about a peg-legged sailor, Peg Leg Joe, who made frequent trips south, encouraging slaves to flee to Canada.[11]

"The main scene of his activities was in the country immediately north of Mobile, and the trail described in the song followed northward to the head waters of the Tombigbee River, thence over the divide and down the Tennessee River to the Ohio," Parks records.

> It seems that the peg-legged sailor would go through the country north of Mobile and teach this song to the young slaves and show them a mark of his natural left foot and the round spot made by the peg-leg. He would then go ahead of them northward and on every dead tree or other conspicuous object he would leave a print made with a charcoal or mud of the outline of a human left foot and a round spot in place of the right foot. As nearly as could be found out the last trip was made in 1859. Nothing more could be found relative to this man.[12]

"The Negro at College Station said that the song had many verses which he could not remember," Parks adds.

> He quoted a number which, either by fault of memory or secret meaning, are unintelligible and are omitted. The ones given are in the phonetic form used by the College Station Negro and become rather simple when is told that the "drinkin' gou'd" is the Great Dipper, that the "wise man" was the peg-leg sailor, and that the admonition is to go ever north, following the trail of the left foot and the peg-leg until "the great big 'un" (the Ohio) is reached, where the runaways would be met by the old sailor.[13]

Think about it. You're an illiterate slave. Maps are forbidden, even if you *could* read them. You're half starved and not even permitted shoes for fear you'll escape. But by traveling at night, following Polaris, the North Star, you'll encounter a series of clearly defined natural landmarks and maybe—just maybe—you'll make it to freedom.

This is a stunning revelation—if true. Wise slaves and former slaves (Texas was, after all, still in the throes of Jim Crow at the time of this article) were masters of self-preservation. Perhaps "Follow the Drinkin' Gourd" means nothing of the kind. Perhaps the old gentleman told Parks what he wanted to hear.

But perhaps it means—as all the best spirituals and gospel music mean—something more still.

Perhaps "Follow the Drinkin' Gourd" and all of the spirituals and gospel music are a secret map out of slavery for all of us, whatever that slavery might be. The lyrics provide a map for freedom for even those of us who don't yet understand them.

If that is indeed the case, then that is yet another compelling argument for their preservation and study.

John Lovell, Jr., says the body of known spirituals comprise "an epic tradition in the class of the Iliad, the Songs of Roland, or the Lays of the Nebelungs."[14]

To know, even a little, the African American, you *must* be familiar first with the spirituals and—later—gospel music.

2. **To understand the historic (and ongoing) psychic damage caused by the demonic institutions of slavery and Jim Crow on America today, it is necessary to study the most powerful contemporary folk expressions of the people most oppressed by these institutions: the spirituals and gospel music.**

Jim Wallis of *Sojourners* once called racism "America's original sin"—"The United States of America was established as a white society, founded upon the genocide of another race and then the enslavement of yet another."[15]

While Wallis probably wouldn't use it, the choice of the word *demonic* is not accidental or casual. In his dissertation "A Tillichian Analysis of White Racism in the South," Albert Truesdale applies theologian Paul Tillich's formula for identifying the demonic in Nazi Germany to slavery and Jim Crow practices in the American South. According to Truesdale, save for the few shining years of Reconstruction, the white South burned considerable energy and resources through the civil rights era denying African Americans access to every comparable "sphere of life identified by the white community as essential to human dignity."[16] The end result, he argues, was that "The creed of white supremacy, by which the South chose to order its society, was a confession of faith."[17]

Of course, as Truesdale points out, the creed ultimately and utterly failed. But when every force in a community—social, spiritual, emotional, creative—is aligned and arrayed in single-mindedly evil behavior, Walter Winks argues that the resulting mob mind-set must be called "demonic."[18] And to fight the supernatural, you must employ the supernatural.

The exceptional historian/soldier Col. Thomas W. Higginson was one of the first to identify the sacred music of African-American slaves. During the Civil War, Higginson writes poignantly about the music of an African-American regiment. And, inherent in what is perhaps the earliest reference to this music as a "spiritual" is this implied sense of the supernatural. He calls these songs "spiritual incantations."[19]

For Cheryl A. Kirk-Duggan, spirituals are "chants of collective exorcism." They are religious incantations even now, she writes, providing indelible images of dogs tearing flesh and high-pressure hoses scouring the skin of people of color singing spirituals:

> . . . Spirituals exposed past injustice and foreshadowed modern racism. People sang Spirituals during the events of 1954–55: Brown v. Board of Education, the Montgomery bus boycott, and the murder of Emmett Till. Singing the Spirituals served as a badge of honor and a flag of defiance when the 101st Airborne troops monitored the halls at Central High for the safety of the Little Rock Nine. From Albany to Birmingham, Greensboro, and Raleigh, freedom fighters sang

freedom songs during the sit-ins and boycotts, the passing of civil rights legislation and the Interstate Commerce Commission desegregation rulings (1957–62). During the March on Washington (1963), thousands of witnesses to the great proclamations for peace, justice and freedom sang. During the Mississippi Freedom Summer led by members of the Mississippi Freedom Democratic Party, even on the floor of the Democratic Convention at Atlantic City, people sang the Spirituals (1964).[20]

Why? Why did the freedom riders choose century-old slave songs instead of the wealth of instantly recognizable modern music available to them?

Because—just as they had done a century earlier—these songs succeeded. Just as slavery was overcome—or "exorcized"—so were the Jim Crow laws and legalized segregation overturned (in part) through the singing of spirituals and gospel songs.

W. C. Handy ("The Father of the Blues") once said on a radio broadcast that he was always inspired by spirituals—and that spirituals did more for the slave's emancipation than all of the guns of the Civil War.[21]

If the Civil War was waged over slavery, it lasted not five years but continued in the South twenty times beyond that. Some in the South spent 100 years fighting against freedom for African Americans. But that 100-year struggle created a cauldron where a marginalized and despised population—despite lynchings, repressive laws, and white-only drinking fountains—brewed all of the great national musics of the United States of America: spirituals, gospel, the blues, jazz, and rock and roll.

3. To truly understand American music, you must first attempt to understand the spirituals and gospel music.

The famed theologian Dietrich Bonhoeffer once called the spirituals the most "influential contribution" made by African Americans to American Christianity.[22]

How far back does that influence go? Consider these learned opinions by three legendary figures:

In 1893, famed Czech composer Antonín Dvořák told the *New York Herald*, "In the Negro melodies in America I discover all that is needed for a great and noble school of music. . . . There is nothing in this whole range of composition that cannot be supplied with themes from this source. This must be the real foundation of any serious and original school of composition to be developed in America."[23]

In 1903, before the widespread acceptance of blues and jazz, W. E. B. Du Bois wrote :

> Little of beauty has America given to the world save the rude grandeur God himself stamped on her bosom; the human spirit in this new world has expressed itself in vigor and ingenuity rather than beauty. And so by fateful chance the

Negro folk-song—the rhythmic cry of the slave—stands today not simply as the sole American music, but as the most beautiful expression of human experience born this side of the seas. It has been neglected, it has been, and is, half despised, and above all it has been persistently mistaken and misunderstood; but notwithstanding, it still remains as the singular spiritual heritage of the nation and the greatest gift of the Negro people.[24]

In the chapters to come, musicians, commentators, musicologists, and composers alike will testify to the origins of modern music, roots that spread through the fertile soil of gospel music, deeper into the dark loam of the spirituals, and down into the very bedrock of original African music itself—religion with rhythm.

Influential writers such as Frederick Ramsey and Charles Edward Smith, Wilder Hobson, Abbe Niles, Miles Mark Fisher, and others may trace the specifics of that musical progression in impressively scholarly terms, but even the amateur can hear in the few extant recordings of authentic spirituals and the early gospel recordings, the foundational elements of authentic American music—improvisation, call and response, the free use of flatted sevenths, and perhaps above all, rhythm.

Or, as the legendary bluesman John Lee Hooker once told *Down Beat* magazine, "You take spirituals and the blues. Maybe I'm wrong, but I think I'm right—the blues come from spirituals. They are the background of all music."[25]

The spirituals and gospel music endure because they matter, because their appeal, their power, cut across the generations, across racial and religious lines, across the ages, across the oceans.

A final example.

Included in *The Story of the Jubilee Singers, With Their Songs*, is "I'm Troubled in Mind":

I'm troubled, I'm troubled, I'm troubled in mind, If Jesus don't help me, I surely will die.
O Jesus, my Savior, on thee I'll depend, when troubles are near me, you'll be my true friend.
I'm troubled, I'm troubled, I'm troubled in mind, If Jesus don't help me, I surely will die.
When ladened with trouble and burdened with grief, To Jesus in secret I'll go for relief.
I'm troubled, I'm troubled, I'm troubled in mind, If Jesus don't help me, I surely will die.

J. B. T. Marsh, who wrote the history of the Fisk Jubilee Singers, also collected many of their songs. Of "Troubled in Mind" he writes:

The person who furnished this song (Mrs. Brown of Nashville, formerly a slave), stated that she first heard it from her old father when she was a child. After he had been savagely whipped—which happened all too often—he always went and sat upon a certain log near his cabin, and with the tears streaming down his cheeks, sang this song with so much pathos that few could listen themselves without weeping from sympathy; and even his cruel oppressors were not wholly unmoved.[26]

Even today, it is difficult to think of that white-haired old gentleman, his back in bloody tatters, whispering this spiritual to Jesus.

And here's the amazing thing: *That heart-cry endures.* More than a century later, it is still sung.

Somewhere between slavery and the 1930s, I believe that the song changes into "Trouble So Hard." Or perhaps this is a different spiritual altogether. Or perhaps, as we shall see in the pages ahead, the great spirituals were never sung the same way twice—snippets and couplets from one spiritual slide easily and naturally into another. But the feel of the song, the progression, the core of the song remains the same.

The Library of Congress, along with Rounder Records, has released a series of projects recorded in the days before television or (in many areas) radio. Much of the music was originally collected by the legendary John Lomax and his son Alan Lomax, who lugged primitive recording equipment across rural America.

In the 1930s, they recorded Vera Ward Hall just outside Livingston, Alabama, singing more than fifty mostly a cappella spirituals, blues, and children's songs. Included on *Afro-American Spirituals, Work Songs, and Ballads*[27] is "Trouble So Hard." It is an electrifying performance, transcendent in the pain and loss apparent in every word:

> *Oh Lord, trouble so hard*
> *Oh Lord, trouble so hard*
> *Don't nobody know my troubles but God*

In *Our Singing Country,* the Lomaxes write that after repeated visits, Hall, a tiny former slave, finally felt comfortable enough to talk in poignant detail about her life:

> I been drug about and put through the shackles, till I done forgot some my children's names. My husband died and left me with nine children, and none of 'em could pull the others out of the fire iffen they fell in. I had mo'n that, but some come here dead and some didn't. Dey ain't a graveyard in this here settlement where I ain't got children buried, and I got children dead in Birmingham and Bessemer.
>
> I mos' blind now and I can't hear good and I ain't never read no verse in no Bible in my life, 'cause I can't read. I sets 'cross the road here from the church and can't go 'cause I'm cripple and blin', but I hear 'em singin'.[28]

The spiritual reappears—though it never really disappears—as a blues song. In *Conversation with the Blues,* revered blues artist Muddy Waters tells Paul Oliver that he sang it as a child growing up in Mississippi's cotton fields:

I'm troubled, I'm all worried in mind
And I never been satisfied, I jest can't keep from cryin'.[29]

It shows up again on Big Bill Broonzy's *Black, Brown and White* as "Trouble in Mind" from 1956.[30]

Finally, Vera Hall's original vocal track resurfaces on techno artist Moby's masterful CD *Play*[31] as "Natural Blues":

Oh Lord, trouble so hard
Oh Lord, trouble so hard
Don't nobody know my troubles but God

The moan from more than seventy years in the distant past helps *Play* sell millions of copies and win a Grammy.

Why? Because this music cuts through every cultural boundary, across every conceivable prejudice, through time itself.

Christa K. Dixon once heard a Dutch concentration camp survivor tell a conference on African-American literature how the humming of the spiritual "Steal Away" "was the code which helped 200 women in the barracks of a German concentration camp preserve their 'soul' while their bodies were submitted to a brutal process ending in annihilation."[32]

In *Deep River,* Howard Thurman tells the story of a visit to India by a group of African Americans. While there, the group called on Mahatma Gandhi. The great man graciously received them, then requested that they sing "Were You There When They Crucified My Lord."[33]

Two nights after the assassination of Dr. Martin Luther King, Jr., Nina Simone performed before a sold-out auditorium in Westbury Music Fair on Long Island. She, like so many other African Americans across the country, closed her concert with the famed gospel song, "Precious Lord, Take My Hand."[34]

When the 1968 riots threatened to burn Detroit to ashes, African-American DJ Martha Jean (The Queen) Steinberg is credited as the most significant calming influence in the city, staying at her microphone hour after hour, playing gospel music and praying with her listeners.[35]

When an African American, James Charles Evers, strode across the stage at Jackson State College to accept the "Loyalist" Democratic party's nomination for governor of Mississippi in 1971, Fannie Lou Hamer, civil rights freedom fighter, broke into "Precious Lord, Take My Hand" and the two embraced on stage to the cheers of the thousands present at the historic occasion.[36]

In the hours following the 9/11 disasters, people all over America struggled with their response. Many, like sociologist Dane Archer at the University of California, Santa Cruz, chose spirituals or gospel music. That evening, Archer was scheduled to teach the first session of his course, "Violence, War and Peace." Just before the first shaken students arrived, Archer retitled the course "On Higher

Ground"—fifteen ways the world is a safer place because of the efforts of a small group of individuals who fought for social change. The class began with Aretha Franklin's soaring rendition of "On Higher Ground."[37]

When the Library of Congress inaugurated the National Recording Registry in January 2003, it included fifty recordings from more than 100 years of American recording, beginning with a trio of cylinders recorded by Thomas A. Edison in 1888. In the opinion of the Library of Congress and their array of experts, among the greatest recordings in history are "Swing Low, Sweet Chariot" by the Fisk Jubilee Singers (1909), recordings of spirituals by John and Ruby Lomax in 1939, and *Precious Lord: New Recordings of the Great Gospel Songs of Thomas Dorsey, Marion Williams, and Others* from 1973—not to mention seminal recordings from gospel-influenced artists such as Aretha Franklin, Ray Charles, Elvis Presley, and several blues artists.[38]

And finally, it was to the spirituals that Dr. King turned in the towering "I Have a Dream" speech that brisk April day in Washington, D.C., so many years ago:

> . . . when we allow freedom to ring, and we let it ring from every village and every hamlet, from every state and every city, we will be able to speed up that day when all of God's children, black men and white men, Jews and Gentiles, Protestants and Catholics, will be able to join hands and sing in the words of the old Negro spiritual: "Free at last, free at last. Thank God Almighty, We're free at last."

> *Surely been 'buked*
> *And surely been scorned*
> *Thank God A'mighty, I'm free at last.*
>
> *But still my soul is a-heaven born,*
> *Thank God A'mighty, I'm free at last*
>
> *Free at last, free at last*
> *Thank God A'mighty, I'm free at last.*
>
> *If you don't know that I been redeemed,*
> *Thank God A'mighty, I'm free at last.*
>
> *Just follow me down to Jordan's stream,*
> *Oh, Thank God A'mighty, I'm free at last.*
>
> *Free at last, free at last*
> *Thank God A'mighty, I'm free at last.*[39]

Why study the spirituals and gospel music?
How can we not?

Chapter Two

Gospel's African Roots

We are almost a nation of dancers, musicians, and poets. Thus every great event, such as a triumphant return from battle, or other cause of public rejoicing is celebrated in public dances which are accompanied with songs and music suited to the occasion. . . .

—Olaudah Equiano, *Africa Remembered*[1]

I learned an African chant from an old Negro woman in Waco, Texas, who had heard it in her childhood. Her grandmother had got it from an old man who had been brought from Africa as a slave. The woman who sang it for me could explain nothing of what the words meant or how they should be spelled. It seems to be a combination of African and English. The air recalls the beating of tom-toms in African jungles.

> *Go fay, go fay!*
> *Ingo-ango fay!*
> *Circle this house in a hoo-sal lay*
> *In a-ingo-ango fay.*
> *Go fay, go fay!*
> *Ingo-ango fay!*
> *Will jew my 'ligion away.*
> *Mumbi, kiki, joki lo,*
> *In a-ingo-ango fay!*

—Dorothy Scarborough[2]

It begins where it *all* began—Africa. The unique combination of music, religion, and worldview necessary to create both spirituals and gospel begins thousands of years ago on the African continent. If, as some have said, that music is the most conservative of all the art forms—change, when it comes at all, comes slowly—then the origins of a distinctively African music are forever lost in the irrecoverable past.

What the early Portuguese (and later, other) freebooters and slavers found along the western African coast from 1500 to 1860 was a complicated patchwork quilt of progressive kingdoms rich in culture and civility, endless forest inhabited only by hunter-gatherer peoples—and everything in between.[3]

The racist myth of savages living in chaotic barbarity, of course, has long since been dashed. Even the early Western explorers gaped in wonder at:

The Wolof States that arose from the ashes of the once mighty Mali Empire along the Senegal River, fielding an army of 100,000 foot soldiers and 10,000 horsemen.[4]

The Oyo, who reigned supreme in the region between the Volta River to the west to Benin and the Niger in the east under various shrewd *alafin*, dominating trade with a ferocious, but well-trained, cavalry.[5]

Beautiful Kumasi, capital of the sprawling **Asante Empire,** where visitors in 1817 encountered a model city, cleaner and more progressive than most in Europe.[6]

The first European and Arab visitors found something else throughout sub-Saharan Africa, from the Cape Verde Islands to the Congo: the ubiquitous presence of music and dance. The cultures, religious beliefs, food staples, architecture, and even clothing may have varied from region to region, but there existed a commonality of music and dance. They also found that—unlike in Europe and North America—most Africans rarely separated music and dance. The two expressive arts are, even now in much of Africa, an interrelated whole, an ongoing expression of daily life.

Not that pan-African music is completely homogeneous. Akin Euba[7] and others are careful to distinguish between the musical styles of those peoples north of the Sahara and those south of the Sahara. Likewise, the music of Egypt and Christian Ethiopia differ markedly from that of the rest of the continent. And from people group to people group within the continent, significant differences exist.

But in the coastal areas south of the Sahara that suffered the most from the depredations of slavers (as we shall see later), there are a remarkable number of musical similarities. Alan Merriam calls them "underlying unities."[8] Melville Herskovits likewise cites the common cultural (including musical) traits of the Akan-Ashanti, Dahomeans, Yoruba, Bini, and others—which he considers the "center of gravity" of the slave trade.[9]

A. M. Jones is even more specific in his exhaustive *Studies in African Music, Volume I.* His careful comparison of two people groups separated by language, geography, and custom—the western Sudanic-speaking Ewe (or Eve) people and the Bantu-speaking Lala tribe—forces him to maintain that even these two distinct nations are singing the "same music":[10]

Anyone with even a moderate ear could tell without analysis that the musics are similar. Anyone familiar with the tribal music of Africa knows that the music of any one tribe is extraordinarily homogeneous in its principles. The Icila dance is absolutely typical of the dancing one may hear on any moonlit night in hundreds upon hundreds of villages in Bantu Africa. That the two musics are one, anybody could have guessed by listening.

. . . in the world of music there exists no barrier at all.[11]

Jones later tracks startling similarities in chorus style, along with "the rhythmic structure, the musical form of the songs, the whole general ethos of the music identity"[12] between these two widely disparate peoples, marveling at the "homogeneity" of the African music system:

If we think of individual tribal music as such, we must think of it as falling within the general context of the unity of African music as a whole. . . . [W]e find it impossible to believe that the emergence of these well-defined chorus styles all over Africa is merely fortuitous. Does it point to a kinship in the remote past? Or is it a key to the movement of migrations?[13]

Perhaps the most definitive work on the subject has been done by musicologists Alan Lomax and Victor Grauer, inventors of Cantometrics. Cantometric ratings enable trained judges to score music on the relative absence or presence of a series of pre-defined musical characteristics.[14] Cantometrics has been widely used to assess musical commonalities and root similarities in the music of hundreds of cultures around the world. Computers then tabulate the results according to a number of factors, including geography.

Using Cantometrics, Lomax reports that "Africa, centering around the style of Equatorial Africa, is seen to be the most homogeneous song style area in the world."[15]

Ultimately, Lomax declares, "The extraordinary homogeneity of African song style is the result of the almost universal use by Africans of the first of these patterns—the highly cohesive, complexly integrated song model."[16]

"Cantometric analysis points conclusively . . . that the main traditions of Afro-American song, especially of the old-time congregational spiritual—are derived from the main African song style model."[17]

Finally, few researchers have studied African music in the field like J. H. Kwabena Nketia, who has traveled throughout the African continent, and who also states definitively:

. . . we find African societies whose musical cultures not only have their historical roots in the soil of Africa, but which also form a network of distinct yet related traditions which overlap in certain aspects of style, practice, basic procedures and contextual similarities. These related musical traditions constitute a family distinct from those of the West or the Orient in their areas of emphasis.[18]

It will take a music as powerful and potent, as deeply interbred and ingrained in the life of a multitude of peoples as this to survive the coming African diaspora and the subsequent efforts of slave owners to eradicate every vestige of Africa from a collective consciousness. (Lomax calls this core African music tradition "the most stable and the most ancient" in the world—and, without a hint of hyperbole—"the most highly developed of the musical languages of mankind."[19])

But survive this tradition does and, in time, it will wield a force and influence like no other in the history of North American music.

At the same time, it is also not wise to think of African music as existing in a vacuum, wholly unchanged and pristine through the centuries. It is unrealistic to believe "that African music was for centuries cut off from the rest of the world; that it existed in some limbo or cultural Garden of Eden, unsullied by outside influences. . . ."[20] Instead, the massive continent was continually subject to outside influences: Hindu merchants from across the Indian Ocean, Moors and other Islamic forces from north and northeast, the Ethiopian Coptic church from the east, and a host of others, as far back as Roman and Grecian times.

Regardless of the specific degree of homogeneity (although this will prove to be an important point in the evolution of spirituals and gospel music and—later—a bone of contention among some scholars), virtually all observers agree that the impact of music on the life of the average African is and has been pervasive to a degree, for the most part, unparalleled in the West. For the African, life and music are inseparable.

The similarities among the dominant musical and dance forms are even more intriguing when the sheer number of African languages is taken into consideration. Various researchers have found hundreds of separate tribes each with its own form of speech among the Bantu languages of western equatorial Africa, hundreds more West African languages, and still more—perhaps hundreds more—languages among the non-Bantu peoples of eastern Africa.[21]

So, when the first Western Europeans left the familiar coasts of the Mediterranean and ventured southward, everywhere and in every language, the explorers, slavers, freebooters, and researchers found the music of Africa.

Of course, the best travel writers don't just observe—they participate. Richard Jobson detailed one such night during his trek along the River Gambia in 1621's *The Golden Trade or A Discovery of the River Gambra, and of the golden trade of the Aethiopians*:

> I went likewise that night [says he], after we had supt, to the maister of the townes house; who had sent unto mee to mend my supper, a brace of Partridges, and finding there the Ballads [*sc.* Xylophones—*Ed.*], or best musicke, and the

younger sort of women gathered together beheld their dancing, and for that they might see we had such pleasures amongst; I tooke one of them by the hand, and daunced with her, whereof they gave great testimony of great gladness, inviting the rest of my company to doe the like.[22]

Among the first to record the commonalities of African music was Mungo Park, a young Scottish doctor with a keen interest in botany. Park followed the Gambia and Niger rivers in 1795, eventually dying in what is now Nigeria in 1806. While traveling inland in West Africa along the Gambia, he spent time among the powerful Mandingoes and described their musical instruments, their love of poetry, and the universal use of rhythm in every song. One distinctive feature of West African music is the African's ability to improvise lyrics. Park's epic quest included a miserably wet day spent under a tree, alone and hungry, deep in the African forest. At last, he was taken in by a kindhearted family of spinners, who fed him. They then created a song about Park's travails, which he later had translated:

> *The winds roared and the rains fell*
> *The poor white man, faint and weary*
> *Came and sat under our tree*
> *He has no mother to bring him milk*
> *No wife to grind his corn*
>
> *Chorus*
>
> *Let us pity the white man*
> *No mother has he to bring him milk*
> *No wife to grind his corn*[23]

Other travelers later discovered that some of their misadventures were made into less flattering songs. Still others reported on the African tradition of singing in code or secret about their oppressors or petty chiefs and officials—apparently part of a long tradition of "secret" communications within African music.

In a relatively few lines, Park may have been the first Westerner to outline several of the basic elements that will identify African music for the next three centuries: alternation of verse and chorus, a preponderance of rhythm, the use of short musical phrases, a call-and-response format, lyrics with secondary meanings, and a joy of improvisation.[24]

Another early explorer, Sir Richard F. Burton, reported the music and dance he heard and saw in the lake regions of central Africa in the late 1850s. On one steamy night west of Lake Victoria, following a light journey and plentiful banquet, he recalled:

> . . . [A] line or a circle of boys and men is formed near the fire, and one standing in the center, intones the song solo, the rest humming a chorus in an

undertone. The dancers plumbing and tramping to the measure with alternate feet, simultaneously perform a treadmill exercise with a heavier stamp at the end of every period: they are such timists that a hundred pair of heels sound like one. At first the bodies are slowly swayed from side to side, presently, as excitement increases, the exercise waxes severe . . . they bend and recover themselves and they stoop and rise to the redoubled sound of the song and the heel-music, till the assembly, with arms waving like windmills, assumes the frantic semblance of a ring of Egyptian Darwayshes.[25]

Burton, who like most of his contemporaries often displayed strong racist tendencies, is still forced to concede that this is still an astonishingly musical country:

. . . it is impossible not to remark the delight which they take in harmony. The fisherman will accompany his paddle, the porter his trudge, and the house-wife her task of rubbing down grain with song; and for long hours at night the peasants will sit in a ring repeating with a zest that never flags, the same few notes and the same unmeaning line. Their style is the recitative, broken by a full chorus, and they appear to affect the major rather than the interminable minor key of the Asiatic.[26]

And later, he offered these general observations about East Africans and their music:

He delights in singing, yet he has no metrical songs: he contents himself with improvising a few words without sense or rhyme, and repeats them till they nauseate: the long, drawling recitative generally ends in "Ah! Ha!" or some such strongly nasalized sound. Like the Somal, he has tunes appropriated to particu-larly occasions, as the elephant hunt or the harvest-home. When mourning, the love of music assumes a peculiar form: women weeping or sobbing, especially after chastisement, will break into a protracted threne or dirge, every period of which concludes with its own particular groan or wail. . . .[27]

What Burton surmised from his epic journeys, later researchers would con-firm—to most Africans, music and dance come as naturally as breathing. It is difficult, if not impossible, to separate religious and secular song in West Africa *because it is* all *religious and it is* all *secular*. John Lovell, Jr., notes that for all of the known spirituals, there are an equal number of surviving African-American "secular" folk songs and that the two forms share many common elements.[28] Few societies in the world approach both secular and religious song and dance with the same vigor as the African.

The indigenous music of Africa, both then and now, has multiple applica-tions. Much of it may be functional and ever-present, but various groups also have a specialized use for music, including a prominent place within various ritualistic or religious customs.

Ultimately, perhaps the main distinction between African and European music is African music's functionality:

"Up to a point all music anywhere has a function: to please the gods, or to make work go better, or simply to give pleasure. Yet there is no doubt that in Africa it is more closely bound up with the details of daily living than in Europe."[29]

All of this bears a direct and verifiable relation to first spirituals and—later—gospel music. But before we can understand spirituals and gospel music, we must first conduct a very quick survey of the roots of the spiritual and gospel—roots sunk deep in the context, lyrics, music, and dance of African music. It is, as one writer puts it, "perilous to speculate about the extent to which the slaves were able to retain certain African customs, adapt new behavioral patterns and amalgamate African and European traditions without examining specific societies in Africa."[30] It is equally perilous—if not impossible—to speculate about African survivals among North American slaves "without a knowledge of the musical traditions of the countries from which the slaves originally came."[31]

Context

For many Africans, religion is not only vital, meaningful, and understandable, "it is not removed from life, but has been deeply integrated into the daily round."[32]

"Ritual is based on worship that expresses itself in song and dance, with possession by the god as the supreme religious experience."[33]

In short, music is inextricably intertwined in African religious practice. Music, as John Roberts wryly notes, is not "essential" in Christian ritual. Impressive, inspiring, sometimes transcendent—yes. Essential—no. Instead, he writes that "many African ceremonies simply could not take place at all without the appropriate music. To give just one example, the spirits are summoned by the drums in both Yoruba and Dahomean ceremonial, each by its own special rhythms. No drums, no spirits—and no ritual."[34]

Roberts offers by way of illustration various Dogon legends, which claim that it was through the drum that God gave Man the gift of speech.

"Words are so powerful, even magical, that African songs tend to be oblique in reference and obscure in meaning, whereas European folk lyrics usually proceed in an orderly narrative fashion."[35]

Consequently, just as African music is ever-present and multifunctional, everyone in a community takes part in the music. The concept of a concert performed solely by skilled musicians to an audience that passively sits and listens is rare in Africa, as is the concept of one voice being more "beautiful" than another. Everyone in a given community sings because everything is part of everyday life. And the most common form of communal singing, particularly in western and central Africa, is what is popularly called antiphonal, or "call and response," a style where the main singer or leader sings a phrase and the group immediately responds.[36]

"Though the call-and-response at one time was probably more common in Europe than now (some scholars see it as closely linked to tribal and communal ways of living)," Roberts notes, "by the time African and European music met in the New World, it had survived in European usage only in a few forms, such as church litanies and ballad refrains."[37]

Not so in most of Africa.

Words

But beyond the style, context, and religiosity of the music, there is a second difference between African folk songs and their Western counterparts, a difference that will, once again, prove significant once the music is carried over the Middle Passage to the Americas. According to Dan Gorlin (founder/director of Alokli West African Dance) and others, the language in many African songs is often old and rife with ancient historical, cultural, and religious references. He likens it to reading Shakespeare or Chaucer without annotations.[38]

"Some African languages have been evolving for a very long time and are interrelated with an elaborate and equally old mythology," Gorlin writes. "As a result, they can be remarkably expressive with very few syllables, so a short phrase may take several lines of English to translate. Languages are often mixed within a single song. It may require a translator fluent in several African tongues to give a subtle interpretation. The original words may have been corrupted or lost altogether when adopted and sung by people who didn't know the original language."[39]

Centuries later, when overseers heard their slaves singing, they dismissed the words out of hand as childish or mere nonsense syllables—thus enabling the slaves to communicate freely. Interestingly enough, still later, researchers trying to prove a white origin to the spirituals hadn't learned the lesson, either. Unable (or unwilling) to recognize or trace "Africanism" in the songs, they too dismissed much of what they heard as merely derivative of Western European sources.

There are many types of African songs and all are sung for various reasons. "Praise songs, songs of insult, boasting songs, litigation songs, mourning songs, topical songs, story songs, love songs, heroic songs and religious songs and the repertoire of drum language constitute an important part of the literature of African peoples created, developed, maintained and transmitted through music," Nketia writes. "There can be no better testimony than that of the central position that music occupies in the cultural life of traditional Africa."[40]

Gorlin, who has studied and taught African song and dance for thirty years, cites a number of examples of the range of lyric content, from "*Ma fui tsa tsa*," an ode to a Mr. Logodzo, who Gorlin says the Eve cite as a "well-known community leader" with many good qualities worth emulating[41] to "*Kayiboe devia me tsi*," a searing attack on a man named Kayiboe, who is accused of molesting a child.[42]

"Songs often praise popular or historic figures or the doers of great deeds, but it takes a truly infamous act to be named in a song like this," Gorlin writes. "Only songs about the most serious crimes will expose the offender by name, since this can effectively destroy a person's life. In those that criticize minor misconduct, singling out individuals is considered unnecessarily rude and limits a song's usefulness. Besides, communities are usually small enough that everyone knows who the song is about anyway."[43]

Shamed and taunted, Kayiboe will eventually leave the village.

Still other songs are inspirational, historic, or religious in nature. In Nigeria in the 1940s, various people groups continued to sing songs about battles from the eighteenth century.[44]

Through the years, researchers have divided the lyrics to most African songs into a series of not always compatible categories. One of what appears to be the most logical of such breakdowns has been proposed by Chief Fela Sowande, who groups song lyrics into the broad categories of ritual, ceremonial, social, functional, and recreational.[45] Of those categories, he writes that "ceremonial" is most often misunderstood by Western readers:

> The ceremonial level consists of a.) public ceremonies which are required in some cases to follow secret rites and thus complete the ritual; and also b.) those ceremonies which have as their focal center the high-ranking spiritual and temporal human regents of psychic forces that control the destinies of the group. Here we have the type of material often referred to as "Praise Songs," but they are more than that. The purpose here is to reactivate and re-energize the psychic links which connect the human representatives with the psychic forces of which they are the regents. Such ceremonies are mostly public, but some have secret rites attached to them as a result of which they are more properly classified under rituals, in so far as the secret rites are concerned.[46]

The words of still other songs sing of governmental edicts and legal slights (real and imagined) from hundreds of years ago.

Explorer/novelist/war correspondent James Barnes took one of the first motion picture cameras to Africa, beginning in April 1913 from Mombassa in then-British East Africa, and emerging in May 1914 at the mouth of the Congo River. Alas, a tape recorder with invaluable tapes was lost, but Barnes took detailed notes about the words and music he heard, which included everything from laments about war to celebrations of food:

"And they love to extemporize, making up such extremely personal lines as 'So-and-so has a big nose,' etc."[47]

Regardless of the category title, the words of most African songs are an integral part of every facet of life. Whether they are singing "cradle songs, songs of reflection, historical songs, fertility songs" or "songs about death and mourning," Samuel Floyd writes that "the aim of African music has always been to translate the experiences of life and of the spiritual worlds into sound, enhancing and celebrating life."[48]

Music

If the songs are ubiquitous, then the music is even more so. The books of the early explorers are filled with the accounts of drums thundering unseen across the forests and savannahs of Africa.

A UNESCO conference in Yaounde, Cameroon, that celebrated the extraordinary diversity and complexity of African music, even among the peoples least touched by the West, cited not just the rhythm-driven African music familiar to even casual listeners, but polyphony of a more contrapuntal nature, harmonies, and a high degree of composition and improvisation—all wrapped in complex melodies.[49]

But until relatively recently, music was infuriatingly ephemeral to those who sought to record and preserve what they heard. Recording devices of any kind were generally not available until the 1890s at the earliest. While the first Western European explorers often wrote about music, there is no way they could make their readers *hear* that music—and few explorers were trained musicians. For the most part, modern researchers must make do with clues in the extant writings of the era, historic artwork and artifacts, and the surviving music in the areas least touched by Western influences. Only by extrapolating from these, and other sources, can we guess what the many and varied musics of Africa sounded like as the first slavers touched on African shores. However, how much that music has changed (either through natural evolution or cultural intrusions) and how representative that surviving musical sample is (depending on the almost unknowable question of how much African music is lost forever) are two questions better left for future researchers.

What is known is still instructive. According to Philip Curtin and others, the great bulk of slaves were taken from along the West African coast, an area stretching from modern Senegal, through southern Angola, but only extending a few hundred miles into the African interior along that coast.[50] That means that the discussion of African music from that time period may be restricted to those nations and kingdoms most affected by slavery.

Fortunately, the kinds of musical instruments used by the various African peoples *are* generally known from historic record (including drawings and carvings) and surviving artifacts. A host of printed resources detail the variety and geographic scope of African musical instruments. The standard classification of instruments by E. M. von Hornbostel and Curt Sachs still remains valid: idiophones (nonmembranous percussion instruments, often made of wood or metal), membranophones (instruments where the sound is created by the vibration of a membrane, including most drums), aerophones (instruments utilizing a column of air as the primary vibrating system, usually accomplished by blowing the air, such as flutes and panpipes), and chordophones (any instrument where the sound is produced by the vibration of a string, including the various forms of harps and lutes), along with at least ten major subdivisions.[51] As Merriam and others point out, African instruments can be found in each category in surprising variety.

Two other general statements have also withstood the test of time. First, in original African music, instrumental soloists and groups have been—and are currently—found in Africa. And second, because there are few songs without words anywhere in Africa, accompanied song is generally considered to be more important than solo instrumental performance.[52]

Beyond those simplistic observations, the problems are quickly made more complex by the differences between even very closely aligned or neighboring people groups. A good example is found in Nigeria, which is dominated by three tribal groups, the mostly Islamic Hausa in the north, the Ibo in the east, and the Yoruba in the west. The Yoruba are known for their mastery of the "talking" drums, the Ibo are famed for their "keyboard dexterity," and the Hausa are famed for their skill at playing various wind and string instruments.[53]

But as Euba writes, "the hour-glass drums used by the *Hausas* had their origins in the dundun drums of the *Yorubas,* and the *Yorubans* have 'borrowed' the *goje,* a string instrument from the *Hausas,* who in turned adopted it from the *Arabs.*"[54] And while there are many similarities with other African music throughout this region, there are some differences in the choral tradition where, in addition to the familiar call-and-response format, many Nigerians sing in unison, with an emphasis on homogeneity.[55] Finally, the Yoruba, Ibo, and Hausa also have different religious beliefs, while the Hausa language differs markedly from the other two.[56]

A number of early writers tried to assign general musical areas within the African continent, large expanses where the music of the various people groups exhibited at least some unifying characteristics. One such attempt identifies eight musical families: Bushman-Hottentot, East Africa, East Horn, Central Africa, West Coast, Sudan Desert, North Coast, and the less well-defined Pygmy.[57] The areas most impacted by the depredations of slavery were, of course, what Merriam calls "West Coast" and, to a lesser degree, "Central Africa."

"It is difficult . . . to know where to draw the line separating the two areas, but the existence of a coastal belt running roughly from . . . the Gambia on the north to Angola on the south, within which music style is reasonably uniform, can certainly be postulated."[58] "Central Africa," by Merriam's definition, includes the Democratic Republic of Congo (formerly Zaire) and the Central African Republic.

It is within the West Coast musical family that various researchers identify what is perhaps the greatest marker of distinctively African music, a marker that will somehow not just endure but flourish in a strange land centuries later. It is a "strong emphasis on percussion instruments," specifically Richard Waterman's concept of "hot rhythm."[59]

Waterman's theories of "hot rhythm" were first published in the *Journal of the American Musicological Society* and have remained pivotal to understanding the distinctives of not just spirituals and gospel, but of blues and jazz as well. Broadly speaking, European music generally only has one rhythm at any given measure, where much of African music is dominated by polyrhythms:

> . . . [while] the accents of European melodies tend to fall either on the thesis or arsis of the rhythmic foot, the main accents of African melodies—especially those of "hot" music—fall between the down- and up-beats. The effect thus produced is that of a temporal displacement of the melodic phrase, in its relationship to the percussion phrase, to the extent of half a beat. The displacement is usually ahead, so that the melodic beat anticipates the percussion stroke, although on occasion the percussion accent is allowed to anticipate the melodic beat. The entire rhythmic configuration is always held together, and the displacement given meaning, by strategically placed melodic accents which coincide with the percussion accents.[60]

The essence of African music, then, is rhythmic tension. Think of the difference between "Tea for Two" and "Oh Happy Day." As John Rublowsky notes, in Western European music, the accents of the melody coincide with the time beats with a metronomic quality. Not so in African music, where the melodic accents are in free rhythm:

"Although the melody itself may be tied to an underlying metronomic beat, this meter does not determine the rhythm. Musical tension is attained by deliberately staggering the main accented beats."[61]

In short, "It don't mean a thing if it ain't got that swing."[62]

Of course, achieving that level of rhythmic freedom requires a single strong, dependable percussion beat, which allows the other musicians to embellish with an array of counter-rhythms.[63]

Related to that are the various musical features of indigenous African music, which Merriam[64] and others have interpreted to help account for the African's love of musical improvisation. He cites a paper by A. M. Jones that maintains that the end result is that in most African songs the melody line in each verse differs slightly.

And despite ferocious attacks on all things African by the slave owners, despite centuries of repression and the deliberate destruction of African culture, language, and religion, Herskovits, Lomax, Waterman, and others believe that this concept of "hot rhythms" endured in the Americas:

> . . . this consists essentially of musical attitudes, values and appreciations carried below the level of consciousness—learned, without having to be taught,

by each generation through imitation of its elders and seldom verbalized or even subjected to conscious scrutiny—it has been relatively impervious to change from without, even by forces strong enough to cause drastic alterations in the contours of the more overt and consciously maintained aspects of African culture.[65]

Or as A. M. Jones writes, "Rhythm is to the African what harmony is to Europeans and it is in the complex interweaving of contrasting rhythmic patterns that he finds his greatest aesthetic satisfaction. . . . [W]hatever be the devices used to produce them, in African music there is practically always a *clash of rhythms;* this is a cardinal principle."[66]

Dance

Uniquely coupled with the music and rhythm of Africa is its dance. In southern Nigeria, for instance, "dance may be taken as the chief method of portraying and giving vent to the emotions, the dramatic instinct and religious fervour of the race."[67] Amaury Talbot says that dance in Africa is what prayer is to many Western European peoples. It enables them to express "their otherwise inarticulate sense of the mystery of existence, the power of the supernatural influences which enfold them, the ecstasy of joy in life—of youth and strength and love—all the deeper and more poignant feelings so far beyond expression by mere words."[68] It is, he says, the spear point where art, life, and the supernatural meet.[69]

The dances described by the likes of Sir Richard Burton, Mungo Park, Henry Stanley, and others appear to closely resemble modern African dances filmed with the latest recording equipment. Jones believes that since so many dances are tied to religious ceremonies, they have had an advantage when compared to other art forms in surviving Western intrusions. Thus, the dances of the Yeve cult of the Ewe (also Eve) people may be a window to the ancient world of African dance.[70]

Talbot's descriptions of dance in southern Nigeria in the 1920s still provide the most vivid re-creation of the dominant form of dance throughout western and coastal Africa. These dances, he writes, appear spontaneously at times of grief and joy, in religious ceremonies, or even when a group of children spontaneously gather.[71]

"To the European eye," he writes, "the ordinary method of dancing appears monotonous and unattractive, since it consists of slowly moving round in a circle—always in the opposite direction to the hands of a clock, *widdershins*—with apparently little variation in the few steps employed. It takes time to appreciate the variety and detail in the different movements and the unceasing, wave-like ripple which runs down the muscles of the back and along the arms to the finger-tips. Every part of the body dances, not only the limbs."[72]

At a victory celebration recorded *In Darkest Africa,* Henry Stanley observes musicians playing drums to accompany an enormous "phalanx" of dancers—

thirty three lines of thirty three men each—stomping in such precision that the ground shook more than fifty yards away:

"I looked at the feet of the men and discovered that each man was forcefully stamping the ground, and taking forward steps not more than six inches long, and it was in this manner that the phalanx moved slowly but irresistibly."[73]

Talbot's description of a particularly widespread dance also perfectly describes the religious dance the "ring shout," which first appeared in the literature during the colonial era in the United States and continues, virtually unchanged, through the modern day. Neither menacing threats from the slave owners nor the seductive attractions of latter-day dances and music have ever fully eradicated this specific dance form among Americans of African descent:

> In some dances the body is held erect, but more commonly the knees are bent. In one variety the main object appears to be never to lift the feet off the ground and to leave a clear, even continuous track. Gestures are rare, and the arms are not used more than the upper part of the body generally.[74]

To the African, dance is—and always has been—more than mere motion. As Sterling Stuckey says, "For the African, dance was primarily devotional, like a prayer. . . ."[75]

It was spontaneous, it was deliberate, it was rarely more than a heartbeat away.

Religion

To the layperson, perhaps the most startling aspect of African life is how many of the nations and people groups are if not wholly monotheistic, at least aware of a primary god above all others. Albert Raboteau writes that in the area of the most severe depredations by slave traders, "similar modes of perception, shared basic principles, and common patterns of ritual were widespread."[76] For all of the witches, forest sprites, and demons that abound in the various mythologies, many of the West African religions shared a belief in a single, most-high god. Even early observers noted the phenomenon: "I have conversed with all ranks and conditions upon the subject of their faith, and can pronounce, without the smallest shadow of doubt, that the belief of one God, and of a future state of reward and punishment, is entire and universal among them."[77]

Alas, only a few first-person accounts of traditional religion by the native peoples of Africa survive. One such account is by Olaudah Equiano, who was kidnapped and enslaved as a boy while living the Benin province (modern Nigeria). Equiano was sold repeatedly and traveled widely before securing his freedom and was eventually involved in the foundation of the Freetown, Sierra Leone, in 1786:

> As to religion, the natives believe that there is one Creator of all things, and that he lives in the sun, and is girded round with a belt, that he may never eat or drink; but according to some, he smokes a pipe, which is our own favorite luxury. They believe he governs events, especially our deaths or captivity; but, as for the doctrine of eternity, I do not remember to have ever heard of it: some however believe in the transmigration of souls to a certain degree.[78]

By contrast, Sir Richard Burton's travels in East Africa into the Lake Regions of central Africa brought him into contact with what he believed were mostly polytheistic societies. "Few, and only the tribes adjacent to the maritime regions, have derived from El Islam a faint conception of the one Supreme."[79]

Perhaps the best-known writer on the topic of African religion is modern theologian John S. Mbiti, who speaks and reads a number of both African and European languages. Mbiti's voluminous research covers more than 300 peoples in Africa, all outside the traditional Islamic and Christian communities. Like Park, he writes that virtually all of these societies have a "notion of God."[80] Since there are no sacred writings in these societies, Mbiti says they are passed on through "proverbs, short statements, songs, prayers, names, myths, stories and religious ceremonies."[81]

Although some societies refer to God as "Mother,"[82] most visualize God as a father, a creator, and a provider in times of need.[83]

"It is generally assumed that God created the heaven as He created the earth. Heaven is the counterpart of the earth, and it is considered by African peoples to be the dwelling place of God. There are stories told all over Africa of how originally heaven and earth were either close together or joined by a rope or bridge, and how God was close to men. These myths go on to explain how the separation came about. . . ."[84]

Certainly, other beliefs were also held. Nketia writes that various nature and prosperity gods are still worshiped among the traditional Ga and Adangme people of Ghana.[85] But a host of researchers on African religion report a general belief in a single (usually) all-powerful god.[86]

One of the most interesting and controversial theories of what will in time be called "slave religion" reportedly shows how the West Africans would eventually adapt so quickly to Christianity once in the Americas and ties that acceptance to both the general African belief in a single creator god and the similarity between the Christian rite of baptism and various West African river cults. In fact, Melville Herskovits writes that in the kingdom of Dahomey, priests of the river cults were among the fiercest opponents of slavery—and were thus actively hunted by slavers to end their resistance. The surviving priests carried their beliefs with them to the Americas.[87] Herskovits also cites ceremonies among the Yoruba, Ashanti, and in Dahomey of many water rituals, including sacred bodies of water requiring pilgrimages and immersion, and then compares them to the importance to allusions of "crossing the River Jordan" found in so many spirituals. Cherokees, whom he mentions many slaves had contact with, also had a river cult.[87]

Ultimately, a generalized picture emerges of the dominant elements of the music, dance, and religion of the majority of the Africans during the time of the slave traders. From this rich mélange sprang the first spirituals and, ultimately, gospel music.

All that remains is for the music to travel from Africa to the New World. It is one of the most shameful journeys in human history.

Slaving

Modern slavery begins with the Portuguese colonization of a few islands in the Gulf of Guinea shortly after 1485. The rich volcanic soils lent themselves to the production of sugar, then a luxury in Europe. But sugar requires vast amounts of backbreaking labor, and few Portuguese were willing to relocate to the tropics. Soon, the settlers were importing a thousand slaves a year from Africa.[88]

The Portuguese originally raided the African coasts for slaves, but the various chieftains quickly convinced the Europeans that it was cheaper to trade than to fight. Luxury goods in demand at African courts included Moorish silk, silver, and other goods, while the rulers of the great states of Mali or Songhay or their tributaries traded anywhere from seven to fourteen slaves per horse, which they prized greatly.[89]

Eventually, sugar production shifted elsewhere, and São Tomé and the other islands should have become backwater footnotes in history. But by the 1570s, the islands had taken on a new role, that of bases for the transport of slaves from Africa to the New World.[90]

Once the great mercantile houses became involved with the exploration (read: exploitation) of Africa, the scope and scale of the trafficking in human cargo exploded. Slavery was fueled by what eventually became known as "the triangular trade," a chillingly efficient commercial system that contributed significantly to the unparalleled technical progress of Western Europe in the eighteenth and nineteenth centuries, although it actually began in a small way as early as the late sixteenth century.[91]

The first "leg" of the triangle began in Western Europe, primarily Liverpool and Bristol, England, where good woven cloth, alcoholic spirits, knives from Sheffield, and a variety of firearms were transported by ship to western Africa where they were exchanged for slaves.

"These slaves were prisoners of war or condemned criminals," Basil Davidson writes. "If they had stayed in West Africa, they would have been domestic or household slaves. . . . African chiefs often exchanged such 'slaves' among themselves. They saw no reason for not selling them to Europeans. The Europeans accordingly found it fairly easy to buy captives."[92]

The second leg of the triangle—the infamous "Middle Passage"—saw these captives transported from Africa to Brazil, the West Indies, or the southern U.S. coastal ports, where they were exchanged by the plantation owners for cotton, sugar, tobacco, rum, and other New World products. From the Americas, the enterprising captains would sail back to Western Europe, their holds primarily laden with slave-grown American products to sell at an exorbitant profit. This was the third and final leg of the triangular trade.[93]

Sometimes the simplest questions are the hardest to answer. How many slaves were torn from Africa and sent to North America? The reason there is no good answer is part and parcel of the enormous ethical and moral issues that stain slavery. To the captains of industry, the plantation owners, and even the great mass of Western Europeans and North Americans at the time, these partic-ular slaves were less than human. Few cared how many were abducted, as long as their sale turned a tidy profit. Consequently, accurate records are rare.

The great chronicler of the African diaspora is Philip D. Curtin, whose pain-staking research has lifted the veil on the Middle Passage, exposing a host of half-understood forces and widely held misconceptions. *The Atlantic Slave Trade: A Census* remains the most comprehensive, exhaustive work on the subject. Curtin spent years gathering existing (usually fragmentary) records and collating them, always with the knowledge that invaluable documents were destroyed, lost, or never kept at all.

Using the more detailed records kept in Brazil (Brazil continued active slav-ing thirty years after the rest of the world), he arrives at the figure of 3,646,800 slaves taken to that country, which is close to earlier estimates from the period provided by Mauro and Goulart.[94] Slaves transported to Spanish Central and South America during the entire period of the slave trade (save for Brazil) total an estimated million and a half.[95] Slaves imported to the British West Indies during this time represent perhaps 1,665,000 more.[96]

While Curtin estimates that in the seventeenth century more than forty per-cent of African slaves were shipped to Brazil, at that time only a tiny percentage were sent to Virginia and South Carolina,[97] the main U.S. ports of entry. By the eighteenth century, South Carolina had become the trade center of the American South—and these slaves apparently came directly from Africa, nearly half from present areas primarily composed of Angola, Bight of Benin (Nigeria, Cameroon, Gabon), the Gold Coast (Ghana), Senegambia (Gambia, Senegal), and the Wind-ward Coast (Liberia, Ivory Coast).[98]

Active slave trading continued in the British Caribbean as well, usually through Jamaica from 1702 to 1807—again, mostly from countries around the Bight of Benin down to Central Africa. As Curtin is quick to point out, however, that is only where the slaves were recorded to have *left* Africa—the remaining records rarely noted where in Africa slaves originally came *from* to be later shipped from ports such as Lagos.[99]

By the first half of the nineteenth century, some better records survive. For instance, the British Foreign Office reported that nearly seventy percent of slaves came from Angola, Congo North, and Mozambique.[100] The slave trade was now dominated by Cuban and Brazilian merchants[101] in part because on March 2, 1807, the United States passed legislation prohibiting the direct importation of slaves into the country. Although slave running continued, numbers probably lessened significantly shortly thereafter. In the United States, a general consensus emerged that it was simply cheaper to encourage slaves to produce more children than to import additional slaves.[102]

How many slaves eventually came into the United States? This is the area that is most complicated of all, says Curtin. Relatively few slaves came directly to the United States from Africa during the seventeenth century.[103] Later, slaves, both unchecked and regulated, came to the United States directly from Africa, through the Caribbean (especially Cuba and Jamaica), and even through Texas. The importation of slaves continued even during Union blockade of the Civil War, although weapons took precedence. Curtin eventually estimates that the direct importation of slaves into the United States from 1451 through the American Civil War into what he calls "British North America" may have totaled about 399,000. But many more came into the United States from Caribbean ports.[104] In all, perhaps just under a million souls were transported from Africa directly or indirectly to North America. J. D. Fage and later writers have accepted Curtin's estimate (which includes a significant plus/minus variable of twenty percent) as the closest scholars may come to a "solid" figure.[105]

(What is the total number of slaves stolen from Africa since the sixteenth century? The documentation suggests a figure near ten million. Curtin takes 269 pages to come to that rough estimate, checking in minute detail an impressive array of sources.[106] This is significantly fewer slaves than most early sources claimed—ranging anywhere from twenty to forty million Africans—but none of those writers cite Curtin's staggering array of sources.)

Regardless of the specific figures, Fage's summary is worth considering. "This was," he writes, "undoubtedly one of the greatest population movements in history, and certainly the largest migration by sea before the great European emigration, also primarily to the Americas, which began to develop after the Napoleanic wars."[107]

Much speculation remains on the identities of the bulk of the original tribes enslaved, but Curtin and others can identify with some certainty that Yoruba, Hausa, Ibo, Bini, Efik, Fanti, Akan, Ashanti, Malinke, Wolof, Bambara, Kru, Mende, Fon, and Gun peoples were heavily taken.[108]

There is, of course, no way to know how many Yoruba or Gun died fighting slavers in their homelands. No accurate records exist of how many Wolof or Ashanti died along the roads to the coast. Nor are there records of how many Ibo or Fanti died shortly after arriving in America, weakened by mistreatment, starved, and exposed to a host of virulent diseases.

However, Curtin believes that, because of extant records kept by the mercantile and trade companies and even the captains themselves, some guess may be made as to the number of slaves who died en route along the Middle Passage. His rough estimates—which are dependent on the port of embarkation, century, and other factors—range from ten to twenty percent known slave losses per voyage. This is an important point, he adds, when historians consider the number of ships that simply vanished.[109] Ironically, mortality rates among slave ship crews was also about twenty percent.[110]

In the end, Curtin believes that the costs of slavery, which were catastrophic in Africa, were also unacceptable in Europe, as any of the great trading houses more concerned with the loss of human life and less concerned with the bottom line easily could have seen:

> If the African disease environment claimed the life of half the European merchants, factors, officials and soldiers sent out to man the slave trading posts, the social cost was already high. If, in addition, the slave trade cost the life of one sailor out of five, each voyage; and if the West Indian disease environment killed about 130 per thousand per annum among the newly arrived soldiers and planters (as British military surveys of the nineteenth century indicate), then the cost to European society was indeed considerable.
>
> It is nevertheless significant that the South Atlantic System was a cruel and wasteful operation—most damaging for the slaves themselves, but deadly even for those who were free and voluntary participants.[111]

Who were these slaves? Researchers know the names of their nations and people groups, but the individual slaves had names as well. They were individuals, tribal leaders, priests, warriors, and farmers. Men, women, and children. Few of their traditional African names survive, but a handful of stories of slaves torn from their homelands do endure.

Philip Quaque—whose letters from 1765–1811 to the Reverend Dr. Daniel Burton of the Society of the Propagation of the Gospel, London, from Cape Coast Castle in the old "Gold Coast" still survive in the SPG's archives. Quaque was a Fanti, at a time when the neighboring Ashanti were in an expansionist mode. He provides a gripping eyewitness account of the funeral of a Gold Coast Fanti chief, which included child sacrifice, and of the Fanti religion itself, which required the constant appeasing of the spirits of the past.[112]

Olaudah Equiano—an Ibo whose memories of his mother reveal a sharp and penetrating intellect:

> I was very fond of my mother, and almost constantly with her. When she went to make these oblations at her mother's tomb, which was a kind of small solitary thatched house, I sometimes attended her. There she made her libations,

and spent most of the night in cries and lamentation. I have been often extremely terrified on these occasions. The loneliness of the place, the darkness of the night, and the ceremony of libation, naturally awful and gloomy, were heightened by my mother's lamentations; and these concurring with the doleful cries of birds, by which these places were frequented, gave an inexpressible terror to the scene.[113]

Osifekunde of Ijebu—who was kidnapped as a child on the coast of Nigeria and later lived in both Brazil and France. His recollections—dated about 1810, though not published for another thirty-five years—talk about the religious practices of the Ijebu. It is rare to find an account of a (former) slave talking about his faith, rather than a Westerner's account of that conversation or an observer simply reporting what he saw on short visits.

The Ijebu, like the Yoruba, acknowledged a single god, supreme in heaven: Obba Oloroun, who had no temples. But it is Oloroun's will, Osifekunde wrote, that governs the universe.[114] More practical are the hundreds of *orisa*, or lesser gods, to whom the Ijebu paid tribute:

The belief in an evil genie exists alongside the adoration of the gods: Elegwa (Yoruba: Elegba or Esu) has neither priests nor temples, but in certain cursed spots, marked by an ugly figure in wood or by some other sign, the passer-by throws down a small loaf which he has soaked in palm oil and circled twice around his head while averting his eyes: it is a sort of expiatory offering which becomes food for the neighborhood dogs.[115]

Granny Judith—was the grandmother of Richard Jones, also known as Dick Look-Up, who was interviewed by the Federal Writers Project in 1937 at the age of ninety-three. Jones recalled in startling detail the stories his grandmother told of Africa:

. . . they had very few pretty things, and . . . they had no red colors in cloth, in fact they had no cloth at all. Some strangers with pale faces come one day and draped a small piece of red flannel down on the ground. All the black folks grabbed for it. Then a larger piece was draped a little further on, and on until the river was reached. Then a large piece was draped in the river and on the other side. They was led on, each one trying to get a piece as it was draped. Finally, when the ship was reached, they draped large pieces on the plank and up into the ship till they got as many blacks on board as they wanted. Then the gate was chained up, and they could not get back.

When they got on board the ship, there were tied until the ship got to sea; then they was let loose to walk about 'cause they couldn't jump overboard.[116]

Ancestor of W. E. B. Du Bois—Although Du Bois never mentions her name, he was haunted by this tiny woman, the wife or mother of his maternal grandfather Tom Burghardt, "who never became reconciled to this strange land; she clasped her knees and rocked and crooned:

Do bana coba—gene me, gene me
Ben d'nuli, ben d' le."[117]

In time, even slavery lost its allure to Western Europeans. Other African products became more valuable, including timber, ivory, and palm oil. First the Danes outlawed slavery in 1792, followed by the British who—in the twin throes of the Industrial Revolution and a sweeping Protestant revivalism—enforced the anti-slaving laws with the corporate zeal of a former addict.[118]

By then, slavery had come to mean something entirely different in the American South.

Slavery on the African continent, while still repugnant, had certain unwritten rules. One of the first Western Europeans to write about those (mostly) universal codes was Mungo Park, who traveled through central African during the peak of British and French slave trading—when 60,000 slaves per year were shipped to the New World.[119] Park wrote that in the lands that he encountered, about one fourth of the population was free, while the remaining three fourths were slaves, who did most of the work:

> I was told, however, that the Mandingo master can neither deprive his slave of life, nor sell him to a stranger, without first calling a palaver on his conduct, or, in other words, bringing him to a public trial; but this degree of protection is extended only to the native or domestic slave. Captives taken in war, and those unfortunate victims who are condemned to slavery for crimes or insolvency, and, in short, all those unhappy people who are brought down from the interior countries for sale, have no security whatever, but may be treated and disposed of in all respects as the owner thinks proper. It sometimes happens, indeed, when no ships are on the coast, that a humane and considerate master incorporates his purchased slaves among his domestics; and their offspring at least, if not the parents, become entitled to all the privileges of the native class.[120]

Throughout western Africa, slaves were regarded as "additions to the social group headed by their master," trusted and loved members of the family unit who could, in time, live to see their descendents free.[121]

"At the highest levels," J. D. Fage writes, "[slaves] could become trusted traders or soldiers or court officials; indeed, they sometimes seem to have been preferred for the important roles. . . ."[122]

But that was not the case in Charleston, South Carolina, or elsewhere in the South. Instead, African slavery had little in common with the brutal North American version. Where in Africa a slave might eventually become wealthy through hard work or become the most trusted adviser of a king, in America slaves would find that their only release was death.

"Even the Arabs," Christopher Small writes,

> whose system of slavery was in many ways closer to the American, were exhorted by the Koran to manumit slaves, and, again slavery was not hereditary. A child

born of slaves could be a full and free member of the household. Those African kings and other rulers who sold prisoners of war and other, to them, surplus subjects to the white adventurers in their huge ships had not the faintest idea of what they were delivering those unfortunates into—a system which equated human beings at best with livestock, to be bought and sold like cattle, not only themselves but their descendants in perpetuity, deprived of any rights through which it might be recognized that they were human. And of course the social and economic ruin brought to West Africa, as one kingdom after another became caught up in the terrible trade, is well documented.[123]

And so, it was with this background that nearly ten million Songhai, Ibo, Yoruba, and Akans left Mother Africa. The songs and rhythms of untold centuries accompanied them across the nightmarish Middle Passage. This opulent heritage, complex and rewarding, driven by rhythm and improvisation, would come to dominate the music of a new world.

Centuries earlier, the conquered Hebrews once cried,

By the rivers of Babylon, there we sat down, yea, we wept, when we remembered Zion.
We hang our harps upon the willows in the midst thereof.
For there they that carried us away captive required of us a song;
and they that wasted us required of us mirth,
saying "Sing us one of the songs of Zion."
How shall we sing the Lord's song in a strange land? (Psalms 137: 1–4)[124]

Somehow a million African slaves, an ocean away from home, shackled in iron and bearing the scars of a thousand cruel whips, *did* sing the Lord's song in a strange land.

"Endowed by African skills and attitudes, he took his misery and grief, his brutal treatment and towering obstacles, and wove them into new songs and melodies."[125]

These "new songs and melodies" became first the spirituals, then gospel music—a new form of hymn for a new world, hymns such as no one had ever heard before.

European music resembles a cathedral, very decidedly a structure, while African music moves like a river, open ended.—Charles Fox[126]

Chapter Three

The Rise of Spirituals in North America

When I was a boy, it was my responsibility to read the Bible to my grandmother, who had been a slave. She would never permit me to read the letters of Paul except, on occasion, the 13th chapter of First Corinthians. When I was older, this fact interested me profoundly. When at length I asked the reason, she told me that, during the days of slavery, the minister [white] on the plantation was always preaching from the Pauline letters—"Slaves, be obedient to your masters," etc. "I vowed to myself," she said, "that if freedom ever came and I learned to read, I would never read that part of the Bible!"

—Howard Thurman[1]

To quench all desire for mutiny in us, they would sometimes decapitate a few of us and impale our black heads upon the tips of the spars, just as years later they impaled our heads upon the tips of pine trees for miles along the dusty highways of Dixie to frighten us into obedience.

Captivity under Christendom blasted our lives, disrupted our families, reached down into the personalities of each one of us and destroyed the very images and symbols which had guided our minds and feelings in the effort to live. Our folkways and folk tales, which had once given meaning and sanction to our actions, faded from consciousness. Our gods were dead and answered us no more.

—Richard Wright[2]

A few nights ago between 10 and 11 o'clock a runaway slave came to the house where I live for safety and succor. I asked him if he was a Christian; "No sir," said he, "white men treat us so bad in Mississippi that we can't be Christians."

—Bishop Alexander Payne[3]

34

While not exactly the holy grail of scholarship, forests of trees have been felled to record the search for the first or earliest spiritual. It is a good idea to pause a moment here and remember Henry Louis Gates Jr.'s words about this quest to "reassemble fragments . . . to engage in an act of speculation, to attempt to weave a fiction of origins and subgeneration. It is to render the implicit as explicit, and at times to imagine the whole from a part."[4]

And, of course, to find it, we must first describe it. What comprised the first spirituals? What did they look like so that when—and if—we find them, we can recognize them?

Still, everything begins somewhere and sometime. It would appear from all available research that spirituals, in the modern sense of the word, began in the plantations of the Southern states from Virginia to Georgia, perhaps in the early or mid-1700s, perhaps earlier still. Perhaps not. But it is the best place to begin our search for the "fiction of origins."

The recorded history of African Americans in the United States begins in 1619 when a Dutch man-of-war robbed a Spanish vessel on the open seas of the North Atlantic. The Dutch privateer pulled into Jamestown, Virginia, to exchange "twenty negars" for supplies, including slaves Antony and Isabella, who later married and in 1624 gave birth to William.[5]

A host of excellent sources detail the lives of antebellum slaves in both the North and the South and all agree that two distinct approaches to slavery quickly emerged in the American colonies. And, because of those approaches, it seems more likely that spirituals were born in the South.

From the Mason-Dixon line northward, slavery was, at best, a footnote. The climate, the heartfelt opposition to slavery by the Quakers, the multifaceted industrial base, and other factors all led to a marginalized impact.[6] Along with indentured servants and family members, slaves worked side by side with their owners on farms and in dairies, they assisted in raising livestock and became bakers, carpenters, cabinetmakers, sawyers, blacksmiths, printers, tailors, and coopers and found work in New England's burgeoning maritime industries.[7]

As Leon Litwack notes, the standard argument for the gradual demise of slavery north of the Mason-Dixon line was that northern farmers lacked both sufficient land and the warm climate to produce cash crops such as cotton, tobacco, rice, or sugarcane—all of which required extensive care and large numbers of people to plant and harvest. However, on the eve of the Revolutionary War, every colony still had slavery—and a host of laws defining it.[8]

Slowly, the tide turned against slavery in the North. Following the American Revolution, an estimated 100,000 slaves were given their freedom, and at least that many fled to Canada or to the western frontier during the ensuing chaos.[9] Fueled by the unceasing efforts of the Quakers and others, the Massachusetts Supreme Court issued a ruling in 1783 that effectively ended slavery in the state.[10] By 1830, only 3,568 African Americans remained slaves in the North, primarily in New Jersey.[11]

Certainly, freedom did not equate with equality in the North. W. E. B. Du-Bois's powerful memoirs and other contemporary accounts depict a chilly netherworld where African Americans lived separate but hardly equal lives, facing naked oppression and ferocious prejudice virtually everywhere.[12] Freedom of movement and property ownership, as well as the ability to vote, worship, or even shop alongside whites, all were often severely restricted.

Or, as one observer sadly noted, even in the absence of outright slavery, "chains of a stronger kind still manacled their limbs, from which no legislative act could free them; a mental and moral subordination and inferiority, to which tyrant custom here subjected all the sons and daughters of Africa."[13]

If legislation mandated a pale sort of freedom for African Americans, it couldn't change the prejudices and biases many Northerners still held. Unfortunately, those discriminatory practices and feelings extended even to the one facet of life that *should* have been inclusive: religion. Christianity, which had originally flourished as a tiny oppressed sect that welcomed both freed person and slave[14] and clearly specified humane treatment for slaves, was unforgivably slow to embrace African Americans in North America.

Consequently, there was little religious tradition among northern African Americans in the colonies until the late 1600s when a few denominations—most notably the Religious Society of Friends (Quakers)—allowed both slaves and freed slaves in their services. By the early 1800s, slavery had become the defining issue in the young republic and families, churches, and sometimes denominations split over admitting slaves and freed slaves to their houses of worship. Some churches limited African-American activities and access, others kept them in dark corners of the balcony or in half-hidden pews near the back of the church and, to their shame, some eventually banned African Americans completely.[15] In 1831, when a New York minister dared to distribute the sacraments to his African-American members first, a near-riot broke out. Most northern seminaries either overtly or covertly prevented African-American applicants. Again, only the Quakers broke ranks, at least publicly, if not in practice, of accepting African Americans as full members.[16] Meanwhile, numerous African-American leaders noted that white abolitionists spent so much of their energy in stinging denunciations of slavery that they—conveniently—overlooked the plight of free slaves in the North.[17]

As in the South, many northern slave owners and non-slave owners alike either believed that African Americans were too primitive intellectually to comprehend Christianity or that while Christianity might benefit a slave's soul, it would only make him a "worse" slave.[18] Both viewpoints meant that little effort was spent on "saving" slaves. As slaves in the North gradually became freemen and -women, opposition to "Christianizing" them rarely flagged. Slave narratives are filled with accounts of African-American preachers being beaten for teaching the Gospels and slave owners fined for "one of the vilest crimes that ever disgraced society . . . [Y]ou have taught a slave girl to read in the Bible."[19]

"What the colonists feared, of course, was the dimly recognized challenge to their distinct status and the mental differentiation upon which it rested," Winthrop Jordan observes. "For by Christianizing the Negro, then by proffering to him even the meager crumbs of religious instruction which were prerequisite to baptism, the colonist was making the Negro just so much more like himself."[20]

In short, once African Americans learned to speak English, began to dress like "proper" colonials, and were saved by the same God, it made it that much harder to blindly consider them subhuman and lay the lash across their backs.[21]

Regardless, northern African Americans gradually, in small numbers, *did* become Christians, in part because of the tireless work of the Quakers (themselves once a heavily persecuted sect), the Church of England's Society for the Propagation of the Gospel, and some of the small new denominations that were making inroads into the colonies. Slowly, African Americans in the North came to worship the Christian God. *How* they worshiped varied widely from state to state and from denomination to denomination, though rarely in full and equal communion with their white counterparts.

This uneasy state of affairs continued until the first flames of the Great Awakening began in the mid-1700s, a fast-burning religious revival fueled by an army of itinerant preachers who—by their very nature—tended to be inclusive rather than exclusive.[22] Some, like George Whitefield, reveled in the numbers of African Americans who found salvation at his early crusades.[23]

Eventually, there were enough free African Americans in the North, particularly in Philadelphia and New York, that they clamored for their own churches. In 1786, an African-American, Richard Allen, a self-taught former itinerant preacher, was called to preach at St. George's Methodist Episcopal, an integrated church in Philadelphia. Allen worked hard to increase African-American membership in the church and it grew from two to forty-two members, who were then instructed to sit in a separate section in the balcony. But when Allen asked for permission to found a separate black church, the white officials elected not to support him. Allen continued to recruit African-American members anyway.[24]

In November 1787, Allen and Absalom Jones and other African Americans arrived as usual to worship at St. George's, but were told to sit in the gallery, which they did. But when they knelt in prayer, they were roughly accosted by "trustees" of the church and eventually forced to leave.[25]

Motivated by this incident and others like it, Allen and his supporters organized their own church, with the help of some whites.[26] Because of the behavior of the people of St. George's, all but Allen and Jones voted to affiliate with the Episcopalian church. Jones joined the majority, but Allen stayed a Methodist.[27] The St. Thomas African Church of Philadelphia was dedicated on July 17, 1794—the first independent African-American church in North America. On March 26, 1796, the church was incorporated as the African Episcopal Church of St. Thomas and was affiliated with the U.S. Episcopalians,[28] with Jones as the pastor.

Richard Allen, the first African-American pastor in the United States, wrote many religious songs at Mother Bethel in Philadelphia. (photo: Rachel Barkley Menjivar)

Allen, meanwhile, raised money for a second church, the Bethel African Methodist Episcopal Church, which was dedicated on July 29, 1794. A few months later, Bethel affiliated with the Methodist Episcopal Church.[29] St. George's continued to send white pastors to Bethel until Allen was ordained by the Methodist Episcopal Church on June 11, 1799. He was the first African American ordained in the United States.[30]

Other African-American churches soon followed, many with ordained ministers, and many soon requested independence to run their own affairs.[31] Most of the white churches and their congregations initially resisted. Finally, Allen—of course—was the first to "free" his congregation, though he had to resort to the courts to do so. In 1816, Bethel Church was granted its independence from St. George's. The congregation immediately voted to refuse all future white preachers in the pulpit or white ministers in charge of their temporal affairs.[32]

Inspired by Bethel's success, other African-American churches sprang up throughout the Northeast, while more African-American denominations were motivated to spin off from their white counterparts. On May 14, 1809, thirteen Philadelphians formed the first African Baptist church, followed in short order by more Baptist churches in other northern cities.[33]

What both whites and African Americans sang in Protestant churches, at least for the first few centuries of religious life in America, were (for the most part) the psalms of David, set to about thirty-five excruciatingly monotonous tunes, without either harmony or musical accompaniment.[34] Most churches had no musical instruments or hymnbooks. The psalms were taught by "lining out" the text—the minister or missionary reading a line of the psalm before it was sung by the congregation—a common practice in a society where few people, free or slave, could read or write.[35]

Eventually, even the dour Puritans tired of a style of singing that alternated between droning and chaotic. "Between 1647 and 1721 the tempo of the singing of the psalms had become unbelievably slow," William Tallmadge notes. "Furthermore, endless numbers of the embellishments were interpolated throughout."[36] A long period of turmoil slowly pushed most congregations toward more singable hymns, led by the musical contributions of the gifted nonconformist English minister Isaac Watts. Watts almost single-handedly revitalized sacred music both in the colonies and in England with his hymnals *Hymns and Spiritual Songs* (1707) and *The Psalms of David Imitated* (1719).[37] Watts fought for the notion that the words in the hymns should be accessible to uneducated and educated alike, unlike John Wesley—who stoutly insisted that the sole function of hymns was to have listeners "lifted up to the level of the Hymn, and made to feel the beauty and inspiration of poetry."[38] It helped the cause immeasurably that Watts was able to write hymns that did both.

While little remains that chronicles the musical practices of the few independent African-American churches of the late eighteenth and early nineteenth centuries, it would appear that those churches initially used the same psalms or hymnbooks as the white churches they were originally affiliated with. But it wasn't long before the pioneering black preachers introduced their own hymnals, hymnals that reflected the newer, more freer hymns and sometimes hearkened back to certain West African musical traditions.[39]

In 1801, Allen published his own hymnal—*A Collection of Spiritual Songs and Hymns Selected from Various Authors by Richard Allen, African Minister*—for the use of his congregation. The new hymnal featured no musical notation for its fifty-four hymn texts and the lyrics were drawn chiefly from existing collections of hymns by Dr. Isaac Watts, the Wesleys, and other hymn writers favored by his African-American congregation. It also included hymns popular with the Baptists, along with the first known printed example of "wandering refrains"— chorus-like refrains added to various hymns that provided an "improvisational quality" to the singing.[40] These refrain lines and choruses, besides being easy to remember, were structured in such a way that members who felt so moved could shout or moan "Yes, Lord" or "Oh, Jesus" in the "empty" spaces in the music and singing.[41] These ornamentations are also found in the musical traditions of West Africa.[42]

A Collection of Spiritual Songs was so popular that a second edition published later that year included ten more texts and some edits of the original fifty-four— but still no melodies. It's possible that Allen, a prolific writer, wrote some of the texts and altered others.[43] Charles Wesley states that Allen's hymns were something new, something powerful:

> . . . [T]here was no slavish imitation of white writers in any of these efforts. The very crudeness of his endeavors demonstrated his desires to be himself. The charge of imitation might be brought against other Negro writers in the earlier part of the century, but Richard Allen was unique in his independence.[44]

One of the earliest depictions of music in these new, mostly African-American, congregations comes, curiously, from Russian diplomat and artist Pavel Svinin, who visited Bethel during the course of a tour of the United States from 1811 to 1813:

> . . . at the end of every psalm, the entire congregation, men and women alike, sang verses in a loud, shrill monotone. This lasted about half an hour. When the preacher ceased reading, all turned toward the door, fell on their knees, bowed their heads to the ground and set up an agonizing, heart-rendering moaning. Afterwards, the minister resumed the reading of the psalter and when he had finished, sat down on a chair; then all rose and began chanting psalms in chorus, the men and women alternating, a procedure which lasted some 20 minutes.[45]

This description, of course, compares unfavorably to the singing in Svinin's Greek Orthodox church back home, and he follows it with a very early (and again not particularly flattering) depiction of the camp meeting in a Philadelphia alley.[46] But as we've seen in our brief overview of African music, the elements the Russian describes in his diary—spontaneous improvising, antiphonal chants, lengthy sections of the service given entirely to singing, and the presence of those indefinable "moans" are all characteristics of West African music.

Another critic of this new music was John F. Watson, who published a tract titled *Methodist Error; Friendly, Christian Advice, To those Methodists, Who indulge in extravagant emotions and bodily exercises* under the pseudonym "A Wesleyan Methodist" in 1819:

> We have too, a growing evil, in the practice of singing in our places of public and society worship, merry airs, adapted from old songs, to hymns of our composing: often miserable as poetry, and senseless as matter . . . Most frequently [these hymns are] composed and first sung by the illiterate blacks of the society.[47]

Watson also deplores the "singing the same verse over and over again with all their might 30 or 40 times . . ."[48]:

> In the blacks' quarter, the coloured people get together, and sing for hours together, short scraps of disjointed affirmations, pledges, or prayers, lengthened out with long repetitive choruses. These are all sung in the merry chorus-manner of the southern harvest field, or husking-frolic method, of the slave blacks. . . .
>
> With every word so sung, they have a sinking of one or other leg of the body alternately; producing an audible sound of the feet at every step, and as manifest as the actual negro dancing in Virginia . . . If some, in the meantime sit, they strike the sounds alternately on each thigh.[49]

Eileen Southern maintains that these stinging remarks could only be aimed at Allen and the African Methodist Episcopal Church since it was the lone independent African-American church at the Philadelphia conference and Allen did not use the approved Methodist hymnal.[50]

But what Allen and his counterparts were composing and what their parishioners were singing during formal services in African-American churches in Boston and Philadelphia were not spirituals. "Although the 'spiritual songs' so beloved by the black Protestant masses were banned from formal church services, many lenient pastors allowed them during week-night services," Southern adds.[51] And as a twenty-year-old slave outside Dover, Delaware,[52] in private meetings and services, Wesley believes that Allen heard the simple, powerful religious songs of slaves, songs like "Steal Away to Jesus" and "Way Down Yonder by Myself I Couldn't Hear Nobody Pray."[53]

Or perhaps Allen and his contemporaries heard something different in the teeming streets of Philadelphia—streets that included slaves and recently freed slaves and African Americans who had been free for a generation or more. Perhaps they heard religious folk songs simple, emotional choruses and refrains that spoke to African Americans like nothing else they'd ever heard, songs, "composed and first sung by the illiterate black of the society." Where were these new songs coming from?

The South

The South—which is where we shall now turn our attention.

The earliest records in the South regularly mention one of the two prerequisite elements necessary for the creation of spirituals: music. Those records are, however, distressingly threadbare as to the other essential element: Christianity. Quite bluntly, virtually nobody in the South much cared what the slaves believed in the seventeenth and early eighteenth centuries, and only a few enlightened souls in the Northeast even bothered to convert interested ex-slaves.[54]

The scant evidence suggests that most slaves initially retained the gods of their ancestors, even as they lost other vestiges of their life in Africa, "but the coherence of traditional religion must have steadily disintegrated under the several pressures of life in a new environment and under a new regimentation."[55]

And it wasn't long after the beginnings of slavery in this "new environment and under a new regimentation" of the South that the slaves' lot rapidly deteriorated:

> The reduction of Africans from servants to hereditary chattel during the first half of the seventeenth century is linked with the rapid conversion of the wilderness, an equally rapid increase in the African population, and the integration of society and work in terms of a feudal vision in which Africans and some others were cast as tillers of the soils and mechanics of the menial, in perpetual service to an agrarian aristocracy.[56]

Some of the initial impetus in the process to dehumanize slaves may have begun with the constant reports of slave rebellions, most notably Toussaint L'Ouverture's extraordinary crusade in Haiti in 1791. But southern slaves, chafing under brutal conditions, constantly fled or rebelled, as extant references beginning as early as the 1650s reveal.[57]

Acclaimed English actress Fanny Kemble's memoirs of her brief marriage to a dashing but violent slave owner in Georgia provide a vivid glimpse of a country that consequently lived in a state of self-imposed siege:

> [A] most ominous tolling of bells and beating of drums . . . on the first evening of my arrival in Charleston, made me almost fancy myself in one of the old fortified frontier towns of the Continent, where the tocsin is sounded, and the evening drum beaten, and the guard set as regularly every night as if an invasion were expected. In Charleston, however, it is not the dread of foreign invasion, but of domestic insurrection, which occasions these nightly precautions. . . . [O]f course, it is very necessary where a large class of persons exists in the very bosom of a community whose interests are known to be at variance and incompatible with those of its other members. And no doubt these daily and

nightly precautions are but trifling drawbacks, upon the manifold blessings of slavery . . . still, I should prefer going to sleep without the apprehension of my servants cutting my throat in my bed, even to having a guard provided to prevent their doing so.[58]

In the South, slave owners believed that to control a conquered people it was necessary to follow the old wartime adage, "Divide and conquer." This was accomplished, as nearly as possible, by separating members of families as well as slaves who came from the various African tribal nations. Slaves thus fragmented and isolated would be less likely to unify and resist.[59] In addition to formal laws forbidding a host of African survivals, slave owners systematically "demeaned the sacred tales of the black fathers, ridiculing their myths and defiling their sacred rites. Their intention was to define man according to European definitions so that their brutality against Africans could be characterized as civilizing the savages."[60]

However, generations of slaves still managed to transmit some African beliefs and customs to their descendents, thus preserving—against all odds—African music, work songs, the ring shout, snippets of various languages, lore, and even religion.[61] African survivals persisted for generations, particularly in isolated communities and on the far-flung plantations of the South.

More successful were the efforts by southern colonies to outlaw the use of African drums, either for communication or entertainment.[62] But no laws could prohibit African Americans from keeping time with their feet or hands. And while many overseers prevented slaves from speaking in the tobacco and cotton fields, they quickly saw the value in the African-influenced work songs, cries, and hollers.

Work Songs, Cries, and Hollers

Some early writers including Dr. Seth Rogers, a Northern surgeon during the Civil War, point to field hollers and work songs as one of the basic components of the spirituals.[63] And it is clear that slaves brought the work songs (also known as hollers, "cottonfield hollers," cries, or "whoops") with them from Africa:

"A slave's call or cry could mean any one of a number of things: a call for water, food, or help, a call to let others know where he was working, or simply a cry of loneliness, sorrow or happiness."[64]

Like most work songs (some captured by Alan Lomax in the seminal field recordings of the Georgia Sea Islands CD),[65] the hollers contained a rhythmic quality that made the work seem easier, be it rowing, picking cotton, or laying railroad ties. Most were performed in the now-familiar "call and response" format.

Noted Ethiopian scholar Ashenafi Kebede differentiates *calls* from *cries*. Whereas calls may have been primarily used to communicate information—to alert a dozing friend of a fast-approaching white overseer—cries, on the other hand,

> express a deeply felt emotional experience, such as hunger, loneliness, or lovesickness. They are half-sung and half-yelled. Vocables are often intermixed in the text. The melodies are performed in a free and spontaneous style; they are often ornamented and employ many African vocal devices, such as yodels, echolike falsetto, tonal glides, embellished melismas, and microtonal inflections that are often impossible to indicate in European staff notation.[66]

Those cries, Kebede believes, may have evolved into the religious songs or spirituals of African Americans. "There is no doubt," he writes, "that these calls were African in derivation and that they were sung in African dialects in the early part of slave history."[67]

Frederick Olmsted Law wrote one of the earliest—and most eloquent—depictions of field hollers in 1853:

> Suddenly [a slave] raised such a sound as I had never heard before, a long, loud musical shout, rising and falling, and breaking into falsetto, his voice ringing through the woods in the clear frosty night air, like a bugle call. As he finished, the melody was caught up by another, and then, another, and then, by several in chorus.[68]

It is important to remember that both the field hollers and work songs could also be religious at the same time. As in Africa, the slave made no distinction between the "religious" and "non-religious" aspects of his or her life. William C. Turner says that Africans believe that music is "numinous"—it manifests as the most primordial force in life and is the providence of deities.[69] Harvest-related elements sometimes appear in the spirituals, just as sacred elements sometimes appear in the work songs and field hollers. Lydia Parrish recorded several heavily rhythmic chain gang work songs while on the Sea Islands off Georgia, including:

> *Drinkin' of the wine-wine-wine*
> *Drinkin' of the wine*
> *O-yes-my Lord*
> *I oughta bin to Heaven ten thousand years*
> *Drinkin' of the wine*

And

> *Ain't but one thing I done wrong*
> *Stayin' in the wilderness mos' too long*
> *I oughta bin to Heaven ten thousand years*
> *Drinkin' of the wine.*[70]

Booker T. Washington writes that in the beginning, African-American music was "spontaneous," a joyful eruption at marriages, a mournful dirge at funerals: "Wherever companies of Negroes were working together, in the cotton fields and tobacco factories, on the levees and steamboats, on sugar plantations, and chiefly in the fervor of religious gatherings, these melodies sprang to life."[71]

Ring Shout

But when the slaves were alone, away from the prying ears of slave owners or overseers, either in their hidden clearings in the pine forest or the forbidden "praise houses" of the early Christian slaves, they continued another African custom, the mystical dance called the "ring shout." Beyond the Africanisms in the dialect and certain melodies, the most demonstrably African survivor from the slaves' earliest days in North America is the ring shout or shout. Even the word *shout* is possibly of African origin—linguist Lorenzo Dow Turner links it to the West African Islamic word *saut*, meaning to move or dance around the *Kaaba*, the building in Mecca holding Islam's holiest artifacts.[72] Depending on the part of the South where it was heard, the term *shout* refers to either the music or the dance or the combination of the two. And whereas few of the chroniclers of the early spirituals were trained musicologists, even the most rudimentary journalist could describe this direct link to African origins.

The ring shout of the slaves was known to take place in hidden groves, the slave praise houses, and—somewhat later—African-American churches. A typical contemporary description of a shout notes that it ". . . consists of a circle of people moving single file (usually counter-clockwise) around a central point, to the accompaniment of singing, stamping and heel clicking." From there:

> The tempo may build up gradually, singing interspersed with exclamations characteristic of some other Negro church services, until it reaches a tense peak close to an ecstatic breaking point. At the high point of the excitement, such exclamations as "Oh Lord!" and "Yes Lord!" turn into nonsense sounds and cries; seemingly wild emotional responses, they nevertheless are related to the music as a whole, and no notation which omits them can give a fair picture of what is heard.[73]

One of the earliest accounts of a ring shout is by Charles Lyell, a visitor to South Carolina and Georgia Sea Islands plantations in 1848, who noted one while recounting how pious Methodist missionaries had effectively ended *all* singing and dancing by slaves.[74]

The most famous description of a ring shout is found the *New York Nation,* May 30, 1867, reprinted in *Slave Songs of the United States,* which recounts an evening "sperichil" being performed while the congregation walks or shuffles in a circle:

The foot is hardly taken from the floor, and the progression is mainly due to a jerking, hitching motion, which agitates the entire shouter, and soon brings out streams of perspiration. Sometimes they dance silently, sometimes as they shuffle they sing the chorus of the spiritual, and sometimes the song itself is also sung by the dancers.[75]

Lydia Parrish compared notes with recent African travelers and became "convinced" that the "shout of the American Negro is nothing more than a survival of an African tribal dance, and that the accompanying chants in their form and melody are quite as typical of Africa as the dance itself."[76] Margaret Creel is even more specific. She writes that the Gullah ring shout is nothing less than a "manifestation" of the West African possession trace.[77]

Regardless of its specific origin, the ring shout became an integral part of the African-American services in the South long before the Civil War, when it became a mainstay of Sunday afternoons.[78] The form was so resilient that it continued deep into the twentieth century[79] and may still be practiced in isolated communities even today.

The ring shout, always accompanied by spirituals, was certainly the most dramatic of all the surviving Africanisms of homesick slaves. It endured in part because, in most states, the slaves worked ferociously to keep its presence hidden from their masters, devising elaborate plans and early warning systems. Some slaves reported using "a wash-tub full of water in the middle of the floor" in an effort "To catch the sound of our voices when sung" during shouts[80] and thus avoid detection by their overseers or masters.

Not all mainstream religious leaders—black or white—were supportive of the shout. After a visit to a "brush arbor church" in the years before the Civil War, African-American minister Daniel Alexander Payne was shocked when the African-American parishioners promptly doffed their coats, formed a ring, and "clapped their hands and stomped their feet in a most ridiculous and heathenish way. I requested the pastor to go and stop their dancing. At his request, they stopped their dancing and clapping of hands, but remained singing and rocking their bodies to and fro." But Payne and his contemporaries simply couldn't suppress so potent a rite.[81]

And because of bonds created in the brush arbors and praise houses and through the ring shouts, the new African Americans were able to survive the loss of their shared languages and customs. In the words of Albert Raboteau, "even as the gods of Africa gave way to the God of Christianity, the African heritage of singing, dancing, spirit possession, and magic continued to influence Afro-American spirituals, ring shouts and folk beliefs. That this was so is evidence of the slaves' ability not only to adapt to new contexts, but to do so creatively."[82]

In the end, the residents of the Big House and the white lawmakers in the southern capitols may have banned drumming, but they couldn't purge rhythm from the African souls. It was rhythm, John Spencer says, that became the religion of African Americans:

In the ring-shouts of the South and the South Carolina and Georgia Sea Islands, rhythm rocked the praise houses and could be heard for miles around all night long. It empowered those who possessed it to endure slavery by temporarily elevating them out of the valley of oppression up to a spiritual summit.[83]

So fiercely did the slaves protect remnants of their African culture that only scraps of information survive about these clandestine meetings, and even those are mostly in the form of whispers and allusions. This forced secrecy would spill into every aspect of the new slave culture in North America and would become so pervasive that when Lydia Parrish visited the Georgia Sea Islands many decades later, it would take several years before the children of slaves would share those songs with her.[84]

Music

While slave owners in both the North and the South were not concerned about the education or religion of slaves, they *were* concerned about their musical abilities. Slaves were compelled to sing and make music on the very ships bringing them from Africa,[85] and they soon adapted to the strange instruments and musical ways of their captors, all the while desperately seeking to preserve their own musical languages.

As in the North, southern slaves were quickly exposed to a variety of Western European musical styles from their arrival in the Americas. In fact, Irving Schwerke notes that the Americas' first song recital (1733) and opera (1735) were heard not in New York or Boston but in Charleston, and that while their counterparts in New England were still struggling to decide whether the act of singing was "an improper, sinful act," the citizens of Charleston developed a thriving classical music community.[86] Of course, slaves on the distant plantations of the vast southern pine forest frontier rarely heard that kind of music, but they certainly served at the lavish balls of the plantation owners and surreptitiously hung outside the doorways of taverns to listen to the music of Western Europeans.

Documents of the era make frequent reference to the music of African Americans, both slave and free, playing for both white and black audiences— although never at the same time![87] But few provide as insightful—as well as sobering—reading as the thousands of runaway slave advertisements from colonial newspapers. The book-length collection *Runaway Slave Advertisements*, beginning with items dated October 15, 1736, provides 468 pages of paid advertisements of (mostly male) slaves fleeing for their lives, usually described by a hideous array of scars, most apparently inflicted by the very masters offering large rewards for their return, dead or alive. A sizable number of the advertisements mention the slaves' musical prowess, usually on the fiddle, although a few drums and fifes are mentioned. But two intriguing ads detail something else:

Virginia Gazette (Purdie), September 8, 1775.

RUN away from the subscriber in Dinwiddie, the 5th day of April last, a dark mulatto man named JEMMY, 5 feet 9 or 10 inches high, well made, has remarkable long feet, the middle toes longer than the rest, which they ride over, has lost part of one of his fore teeth, which occasions the next to it to look blue, is a very artful fellow and will probably endeavor to pass for a freeman; he is very fond of singing hymns and preaching, and has been about Williamsburg ever since he went off, passing by the name of James Williams. Whoever apprehends the said slave, and secures him so that I get him again, shall have 40 s. reward, and if deliver to me in Dinwiddie, 4 1.[88]

Virginia Gazette (Purdie), May 29, 1778.
Two Hundred DOLLARS Reward.

RUN away from the subscriber in Northumberland, two Negro men, viz. JOE, a tall black fellow, who has a fine smooth address, a hole in one of his cheeks and is very artful. He can read a little, is fond of singing hymns, and exhorting his brethren of the Ethiopian tribe.[89]

In time, slave musicians were as common—and as necessary—as drivers, craftsmen, and preachers on Southern plantations and enjoyed the same status. One slave stated that every farm had a "resident" fiddler.[90] A traveler on the Washington, D.C., to Charleston road during the 1850s once claimed that he didn't see a white orchestra during the course of the entire journey.[91] Slaves provided music both for the frequent balls at the plantations and the even more common "frolics" in the slave quarters. And while the plantation owners and their children might rehearse the classics at home, they depended on the slaves for dance music.[92]

Consequently, slave "musicianers" often enjoyed greater status, privileges, earning potential, and even freedom of movement than their fellow slaves,[93] despite frequent criticism from white (and sometimes black) preachers.[94]

And for the slaves, who apparently continued their ancient traditions of melding the sacred and the profane in all things, the distinctions between dance music and religious music were artificial at best. There were many instances of slaves who fiddled on Saturday and preached on Sunday—to virtually the same audience each time.[95]

Religion

The most striking element of slavery in the South was the vast plantation system. The size was necessary to make possible the cultivation of labor-intensive crops like cotton and tobacco. Most of the plantations were separated by long distances, which tended to separate slave populations even further. Still, only a few plantations had hundreds of slaves, and ownership in the so-called "planter class" required ownership of just twenty slaves.[96] Just under half of all slaves were owned by planters who owned thirty or more slaves.[97] The sheer number of slaves, particularly "field slaves" who rarely came to the Big House, a policy of absentee ownership, and the diversified tasks of the slaves meant that few owners had direct contact with their slaves (outside of their personal servants), and little direct interaction or supervision occurred.[98] In some areas, particularly the Georgia Sea Islands, the climate was considered so unhealthy to Western Europeans that "it was not uncommon for a plantation with six or seven hundred slaves to have no more than one or two whites living on it."[99]

One unintentional result of the plantation system, which was transported virtually untouched from the Celtic fringes of Scotland and Ireland to the American South, was that religious education of slaves—while not necessarily always discouraged—was virtually nonexistent.[100] In fact, the typical Southerner—white *or* African American—was simply not much of a churchgoer in those days. In *Cracker Culture*, Grady McWhiney details contemporary reports outlining the scarcity of Bibles (or any books) in the South and that "the average of their going to church was once in seven years. Several between 30 and 45 years old had heard but one or two sermons in their lives. Some grown up youths had never heard a sermon or a prayer until my visit."[101]

"All over the planting districts," insisted a Northerner who visited the South in the 1850s, "very few attend church, and very few of the churches have constant preaching." He noted that in Albany, Georgia, a town of some twenty stores that exported annually "12,000 bales of cotton," only thirty-nine people (including three blacks) attended the Methodist church, the only one open on "a beautiful Christmas Sabbath . . . There were three thousand souls within sound of a church-going bell, had there been one. Where were they?" This same man charged that only forty-eight people attended the Presbyterian church, the only one in Dublin, Georgia, a town of some two thousand inhabitants, and that at Oglethorpe, "a smart young city at the termination of the Southwestern railroad, where there was a population of over three thousand, there was no church service during the Sabbath I spent there."[102]

Visitors offered various explanations for the Southerner's impiety. One traveler remarked that Sunday in the South "seemed a day on which people loved to get drunk." Another found "that many of the people were accustomed to be intoxicated Saturday night, and therefore, were unable to attend church on the Sabbath." As still another Northerner pointed out: "The Sabbath [in the South] is rather a day of recreation and pastime with the slaves . . . in which they visit each other, and spend the day in a very unbecoming manner—following closely the example of their parents."[103]

Ultimately, McWhiney notes, neither southern plantation owners nor poor whites were so much irreligious as they were indifferent about church attendance. The most popular denominations of the South required little more than a belief in Jesus and baptism as prerequisites for eternal salvation. "Such beliefs fostered a more tolerant and relaxed set of religious practices than those found in New England. Most Southerners were compelled by neither conscience nor community pressure to be especially pious. They attended church or stayed home at their own convenience and pleasure."[104]

Eugene Genovese and others follow Luther P. Jackson's outline and place the beginnings of any significant efforts to convert slaves at or about 1750. Jackson then divides the history of black Christianity in Virginia into three periods: 1750–1790, 1790–1830, and 1830–1860:

1750–1790
Great Awakening, first evangelical work of Baptists and Methodists

1790–1830
Evangelical work of slaves slows with rise in Southern antislavery feelings, particularly following the revolt spurred by Nat Turner, a prominent African American Christian. Most mainline Southern churches buckled under the pressure from slaveholders to accommodate proslavery church leaders.

1830–1860
Jackson posits renewed support for approved religious proselytizing of slaves.[105]

In recent years, the question has been debated regarding the extent to which Christianity actually penetrated and transformed the slave community. The Great Awakening and the subsequent revivals (see below) led to the conversions of many plantation owners as well. Of course, how much those conversions benefited slaves is uncertain, and simmering hostility to Christianity among slaves probably never totally dissipated.[106] Likewise, the percentage of African Americans who became devout Christians (or at least publicly professed such a conversion) is also in doubt. In the early 1840s, Charles Colcock Jones reports that only a small minority of slaves attended churches, and in some areas of the South there were no churches at all. Not, as he wryly notes, that the preaching of whites made much of an impact on those slaves in attendance.[107] Regardless, only about 468,000 slaves claimed church membership in 1859, and by 1900 that number had risen only to 2.7 million members in an African-American population of 8.3 million.[108]

Part of the problem in winning slaves over to Christianity was in the *kind* of Christianity espoused, especially by many Southerners. Some very early writings on slavery emphasize the importance of slaves obeying their masters above all else.[109] Perhaps the most obvious example is found in the journals of Charles

Colcock Jones from 1837 where he reprints a part of a slave "litany" from a religious service involving slaves:

Q: What are the Servants to count their Masters worthy of?
A: All honour.
Q: How are they to try to please their Masters?
A: Please them well in all things, not answering again.
Q: Is it right for a Servant when commanded to do anything to be sullen and slow, and answering his Master again?
A: No.
Q: But suppose the Master is hard to please, and threatens and punishes more than he ought, what is the Servant to do?
A: Do his best to please him.[110]

Instead of following the teachings of Jesus, former slave William Wells Brown tells stories about how slave owner Daniel D. Page, the owner of a pew at First Presbyterian Church in St. Louis, once whipped a slave named Delphia nearly to death—even though she also attended that same church. Much later, when she'd painfully recovered from her wounds, she resumed attending First Presbyterian and Page's fellow parishioners saw nothing wrong with his actions.[111]

But Brown and most of his fellow slaves instinctively knew that slavery and Christianity were incompatible: "[The slaves] regarded the religious profession of the whites around us as a farce, and our master and mistress, together with their guest [a traveling preacher], as mere hypocrites."[112]

The slaves, who knew everything that went on in the Big House, saw the hypocrisy of American Christianity: slaveholders who were touted as exemplary Christians but who murdered and bedded their slaves, churchgoing slaveholders who sold their slaves in Georgia and South Carolina for church and mission fund-raisers even as the slaves squalid quarters were searched for Bibles.[113]

Despite regular doses of this self-serving religion, one that "cobbled together" a series of "questionable bits of Christian theology," most slaves were simply too smart to accept it wholeheartedly and "the vast majority . . . never for a moment accept[ed] it." As Christopher Small notes, not even generations of propagandizing could erase African-Americans self-knowledge of the "grievous offence that was committed against them." Instead, the slaves retained "those fragments of African religion that remained functional to their needs" and "pieced together from those fragments of orthodox belief" to create something that *would* help them survive, something of real value.[114]

The resulting belief system became the African-American church and the spirituals became its music. This religion radically reshaped the bad theology that had often been given to the slaves and provided instead the lone form of "resistance to the dehumanizing oppression, degradation, and suffering of slavery."[115] John Lovell, Jr., describes this new religion, which combined the best elements of two traditions, as "a lateral, not a forward pass."[116] Not better, not worse, but new. Wyatt Tee Walker calls this unlikely combination "Jesus-faith" and says its theology was preserved in the spirituals. The Jesus-faith "served to insulate the antebellum slave from the real temptation of collective suicide."[117]

Just as in their cuisine, African Americans took the scraps left to them and in their stewpots created a feast:

> Slavery in the New World, a veritable seething cauldron of cross-cultural contact, however, did serve to create a dynamic of exchange and revision among numerous previously isolated Black African cultures on a scale unprecedented in African history. Inadvertently, African slavery in the New World satisfied the preconditions for the emergence of a new African culture, a truly Pan-African culture fashioned as a colorful weave of linguistic, institutional, metaphysical, and formal threads. What survived this fascinating process was the most useful and most compelling of the fragments at hand.[118]

Not all African Americans completely gave up the old beliefs. African motifs, myths, beliefs, and customs survived for centuries in America. Additionally, as with many Central and South American cultures where Roman Catholicism blended easily with indigenous beliefs, sometimes slave belief systems were expansive enough to incorporate elements of both. R. Emmet Kennedy tells of an African-American man in the 1920s who believed that the sun did a "sun shout" or "sun dance" on Easter Sunday morning when "the sun rose above the horizon and looked upon the worshipful earth, dancing for very joy at the Resurrection of the Son of Man."[119] According to Kennedy, George Riley faithfully awoke before dawn to try and see the celestial event each Easter. And, when he finally claimed to have witnessed the miraculous event, he remained in an ecstatic state for hours: "All day long his voice could be heard through the house chanting, 'He Never Said a Mumblin' Word,' with a spirit that seemed to express a feeling of adulation rather than a feeling of commiseration which the words naturally inspire."[120]

This revolutionary new religion was not the result of African Americans becoming West European-styled Christians, it was the result of slaves *refashioning* the Christian religion to make it applicable to their own peculiar institution—slavery.[121] And, like every new revolutionary movement, it needed marching music—spirituals.

Sterling Stuckey and others believe that by adopting the white man's religion—at least outwardly—slaves were finally provided the perfect cover to continue to practice elements of their native faiths:

> The very features of Christianity peculiar to slaves were often outward manifestations of deeper African religious concerns, products of a religious outlook toward which the master class might otherwise be hostile. By operating under cover of Christianity, aspects of Africanity, which some considered eccentric in movement, sound and symbolism, could more easily be practiced openly.[122]

Baptist preacher. Alma Plantation, False River, Louisiana, July 1934 (photo: Alan Lomax, Library of Congress Lomax Collection)

In fact, Stuckey writes that the earliest slave preacher/pastors were probably equated by slaves with "priest-kings" from their native lands; this explains their long hold over their congregations, because "if the African religious leader was to operate in the open, the safest cloak to hide behind was that of Christianity. African religious leaders predominated in slavery and in that oppressive environment orchestrated their people's transformation into a single people culturally."[123]

Like Stuckey, W. E. B. Du Bois writes of the priest/medicine man who appeared on the plantations to heal the sick and serve as an interpreter to the Unknown, a "bard, physician, judge and priest, within the narrow limits allowed by the slave system."[124] From the preacher then rose the African-American church, which "was not at first by any means Christian nor definitely organized," a church that, after a lapse of many generations, eventually *became* Christian.[125]

M. J. Herskovits in *Man and His Works* offers a different spin on the slow transformation from native beliefs to European Christianity among slaves. He cites examples throughout West African nations where gods are frequently borrowed and swapped among the different tribes, their different aspects and powers easily assimilated into existing myth structures. Christianity, he suggests, should be no different:

> West African gods are often described by the members of a tribe as having taken over from another people, and one native explanation why this was done shows such insight into the psychology of the matter that it should be noted here. When one group conquered another, the superior power of the gods of the conquerors was self-evident, and it was thus to the advantage of the conquered to appease them.[126]

While church attendance and denominational membership are generally effective indicators of the percentage of the white population professing Christian beliefs at any given time, it may or may not be equally adequate when trying to represent the number of African-American believers. Numerous observers point out the small number of African Americans attending sanctioned churches, but as William H. Tallmadge and others note, actual church membership is not a prerequisite for salvation in most Protestant denominations. In fact, active church membership "might actually have inhibited the creation of spirituals by circumscribing the singing and limiting it to the singing of regular denominational hymns in the traditional manner."[127] Many slaves preferred their own, often hidden, services instead.

Miles Mark Fisher's controversial but compelling *Negro Slave Songs in the United States* raises the issue that many more slaves may have become Christians—or at least embraced a form of Christianity—through the ubiquitous, if rarely studied—secret meetings of the "African cult."[128]

"Native African secret meetings had brought Christianization to American Negroes," writes Fisher. "They supplied all of the sacred ministries to which

Negroes had been accustomed at home when they were sick, when they 'married,' and when they died. Negroes needed the comfort of group fellowship in order to condition themselves to slave situations."[129] Therefore, when the revivals of the early 1700s reached the South, Fisher believes that "the camp meetings were definite rivals of the African cult."

Renewed efforts to bring Christianity to the slaves began only with the Great Awakening of 1730–1750, which attempted to end decades of neglect, mingled with occasional outbursts of outright hostility, in the United States. The Great Awakening, really a series of widely scattered revivals triggered by the extraordinary visits by itinerant Anglican preacher George Whitefield, somehow knit the Scots and Irish of the middle southern colonies with their dour English brethren in New England, Pennsylvania Dutch Lutherans with the new Baptist and Methodists, middle class and poor, slaves and masters, into one movement—at least temporarily.[130]

At the center of these revivals was the Englishman Whitefield, who had given up a career on the stage when he became a Christian. In New England, he drew as many as 8,000 listeners a day for months to his heavily theatrical, often impromptu, sermons in a culture with little or no theatrical tradition.[131] Whitefield was said to be so compelling that one of his sermons even prompted the notoriously penurious Benjamin Franklin to tithe lavishly.[132]

Spurred by Whitefield, the revival spread into the South, which, as we have seen, "was populated by lukewarm Anglicans and African slaves trying to hold on to their indigenous religious practices."[133] Gifted preachers like Shubal Stearns and Daniel Marshall (the Carolinas) and Samuel Davies (Virginia), who was particularly concerned about the souls of slaves,[134] began a tradition of religious involvement in the South that continues today.

Although the Great Awakening eventually ran its course, Whitefield continued to visit the colonies in 1764 and 1770 and various smaller revivals smoldered briefly throughout North America until they merged into the so-called Second Great Awakening, which flared out of New England about 1790 and roared west into the frontier of the Ohio Valley.[135] Like its predecessor, its basic tenets were a reliance on the Bible, the "insistence on personal, emotional conversion," and a missionary imperative.[136]

In time, the revivals spread to tiny Cane Ridge, Kentucky, a small town northeast of Lexington, where it morphed into the legendary Cane Ridge Camp Meeting revival. Presbyterians joined Baptists and Methodists for a spontaneous revival "that attracted tens of thousand of isolated, sensation-starved frontier people," which lasted a full week and forever changed the shape of revivalism in the United States.[137]

These new revivals were inclusive, joyous, nonauthoritarian, and highlighted by long sessions of the rapturous singing of up-tempo songs designed to appeal to the large crowds of usually illiterate frontiersmen, yeomen, and slaves. Perhaps these revivals attracted the slaves more than previous (admittedly half-hearted) attempts because, for the first time, they were allowed full physical as well as verbal expression of this newfound religious ecstasy.[138] By contrast, some southern colonies had strict laws about the assembly of slaves and more than one plantation prohibited any gathering, no matter how religious. Slaves still adopted Christianity in large numbers at the camp meetings,[139] as did their masters and overseers who, either through zeal or guilt, then allowed the wholesale conversions of their slaves.

For many white Americans, this was the first time they had ever been in such close contact with this many African Americans. In time, owing to white complaints, some of the more popular camp meetings set up separate tents for African American participants. One such tent in the Midwest is described by English author Frances Trollope, Mark Twain's favorite travel writer and mother of the novelist Anthony Trollope, in an account of her life in the United States from 1827 to 1831, *Domestic Manners of the Americans*. This was the best-selling travel book of its day in both countries (if reviled in the United States) because of its remarkably perceptive and witty—though not without prejudice— observations. This is a section from a very early, sharply drawn account of a camp meeting in 1829:

> One tent was occupied exclusively by Negroes. They were all full-dressed, and looked exactly as if they were performing a scene on the stage. One woman wore a dress of pink gauze trimmed with silver lace; another was dressed in pale yellow silk; one or two had splendid turbans; and all wore a profusion of ornaments. The men were in snow white pantaloons, with gay coloured linen jackets. One of these, a youth of coal-black comeliness, was preaching with the most violent gesticulations, frequently springing high from the ground, and clapping his hands over his head. Could our missionary societies have heard the trash he uttered, by way of an address to the Deity, they might perhaps have doubted whether his conversion had much enlightened his mind.[140]

Still, most foreign visitors were impressed by what they saw at camp meetings, including those of the subsequent Second Awakening, especially since Europeans had nothing to compare with these vast meetings in the frontier that included both black and white worshipers.[141]

The music sung at the various revivals and camp meetings varied widely, as indicated in the various histories of the movement, often depending on both the location and the backgrounds of the evangelists involved. The first and still one of the best definitions of what became known as a camp-meeting song or hymn is from Louis F. Benson:

> Spontaneous song became a marked characteristic of the camp meetings. Rough and irregular couplets or stanzas were concocted out of Scripture phrases and everyday speech, with liberal interspersing of Hallelujahs and refrains. Such

ejaculatory hymns were frequently started by an excited auditor during the preaching, and taken up by the throng. . . .[142]

The literary form of the Camp Meeting Hymn is that of the popular ballad or song in plainest everyday language. . . . The refrain or chorus is perhaps the predominant feature, not always connected with the subject-matter of the stanza, but rather ejaculatory. In some instances such a refrain was merely tacked on to a familiar hymn or an arrangement of one. . . .[143]

In both the Deep South and on the western frontier, the conditions shaped the music. The fast-paced songs featured simple refrains and choruses, which were well suited to group singing.[144] The refrains and choruses were patchworked together from existing hymns and easily remembered from meeting to meeting—all necessary in a mostly illiterate culture used to the "lining out" of hymns (when they sang at all). Additionally, many of the camp meetings were held at night, lit only by flickering torches—another reason to avoid complicated hymnals and sheet music. These simple "spiritual songs" did eventually give way to tune books in the 1830s and 1840s.[145]

But the presence of slaves (and, in the North, former slaves) at the various, far-flung camp meetings and revivals would spark a controversy in the study of spirituals and gospel music that wouldn't die down until late in the twentieth century. Certain scholars claimed that the slave participation was a pivotal clue in proving that the spirituals, rather than being the products of African Americans, where actually songs adopted or created by the slaves *after* hearing these camp-meeting songs, which they then transformed into spirituals. In fact, they argued that the common source for *both* the black and white spirituals lay in camp meetings and white southern rural churches. Other scholars disagreed, arguing instead for an African origin of the spirituals.

The debate pitted Guy B. Johnson, George Pullen Jackson, and Newman I. White on the side of a white origin for black spirituals versus Nicholas George Ballanta, Lorenzo D. Turner, Melville Herskovits, John and Alan Lomax, Dorothy Scarborough, and others on the side of African origins for the spirituals. One of the many difficulties in shaping the argument lay in the fact that the camp-meeting hymn developed quickly within an oral tradition. Firsthand reporting from the camp meetings from eyewitnesses trained in music is rare and only occasionally conclusive.[146]

At the heart of the argument is Jackson's claim that he had identified 116 primarily shape-note melodies and texts popular during the camp meeting era and matched them with 116 spirituals out of a possible 893 known spirituals[147]: "I think we are justified in looking on Negro dramatic singing as a racial emphasis and nothing more," Jackson writes. "I believe it is erroneous to state, as does John Work, that the American negroes' dialogue patterns in song are 'unquestionably African in origin.'"[148]

But later writers and music theorists including Alan Lomax[149] and William H. Tallmadge, using more modern methods of musical analysis, have proven—if anything—that the opposite is true. Not only is the identifying structure of the camp-meeting song actually of African origin, 100 of Jackson's 116 hymns "possess structural characteristics of black vocal practice."[150]

And, when what would become known as spirituals *did* incorporate pieces of melody lines or the odd rhymed couplet from well-known hymns of the day,

> this material was immediately subjected to a molding process, bringing it in line with established musical practices developed from African sources: call-and-response, increased rhythmic flexibility, the use of handclapping for percussion (which can lay claim to being the *major* African percussive practice, and which was reported in black U.S. religious music by the eighteenth century), and the emphasis on possession states as a form of worship and a sign that the spirit was present.[151]

Other arguments have also been slowly put to rest. The claim that because some of the camp-meeting songs were published before the first collection of spirituals saw print means they were composed earlier does not take into account the very obvious fact that the spirituals were a body of ever-changing work belonging to a segment of the population that was systematically kept illiterate with no access whatsoever to the publication centers in the Northeast.[152]

Another salient point, this one from musicologist Richard Waterman, combines cultural and psychological arguments. Waterman contends that the original notation of spirituals was primarily accomplished by "New World transcribers" who wrote down the songs with a "predisposition" to their "own traditions of written music":

> Written music is a more or less faithful symbolization of psychological, not acoustic, musical realities, and the closer the perception patterns of the transcriber are to those of the person performing the music, the closer will his manuscript come to expressing the authentic musical intentions of the music. If the listener is aware of only one possible way of patterning music, all the music he hears will seem to him to fit into this, and anything which does not fit will be dismissed as incomprehensible and meaningless.[153]

Perhaps the most eloquent arguments for the African origins of spirituals comes from R. Nathaniel Dett, the gifted African-American composer. In *The Dett Collection of Negro Spirituals, Third Group,* he carefully outlines a variety of reasons that demolish the notion that this music must have come from white composers. To the assertion that the spirituals were derived from the hearing of hymns by Sankey and Moody, Dett responds that "if the revival hymns of these two evangelists had had the vitality to produce the spiritual, they would have also had the vitality to have survived their own period. Moody and Sankey hymns have disappeared from our music, while the spiritual seems ever to gain in favor, not only at home, but also abroad."[154]

Dett also argues that where sacred music had long since excised rhythm in an effort to differentiate itself from secular music, the unmistakable rhythm found in virtually all spirituals is such that the art form could not possibly have come from the long-standing tradition of dignified ecclesiastic counterpoint.[155]

And finally, perhaps most tellingly, Dett reminds us that the "one outstanding rhythmic characteristic of the spiritual—syncopation—which in caricature has marked several distinct periods in American popular music, the age of minstrelsy, of ragtime, of jazz, and lately of 'swing' music. This one idiom is of itself sufficient to stamp all Negro music as unique."[156]

Even one of the earliest proponents of the theory that spirituals were of African origin, musicologist Henry Krehbiel, notes some similarities between the spiritual "Lord, Remember Me" and Stephen Foster's popular "Camptown Races," composed in 1850. But as we shall see, there is no known date for the composition of "Lord, Remember Me"—or virtually any other spiritual, for that matter. Nor is there proof that the transcribed version of a given spiritual is the definitive one. At best, it was a snapshot of what that particular spiritual sounded like at that point in time, at that particular place in time.[157]

Perhaps the most extreme pronouncement on the subject was published in a national magazine in 1936, which flatly stated that the "stream of Negro music in America starts and finishes with white men."[158] And certainly the melodies of a few of the thousands of known spirituals bear more than a passing resemblance to certain popular songs of the eighteenth and nineteenth centuries, both sacred and profane. It would be strange if they didn't—in the days before copyright law, penning new lyrics to favorite songs was a respected gentlemanly pastime and included such proponents as Benjamin Franklin, who played guitar and harp and invented the "Glass Harmonica" or "Glassy-chord."[159] But as Chase and others point out, Foster once worked on a steamboat wharf checking cotton bales unloaded by African-American roustabouts who doubtless sang work songs and proto-spirituals. Foster didn't begin composing until 1845—perhaps decades after the musical idiom we would later know as spirituals first began to be noted.

Some scholars still debate the origins of the spiritual, even today. A more recent take on the subject is by John F. Garst, "Mutual Reinforcement and the Origins of Spirituals" from 1986, which argues that spirituals can have neither a wholly African nor wholly Western European origin and uses, by way of proof, the illustration of a blue-eyed child with a blue-eyed father and brown-eyed mother: "When there is a double heritage, neither is invalidated by the other."[160] But in 1992, Anne Dhu Shapiro applied the Samuel Bayard "tune-family" concept—the now widely accepted notion that a number of related melodies may evolve from a single original "air"—to spirituals. Shapiro, who writes extensively on musical tune-families, notes that, unlike many of their white spiritual counterparts, "the majority of nineteenth-century Negro spirituals do not fall easily into tune-family categories."[161]

Bolstered by similar findings in recent years, those arguing for African origins have slowly won the day, though the debate died hard. But this is not a tempest in a teapot—the dry academic argument where the objections are so fierce because the stakes are so low. At the heart of the matter is whether there are *any* truly American original music forms: spirituals, blues, jazz, gospel, and/or rock and roll.

Preaching

The final necessary element in the creation of spirituals may or may not be the last element introduced chronologically into the equation: preaching. There were black preachers in the South before the Great Awakening, both in the hidden (and sometimes not so hidden) praise houses and the established "free" black churches. With the rise in the number of Christians (again, both in the brush arbors and denominational churches) in the South following the Great Awakening, the African-American preacher began to assume an increasingly more significant role, both in the community and in the formation of the spiritual itself. There was, for instance, Andrew Marshall, a free African-American pastor of the First African Baptist Church in Savannah, Georgia, until his death in 1856. Marshall was "greatly respected" by the townspeople and an "idol" to his congregation of slaves.[162]

The origins of true black preaching, many scholars maintain, are not to be found in the dolorous homilies of white Anglicans or Episcopalians but, once again, in Africa.

Winifred D. Bennett's *A Survey of American Negro Oratory* ties the presence in Africa of the following traits during religious ceremonies—shouting and dancing, the presence of a highly emotional audience, impressive oratory, and audience interaction, among others elements—to the presence of similar traits in African-American preaching.[163] Jon Michael Spencer, who has written extensively on African-American preaching, states that there are startling "commonalities" between the rhythmic, melodic preaching of African-American preachers and the folk songs of West Africa:

> That black preachers intoned their sermons and prayers is no historical novelty, for their African ancestors chanted oral history and folk stories, and their African-American progeny moaned bluesy hollers and vendors whooped street cries. Additionally, just as Africans chanted tribal laws, folk stories, and proverbs, so have black preachers intoned biblical laws, Old Testament stories, and folkloric exempla.[164]

Just as West Africans perpetuated their histories through song, so did African-American preachers preserve the slave experience in sermons and spirituals.[165] W. E. B. Du Bois admits that "many of the old customs" of Africa still "cling" to the African-American church. It is the combination of African survivals and the fact that the African-American church is "the sole surviving social institution of the African fatherland that accounts for its extraordinary growth and vitality."[166]

Historic literature and diaries are full of casual observers transcribing the sermons of African-American preachers in the eighteenth and nineteenth centuries, though usually through the filters of racism, often mocking the theological concepts, demeaning the participants, and attempting to phonetically spell out the black dialect of the day. One notable account is from the journal of Edward King, who traveled widely across the South in the days following the Civil War. Below is an excerpt of a sermon he heard in Zion Hill, a village between Richmond and Petersburg:

> Then he began preaching against hypocrisy. He seemed especially to chide the women for becoming converted with too great ease. "Woe!" he cried, "woe unto dat woman what goes down into the water befo' she ready; woe unto her!" with a long, singing descent on the last words; and then he added, sotto voce, "Dat what make so many women come up stranglin' an' vomitin' an' pukin' outen de water; de debbil dat still in 'em git hole on 'em, an' shake 'em an' choke 'em under de water! Let no woman shout for Jesus what don't know 'bout Jesus! It's one thing that to git to Heaven, but it's anudder to git in! Don' ye know what Heaven is? Heaven's God! We must know what we is preachin' about, an' ef we don't we ought to SET DOWN!" (This with terrific emphasis.)
>
> In describing the creation, he said: "Breddren, it's now 12,877 years since de good Lord made de world, an' de morning stars sung togedder. Dat wa'n't a month age! I wasn't dar den!" (thus illustrating with sublime scorn the littleness of man), "but by de grace of God, I'll git dar by 'n' by!" *(Here his voice was faint and suggestive of tearful joy.)* "to join de mornin' stars, an' we'll all sing togedder!
>
> "Oh yes! Oh, yes! Heaven's God made de world an' de fullness darof, an' hung it up on de high hooks of heaven. Dar wa'n't no nails dar; no hammer dar; no nothin' but de word of God." In hinting at the terrors of death to the unconverted, he sang wild word-pictures which had a certain rude force even for us, and then shrieked out these sentences: "Ef de brudders don't want to die in de dark, dey must git Christ to hole de candle. God's grace shall be de candle in de good brudder's heart. Devils may howl, lions may roar, but nothing shall daunt dat brudder's heart. Angels shall come down with lighted candles in deir hands to congratulate de brudder." Then, once more screaming and dancing and weeping, he uttered these words: "Die right, brudder, 'n yo' shall not die in de night; yo' shall die in eternal day. Ef Christ don't bring enough, den God will come wid his candle; an' ef dat ain't enough, den de Holy Ghost'll come wid his candle, too, an' dar can't be no more night wid dat brudder's soul."[167]

Even in this sometimes condescending passage, one of the great identifying markers of black preaching is soon evident: rhythm. "Rhythm is the element that gives black preaching locomotion and momentum," Spencer writes. "Without it, preaching would not only be static, it would hardly have an audience."[168]

Rhythm in African-American preaching conveys the urgency and fervor of the preacher. As with African song, a rhythmic feel can be accomplished a number of ways—by stretching words out, by jamming words together, and by the use of dramatic pauses. The rhythm can also be emphasized with a tapping foot or a hand pounding on a pulpit.[169] Black preachers used whatever was necessary to convey the message and connect with the congregation.

"In the black church," Paul Carter Harrison writes,

> the preacher mobilizes the power of the word for incantative purposes or exorcism, blessing or curse; and though much of it is done through innuendo, his images are complete and he appears as a total force. He employs *Drum*—the timbre of rolling vowels, foot-stomping, hand-clapping—*Dance*—transporting himself, at times, up and down the aisles—and *Song*—the pitch and modulations of his voice intoning the breath of the spirit—putting together the necessary ingredients for the ritual.[170]

"[The old-time African American preacher] was illiterate," William Pipes notes, "he reflected the African heritage. Rules of logic and education did not hamper him; his sermons were the product, for the most part, of his imagination. For him, classical standards of rhetoric did not exist; his speeches were *imaginative, emotional,* and *filled with imagery;* word pictures became the keys to the minds of the Negro audience."[171]

And like the spirituals themselves, so many of them based on the classic African call-and-response model, the preacher and the congregation maintained a continual dialogue throughout the service. But more than simply acknowledging the sermon's points, African-American congregations early on began to "preach back" to the pastor.[172] In African-American preaching, those congregational responses are not random but have, over time, come to assume a complicated language all their own. Researchers have analyzed the patterns of give-and-take in the best African-American sermons, and identified three distinct response patterns or *sermonphones:*

1. *One-word sermonphones.* The most popular sermonphone is probably "well." An African-American preacher, in the throes of a particularly powerful passage, may suddenly retreat from the lectern briefly to collect his thoughts. If the congregation believes the service is progressing appropriately, someone in the back may shake his or her head and say, with obvious admiration, "Well." Other worshipers may then join in, turning the word into a chorus.
2. *Phrase sermonphones.* Phrase sermonphones are much more specialized than one-word sermonphones. A preacher who is going well may expect

Baptist congregation. Alma Plantation, False River, Louisiana, July 1934 (photo: Alan Lomax, Library of Congress Lomax Collection)

to hear such phrases as "Preach it," "Tell it," "Thank you, Jesus," or "Carry me, Lord" by way of affirmation.

3. *Nonarticulated sermonphones.* This area includes expressive nonverbal sounds variously described as "mooning," "mourning," "whooping," "turning," and "zooming."[173]

The entire service in many African-American churches, while still depending on spontaneity, is carefully crafted toward a specific goal. "In the vernacular of the culture," William C. Turner writes, "preaching of this type must 'start low, go slow, climb higher and strike fire.' If this does not occur, the speaker is often thanked for a 'talk' as a means of communicating the corporate judgment that true preaching, alas, has not taken place."[174] The service can then be likened to a symphony, with each movement propelling the listener toward a predetermined climax.

Turner maintains that African-American "preaching is musical" and that "music is one of the instruments bridging the chasm between the world of human beings and God who speaks to them through preaching. Music in black preaching establishes a direct link between the spirit within the preacher, the word that is uttered, and the worshiping congregation."[175]

In that impassioned and fertile setting, how could spirituals *not* occur?

Some observers, such as Spencer, assert that "a substantial number of spirituals evolved via the preaching event of black worship." Some spirituals, he writes, were the result of the black preachers and lay leaders crafting successful word and music combinations ahead of time to teach to their flocks. Others, however, resulted from "extemporaneous sermonizing, which crescendoed little by little to intoned utterance." Combined with the supportive sermonphones, the congregation would join in the process, picking and spontaneously shouting out beloved or familiar couplets and phrases.[176]

Then, as now, the input of the congregation is crucial for the communal celebration. "This melodious declamation," Spencer writes, "delineated into quasi-metrical phrases with formulaic cadence, was customarily enhanced by intervening tonal responses from the congregation. Responsorial iteration of catchy words, phrases, and sentences resulted in the burgeoning of song, to which new verses could be contemporaneously adjoined."[177] Some of these new spirituals were quickly forgotten, but the best new songs would be remembered and repeated again and again in the years to come. Spencer says it is a process that continues today in African-American churches.[178] In *Sacred Symphony: The Chanted Sermon of the Black Preacher,* Spencer compares transcriptions of African-American sermons from 1862, 1864, and 1938 with sixteen sermons by various modern Baptist, Holiness, and Pentecostal preachers from the Sea Islands of South Carolina to Los Angeles. The comparison reveals a remarkably similar style, one where rhythm and melody are paramount.[179]

The seminal collection of spirituals, *Slave Songs of the United States,* contains an early description of how spirituals were created, but only after admitting that the "intonations and delicate variations of even one singer cannot be reproduced on paper" in this description of a worship service led by former slaves:

> There is no singing in parts, as we understand it, and yet no two appear to be singing the same thing—the leading singer starts the words of each verse, often improvising, and the others, who "base" him, as it is called, strike in with the refrain, or even join in the solo, when the words are familiar. When the "base" begins, the leader often stops, leaving the rest of his words to be guessed at, or it may be they are taken up by one of the other singers. And the "basers" themselves seem to follow their own whims, beginning when they please and leaving off when they please. . . .[180]

Hampton Institute graduate Harris Barrett, who worried in 1912 that the spirituals were dying, once wrote that it was still possible to see spirituals spontaneously arise in African-American services:

> I have sat in a gathering where everything was as quiet and placid as a lake on a summer day, where the preacher strove in vain to awaken an interest; I have heard a brother or sister start one of these spirituals, slowly and monotonously; I have seen the congregation irresistibly drawn to take up the refrain; I have seen the entire body gradually worked up from one degree of emotion to another until, like a turbulent, angry sea, men and women, to the accompaniment of the singing, and with shouting, moaning and clapping of hands, surged and swayed to and fro. I have seen men and women at these times look and express themselves as if they were conversing with their Lord and Master, with their hands in His; and to those benighted souls it was as real as any experience of their lives.[181]

The spirituals are, Spencer explains, the inevitable outcome of the African-American worship service when a "trilogy" of essential events is triggered—"the Holy Spirit moves the black preacher and the black preacher speaks to the congregation and the congregation responds with 'Amen.'"[182] The black church accomplished this by "using the power of the Holy Spirit to transform black suffering and equate it with the suffering of Jesus"[183] in a "ritual nearly as rigid and unvarying as that used by the Catholic and High Lutheran services."[184]

"The spirituals are songs about black souls, 'stretching out into the outskirts of God's eternity' and affirming the Word that makes you know that you are a human being—no matter what white people say," writes James H. Cone.

> Through the song, black people are able to affirm that Spirit who was continuous with their existence as free beings; and they created a new style of religious worship. They shouted and they prayed; they preached and they sang, because *they had found something.* They encountered a new reality; a new God not enshrined in white churches and religious gatherings.[185]

Ultimately, our question becomes: What was this *something* that began long before the Great Awakening, this something that incorporated African melodies, rhythm, antiphonal singing, work songs, and (perhaps) snippets of other musical forms of the eighteenth and nineteenth centuries? What was this *something* involving music and spirituality that was developing beyond the slave quarters, through the virgin southern pine forest, and deep in the hidden hills and dales, far from the master's suspicious ears, miles from the Big House, on the scattered plantations of the American South? United against an implacable enemy, Ibo and Ashanti and the scatterings of a hundred more nation tribes, created *something* that kept hope alive. Together, they heroically retained and nurtured the primal features of their shared African heritage, incorporated Christianity's basic tenet—hope—to insure that "the new reality could be interpreted and spiritual needs at least partially met."[186]

The answer, of course, is that *something* is the spiritual.

So—back to our original question: When do spirituals begin?

Perhaps they begin within hours of arriving from the auction block on a plantation in South Carolina's lowlands or Virginia's piedmont. Away from the eyes of overseers and their new masters, slaves swapped tales of the crafty spider Anansi, who outwitted the lion, solemnly recited the feats of Eshu of the Yoruba, danced the mysterious ring shout, and sang—sometimes the songs of their ancestors, sometimes Christian songs, sometimes a wonderful combination of both.[187]

Perhaps the spirituals don't begin until the first slave churches, where unnamed African-American preachers combined African stories of the eagle who magically healed an old woman with stories of Moses, David, and Jesus in a rhythmic singsong to the encouragement of his tiny congregation.

Perhaps the spirituals begin in both places, everywhere, at once.

The important thing is not that the spirituals began but that they *are.*

First Spirituals

Following the Great Awakening, a few accounts survive of slaves singing the new Watts hymns in New England[188] but almost none in the South where, instead, contemporary writers continue to bemoan the slaves' lack of piety.[189] "By 1800, the opposition to giving the slaves religious instruction was disappearing as the tide of evangelical revival rose steadily," Dena Epstein writes.[190] This finally clears the way for slaves to sing religious songs openly. She cites the two earliest known examples of "distinctive" religious singing among slaves (as opposed to singing the popular hymns and psalms of the day) in an account by George Tucker in 1816, who watched a group of thirty chained slaves walk past the steps of the courthouse in Portsmouth, Virginia, "singing a little wild hymn of sweet and mournful melody; flying by a divine instinct of the heart, to the consolation of religion."[191]

A second account comes from the Quaker (and Underground Railroad organizer) Levi Coffin in 1821, who heard as "the Negroes broke out with one of
their plantation songs, or hymns, led by Uncle Frank . . . a sort of prayer in
rhyme, in which the same words occurred again and again."[192]

Neither, of course, is that elusive "smoking gun," the definitive first mention
of what is now known as the spiritual—and Coffin's account was written at least
forty years after the fact. Consequently, Epstein credits the following report from
1830, written by a visitor to Charleston, who describes in detail the religious
songs of a group of African Americans one Sunday evening, as being the first
definitive account of a unique musical form:

> . . . the religious fervor of the Negroes does not always break forth in strains
> the most reverential or refined. The downfall of the archfiend forms the principal
> topic of their anthems. A few lines recollected at random may serve as an exam-
> ple, as—

> *Sturdy sinners, come along,*
> *Hip and thigh we'll pull him down,*
> *Let us pull old Satan down,*
> *We shall get a heavenly crown, &c, &c,*

> *Old Satan, come before my face*
> *To pull my kingdom down*
> *Jesus come before my face*
> *To put my kingdom up.*
> *Well done, tankee, Massa Jesus,*
> *Halleluja, &c.*[193]

Musician and musicologist John W. Work dates the origins of spirituals earlier still, using methods other than extant publications and memoirs. According
to Work, a colony of freed slaves (mostly from Kentucky, Pennsylvania, and
South Carolina) was voluntarily transported to Samana Bay in Haiti. The group
remained isolated from the native peoples and preserved its dialect. According
to Work, at some point in the past, the colony ceased singing spirituals during
church but continued to sing them at cornhusking parties. When an American
organization visited the isolated colony in the 1930s, the descendents of the original colonists sang for them a number of spirituals, including "Roll Jordan Roll":

> This is important. Since this colony has existed in comparative isolation, the
> singing of spirituals is significant. If "Roll Jordan Roll" was taken to this colony
> in 1824 in the state in which it now exists in America, it must have been generally
> known. The number of years before 1824 which it must have taken first for the
> process of unconscious perfection and standardization, the development cycle
> [previously] discussed, and, second, for the extremely gradual dissemination of
> the spiritual over widely separated sections of the country would unquestionably

lead us to the possibility that "Roll Jordan Roll" is an eighteenth century creation.[194]

During and following the Civil War, Union officer Col. Thomas W. Higginson wrote extensively about spirituals he heard in camp while commanding the
South Carolina Volunteers. In an article from 1867, he noted that he had heard
of the "class of songs" called "Negro Spirituals" for "many years" prior to the
Civil War.[195]

John Lovell, Jr., concludes that it is "emphatically clear" the spiritual existed
"a century or more before 1867" as "independent folk song, born of the union
of African tradition and American socioreligious elements."[196]

Lydia Parrish also proposes a colonial-era beginning for spirituals. She cites
South Carolina as a possible "nursery" for spirituals because the majority of
African Americans in the Sea Islands and along the South Carolina coast are
Baptists, and Charleston was the site of intense Baptist evangelizing efforts from
1684 to 1746.[197]

A second proof of pre-1776 colonial origins for the spirituals, Parrish claims,
is the appearance of many spirituals in Prof. C. L. Edwards's *Bahama Songs and
Stories* (Boston: 1895), compiled from the descendents of slaves belonging to the
earliest families in the Bahamas, many of whom were "loyalists" who fled there
during the American Revolution.[198]

In *Negro Slave Songs in the United States*, Miles Mark Fisher supplies what is
probably the earliest proposed date for the origination of spirituals. Fisher posits
that the first spirituals came to North America with the arrival of the first African
Americans in Virginia in 1619.[199] Although he is unable to provide physical or
musicological evidence of such a date—if, indeed, any exists—Fisher's thesis that
spirituals arrived, at least in their most basic form, with the first African Americans resonates with all we know about African culture.

At some point, as the first slaves were reluctantly exposed to Christianity in
the years that followed, the songs to their ancestors and African gods became the
songs of Jesus and Moses. It would appear that these proto-spirituals would be
further shaped by the corresponding rise of two early institutions: the religious
revivals of the eighteenth century and the subsequent establishment of the African-
American preacher and his church.

For serious collectors such as John A. Lomax and his son Alan, who heard
most of the world's great music in their lifetimes, the question of the "first spirituals" was an academic one at best and hardly worth pursuing:

> Whatever their origin, whatever their structure, whatever their compo-
> nents—there can be no question in the minds and hearts of those who have heard
> them that in the Negro spirituals American folk art reaches its highest point.
> Indeed, we assert that these songs form the most impressive body of music so far
> produced by Americans, ranking with the best of music anywhere on this earth.[200]

What is known is that this something—these spirituals—were and are special. They have endured to this present day. The question is, then, why? R. Nathaniel Dett, himself a composer, believed he knew the answer:

> The difference is this—that while with other races folk singing was only one of the avenues of soul expression, with the Negro, it was the sole avenue of emotional relief. With other races, the making of the folk song was incidental to life; with the creators of the spiritual, it was life itself.
>
> On the plantation, the makers of these songs were slaves, hirelings, chattel, with minds and bodies subject to the wills and whims of their masters. At their own "meetings," often held in secret, they were utterly themselves, and thoughts and impulses and emotions burst forth with an exuberance all the more terrific by reason of having been suppressed. This gave to the spiritual an intensity of projection comparable to no other folk expression in the world.[201]

Chapter Four

What Spirituals Are,
What Spirituals Mean

The plantation songs known as "Spirituals" are the spontaneous outburst of intense religious fervour. . . . They breathe a child-like faith in a personal Father, and glow with the hope that the children of bondage will ultimately pass out of the wilderness of slavery into the land of freedom. In singing of a deliverance which they believed would surely come, with bodies swaying, with the enthusiasm born of a common experience and of a common hope, they lost sight for the moment of the auction block, of the separation of mother and child, of sister and brother. There is in the plantation songs a pathos and a beauty that appeals to a wide range of tastes, and their harmony makes abiding impression upon persons of the highest culture. The music of these songs goes to the heart because it comes from the heart.

—Booker T. Washington[1]

They that walked in darkness sang songs in the olden days—Sorrow Songs—for they were weary at heart. And so before each thought that I have written in this book, I have set a phrase, a haunting echo of these weird old songs in which the soul of the black slave spoke to men. Ever since I was a child, these songs have stirred me strangely.

—W. E. B. Du Bois[2]

The singing deacon intones his lines in a rumbling voice that pulls the whole congregation up into mellow cadences, and, although here, too, each singer is decorating the melodic line with his own tunes and quavers, he feels the texture of the whole sound and, without reflection or intent, his individual voice blends with that of his fellow-worshipers to produce a rich tower of sound. With the Negroes there is a sense of singing together, of blend—perhaps this is one of the profoundest differences between all whites and all Negro folk-singing.

Essential to the blend of voices is the "beat," the regular pulsing rhythm that runs through the Negro surge-singing (as through all their music) and which one cannot feel in the white lining hymns. The beat is extremely slow, but it is very regular and very impressive, and it binds all the voices together and makes the ancient melody roll forward like a tremendous wave in midsea, towering up and up, cresting, then subsiding into quiet, though retaining all its strength. In the quiet one hears the gentle and insistent tap-tap-tap of a single foot upon the bare, board floor.

—John A. and Alan Lomax[3]

Sometime after the arrival of African slaves on the North American continent—but long before the beginning of the American Civil War—the African-American musical form known as the spiritual assumed an identifiable shape. Unfortunately, this was before the advent of audio recordings, so researchers can only surmise what early spirituals sounded like by using extant descriptions and a few recordings made decades later in isolated churches throughout the South. Still, what has survived gives us an idea what the spirituals said and at least a hint of their music.

On the eve of the Civil War, spirituals were being performed by slaves, as they apparently had been for decades, in both hidden churches and brush arbor services and in the "authorized" or sanctioned African-American churches on southern plantations, in various towns and cities, and—occasionally—in small independent black communities.

Taken on its own, the word *spiritual* refers to one of the three kinds of sacred songs sanctioned in the New Testament church: "Let the word of Christ dwell in you richly in all wisdom; teaching and admonishing one another in psalms and hymns and spiritual songs, singing with grace in your hearts to the Lord."[4]

Not all scholars agree with using the term *spiritual* to describe this music. Lydia Parrish, who first began going to Saint Simons of the Georgia Sea Islands in 1912, was the founder of the Spiritual Singers Society of Coastal Georgia. She purposefully avoided the use of "spirituals"—referring instead to "slave songs," "slave hymns," "plantation songs," "ballads" (or "ballats), and, especially, "anthems." At the time of writing *Slave Songs of the Georgia Sea Islands,* Parrish said the songs were still called "ant'ems" in both Georgia and the Bahamas. The term *spirituals,* she believes, may have originated in South Carolina[5] where the first, and most influential, collection of spirituals *(Slave Songs of the United States,* first published in 1867) originated.

One of the first known mentions of the word *spirituals* is in W. F. Allen's article "The Negro Dialect" from *Nation,* published December 14, 1865. In it,

Allen, one of the three authors of *Slave Songs of the United States,* (under the pseudonym "Marcel"[6]), matter-of-factly mentions both "sperituals" and "running sperichils" (which he relates to ring shouts).

Both "sperituals" and "sperichils" are also mentioned in Allen's introduction to *Slave Songs of the United States.*[7] Eileen Southern notes that since none of the authors of *Slave Songs* spent time defining it, "the term must have been in common usage by the 1860s."[8] Incidentally, of the influential (and now widely quoted) articles that preceded the publication of the book,[9] only "The Negro Dialect" actually used the term "sperituals." We will examine *Slave Songs of the United States* more fully in Chapter Five.

Composition

There are a number of definitions of the religious-based African-American folk music that first came to the general public's attention in the late 1860s. One scholar described spirituals as "Musical poems, not attributable to any specific poet or composer, of the early Afro-American's view of life which, through the evolution of their fame and usage, acquired set arrangements of melody, form, harmonic treatment, and text."[10]

From a lyric standpoint, John Lovell, Jr., characterizes them as possessing "a careful organization of a vivid first line, a middle refrain line, and a chorus. The repetitions are mainly singing devices, memory aids, and means of enlisting and holding the support of the group. These methods appear in many folk songs, but in the spiritual they are generally meshed with originality and taste."[11] Southern adds the distinguishing characteristic that most spirituals feature four-line stanzas in the *aaab* rhyme scheme (three repeated lines and a refrain) or the *aaba* format (two repeated lines, one new line, then a repeat of the first).[12] The structure of both rhyme patterns encourages frequent use of the now-familiar African call and response (or, as some observers call it, "call and recall"[13]) format, with alternating solo verses with refrains.[14]

However, neither the *aaab* nor the *aaba* rhyming sequences are universally applicable, as Southern is quick to add. For instance, not all spirituals feature rhyme schemes. Since most spirituals grew out of spontaneous pastor/congregation interactions, rhymed couplets apparently were not valued as highly as an honest expression of faith. "Since the lead singers extemporized the words of a song as they went along," she writes,

> they had no time to think about rhyme, so great was their concern for the ideas they wanted to express. Perhaps during the choral response they could think ahead a bit, but not always to the extent of perfecting the rhyme. The next time the song was sung, the leader might improvise different words in response to a different set of circumstances, or a different person might lead the singing.[15]

Likewise, from the various collections of spirituals made at the time, it appears that certain popular phrases, lines, and couplets reappear so often that scholars such as Southern have named them "wandering verses" and their original settings are, not surprisingly, even more difficult to trace. Such phrases include "the lonesome valley," "the New Jerusalem," and "the ship of Zion."[16] The writers who advocated a Western European origin to all spirituals pointed to these "wandering verses" and the presence of sometimes recognizable snippets from the popular hymns of writers such as Watts as further proof of their thesis. But since the Bible is the common source of most lyrics in both traditions, that connection is tenuous at best. And when there is a recognizable white hymn referenced in a spiritual, Southern terms it a "refashioning" of both the lyrics and motives of the original hymn (or hymns)—and not just an alternative version:

> The spiritual is another song type with its own text, music, and distinctive stylistic features. Typically, the melodies of the slave songs represent original composition rather than a borrowing of old tunes. Not that the slaves were averse to appropriating tunes for their improvised songs from other repertories of the period—popular songs, Anglo-American songs, and even hymns. But, as song collector Thomas W. Higginson pointed out, "As they learned all their songs by ear, they often strayed into wholly new versions, which sometimes became popular, and entirely banished the others." In essence, the plantation songs were reshaped by the process of "communal recreation" into characteristic African American folk songs, no matter what the original sources of text and melodic materials.[17]

In a similar vein, one of the first collectors of spirituals commented that African Americans keep "exquisite time" and "do not suffer themselves to be daunted by any obstacle in the words. The most obstinate Scripture phrases or snatches from hymns they will force to do duty with any tune they please, and will dash heroically through a trochaic tune at the head of a column of iambs with wonderful skill."[18]

Music

From a musical standpoint, an all-encompassing description of spirituals is an even more slippery proposition. Exactly *what* the melodies of the spirituals sounded like is elusive at best, particularly in the days prior to the Civil War. Even that most meticulous of all researchers, Dena J. Epstein, can only offer fragmentary descriptions that provide tantalizing clues to the sacred music of slaves—despite a lifetime spent in examining travel accounts, missionary reports, letters, memoirs, fiction, newspapers, and slave narratives.[19] Epstein's sources prior to the Great Awakening of 1740 almost invariably feature clergymen and missionaries denouncing the "idolatrous" singing (and dancing) on Sunday by slaves, but precious little of exactly what this "idolatrous" music sounds like.[20]

The deep, dark waters of music theory are perilous even for trained musicians, but a few observations may be helpful as long as the listener remembers
that, when it comes to spirituals, as W. E. B. Du Bois writes, "The songs are
indeed the siftings of centuries; the music is far more ancient than the
words . . ."[21] and not always translatable by Western-trained musicians.

Jon Michael Spencer and others write that the primary melodic mode utilized
in the transcribed spirituals is pentatonic, even though some spirituals only use
a portion of the scale[22]—although, again, this observation must be viewed with
an eye toward the prejudices of musicians schooled exclusively in European-
styled conservatories. Ordinarily, the major or pentatonic scale produces lighter,
more upbeat melodies. But contemporary accounts indicate that many of the
spirituals sounded instead melancholy and apparently in a minor key—or something altogether different. William Francis Allen struggled to capture the music
of the spirituals, writing, "what makes it all the harder to unravel the thread of
melody out of this strange network is that, like birds, they seem not infrequently
to strike sounds that cannot be precisely represented by the gamut, and abound
in 'slides from one note to another, and turns and cadences not in articulated
notes.' "[23]

Although John W. Work claimed it was "impossible" to accurately record the
"extravagant *postamenta*, slurs and free use of extra notes" found in spirituals, he
was much interested in studying the scales commonly used by slaves in their
composition:

> [The slave composer] unconsciously avoided the fourth and seventh major
> scale steps in many songs, thereby using the pentatonic scale. But there were
> employed notes foreign to the conventional major and minor scales with such
> frequency as to justify their being regarded as distinct. The most common of these
> are the "flatted third" (the feature note of the blues) and the "flatted seventh."[24]

The resolution to this apparent dichotomy in the perception of spirituals in
a major or minor key is found in the African survivor known as the famed "blue
note"—certain tones in the major and pentatonic scale "flattened" or "bent" to
a lower pitch.[25] Using the transcriptions of the spirituals in *Slave Songs of the
United States*, Southern says that the seventh tone of the scale is "flatted, indicat-
ing that the tone was sung lower than normally."[26] The legendary blues artist
W. C. Handy described the "curious, groping tonality" of the "blue note" as a
"scooping, swooping, slurring tone" and identified it as one of the markers indi-
cating the African origins of the practice, whether it was used by African Americans in spirituals or the blues.[27]

Still, the writers who first chronicled spirituals in the 1860s often commented
that many of the songs were sad and in a minor key, and the misconception that
all spirituals were in a minor key has lingered to the present day. But other
than Lucy McKim Garrison, few early collectors were trained musicians. Henry

Krehbiel's study shows that spirituals in minor keys did *not* predominate—it only sounded so because of their sad nature and "alien" (to Western-trained ears, anyway) progressions and changes. Krehbiel drew from the major collections of spirituals of the day —*Slave Songs of the United States, The Story of the Jubilee Singers, Religious Folk Songs of the Negroes as Sung on the Plantations* (originally *Cabin and Plantation Songs*), *Bahama Songs and Stories*, and *Calhoun Plantation Songs*—and examined 527 spirituals. His trained analysis of the "intervallic structure of their melodies" produced the following table and effectively ended the notion that the majority of spirituals were performed in a minor key:

Ordinary major	331
Ordinary minor	62
Mixed and vague	23
Pentatonic	111
Major with flatted seventh	20
Major without fourth	78
Minor with raised sixth	8
Minor without sixth	34
Minor with raised seventh (leading-tone)	19[28]

As with anything else related to the spirituals, it is hard to make sweeping generalizations about the music. Still, it seems clear that most spirituals were not sung in unison. Instead, Southern writes that what most spirituals featured should be termed *heterophony*, where slaves "followed the lead melody for the most part but allowed themselves to wander away from it when its tones were too high, or when the text called for special emphasis, or simply when their whims indicated the need for more variety."[29]

There does, however, seem to be some agreement on the nature of spirituals when the focus is instead on the rhythm or beat of the music when compared to other forms of folk music. The spirituals show a preference for simple duple meters, with the time kept by the patting of a hand or a tapping of a foot.[30] That pronounced "beat" is one of the seven basic characteristics of a true spiritual, according to Wyatt Tee Walker:

1. Deep Biblicism
2. Eternity of Message
3. Rhythmic
4. Given to improvisation
5. Antiphonal or Call and Response
6. Double, or Coded Meaning
7. Repetitive
8. Unique imagery[31]

To those identifying characteristics, Albert Raboteau would add polyrhythms, syncopation, and ornamentation.[32]

Former slave Robert Anderson's memoirs provide intriguing insights into the music-making process of spirituals. He claimed that virtually all slaves had musical talent and were capable of creating music appropriate to the task at hand—be it lullabies, marching songs, work songs, and new melodies for spirituals:

> The slaves knew nothing about music from the standpoint of a musician, but all of them could sing and keep time to music, improvise extra little parts to a melody already known, or make up melodies of their own. They liked the weird and mysterious in religion and wove this feeling into the melodies that were improvised as a means of expressing their feelings.[33]

There were also a number of different kinds of spirituals. Certain spirituals were created expressly for a worship service, while others were preferred for the rare moment of rest. Some spirituals were only sung at baptisms and weddings, some for slave funerals (which included many practices virtually unchanged since Africa), and still others—"ring spirituals," "running spirituals," or "shout spirituals"—were reserved for the ring shout.[34] Some spirituals in particular became inextricably linked with the ring shout, including "Oh, We'll Walk Around the Fountain"; "I Know, Member, Know Lord"; "The Bells Done Ring"; "Pray All the Members"; "Go Ring That Bell"; and "I Can't Stay Behind."[35]

Other collectors and commentators, such as John W. Work, employ a different system to categorize spirituals. Work roughly divides spirituals into three groups (with representative examples):

Call and response (most common)
"Great Camp Meeting"
"Shout for Joy"
"Good Morning Everybody"
"Swing Low, Sweet Chariot"
"Sittin' Down Beside the Lamb"

Slow, sustained long-phrase melody (least common)
"Deep River"
"Nobody Knows the Trouble I Seen"
"My Lord, What a Morning"
"Were You There?"

Syncopated Segmented Melody (most popular)
"Shout All Over God's Heab'n"
"Little David Play Yo' Harp"
"Ain't Goin' Study War No Mo'"
"Ol' Ark's a-Moverin' "[36]

A final characteristic of the spiritual is its loose, unstructured nature. While a pastor or designated song leader might start the song and select the tempo and pitch, members of the congregation in most African-American churches felt free to jump in at any time and take the spiritual in a new direction or begin a new song altogether.[37] The fact that virtually none of the slave churches or brush arbor meetings are recorded as having accompanying instrumentation (and some groups banned instruments altogether for theological reasons) was another factor in the freewheeling nature of spirituals. No instrumental accompaniment meant that the music could go wherever the spirit led. This gave each service an air of expectancy and excitement not found in more formal, liturgy-led services.

"The flexible, improvisational structure of the spirituals gave them the capacity to fit an individual slave's specific experience into the consciousness of the group," adds Raboteau.

> One person's sorrow or joy became everyone's through song. Singing the spirituals is therefore both an intensely personal and vividly communal experience in which an individual received consolation for sorrow and gained a heightening of joy because his experience was shared. Perhaps in the very structure of many spirituals one can see articulated this notion of communal support. In the pattern of overlapping call and response, an individual extemporizes the verses, freely interjecting new ones from other spirituals. Frequently, before he was finished, everyone else would be repeating a chorus familiar to all.[38]

And, because the spirituals were so fluid, even the meaning of the words might change from service to service, without nullifying the original meaning.[39] No other known musical style could convey the complex beliefs of the slave in such "moving, immediate, colloquial, and, often magnificently dramatic terms."[40]

Words

For a people purposefully kept illiterate and only given bits and pieces of the Bible, the African-American slaves had a limited number of sources to draw upon as inspiration for the words they sang in their spirituals. The bulk of the lyrics are typically drawn from stories in the Old and New Testaments of the Christian Bible, the natural world around them, and personal religious testimony and experiences.[41]

Within that continuum, there is still a great deal of room for creativity. One observer places the thousands of extant spirituals into the following categories to illustrate this very point:

> Lyrics of Sorrow, Alienation, and Desolation
> Lyrics of Consolation and Faith
> Lyrics of Resistance and Defiance
> Lyrics of Deliverance
> Lyrics of Jubilation and Triumph
> Lyrics of Judgment and Reckoning

Lyrics of Regeneration
Lyrics of Spiritual Progress
Lyrics of Transcendence[42]

"In their adept mixing of naivete, dignity and sophistication—qualities of the tragic and the epic—the semantics of the spirituals run the gamut from the magnificently simple, to the ambiguous, to the utterly confounding," writes Erskine Peters.[43]

In the years following the Civil War, as more of the former slaves became literate, some of the older slaves distrusted written spirituals and hymns, claiming the printed page interfered with the direct intervention of the Holy Spirit. Jeannette Robinson Murphy's interview with an elderly woman who had once been a slave in Kentucky reveals the depth to which those slaves cherished the "mystery" of the services:

> Us ole heads use ter make 'em on de spurn of de moment, after we wrassle wid de Spirit and come thoo. But the tunes was brung from Africa by our granddaddies. Dey was jis 'miliar song . . . dey calls 'em spirituals, cause de Holy Spirit done revealed 'em to 'em. Some say Moss Jesus taught 'em, and I's seed 'em start in meetin'. We'd all be at the "prayer house" de Lord's Day, and de white preacher he'd splain de word and read whar Ezekiel done say—
> Dry bones gwine ter lib again.
> And honey, de Lord would come a-shining thoo dem pages and revive dis ole nigger's heart, and I'd jump up dar and den and holler and shout and sing and pat, and dey would all cotch de words and I'd sing it to some ole shout song I'd heard 'em sing from Africa and dey'd all take it up and keep at it, and keep a-addin to it and den it would be a spiritual. Dese spirituals am de best moanin' music in de world, case dey is de whole Bible sung out and out.[44]

But in the dangerous lives of the slaves, singing "the whole Bible sung out and out" could mean your death warrant at the hands of a capricious overseer. The spirituals contain some of the greatest, most evocative religious poetry of all time. But they were also part of the greater African-American slave communications system, an extraordinarily complex secret language that enabled these brutally oppressed people to survive—and flourish.

And, as John Storm Roberts continually cautions, just because a certain spiritual was captured on a single plantation in 1863 does not mean that that is the definitive form of that spiritual—if, indeed, a "definitive" form exists. Most transcribed spirituals were little more than snapshots.[45] It might have been the last known performance of that spiritual. It might have been the first. In the years to come, this spiritual's melody and lyric might transform and evolve until it becomes unrecognizable to the congregation where it first appeared.

Equally perilous is the presumption of assigning definite meaning to the words of a given spiritual. Working from the assumption that many of the surviving spirituals may have had multiple layers of meaning to the informed listener places the reader on much safer ground. And to admit that certain spirituals are inspired—or, as the Holiness preachers might say, *anointed*—is perhaps the sanest course of all.

"It is highly significant that with all the Biblical characters, incidents, parables, sermons and historical features to choose from, the slave, in thousands of songs, selected relatively few and turned these to only a few ends," John Lovell, Jr., writes. "The secret of his genius was in the skill of his adaptations, not in the volume of his selections. He could take the same character or incident and give it many dazzling facets. He was more interested in genial touches than in serious sermonizing. His sense of the grotesque or humorous and his comparisons of some Bible personality with ridiculous or hidden aspects of his own world were often the key to his final treatment."[46]

To understand the spirituals, the reader or singer is best served by understanding the language of the slaves who sang them. In *Black Song: The Forge and the Flame* Lovell reminds us that no one not born and reared in a particular folk community can truly understand the significance of that community's folk songs. It doesn't mean we can't sing or appreciate or study them—but we'll always be looking through a glass, darkly.[47]

The language established by enslaved African Americans was a colorful blend of African syntactical features and words, carefully created "code" words, and the dialect that resulted from generations of illiterate slaves taught only the barest necessities of spoken English. This code made communication between slave groups easier and served to effectively conceal African-American goals and dreams. Out of direst necessity, it spread to the black church as well.[48] "Even today," writes Grace Sims Holt, "a white person visiting a rural or ghetto church might find it difficult if not impossible to decipher or interpret the 'code' talk of the preacher."[49] And with the spirituals, slaves were able to create a wonderfully effective "clandestine theology,"[50] using that code to outsmart their captors.

As we have mentioned earlier, there is African precedent for this "double-voicedness." African myths, riddles, and proverbs are filled with stories of weak but clever animals outwitting their stronger counterparts, some of which found public expression in the Brer Rabbit stories.[51] Naturally, common knowledge of those tales and their secret meanings found their way into the spirituals and work songs of the slaves. "Communication in song was certainly safer than direct talk," writes Russell Ames, "and slaves could further disguise their messages by singing about animals instead of about themselves. Almost any apparently innocent and comical lines could be used to pass along word of an illegal meeting and to advise caution."[52] Years after slavery, the use of animals to convey deeper truths remained strong in the African-American community. The following bit of poetry says much about the black ability to survive as strangers in a strange land:

De white man done drive off de Injun,
Done mos' drive off de fox,
But Brer Rabbit, he say he gwine stay.[53]

It wasn't long before what began as a survival mechanism among slaves became, if not a weapon, then at least a treasured asset. To describe it, Henry Louis
Gates, Jr., coined the word "Signifyin(g)." Signifyin(g) refers to the particularly
African-American concept of combining a multitude of meanings, including
speaking on multiple levels (especially in the presence of whites), self-reference,
and identification of (apparently) arbitrary words, phrases, concepts, the sheer
joy of language, the ability to riff or improvise around someone else's words or
music, and the ability to co-opt words and concepts that have meant something
to whites and transform them into something entirely different.[54]

"Signifyin(g) is black double-voicedness; because it always entails formal re-
vision and intertextual relation," Gates writes, "and because of Esu's double-
voiced representation in art, I find it an ideal metaphor for black literary criticism for the formal manner in which texts seem concerned to address their antecedents. Repetition, with a signal difference is fundamental to the nature of
Signifyin(g) . . .".[55] Gates calls Signifyin(g) a "rhetorical practice" designed to
protect sensitive information from outsiders.[56] An instinctive understanding of
this "practice" enabled slaves standing in front of overseers to feign ignorance
and yet at the same time exchange valuable information through spirituals, work
songs, and "pidgin" English. Or, as some older African Americans once said, "A
heap see and a few know."[57] Spirituals, then, besides their very obvious religious
mandate, "communicate ethnic identity" within the community:

> . . . Black slaves used the spirituals to imitate life, to remake reality, and to
> know art as life. This experience of true soul theology or self-consciousness, often
> cloaked in silence for the sake of survival, comes alive in the Spirituals as func-
> tion, useful art affording glimpses of true humanity. Slave bards produced more
> than six thousand extant Spirituals despite the prohibition of slave education. So
> many exist because there was so much to say, to share, in codes that those beyond
> the community were not privy to understand.[58]

As a result, it is difficult to look at what appears to be—on the surface—even
the most straightforwardly narrative spiritual and not wonder for a moment if
there is not something else there. Topical spirituals, including those related to
the birth of Jesus, would seem to be about exactly what the words purport to
describe. Work considers "O Mary, What You Goin' to Name That Pretty Little
Baby?" or "Wasn't That a Mighty Day When Jesus Christ Was Born" the equal
to any Western European Christmas carol.[59] But Christa K. Dixon hears both a
hint of the slaves' anguish and a group recollection of the camp meeting revivals
in "Mary Had de Leetle Baby":

> *Mary had de leetle baby*
> *Born in Bethlehem*
> *Eb'ry time de baby cry*
> *She rock in a weary lan'*
> *Ain't dat a rockin' all night*
> *Ain't dat a rockin' all night*
> *Ain't dat a rockin' all night*
> *All night long!*[60]

Even more intriguing are "Go Tell It on de Mountain"[61] and "Rise Up, Shepherd, an' Foller."[62] To slaves yearning to be free, might lines like "When I was a seeker, I sought both night and day, I ask de Lord to help, An' He show me de way" and "If you take good heed to de angel's words, Rise up, shepherd, an' foller, Yo'll forget yo folk, yo'll forget yo' herds, Rise up, shepherd, an' foller" resonate in ways *beyond* their apparent surface meaning?

The theory that virtually every spiritual was a veiled reference to escaping to freedom had as its greatest proponent in the great African-American author and preacher Miles Mark Fisher. Some of Fisher's supporting examples, such as "Let Us Break Bread Together on Our Knees," seem obvious in retrospect. The Christian act of communion is tied neither to the solar calendar nor does it have a directional mandate, so Fisher believes that in the lines

> *When I fall on my knees, with my face to the rising sun*
> *Oh Lord, have mercy on me*

the phrase "with my face to the rising sun" is probably a coded signal for a secret meeting of the "African cult."[63] Similar interpretations by Fisher of other spirituals, however, depend on detailed knowledge of both when and where specific spirituals were actually composed, information that most scholars maintain is difficult, if not impossible, to ascertain.

However, there are certain spirituals that *do* appear to have multiple meanings. Both Fisher and Earl Conrad suggest that the legendary Harriet Tubman may have authored "Go Down, Moses," which soon became her "special" song:

> *Dark and thorny is de pathway*
> *Where de pilgrim makes his ways*
> *But beyond dis vale of sorrow*
> *Lie de fields of endless days*

Supposedly, when slaves heard this spiritual, they were to begin preparations for leaving immediately. Tubman is also supposed to have promoted the spiritual "Wade in the Water" to demonstrate how to throw bloodhounds off the scent.[64]

Dorothy Scarborough recounts how the eighty-year-old head of the Baptist Publication Society for African Americans told her in the early 1920s how "Steal

Away" became a signal for a secret religious meeting during the slave era.[65] But Russell Ames believes that "Steal Away"—which is recorded as having been sung during Nat Turner's slave rebellion in Southampton County, Virginia, in 1831— may have been composed by the charismatic Turner himself.[66] Ames's examination of these lyrics, if correct, reveals an extraordinary level of Signifyin(g):

> *CHORUS*
> *You mought be a Carroll from Carrollton*
> *Arrive here night afo' Lawd made creation*
> *But you can't keep the world from moverin' around*
> *And not turn her [Nat Turner] back from the gaining ground*
>
> *You mought be rich as cream*
> *And drive you a coach and four-horse team,*
> *But you can't keep the world from moverin' around*
> *And not turn her back from the gaining ground*
>
> *You mought be reader and writer too,*
> *And wiser than old Solomon the Jew,*
> *But you can't keep the world from moverin' around,*
> *And not turn her back from the gaining ground.*
>
> *And your name might be Caesar sure,*
> *And got you cannon can shoot a mile or more,*
> *But you can't keep the world from moverin' around,*
> *And not turn her back from the gaining ground.*[67]

Ames writes that the lyrics of the first line are obviously making sly fun of the aristocratic Carroll family. Less clear is the refrain. It is tempting to pass these off as nonsense words, but since the oft-repeated choruses are the "heart" of most spirituals, Ames is not so sure:

> "You can't keep the world from moverin' around" could well be a way of saying to the masters, "You can't stop change; you can't keep us from rebelling and escaping." The last line—"And not turn her back from the gaining ground"—seems to repeat the idea, but this is an odd and obscure line, phrased with an awkwardness rare in slave songs. Probably "not turn her" really stood for "Nat Turner," repeated over and over again. So believes Lawrence Gellert, from whose extraordinary collection this song comes to us.[68]

Ames and Gellert make a compelling argument—if the slave owners only knew what was being said about them! Still, in the days following Turner's rebellion, a number of spirituals were banned. Ames notes that by the advent of the Civil War, slaves were incarcerated in Georgetown, South Carolina, just for singing the spiritual "We Shall Be Free":

My father how long
Poor sinner suffer here?

And it won't be long
Fore de Lord will call us home.

We'll soon be free
De Lord will call us home.[69]

Ames mentions another possible slave "message" song, the spiritual "Good News, Member" (first mentioned in *Slave Songs of the United States* as #119), which might have been used to report that a friend or family member had escaped:

Good news, member, good news, member;
Don't you mind what Satan say.
Good news, member, good news, member;
I heard from heaven today.

My brother have a seat and I so glad,
Good news, member, good news.

My Hawley have a home in Paradise;
Good news, member, good news.[70]

Other songs, linked by various writers to escaping slavery, include "Steal Away to Jesus," "Swing Low, Sweet Chariot," "Seeking for a City," "Run to Jesus," "Brother Moses Go to de Promised Land," "Oh Sinner, You'd Better Get Ready," and, as mentioned in Chapter 1, "Foller de Drinkin' Gou'd." It is entirely possible, of course, that when escape attempts were brewing, old songs were given new, perhaps detailed, lyrics that outlined specific points of departure or times.[71] The vast majority of these—if they were ever written down—were "systematically" destroyed, along with all of the other records of the Underground Railroad.[72] The risks of discovery were simply too great.

Even the songs that passed easily among religious, play, and work-related situations were infused with a multiplicity of meanings. According to folk historians Frank and Doug Quimby, "Hambone" ("Ham bone, ham bone, wha's you been?/All roun' the worl' an' back again") is a "bitter commentary" on the journey of a single hambone carefully passed among slave cabins, giving flavor to other foods until it disintegrated; "Ragged Leevy" is a penetrating comment on slave life; "Ole Tar River" probably dates from Underground Railroad days; and "Shout, Daniel" referred not to the biblical Daniel but to a slave by the same name busy trying to escape an angry overseer.[73] "In Bolton," Art Rosenbaum writes in the Forward to *Slave Songs of the Georgia Sea Islands*, "it is still understood by the McIntosh County Shouters that 'kneebone bend' in the shout song 'Knee-bone' refers to their slave ancestors kneeling to pray in the wilderness when they found themselves slaves in a strange continent. . . ".[74]

It is possible to read too much into the spirituals, just as the vague writings of Nostradamus have been used to "prove" just about any prophetic notion in recent years.

Nonetheless, it is possible to actually date some spirituals to within a few decades, especially those that refer to specific people or events. For instance, the modern railroad was not introduced into the United States until the late 1820s, and no railroad lines made it into the Deep South until the 1830s and 1840s. Slaves and masters alike shared a fascination with the sound, speed, and power of the new "iron horses," though few slaves were ever allowed free run on a train. Logically, spirituals referring to railroads—"Git on Board, Little Children" (also called "The Gospel Train"), "Same Train," "When the Train Comes Along" ("I may be blind and cannot see, But I'll meet you at the station, When the train comes along"), "How Long de Train Been Gone," and others—must be no earlier than this period.[75] The words to "Git on Board, Little Children" have a particularly poignant quality and may reference the Underground Railroad as well:

> De fare is cheap, an' all can go, De rich an' poor are dere,
> No second class aboard dis train, No differunce in de fare.

But perhaps the greatest lyrical gift of the spirituals may have been their unknown composers' extraordinary ability to transform the heroes (and villains) of the Bible into a shared experience that not only taught theology but created a universal literature, an ethical model, and a method of disseminating information as well as providing a precious few moments of respite and entertainment and a source of succor to the afflicted and abused.

This was accomplished, like virtually everything the slaves accomplished, through taking the scriptural scraps given to them by their overseers and refashioning them, through the filter of their shared African memories, into something altogether new and powerful that would sustain them as African Americans living as slaves. This radical new imaging of the stories of the Bible is one of the greatest gifts of the spirituals. It strips away two thousand years of accumulated tradition to return to the ethos of the first-century Christians (or Followers of the Way), men and women who knew Jesus of Nazareth on a personal level, men and women for whom the giants of the Old Testament were just as real and vital as family members, men and women who lived in an ineffable *now*, believing every moment would see the return of the crucified Christ.

In the sprawling cast of Old and New Testament luminaries, slaves found stories and personalities expansive enough and rich enough to match the "traditional epic treatment" of their African ancestors.[76] Charshee Charlotte Lawrence-McIntyre calls them "metonymic devices"—metaphors that allowed the African Americans to infuse the biblical figures and tales with additional layers of meaning decipherable only to the code-initiated slaves.[77] Like Miles Mark Fisher, Lawrence-McIntyre asserts that many of the most common figures in the spirituals always carry this metonymic overlay:

Satan	= slave master
King Jesus	= slave benefactor
Babylon	= winter
Hell	= further South
Jordan (River)	= first step to freedom
Israelites	= enslaved African Americans
Egyptians	= slaveholders
Canaan	= land of freedom
Heaven	= Canada (north)
Home	= Africa[78]

"Satan is not a traditional Negro goblin," writes John Lovell, Jr., "he is the people who beat and cheat the slave. King Jesus is not just the abstract Christ, he is whoever helps the oppressed and disfranchised, or gives him a right to his life. Babylon and Winter are slavery as it stands—note 'Oh de winter, de winter, de winter'll soon be over, children'; Hell is often being sold South, for which the sensitive Negro had the greatest horror. Jordan is the push to freedom."[79]

But again, it is best not to definitively assign any one trait or identification to any specific concept in the spirituals. When the creative geniuses who composed the spirituals dealt with the multifaceted personalities that populate the Christian Bible, they rarely restricted themselves to just a single interpretation of any biblical event or person. The slaves were intentional about who they sang about. Some otherwise intriguing personalities, such as the flawed, tragic, but ultimately heroic King Saul, almost never appear in the spirituals, nor do many of the twelve disciples, save for Peter. However, Old Testament figures such as Daniel, David, Joshua, Jonah, Moses, and Noah dominate the extant songs. Levine says this "Old Testament bias" is because these men

> were delivered in this world and delivered in ways which struck the imagination of the slaves. Over and over their songs dwelt upon the spectacle of the Red Sea opening to allow the Hebrew slaves to pass before inundating the mighty armies of the Pharaoh. They lingered delightedly upon the image of little David humbling the great Goliath with a stone—a pretechnological victory which postbellum Negroes were to expand upon in their songs of John Henry.[80]

Some of their heroes were obvious choices, such as Samson, blinded and in chains, toppling the palace of his captors.[81] Others were more unlikely, such as the bewildered Noah ("Norah"), steadfastly building an ark, faithfully following the Lord's commands, despite the derision of his neighbors:

> *Oh God comman' Brother Norah one day*
> *Oh hist the windah let the dove come in*
> *An tol' Brother Norah to build an ark*
> *Hist the windah, let the dove come in*[82]

And, over and over, the slaves told and re-told the great stories of Moses and Daniel—Moses leading the Children of Israel out of bondage, Daniel delivered from the lion's den. "The similarity of these tales to the situation of the slaves was too clear for them not to see it," Levine adds, "[and] too clear for us to believe that the songs had no worldly content for blacks in bondage."[83]

> *He delivered Daniel from de lion's den*
> *Jonah from de belly ob de whale*
> *And de Hebrew children from de fiery furnace*
> *And why not every man?*

What is nearly as amazing is that the slaves' overseers didn't hear the obvious notes of rebellion in these songs. But then, to admit the spirituals were something other than gibberish or nursery school rhymes would have demolished the slave owners' carefully constructed mythology that African Americans were subhuman. (Following the Nat Turner revolt, a delegate to the Virginia legislature once boasted, "We have as far as possible closed every avenue by which light may enter slaves' minds. If we could extinguish a capacity to see the light our work would be completed; they would then be on a level with the beasts of the field.")[84] Consequently, the slaves sang inflammatory spirituals like this one, within earshot of their masters, at every turn:

> *Then Moses said to Israel*
> *When they stood upon the shore,*
> *"Your enemies you see today,*
> *You'll never see no more."*
>
> *Then down came the raging Pharaoh,*
> *And you may plainly see,*
> *Old Pharaoh and his host*
> *Got lost in the Red Sea.*
>
> > *Didn't old Pharaoh get lost, get lost*
> > *Didn't old Pharaoh get lost in the Red Sea?*

"It is hardly possible that the slaves made no connection between themselves and the Israelite slaves. Indeed, the escape of the Israelites and the destruction of Pharaoh's 'patter-rollers'* was repeatedly described in Negro spirituals, while their whole enslaved people was referred to as 'my army.'"[85]

---

*"Patter-rollers," "pater-rollers," or "padder-rollers" were the feared white vigilantes or "patrol officers" who roamed the Southern countryside at night, empowered by custom or legal precedent to apprehend, punish, and return any slaves they encountered.

(There will be an eerie parallel a century later when members of the under-ground church in Nazi Germany would hear sermons about the God-protected little boy David and the powerful giant Goliath. In that one-sided battle, the persecuted Confessing Christians understood what the symbols meant, even if the Gestapo spy in their midst did not. As long as the pastor stayed within the framework of the Old Testament story, he could not be denounced as "subver-sive.")[86]

Despite the danger, Frederick Douglass recalled singing songs of deliverance in front of his abusive owner, "Mr. Freeman."

A keen observer might have detected in our repeated singing of

> *O Canaan, sweet Canaan*
> *I am bound for the land of Canaan*

something more than a hope of reaching heaven. We meant to reach the *north*—and the north was our Canaan.

> *I thought I heard them say*
> *There were lions in the way*
> *I don't expect to stay*
> *Much longer here.*
> *Run to Jesus—shun the danger*
> *I don't expect to stay*
> *Much longer here.*

was a favorite air, and had a double meaning. In the lips of some, it meant the expectation of a speedy summons to a world of spirits; but, in the lips of *our* company, it simply meant a speedy pilgrimage toward a free state, and deliver-ance from all the evils and dangers of slavery.[87]

It is not surprising, then, that perhaps the most common image found in the spirituals is the deliverance of a chosen people. The core message of the spirituals may indeed be God's ultimate liberation of the suffering slave. "The message of liberation in the spirituals is based on the biblical contention that God's righ-teousness is revealed in his deliverance of the oppressed from the shackles of human bondage," writes James H. Cone.[88]

The universe of the spirituals revolved not around the man and woman in the Big House or the sadistic overseers in the field. It instead focused on "God and Jesus and the entire pantheon of Old Testament figures who set the stan-dards, established the precedents and defined the values; who, in short, consti-tuted the 'significant others.' "[89] And, in that regard, the stories of the Bible were a "gold mine" for the slave composers.[90]

A second reason for the enduring power of the spirituals is the absolute, often tender familiarity the slaves enjoyed with the men and women of the Bible. They *lived* these stories. They sang of King Jesus, Weeping Mary, Brudder Joshua, and the others in the most intimate terms. Even Death is personified:

> *Oh Deat', he is a little man*
> *And he goes from do' to do'*
> *He kill some souls and he wounded some*
> *And he lef' some souls to pray.*[91]

One of the most charming, if a little unsettling, uses of intensely personal imagery in the spirituals depicts a race between the narrator and Satan:

> *Ole Satan is a busy ole man*
> *He rolls stones in my way*
> *Moss' Jesus is my bosom friend*
> *He roll 'em out o' my way.*[92]

Few songs of the Nativity narratives from *any* era or culture have the gentle, sweet-spirit magic of lines like "Mary, what you goin' to name that pretty little Baby?" This compelling merging of the sacred and the profane, of spirit and flesh, is one of the most endearing qualities of spirituals. "Such intimacy between man and God is extraordinarily pronounced in Negro spirituals compared with other folk songs," notes Ames. "No doubt this is partly explained by the slaves' extreme sufferings, but it must also have had its origins in Africa where relations with supernatural beings are personal and intimate. In West African religions today, the spirit world overlaps with the human world, and gods, ancestors, and other spirits are close at hand all the time. So they are also in the spirituals . . .".[93]

This was possible, of course, because the slaves were able to separate the gold from the dross of Christianity. The slave composers quickly identified with the "real" Jesus Christ, the one written about in the Gospels of the New Testament, not the Jesus described in the sermons of white preachers. African-American slave Christianity was built on a compassionate and suffering Jesus,

> . . . a promulgator of freedom and peace and opportunity, a son of an omnipotent Father. Christ and his Father had proved themselves. They had brought justice out of many impossible situations and could and would bring it bold out of slavery, when the time came. They were already bringing it out, to some extent, since they were guiding so many black people [runaways] to the realms of freedom.[94]

It is this empathy with King Jesus that created some of the greatest spirituals, those depicting the Crucifixion. To African Americans, to be unjustly accused and nonchalantly murdered was an all-too-regular occurrence:

Those cruel people! Those cruel people!
Those cruel people! Those cruel people!

Hammering! Hammering! Hammering!

They crucified my Lord, They crucified my Lord, They crucified my Lord.
They nailed him to the tree, They nailed him to the tree, They nailed him to the tree.
You hear the hammers ringing, You hear the hammers ringing,
You hear the hammers ringing.
The blood came trickling down, The blood came trickling down,
The blood came trickling down.[95]

Another spiritual that resonated with slaves was the curious "He Never Said a Mumblin' Word." Although the four gospel accounts report that Christ *did* speak at different times during His trial and crucifixion, the slave composers instead chose to emphasize His silence:

They led Him to Pilate's bar
Not a word, not a word, not a word.
They led Him to Pilate's bar
Not a word, not a word, not a word.
They led Him to Pilate's bar
But He never said a mumblin' word, Not a word, not a word, not a word.[96]

But it is perhaps in "Were You There When They Crucified My Lord?" that the spiritual finds its greatest expression on this subject:

Were you there when they crucified my Lord?
Were you there when they crucified my Lord?
Sometimes it causes me to tremble, tremble, tremble
Were you there when they crucified my Lord?

Were you there when they nailed Him to the tree?
Were you there when they nailed Him to the tree?
Sometimes it causes me to tremble, tremble, tremble
Were you there when they nailed Him to the tree?[97]

There are a number of reasons for the power of this spiritual. Christa K. Dixon notes that while the biblical account never refers to the Roman cross as a "tree," the tree image must have had a chilling psychic connection for slaves who had seen friends and family members hung and lynched in trees.[98] That connection endured for their children and children's children in the South of Jim Crow through the late 1960s.

"Were You There When They Crucified My Lord?" is a vivid example of another reason why the spirituals are singular in their power: they convey a sense of the immediacy of the event. The narrator is there, witnessing this awful event in real time. Some of the greatest spirituals have a first-person, present-tense urgency that makes them compelling hundreds of years later. Save for a very few exceptions (for instance, "Amazing Grace" and, later, "The Old Rugged Cross"), the hymns and the sacred songs of the white churches prefer a more manageable (and more comfortable) distance between the composer and his or her subject matter.

To the slave, space and time were irrelevant, as it was to the Renaissance painters who placed fifteenth-century garb on Christ and the Apostles. "There was an immediacy about their relationship to biblical persons which allowed for intimacy in the midst of estrangement," writes Dixon. Slaves didn't sing *about* David, they sang *to* David: "Lil David, play on yo' harp, Hallelu, hallelu."[99] Lawrence Levine calls it "sacred time," an understanding of the infinite *now* that enabled slaves to equate President Abraham Lincoln with Father Abraham and Harriet Tubman with Moses in a place where past, present, and future are all one. The slave actually witnesses Christ being crucified—"It causes me to tremble," even now.[100] As one writer put it, "Another remarkable quality of Negro spirituals . . . is their immediacy—the sense that Biblical history is taking place right before your eyes or even that you are included in the action."[101]

"For the slaves, then, songs of God and the mythic heroes of their religion were not confined to a specific time or place, but were appropriate to almost every situation."[102] Time extends upward to allow communication with God and downward to allow the archetypal ancestors to be continually re-enacted and recovered at the same time—sacred time. "For the slaves, then, songs of God and the mythic heroes of their religion were not confined to a specific time or place, but were appropriate to almost every situation."[103]

This concept, as expressed through the spirituals, enabled the slaves to soar beyond their chains and inextricably tie their lives both with the lives of the biblical saints in the past and John the Revelator's vision of the heavenly kingdom to come. "The spirituals are the record of a people who found the status, the harmony, the values, the order they needed to survive by internally creating an expanded universe, by literally willing themselves re-born," writes Levine.[104]

The spirituals were thus essential in creating a shared consciousness—and a shared community. All shared in the passion of Christ, all crossed the Red Sea with Moses, all looked to be free—be it in heaven or in Canada—together.

"Standing the storms of life as a group is much easier than standing them individual by individual," declares John Lovell, Jr.

> The slave poet and all his singers knew that the breaking down of the group morale of the slaves was considered to be a necessity of the governing classes. If the master and the overseer could handle them one by one, they could inflict upon them all any kind of discipline. But if they held together as a group, their resistance would be hard to overcome. Thus they sang,

> > *We'll stand the storm,*
> > *It won't be long,*
> > *We'll anchor by and by.*[105]

Baptist Congregation. Alma Plantation, False River, Louisiana, July 1934 (photo: Alan Lomax, Library of Congress Lomax Collection)

And if they do "stand the storm," something wonderful happens. Lovell believes that the "really significant poetry" is found in the spirituals that celebrate heaven:

> Take a simple spiritual like "I Got Shoes." "When I get to heav'm" means when I get free. It is a Walt Whitman "I," meaning any slave, present or future. If I personally don't, my children or grandchildren, or my friend on the other end of the plantation will. What a glorious sigh these people breathed when one of their group slipped through to freedom! What a tragic intensity they felt when one was shot down trying to escape!
>
> So, the group-mind speaks in the group way, all for one, one for all. "When I get to heav'm, gonna put on my shoes . . ." that means he has talents, abilities, programs manufactured, ready to wear. On [Frederick] Douglass' plantation, the slaves bossed, directed, charted everything—horse-shoeing, cart-mending, plow-repairing, coopering, grinding, weaving, "all completely done by slaves." But he has much finer shoes than that which he has no chance to wear. He does not mean he will outgrow work, but simply that he will make his work count for something, which slavery prevents. When he gets a chance, he says, he is going to "shout all ober God's heav'm"—make every section of his community feel his power. He knows he can do it.[106]

There are many more spirituals, thousands more. There are spirituals celebrated for haunting beauty of the melody: "Deep River" and "Swing Low, Sweet Chariot." There are spirituals celebrated for the quiet power of their words: "Lay This Body Down" ("I walk in de moonlight, I walk in de starlight, I lay dis body down. I know de graveyard, I know de graveyard, When I lay dis body down."). And there are epic spirituals with dozens, perhaps hundreds of verses that tell the story of not just one nation, but two: "Go Down, Moses."

In summation, Lovell makes a thoughtful observation:

> The Negro slave is the largest homogenous group in a melting-pot America. He analyzed and synthesized his life in his songs and sayings. In hundreds of songs called spirituals, he produced an epic cycle; and, as in every such instance, he concealed there his deepest thoughts and ideas, his hard-finished plans and hopes and dreams. The exploration of these songs for their social truths presents a tremendous problem. It must be done, for, as in the kernel of the Iliad lies the genius of the Greeks, so in the kernel of the spiritual lies the genius of the American Negro.[107]

Legendary African-American speaker/author/freedom fighter Frederick Douglass, ca. 1879 (photo: George K. Warren, National Archives Gift Collection)

Chapter Five

The American Civil War

But it is in religion that the African pours out his whole voice and soul. A child in intellect, he is a child in faith. All the revelations of the Bible have to him a startling vividness, and he will sing of the judgment and the resurrection with a terror or a triumph which cannot be concealed. In religion he finds also an element of freedom which he does not find in his hard life, and in these wild bursts of melody he seems to give utterance to that exultant liberty of soul which no chains can bind, and no oppression subdue.

—Unsigned article, *Dwight's Journal of Music*, November 15, 1856[1]

Like tears, [spirituals] were relief to aching hearts. Personally, I think these spirituals did more for our emancipation than all the guns of the Civil War.

—W. C. Handy[2]

The passage of time has softened the passions that raged during the Civil War, but for the participants on both sides, it consumed Americans—slave and free—like nothing that had gone before and like nothing ever would again. The War Between the States, The States Rights War, the Civil War remains, for many, the defining moment in American history. But for those most directly affected by its outcome, the slaves, it was nothing less than a struggle between good and evil, life and death, freedom and bondage. How pernicious was this slavery? Historian Stanley M. Elkins writes that the only comparable shared collective experience in recent American history was the Nazi concentration camp. "The concentration camp was not only a perverted slave system," he writes, "it was also—what is less obvious but even more to the point—a perverted patriarchy."[3] It was a system that forced children into the fields to work

94

at age six. It was a system that routinely starved, overworked, and brutalized slaves until few lived into their late forties.[4] White-haired Uncle Tom of *Uncle Tom's Cabin* was an anomaly in slave life.

Enough books have been written on the American Civil War to fill a library and the merits and failings of its various participants have been debated in the great academic journals for more than a century. But there were other heroes besides the great political leaders and generals, otherwise ordinary men and women who risked their lives for the lives of strangers. Two of the best known, Sojourner Truth and Harriet Tubman, are only representative of the unknown thousands who dared to free the slaves and work along the famed Underground Railroad. Sojourner Truth served as a spy for Union regiments and tirelessly lectured (and sang) to raise money for distribution in Union camps.[5]

Tubman, who is forever linked with the spirituals, is worth a special mention. No fugitive slave was ever caught under the watch of the tiny African American, her back and shoulders ribboned from the beatings of numerous masters. Half starved as a child, uneducated, narcoleptic, partially deaf from a blow, and missing her front teeth, Tubman served as nurse, spy, and guerilla fighter in the cause of freedom.[6] In the course of her shadowy career, the woman dubbed "General Tubman" by John Brown and "Moses" by others led untold hundreds of slaves to freedom along the Underground Railroad.[7] Her friends called her "Old Chariot"—a chariot being *any* means a slave could be conveyed North. According to Earl Conrad, when slaves sang the spiritual

> *I looked over Jordan and what did I see,*
> *Coming for to carry me home,*
> *A band of angels coming after me,*
> *Coming for to carry me home*

the "band of angels" was Tubman, or another conductor, leading them to freedom.[8]

Tubman led more than slaves. She once commanded more than 300 African-American soldiers on a successful raid up the Combahee River, freeing more than 750 slaves.[9] "When the Negro put on the 'blue,' Moses was in her glory and traveled from camp to camp, always treated in the most respectful manner," William Still writes. "The black men would have died for this woman, for they believed she had a charmed life."[10] While in Canada in 1860, Still once encountered several slaves Tubman had personally led to safety—all of whom believed she possessed a supernatural power. When someone in Still's party asked one of the now-free slaves if they'd feared capture along the way, the man replied:

> "Oh no," said he. "Moses got de charm."
> "What do you mean?" we asked.

He replied, "De whites can't catch Moses, kase you see she's born wid de charm. De Lord has given Moses power."[11]

Charmed or not, Tubman used spirituals as signal songs in her journeys. "One could go through every major experience of Harriet Tubman and find that she expressed her victories in songs; songs that are now known to us as spirituals," writes Conrad. "Music was a means, a leverage, a shrewd resort; it was a mask for the real Negro who was, beneath the melody, thinking, planning and advancing."[12]

In time, Tubman's fame (or notoriety) reached beyond the United States. William Still, the ardent abolitionist and head of the Philadelphia branch of the Underground Railroad, received a letter in March 1857 from one of Tubman's many friends:

> I have been very anxious for some time past, to hear what has become of Harriet Tubman. The last I heard of her, she was in the State of York, on her way to Canada with some friends, last fall. Has thee seen, or heard anything of her lately? It would be a sorrowful fact, if such a hero as she, should be lost from the Underground Rail Road. I have just received a letter from Ireland, making inquiry respecting her.[13]

Tubman died March 10, 1913, with Eliza E. Peterson, leader of the national African-American temperance organization, and two ministers present. With her waning strength, she is said to have conducted her own service, closing with the singing of "Swing Low, Sweet Chariot."[14]

Tubman's other "signature" spiritual, "Go Down, Moses," has the distinction of being the first spiritual published with music in the United States. In September 1861, the American Missionary Association assigned the Reverend Lewis C. Lockwood, an employee of the Young Men's Christian Association, to Fortress Monroe, near present-day Hampton, Virginia. There he transcribed Tubman's "Go Down, Moses." The first stanza was published in the *National Anti-Slavery Standard* on October 12, 1861. On December 2, Lockwood sent the complete twenty stanzas to the YMCA secretary in New York City, who then forwarded it to the *New York Tribune,* which printed the complete text. Both words and music were published by the *National Anti-Slavery Standard* on December 14, 1861.[15]

Tubman was friends with Col. Thomas W. Higginson, one of an incredible group of minds gathered during the early days of the Civil War in or near Port Royal, South Carolina. Their presence there would serve as one of the most significant milestones in African-American music in the United States. In addition to Higginson, commander of the South Carolina Volunteer Regiment, a Harvard graduate, minister, and ardent abolitionist, Port Royal and the surrounding islands would be the home of such perceptive observers as Charlotte

Forten, a young black teacher from Philadelphia; Laura M. Towne, an African-American teacher from New Jersey; teacher and author Elizabeth Botume; and Lucy McKim Garrison, one of the coauthors of *Slave Songs of the United States*. All played important roles in the history of spirituals and gospel music.

Most Americans were only "dimly aware" that such a thing called "spirituals" even existed on the eve of the Civil War, and much of what passed as African-American music was actually white-composed parodies composed expressly for the minstrel theater so popular during this era.[16] The field reports from Higginson and others "shattered" the "closed society" that had been the American South and made available reports of this music to sympathetic northern readers.[17]

After the war began, the Union blockade of the South was soon followed by the fall of a number of Confederate fortresses and ports up and down the Atlantic seaboard. When Major-General Benjamin F. Butler took Fortress Monroe on May 24, 1861, three slaves crossed the Union lines to safety. Butler eventually termed them "contrabands of war," unleashing a flood of slaves into Union camps all along the Atlantic coast and elsewhere.[18] The term *contrabands* soon caught on in the press. When the South Carolina Sea Islands fell to Union forces, the military governor was authorized to raise five regiments from the ranks of the contrabands on the islands. In January of 1863, Colonel Higginson was chosen to lead the First South Carolina Colored Volunteers, the first African-American soldiers authorized by the War Department, organized days before the famed Massachusetts 54th Regiment.[19] A fierce advocate of both abolitionism and women's suffrage, Higginson, who had once met John Brown while working to free slaves in Kansas, wrote elegant articles and surprisingly contemporary memoirs that vividly described shouts and hitherto unknown spirituals[20] and did much to spur national interest in the music of slaves.

On one forced march, Higginson tells how his men sang, in rapid succession, "John Brown's Body," "What Make Old Satan for Follow Me So?" "Marching Along," "Hold Your Light on Canaan's Shore," "When This Cruel War Is Over,"

> . . . yielding presently to a giant burst of the favorite marching song among them all, and one at which every step instinctively quickened, so light and jubilant its rhythm—

> *All true children gwine in de wilderness*
> *Gwine in de wilderness, gwine in de wilderness*
> *True believers gwine in de wilderness*
> *To take away de sins ob de world*

> ending in a "Hoigh!" after each verse, a sort of Irish yell. For all the songs, but especially for their own wild hymns, they constantly improvised simple verses, with the same odd mingling—the little facts of to-day's march being inter-

woven with the depths of theological gloom, and the same jubilant chorus annexed to all; thus—

> We're gwine to de Ferry
>> De bell done ringing
> Gwine to de landing
>> De bell done ringing
> Trust, believer
>> O, de bell done ringing
> Satan's behind me
>> De bell done ringing
> 'T is a misty morning
>> De bell done ringing
> O de road am sandy
>> De bell done ringing
> Hell been opened
>> De bell done ringing

and so on indefinitely.[21]

Higginson's carefully described notes on dozens of various spirituals, how they were sung, and when they were sung remain invaluable for researchers even today. Even his offhand comments about specific spirituals are perceptive:

> But of all the "spirituals" that which surprised me the most, I think—perhaps because it was that in which external nature furnished the images most directly—was this. With all my experience of their ideal ways of speech, I was startled when first I came on such a flower of poetry in that dark soil.

XVII. I Know Moon-rise

> I know moon-rise, I know star-rise
>> Lay dis body down
> I walk in de moonlight, I walk in de starlight
>> To lay dis body down
> I'll walk in de graveyard, I'll walk through de graveyard
>> To lay dis body down
> I'll lie in de grave and stretch out my arms
>> Lay dis body down
> I go to de judgment in de evenin' of de day
>> When I lay dis body down
> And my soul and your soul will meet in de day
>> When I lay dis body down

"I'll lie in de grave and stretch out my arms." Never, it seems to me, since man first lived and suffered, was his infinite longing for peace uttered more plaintively than in that line.[22]

In addition to providing the words to such important spirituals as "Lord, Remember Me," "Many Thousand Go," and "Rain Fall and Wet Becky Lawton," Higginson notes, for instance, on "Blow Your Trumpet, Gabriel" that he'd first heard it in his "boyish days" (in the Northeast), providing another valuable clue in the ongoing effort to date the spirituals.[23] Likewise, in his short discussion of "We'll Soon Be Free" ("We'll soon be free, we'll soon be free, we'll soon be free, When de Lord will call us home"), he mentions that a young drummer explained to him that the freed slaves understood the symbolic nature of the words while singing it in front of their masters, "Dey tink *de Lord* mean for say *de Yankees*."[24] Higginson also reports on his delight at being present at the birth of a spiritual, a spontaneous song called "The Driver" that emerged while he was being rowed from Beaufort to Ladies's Island.[25]

Preservation of the spirituals became a religious quest for Higginson, who insisted that "history cannot afford to lose this portion of its record." Of the spirituals, he writes, "There is no parallel instance of an oppressed race thus sustained by the religious sentiment alone. These songs are but the vocal expression of the simplicity of their faith and the sublimity of their long resignation."[26]

Among the first civilians to visit the Sea Islands in the summer of 1862 were Miller McKim and his daughter Lucy, then just nineteen. The McKims were sent to Port Royal at the behest of Philadelphia abolitionists, who sought information about the contrabands' needs for teachers and supplies. Lucy McKim (later Garrison) was, particularly for the era, both well educated and an extremely accomplished musician.[27] Apparently already familiar with spirituals, she spent her few weeks on the Sea Islands wisely and productively, and quickly became enraptured with the music she was hearing. Not only did she begin collecting the spirituals, she began touting them to the popular magazines and newspapers of the day. Her letters were among the first to seriously try and accurately reproduce "the odd turns" she was hearing. "The musician was perceptive and sensitive enough to appreciate a musical style so vastly different from any she had known," writes Epstein, "while the girl abolitionist responded with deep sympathy to the human warmth, the sadness and the beauty of the songs."[28]

After her return home to New Jersey, McKim joined her collection of spirituals with the even larger one of her cousin, Charles P. Ware, one of fifty-seven teachers and missionaries recruited by the Education Commission for Freedmen and another avid collector, even as she continued to solicit new songs from her friends in Port Royal.[29] The third name on the cover of the book that would eventually become *Slave Songs of the United States* was William F. Allen, a noted scholar, musician, and one of the few men of his era who had had experience writing down folk songs. Allen also lived for several years among the contrabands and contributed the lengthy, oft-quoted introduction to *Slave Songs of the United States*.[30]

Although *Slave Songs* didn't create much of a stir upon its publication in 1867, it is today regarded as a milestone not just in African-American music but in modern folk history. The authors were uncommonly "modern" for the era, earnestly trying to capture the essence of the music they were hearing and re-freshingly free of the racial prejudice and stereotyping common among even much later collectors. *Slave Songs*, and its subsequent reprintings over the dec-ades, gave the world its first taste of such memorable spirituals as "Roll, Jordan, Roll," "Michael, Row the Boat Ashore," "Nobody Knows the Trouble I've Had," "Jacob's Ladder," "I'm Troubled in Mind," "Rock o' My Soul," "The Good Old Way"—136 spirituals in all.

Lucy McKim Garrison, William F. Allen, and Charles P. Ware were more than just collectors. They studiously divided the spirituals by the regions where they were collected, including a startling set of religious folk songs in Creole French from Louisiana. They carefully noted who provided the songs (including Higginson) and, where applicable, added notes about the subject or singer of a spiritual. Musicologist Harold Courlander once termed the importance of *Slave Songs of the United States* as being "something like our first orbital lunar flight."[31]

Even in 1867, the authors were lamenting the loss of "genuine" slave and plantation songs—and the rise of "spurious imitations, manufactured to suit the somewhat sentimental taste of community." A great number of spirituals transcribed in the spring of 1866 in Richmond, Virginia, were apparently lost with the sinking of the *Wagner*. "In making the present collection," noted Allen in the introduction,

> we have only gleaned upon the surface, and in a very narrow field. The wealth of material still awaiting the collector can be guessed from a glance at the localities of those we have, and from the fact, mentioned above, that of the first forty-three of the collection, most were sung upon a single plantation, and that it is very certain that the store of this plantation were by no means exhausted.[32]

The authors attempted to collect the spirituals directly from the singers themselves wherever possible. They documented that, for instance, "Roll, Jordan, Roll" was sung in South Carolina and Florida but not in North Carolina.[33] The largest collection was compiled by Ware, primarily at Coffin's Point, Saint Hel-ena Island.[34] Allen, very astutely (for the time) attributes a directly African origin for a number of the melodies, most notably "The Trouble of the World," "Hold Your Light," "Go in the Wilderness," "Becky (or Becca) Lawton," "Shall I Die," and "'Round the Corn, Sally."

"'O'er the Crossing' (No. 93) may very well be purely African in origin," he notes. "Indeed, it is very likely that if we had found it possible to get at more of their secular music, we should have come to another conclusion as to the pro-portion of the barbaric element."[35] (However, Higginson claimed to have never heard a "secular" song among the Port Royal freedmen.)

As for the individual spirituals, some of the annotations are equally informa-tive. For the haunting air "Lay This Body Down," first noted by Higginson, the

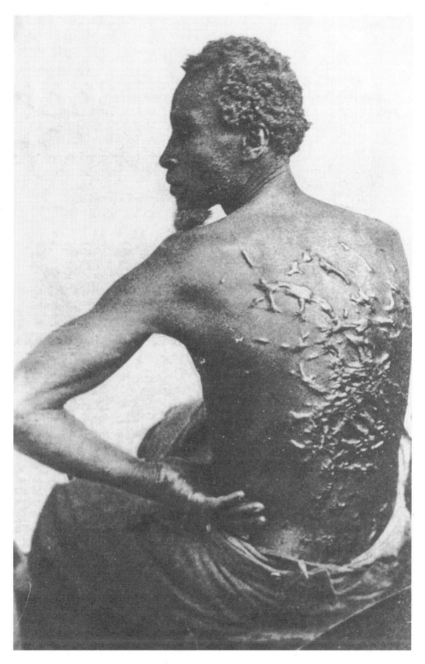

Peter, Baton Rouge, Louisiana, April 1863. Not even savage whippings could deter slaves from singing. (photo: the National Archives)

authors added a lengthy history. They suggest, for instance, that "Lay This Body Down" may have been the song heard by reporter W. H. Russell of the *London Times* and mentioned in his book *My Diary North and South* (first published in 1863):

> The writer was on his way from Pocotaligo to Mr. Trescot's estate on Barnwell Island, and of the midnight row thither he says:
>
> "The oarsmen, as they bent to their task, beguiled the way by singing in unison a real negro melody, which was unlike the works of the Ethiopian Serenaders as anything in song could be unlike another. It was a barbaric sort of madrigal, in which one singer beginning was followed by the others in unison, repeating the refrain in chorus, and full of quaint expression and melancholy:
>
> > *Oh your soul! Oh my soul! I'm going to the churchyard*
> > *To lay this body down*
> > *Oh my soul! Oh your soul! We're going to the churchyard*
> > *To lay this nigger down.*
>
> "And then some appeal to the difficulty of passing the 'Jawdam' constituted the whole of the song, which continued with unabated energy during the whole of the little voyage. To me it was a strange scene. The stream, dark as Lethe, flowing between the silent, houseless rugged banks, lighted up near the landing by the fire in the woods, which reddened the sky—the wild strain, and the unearthly adjurations to the singers' souls, as though they were palpable, put me in mind of the fancied voyage across the Styx."[36]

One of the most intriguing spirituals in the collection is number fifty-two, the mournful, plaintive "Shall I Die?" which shows up only rarely in other collections. The authors say it was "a great favorite on the Capt. John Fripp plantation," commenting on its "simplicity, wildness and minor character," which suggests an African origin:

> *Believer, O shall I die? O my army, shall I die?*
> *Jesus die, shall I die? Die on the cross, shall I die?*
> *Die, die, die, shall I die? Jesus da coming, shall I die?*
> *Run for to meet him, shall I die? Weep like a weeper, shall I die?*
> *Mourn like a mourner, shall I die? Cry like a crier, shall I die?*[37]

More familiar to modern listeners is "The Good Old Way," a spiritual made famous by the movie *O Brother, Where Art Thou?*:

> *As I went down in de valley to pray,*
> *Studying about dat good old way,*
> *When you shall wear de starry crown,*
> *Good Lord, show me de way.*

O mourner/sister let's go down, let's go down, let's go down,
O mourner/sister let's go down,
Down in the de valley to pray.[38]

Ultimately, all of the spirituals found in *Slave Songs of the United States* are worth additional study. Whatever the limitations of this seminal collection, Dena J. Epstein is quick to note that "[s]ympathetic appreciation for exotic folk musics was rare" during this era and that "the editors of *Slave Songs* were far in advance of the musical community in general."[39] Allen echoes those sentiments in his introduction, proclaiming that all of the spirituals in the collection are priceless in tracing the life and development of the African-American slave.

"The wild, sad strains tell, as the sufferers themselves could, of crushed hopes, keen sorrow, and a dull, daily misery, which covered them as hopelessly as the fog from the rice swamps," he writes. "On the other hand, the words breathe a trusting faith in rest for the future—in 'Canaan's air and happy land.' To which their eyes seem constantly turned."[40]

There were other teachers and missionaries in the South Carolina and Georgia Sea Islands, along with Fortress Monroe and the other Union camps that soon burst at the seams with suddenly free slaves. Among them was Laura M. Towne, who spent thirty years keeping famed Penn School going, often with her own money, and who was dearly beloved by the students. Towne was a good friend of the McKims and once dined with Col. Robert Gould Shaw in the days before the all-black Massachusetts 54th Regiment made its brave, if doomed, assault on Fort Wagner (as seen in the movie *Glory*).

Towne provided some of the songs in *Slave Songs of the United States* and wrote a wonderful book about her twenty years in the Sea Islands.[41] Towne's contributions include a vivid description of a shout and a discussion of the slave religion as it is voiced in the spirituals. In one touching story, she tells of an interview between a Union officer and a former slave. The slave had been much abused by his former master:

"Well," said an officer standing by, "we have caught him and now what shall we do with him?" "Hang him, hang him—hanging is too good for him," cried the Negro, in great excitement. "Well," said the officer, "he shall be hung, boy, and since he injured you so much, you shall have a chance now to pay him back. You shall hang him yourself, and we'll protect you and see it done." "Oh no, can't do it—can't do it—can't see massa suffer. Don't want to see him suffer."[42]

In another diary entry, Towne reported a conversation between a former slave and his one-time master. The slave had confidently expressed the hope of going to heaven someday, but the owner had sneered at the thought of Jesus taking "d—d black niggers into heaven." The slave stood his ground and replied that "he felt sure of one thing, they would be where Christ was, and even if that was in hell, it would be a heaven, for it did not matter what place they were in if they were only with Christ."[43]

Like Higginson, Henry George Spaulding was a Unitarian minister. As a member of the U.S. Sanitary Commission during the Civil War, he visited Port Royal, Saint Helena, and Beaufort in the South Carolina Sea Islands in 1863 while with the navy. Spaulding recorded numerous spirituals for *Slave Songs,* including the first known transcriptions of "O Lord, Remember Me" and "The Lonesome Valley." His article "Under the Palmetto" for the *Continental Monthly* in August 1863 is another important early resource in the history of spirituals.

"The words of the shout songs are a singular medley of things sacred and profane," he writes, "and are the natural outgrowth of the imperfect and fragmentary knowledge of the Scriptures which the Negroes have picked up.

> The tunes to which these songs are sung, some of them weird and wild— "barbaric madrigals"—while others are sweet and impressive melodies. The most striking of their barbaric airs it would be impossible to write out, but many of their more common melodies are easily caught upon being heard a few times. This music of the Negro shout opens a new and rich field of melody—a mine in which there is much rough quartz, but also many veins of sparkling ore.[44]

But perhaps the most penetrating observer, certainly from a modern standpoint, was Charlotte Forten, one of the first African-American teachers sent to the Sea Islands of South Carolina in 1862 by the New England Freedmen's Aid Society. The Forten family was well known and well regarded in Philadelphia and was closely allied with Higginson, John Greenleaf Whittier, and William Lloyd Garrison. Charlotte was an accomplished musician and teacher, and her detailed, sometimes introspective memories of a year and a half spent among the contrabands on Saint Helena Island were first published in *Atlantic Monthly* during the Civil War. They were not collected and released as a book until 1953.[45]

Among the many spirituals Forten describes is from this depiction of a service at a Baptist church where the "people came in slowly; for they have no way of knowing the hour, except by the sun." What follows is a fine example of the fluid, yet intensely personal nature of the spirituals:

> The people sang, "Roll, Jordan Roll," the grandest of all their hymns. There is a great rolling wave of sound through it all.

> > *Mr. Fuller settin' on de Tree of Life,*
> > *Fur to hear de ven Jordan roll.*
> > *Oh, roll, Jordan! Roll, Jordan! Roll, Jordan roll!*
> > *Oh, roll, Jordan! Roll, oh, roll, Jordan roll!*
> >
> > *Little chil'en, learn to fear de Lord,*
> > *And let your days be long.*
> > *Oh, roll, Jordan! Roll, Jordan! Roll, Jordan roll!*

Oh, march, de angel, march! Oh, march, de angel, march!
My soul arise in heab'n, Lord,
Fur to hear de ven Jordan roll!

The "Mr. Fuller" referred to was their former minister, to whom they seem to have been much attached. He is a Southerner, but loyal, and is now, I believe living in Baltimore.[46]

Another fascinating snippet detailing the use of spirituals comes from her depiction of a contraband Christmas celebration. Forten tells how, following the distribution of the humble presents, the children sang a series of spirituals, including "a very singular one":

I wonder where my mudder gone;
    Sing, O graveyard!
Graveyard ought to know me;
    Ring, Jerusalem!
Grass grow in de graveyard;
    Sing, O graveyard!
Graveyard ought to know me;
    Ring, Jerusalem!

They improvise many more words as they sing. It is one of the strangest, most mournful things I ever heard. It is impossible to give any idea of the deep pathos of the refrain—"Sing, O graveyard."

In this, and many other hymns, the words seem to have but little meaning; but the tones—a whole lifetime of despairing sadness is concentrated in them. They sing, also, "Jehovah, Hallelujah," which we like particularly—

De foxes hab holes,
And de birdies hab nests,
But de Son ob Man he hab no where
To lay de weary head.

CHORUS

Jehovyah, Hallelujah! De Lord He will purvide!
Jehovyah, Hallelujah! De Lord He will purvide!

They repeat the words many times. "De foxes hab holes." And the succeeding lines are sung in the most touching, mournful tones; and then the chorus—"Jehovyah, Hallelujah"—swells forth triumphantly, in glad contrast.

Christmas night, the children came in and had several grand shouts. They were too happy to keep still.[47]

Obviously, the spirituals were sung elsewhere in the Civil War besides the Sea Islands. President Abraham Lincoln, "Father Abraham," sang regularly with

The first great collections of spirituals were assembled at the various contraband camps. Contraband School of Freedman's Village, Arlington, Virginia (photo: Mathew Brady Collection, the National Archives)

a group led by White House employee Aunt Mary Dines. Dines, who could also write music, worked at the contraband camp on Seventh Street, where the Lincolns sometimes stopped on their way to the summer White House.[48] On one occasion, at an impromptu religious service at the camp, Dines led the singing, including "Nobody Knows the Trouble I've Seen," "Swing Low, Sweet Chariot," "Didn't My God Deliver Daniel?" "I've Been in the Storm So Long," "Steal Away," and "Every Time I Feel the Spirit," while Lincoln, "choked with emotion," wept openly. On another occasion, when the group sang, "John Brown's Body" and "I Thank God I'm Free at Last," Lincoln is reported to have bowed his head.[49] And during Emancipation Proclamation ceremonies, on January 1, 1863, the accounts of the various ceremonies include at least one where "Go Down, Moses" (called "The Song of the Contrabands" by the *New York Times*) was sung.[50]

Most accounts of the famed African-American 54th Regiment of the Massachusetts Volunteer Infantry end with the gallant charge on Fort Wagner. But the attack failed and, surrounded and outgunned, some of the regiment surrendered. Most were bayoneted on the spot, but a few were shipped to the Confederate prison in Charleston. Years later, a white officer told their story, how the small band of half-starved survivors continued to sing "Union songs" during the day and their own songs at night:

Often after nine o'clock at night, when by the rules we were confined in our quarters, I have been aroused from a doze by the singing of the colored prisoners. At such times, the voices coming down from the upper floors of the jail sounded very sweet, and there was a certain weird, indescribable sadness in the minor key melodies, that told of camp-meeting days and the religious hope that seemed to be confined exclusively to these poor fellows.[51]

(Another little-known footnote of the story is that after the fall of Charleston, the survivors were moved in the dead of winter to a prison near Florence, where all starved together. Florence briefly housed about 15,000 prisoners, and at least 3,000 died—a mortality rate of eleven percent per month. The men were moved still again to North Carolina. Finally, only a handful survived to go to the most dreaded prison of all —Andersonville—where the jailers boasted of "killing more Yankees than Lee in Virginia."[52])

But the African-American regiments knew more successes than failures in their short years of operation. Spirituals accompanied the Massachusetts 55th's triumphant entry into Charleston on February 22, 1865. One participant wrote that, "It was one of those occasions which happen but once in a lifetime, to be lived over in memory forever."[53]

When the Confederate forces pulled out of Richmond on April 2, among the first Union forces to enter was the Fifth Massachusetts Cavalry, who entered the city singing:

> *De massa run, ha! ha!*
> *De darkey stay, ho! ho!*
> *It must be now de kingdom comin',*
> *An de yar of Jubilo.*

A few hours later, hundreds of residents and elements of the Fifth Massachusetts Cavalry spontaneously gathered outside the infamous Lumpkin's Jail in Richmond's sprawling slave market. From inside, imprisoned slaves sang gustily:

> *Slavery's chain done broke at las'*
> *Broke at las'!*
> *Broke at las'!*
> *Most done waiting for de Morning Star!*
> *Gonna praise God till I die!*

The crowd outside joined in the song until the soldiers broke open the pens and freed the slaves.[54]

Among the first visitors to the still-smoldering ruins of Richmond in the days following its fall was President Abraham Lincoln, instantly recognizable to black and white alike with his long black coat and now-familiar tall silk hat. The African-American population was immediately galvanized. "Here, at least, was the man who had set them free," writes Philip Van Doren Stern, "this was the long awaited Messiah, whose coming had been foretold in many a secretly worded spiritual sung at nightfall on thousands of plantations throughout the South. Here, in person, was the Father Abraham of their hopes and dreams." Observers of the scene reported that the African Americans spontaneously broke into hymns and spirituals at the sight.[55]

Among the many participants who wrote passionately about their experiences during the Civil War was Col. George W. Williams, who became Judge Advocate of the Grand Army of the Republic. In a section describing the history of African-American soldiers in the Union armies, he writes: "Unable to harness his thoughts to the polished and balanced phrases of refined expression, the Negro turned the impetuous current of his feeling into rhyme. He did not speak, he gurgled, cried, and sang out of his soul."[56]

But Williams's elegant writing can't disguise the horrific losses suffered by African-American troops who were repeatedly thrown into hopeless situations where they died bravely. Few of the African-American soldiers who marched steadfastly into the charnel house that was the Crater at Petersburg survived the day.

Following the long trench warfare that marked the Petersburg campaign, Lee's battered Army of Northern Virginia slipped out of the town during the night. "At early dawn, Birney's Negro troops were led against Petersburg," recalls Williams, "but there was no enemy to dispute their entrance. The Negro population gave the black soldiers in blue a most cordial welcome. They were greeted with tears and cheers, with prayers and praise, with songs and phrases of high-sounding adulation." Birney's men soon pulled out of Petersburg and were among those in hot pursuit of the Army of Northern Virginia when Lee finally surrendered his famished troops at Appomattox Court House.[57]

That evening, groups of musicians from Lee's army performed for their Union counterparts. Later, several African-American bands strolled over to the ragtag Confederate camp and performed for them as well.[58] "After the Confederate army had been paroled, the Negro troops cheerfully and cordially divided their rations with the late enemy," notes Williams, "and welcomed them at their campfires on the march back to Petersburg. The sweet gospel of forgiveness was expressed in the Negro soldiers' intercourse with ex-rebel soldiers, who freely mingled with the black conquerors. It was a spectacle of magnanimity never before witnessed among troops that had hated and actually murdered one another."[59]

The war destroyed most of the South's communications systems, but word of the rebels' surrender spread quickly through the slave "grapevine telegraph." Booker T. Washington remembered that the slaves sang their spirituals with even greater frequency in those hours and days before his plantation was finally notified:

[The singing of spirituals] was bolder, had more ring, and lasted later into the night. Most of the verses of the plantation songs had some reference to freedom. True, they had sung those same verses before, but they had been careful to explain that the "freedom" in these songs referred to the next world, and had no connection with life in this world. Now they gradually threw off the mask, and were not afraid to let it be known that the "freedom" in their songs meant freedom of the body in this world.[60]

But the joy in the slave quarters was short lived. Lincoln was assassinated on April 14 and died within hours. The hastily organized funeral ceremonies at the White House were followed by a vast procession, taking the body to the Capitol. At the head of the column was the 22nd Colored Regiment, which had distinguished itself for bravery during the Battle of Richmond.[61] None felt the loss more keenly than the former slaves on South Carolina's Sea Islands. Teacher Laura Towne's meticulous diary captured their grief like few other accounts:

On the island here they are inconsolable and will not believe he is dead. In the church this morning they prayed for him as wounded but still alive, and said that he was their Saviour—that Christ saved them from sin, and he from "Secesh,"* and as for the vile Judas who had lifted his hand against him, they prayed the Lord the whirlwind would carry him away, and that he would melt as wax in the fervent heat, and be driven forever from before the Lord.[62]

A few days later, Towne was approached by an elderly former slave who tried, with his broken English, to explain what he was feeling. "Lincoln died for we," he said. "Christ died for we, and me believe him de same mans."[63]

One war was finished, but for the suddenly freed African American, another was about to begin.

---

*"Secesh" is a corruption of Secessionist.

Chapter Six

Reconstruction, the Jubilee Singers, and Minstrelsy

The Negro would deserve well of this country if he had given it nothing but the melodies by which he will be remembered long after the carping critics who refuse to admit that he is capable of intellectual progress are forgotten. His songs of a religious nature are indisputable proofs of the latent power for an artistic development which his friends have always claimed for him. They are echoes from the house of bondage, cries in the night, indistinct murmurs from an abyss. They take directly hold upon the Infinite. They are sublimest and most touching when they partake of the nature of wails and appeals. They have strange hints and gleams of nature in them, mingled with intense spiritual fervor.

Edward King, *The Great South*, 1879[1]

Fifty years from now, when every vestige of slavery has disappeared, and even its existence has become a fading memory, American and probably Europe, will suddenly awake to the sad fact that we have irrevocably lost a veritable mine of wealth through our failure to appreciate and study from a musician's standpoint the beautiful African music, whose rich stores will then have gone forever from our grasp.

—Jeanette Robinson Murphy, 1899[2]

If morning stars sing together, who shall say that minstrel men may not lead parades through pearly gates and up streets of gold?

—W. C. Handy[3]

. . . in the Jubilees and their songs, America has produced the perfectest flower of the ages.

—Mark Twain, 1897[4]

110

The improbable, heady years of 1867 through 1877 during Reconstruction (Du Bois called them the "mystic years") had a dreamlike quality in the South. African Americans resisted, to an extraordinary degree, the very human tendency to exact a well-deserved revenge on their former masters. Instead, on the "Gullah Islands" off South Carolina and Georgia and elsewhere, the freed slaves sang what Margaret Creel called their "Marseillaise," an "exhilarating" spiritual that was triumphant rather than vengeful:

> *De Talles' tree in Paradise*
> *De Christian calls de Tree ob Life,*
> *An' I hope dat trumpet blow me home*
> *To my New Jerusalem!*
>
> *Paul and Silas jail-bound*
> *Sing God's praise both night and day*
> *An' I hope dat trumpet blow me home*
> *To my New Jerusalem!*[5]

For Creel, the meaning of "New Jerusalem" shifted in the days following the Civil War from a spiritual of a heaven to come to something altogether new and different during Reconstruction. "But when the freed people sang 'New Jerusalem' at the Emancipation Jubilee on New Year's Day in 1866," she notes, "it was their earthly future and enthusiasm for their long-awaited freedom that filled their thoughts and expectations. The Tree of Life was the tree of liberty, as paradise was a land free of bondage."[6]

To northern teacher Elizabeth Botume, the song, which erupted repeatedly and spontaneously in the streets filled with jubilant freedmen on New Year's Day, was prophecy fulfilled:

> According to their spiritual, they had "fought for liberty," and this was their "New Jerusalem," of which they so often sang. Even the poorest, and those most scantily clothed, looked as if they already "walked that golden street," and felt "that starry crown" upon their uncovered heads. It was indeed a day of great rejoicing and one long to be remembered. These people were living their "New Jerusalem."[7]

To most African Americans, the spirituals, first sung in the secret meetings and brush arbor churches, very clearly explained that their faith had been the catalyst that "wrought the miracle of emancipation"—even more than "Marse" Lincoln's armies.[8]

> *Walk in, kind Savior*
> *No man can hinder me!*
> *Walk in, sweet Jesus*
> *No man can hinder me!*

See what wonder Jesus done
O no man can hinder me!
See what wonder Jesus done
O no man can hinder me![9]

And, as before, the spirituals served the newly freed slaves in other ways, as well. Botume writes of a time when, in the days following the Emancipation Jubilee, a young African-American sergeant, recently returned from the army, died unexpectedly:

> His friends immediately assembled and held a watch-meeting, which they call "a setting-up." All night long we could hear their solemn chanting and clapping of hands as they beat the time. They had a praise meeting before the house, as they believe the spirit remains with the body until daylight, when it takes leave and goes home to the heavenly Father as the morning stars go out.
>
> The comrades of the young sergeant wished to bury him with military honors, so they waited until the next night at midnight. They had a long procession, with torches and a muffled drum. Then all the women and children straggled along, singing their spirituals. It was a somber sight as this sable procession wound around through the grove. As the tones of their spirituals reverberated through the arches of this "God's first temple," I was reminded of the Pilgrim's March in *Tannhauser*.[10]

But in short order, the long-feared backlash began. The woefully understaffed, financially inadequate Freedmen's Bureau (1865–1872) was supposed to be "an Urban League, CEO, WPA and Rosenwald Foundation all rolled up into an early NAACP."[11] Despite the efforts of Charles Sumner and Thaddeus Stevens, who tried to bring the vote and "a mule and 40-acres" to the newly freed slaves, none of this was granted—or, if granted, was soon taken away by southern lawmakers. Grizzled, one-armed Gen. O. O. Howard, head of the Freedmen's Bureau, following President Andrew Johnson's pardons of the South Carolina planters, reluctantly went to tell the former slaves that their lands were being confiscated and returned to the original owners. The slaves responded by singing "Nobody Knows the Trouble I've Seen" as Howard wept.[12]

The worst was yet to come. Despite President Johnson's veto, the fourteenth Amendment, which eliminated race as a condition for U.S. citizenship and prohibited states from violating due process or equal protection of African Americans, was passed. Throughout the South, terrible race riots followed and dozens, perhaps hundreds, of African Americans were murdered

The Reconstruction Acts were first passed then swiftly negated by the men charged with carrying them out. The Freedmen's Bureau dissolved in 1872. And after various political compromises, military protection was no longer available to African Americans in the South after 1876. Old regimes returned and exacted a horrific vengeance for losing the Civil War on the only people handy who couldn't fight back: the freed African Americans. Lynchings, the Ku Klux Klan, restrictive Jim Crow laws, and the "Black Codes" followed in short order.[13] One by one, white Southerners stripped all political, cultural, and economic entities and organizations from African Americans save one: the church. Freed slaves flocked to the "established churches" (including the African Methodist Episcopal and the Methodist church), but most enthusiastically to the Baptist church.[14]

In time, with every other avenue denied them, *all* African-American life in the South revolved around the church, including social activities such as picnics, all-day sings, sports, travel, and dinners—while in the North, the churches became centers for political activism as well.

The church provided, as it had during slavery, an emotional outlet for those who were oppressed on all sides. "Testifying" sessions enabled African Americans to vent their frustrations and pain. "The entire concept was built around an intimate community, a subculture within the larger eco-system," notes Richard Raichelson. "The philosophy of the church reinforced this sense of community, for by nature of its doctrines—which shunned things of a worldly nature—it kept the group together."[15] In the South and parts of the North, the church was the only place where large numbers of African Americans could freely assemble. As the remaining viable entity representing African Americans, the black church "provided leadership training and burial societies, insurance companies," and even supported a number of small African-American business enterprises.[16]

Not surprisingly, from the black church's earliest beginnings in the brush arbors, African-American ministers consequently exerted far-reaching influence over their congregations, in everything from music to politics, and—particularly in the South—served as the lone spokesmen for their constituents in a white-dominated world.[17]

Despite serious efforts to eradicate it within the African-American community, illiteracy was still a problem, particularly among the older freed slaves. Thus, the ancient process of "lining out" spirituals by preachers continued unabated for many years after the Civil War. And the spirituals, which had never disappeared, flourished once again. One contemporary observer at an African-American church marveled at the singing, writing that it was "music full of unpremeditated and irresistible dramatic power."[18]

One of the most acute observers of the postbellum African-American church was Edward King, a well-known journalist, novelist, and war correspondent. King was well traveled in the United States and abroad; his monumental travel diary *The Great South* resulted from a series of articles first published in *Scribner's Magazine* between 1872 and 1874. Here he describes in detail African-American churches and their services from Virginia to Texas during the course of his travels. More than a decade after the Civil War, his description of the spirituals recalls earlier depictions, where the "simplest hymns are sung with almost extravagant intensity." And, as before, the spirituals were primarily improvised by preacher and congregation during the impassioned worship services:

But few were ever written; they sprang suddenly into use. They arose out of the ecstasy occasioned by the rude and violent dances on the plantation; they were the outgrowth of great and unavoidable sorrows, which forced the heart to voice its cry; or they bubbled up from the springs of religious excitement. Sometimes they were simply the expression of the joy found in vigorous, healthy existence; but of such there are few. The majority of the Negro songs have a plaintive undertone.[19]

But forces and events were already gathering that would attempt to change the spiritual. Particularly in the larger southern metropolitan areas, as the first great African-American churches were established, some of the freed slaves found themselves uncomfortable singing the old songs; others found them demeaning and an unwelcome reminder of a dark past. David Macrae was a Scots traveler in the United States in the years following the American Civil War. At the famed Broad Street African Church in Richmond, he noted that the music was "tamer" and that the more than one thousand worshipers in attendance that day sang mostly the hymns of Isaac Watts.[20] "These plantation hymns are less sung now than they used to be, and will probably before long be numbered amongst the things of the past," he wrote in his diary. "The young Negroes are being educated and want a higher kind of psalmody; and even the older people, in some cases, are drawing back from hymns that are so much connected in their minds with slavery."[21]

However, at a rural camp meeting near "Poplar Springs" some days later, Macrae also heard the older religious songs and recorded a prayer by "Sister Nancy Brooks" that captures the former slaves' complex concept of "sacred time":

O Father Almighty! O sweet Jesus! Most gloriful King! Will you be so pleased as to come dis way and put your eye on dese yere mourners? O sweet Jesus, ain't you de Daniel's God? Didn't you deliber de tree chill'un from de firey furnish? Didn't you hear Jonah cry from the belly ob de whale? Oh, if dere be one seeking mourner here dis afternoon, if dere be one sinking Peter, if dere be one weeping Mary, if dere be one doubting Thomas, won't you be so pleased to come and deliber them? Won't you mount your gospel horse an' ride round' de souls of dese yere mourners, and say, "Go in peace, and sin no more?" Won't you be so pleased to come wid de love in one han' and de fan in de odder han' to fan way doubts? Won't you be so pleased to shake dese yere souls over hell, and not let 'em fall in?[22]

Eventually, the African-American churches split over musical styles as well. The more educated African-American church leaders and the larger urban congregations opposed the more spontaneous musical and worship styles of many (often the more rural) blacks, while others retained the hymnals of the parent denominations. The most vocal opponent of the spirituals was Bishop Daniel

A. Payne of the American Methodist Episcopal Church, an influential African-American clergyman, author, and first president of Wilburforce University, making him America's first African-American college president. Bishop Payne spoke out vehemently against spirituals, calling them "ring" songs sung by "fist and heel worshipers." He denounced them as "cornfield ditties" and "voodou dances."[23] Payne tells of breaking up a rural "bush meeting" in January 1878, where the parishioners "formed a ring" and "stamped their feet in a most ridiculous and heathenish way." Payne forced the pastor to stop the ring shout and sternly lectured those in attendance, saying that this "was a heathenish way to worship and disgraceful to themselves, the race, and the Christian name."[24] Later, Payne and the young pastor argued over the ring shout:

[H]e said: "Sinners won't get converted unless there is a ring." Said I: "You might sing till you fell down dead and you would fail to convert a single sinner, because nothing but the Spirit of God and the word of God can convert sinners." He replied: "The Spirit of God works upon people in different ways. At camp-meeting there must be a ring here, a ring there, a ring over yonder, or sinners will not get converted."[25]

Payne also includes one of the "cornfield ditties" by way of proving his point:

Ashes to ashes, dust to dust;
If God won't have us, the devil must.
I was way over there when the coffin fell;
I heard that sinner as he screamed in hell.[26]

Still, the spirituals endured, particularly in the smaller, country churches. But their survival was by no means assured in the latter half of the nineteenth century. Two radically different cultural forces emerged that threatened their continuation as a unique, readily identifiable African-American religious folk music: the rise of the Fisk University Jubilee Singers phenomenon and the ongoing co-opting of African-American culture by the minstrel movement.

The Fisk Jubilee Singers

For all of the care and love that went into Slave Songs of the United States, its publication passed relatively unnoticed by the public at large, save for a few abolitionist newspapers and magazines—which, once freedom for slaves was won, themselves became obsolete in the years following the Civil War. What finally made the spirituals a household name in the latter half of the nineteenth century were the unceasing efforts of an unlikely band of former slaves and the children of slaves, the Fisk Jubilee Singers.

The story of the Jubilee Singers is one of the few bright spots in the otherwise grim history of post-Reconstruction African-American history. It begins with the founding of the American Missionary Association in 1846 in Albany, New York. In the years to come, the AMA chartered seven colleges and schools of theology: Berea College, at Berea, Kentucky; Hampton Institute, Hampton, Virginia; Fisk University, Nashville, Tennessee; Atlanta University, Atlanta, Georgia; Talladega College, Talladega, Alabama; Tougaloo University at Tougaloo, Mississippi; and Straight University, New Orleans, Louisiana. Fisk opened in January 1866, and was chartered as a university the following year.[27]

Despite sacrificial efforts by all involved, Fisk, like the other African-American schools, soon found itself in serious financial troubles. The school turned to First Sgt. George Leonard White, a Union veteran of the bloody battles of Gettysburg and Chancellorsville, who had worked for the Freedmen's Bureau in Nashville. White originally volunteered as a music teacher at Fisk but became its treasurer as well when the school was chartered.[28]

White remained as a music teacher and quickly realized that many of the students were gifted singers. He handpicked some of the best for special, more-intensive music and vocal training. This was followed by a series of carefully chosen concerts, including a choir trip to Memphis in 1869. Another concert, this to the National Teachers' Association of the United States convention in Nashville, received a mixed response. Some attendees howled their displeasure at seeing African Americans on a stage, while others clamored for the singers to open *all* of the convention's sessions.[29] For the first time, perhaps at the suggestion of the famous Hutchinson Family Singers,[30] White began to see the possibilities of touring with the group as a fund-raising venture.

Unfortunately, early performances north of the Ohio River met with indifferent success and insufficient donations. Many hotels refused the small choir admittance and a number of the singers suffered due to the cold weather. Until November 1871, they did not even have a true name—one Cincinnati paper had dubbed them "a band of Negro minstrels who call themselves Colored Christian Singers."[31] After long hours of agonizing over various choices, White at last decided to name them "the Jubilee Singers," a clear reference to the Old Testament "Year of Jubilee" in the Book of Leviticus and a popular phrase in African-American spirituals.[32]

As the newly named Jubilee Singers slowly worked east, the tide turned in their favor. In New York, they were enthusiastically sponsored by the Reverend Henry Ward Beecher, which prompted newspapers such as the *New York Herald* to support their appearances.[33] Preliminary to a quick trip to Boston for a concert in the Music Hall, Beecher wrote to a Boston friend: "They will charm any audience, sure; they make their mark by giving the 'spirituals' and plantation hymns as only they can sing them who know how to keep time to a master's whip. Our people have been delighted."[34] Another supporter, Dr. Theodore L. Cuyler, told the *New York Tribune* that during the Jubilee Singers' concert in his church (Lafayette Avenue Presbyterian of Brooklyn) in early December 1871,

I never saw a cultivated Brooklyn assemblage so moved and melted under the magnetism of music before. The wild melodies of these emancipated slaves touched the fount of tears, and gray-haired men wept like little children.

Allow me to bespeak a universal welcome through the North for these living representatives of the only true native school of American music. We have long enough had its coarse caricatures in corked faces; our people can now listen to the genuine soul-music of the slave cabins, before the Lord led his children "out of the land of Egypt, out of the house of bondage!"[35]

However, it was probably not the "wild melodies" of the spirituals that the Jubilee Singers sang, especially during the early days of the group's existence. Existing playbills included mostly more sentimental fare, including "Home Sweet Home," "Old Folks at Home," "The Battle Hymn of the Republic," and a "Temperance Medley."[36] In fact, when the group that became the Jubilee Singers would close early rehearsals with spirituals, some faculty members discouraged them from continuing.[37] The spirituals were initially only performed as encores to the more "cultural" music, such as *Esther, the Beautiful Queen* by William B. Bradbury.[38] It wasn't until a performance at Oberlin College where the audience's enthusiastic response to the spirituals was so overwhelmingly positive that the Singers made them the centerpiece of future performances.[39]

Even then, what the Jubilee Singers mostly sang were classical arrangements of the original spirituals—like the light arias sung by modern college glee clubs in the European "art song" tradition—later arranged in standard SATB (Soprano, Alto, Tenor, Bass) harmonies by respected church musician Theodore Seward. Seward carefully smoothed out the arrangements, irregular measures, and odd tempos and later boasted that his arrangements were "entirely correct."[40] And perhaps they *were* faithful reproductions of what the Jubilee Singers were performing—but the end results could not accurately be called "spirituals." Seward was aware of comments that claimed he had made the music "too good" and responded that the differences between what most African Americans sang in southern churches and the music of the Western European classical tradition was a difference in degree of "culture":

> The Jubilee Singers, no doubt, represent the highest average of culture among the colored people, but the singing of these songs is all their own, and the quickness with which they have received impressions and adopted improvements from the cultivated music that they have heard, only affords an additional illustration of the high capabilities of the race.[41]

Still, the public (for the most part) loved what they heard and gave generously. The Jubilee Singers even performed "Go Down, Moses" for the embattled President Ulysses Grant[42] before finally returning to Nashville. Their triumphant return, unfortunately, was marred by an ugly incident at the Louisville train station where a "cursing mob of one or two thousand people" harassed them for purchasing first-class tickets and daring to sit in an unoccupied sitting room while waiting for the train.[43]

The years that followed contained more successful concert tours. One of their most devoted fans was Samuel Clemens/Mark Twain, who was known to break into spirituals at inopportune times (such as at formal state dinners).[44] One of the most charming sections of Gustavus Pike's original *The Singing Campaign for Ten Thousand Pounds or The Jubilee Singers in Great Britain* is a letter of reference from Clemens to various English booking agents on behalf of the Jubilee Singers:

> I heard them sing once, and I would walk seven miles to hear them sing again. You will recognize that this is strong language for me to use, when you remember that I never was fond of pedestrianism, and got tired of walking that Sunday afternoon, in twenty minutes, after making up my mind to see for myself and at my own leisure how much ground his grace the Duke of Bedford's property covered.
>
> I think these gentlemen and ladies make eloquent music—and what is as much to the point, they reproduce the true melody of the plantations, and are the only persons I ever heard accomplish this on the public platform. The so-called "negro minstrels" simply mis-represent the thing; I do not think they ever saw a plantation or ever heard a slave sing.
>
> I was reared in the South, and my father owned slaves, and I do not know when anything has so moved me as did the plaintive melodies of the Jubilee Singers. It was the first time for twenty-five or thirty years that I had heard such songs, or heard them sung in the genuine old way—and it is a way, I think, that white people cannot imitate—and never can, for that matter, for one must have been a slave himself in order to feel what that life was and so convey the pathos of it in the music.[45]

The Jubilee Singers' subsequent tour of the British Isles in 1873 included an unexpected private concert for Queen Victoria, arranged by George John Douglas Campbell, the eighth Duke of Argyll. The little band sang "Steal Away to Jesus," "Go Down, Moses," "John Brown," and a chanted version of "The Lord's Prayer"—and thereby received the stamp of approval for all future concerts abroad.[46] Among those who received and entertained them or heard them in concert were the Prince and Princess of Wales, author George MacDonald (whose wife wrote a play, which the family performed, in their honor), the Reverend C. H. Spurgeon, Jenny Lind, and Prime Minister W. E. Gladstone. Newspaper coverage was almost uniformly favorable.[47] The group continued to tour the United States for many more years as well, spawning a number of successful (including college groups representing Hampton and Tuskegee) and less successful imitators.

As for Theodore Seward, although his approach has since been repudiated by folklorists and musicologists alike, Dena J. Epstein's careful examination of records and reviews by American audiences who did, on rare occasions, hear authentic spirituals in performance reveals that the public simply was not ready for the "irregular rhythms, rhapsodic singing, rasping voices and bodily movement" of the true spirituals.[48] The Jubilee Singers and their performances were about as "authentic" as most audiences at that time could handle.

The influence of the Fisk Jubilee Singers can hardly be overstated. Within two years of the Jubilee Singers' first concert tour, Sandra Graham has found a dozen or more imitators, including the National Jubilee Singers, the Tennesseans, the Jackson Jubilee Singers, the North Carolinians, Sheppard's Colored Jubilee Singers, Slayton's Jubilee Singers, the Centennialites, and the Alabama Jubilee Singers.[49] In the fall of 1872, George White writes of attending a concert by the New Canaan Jubilee Singers in New York, who had allegedly already earned $43,000.[50] Everybody wanted in on the Jubilee phenomenon.

W. E. B. Du Bois, who grew up in the Northeast, once wrote prior to attending Fisk University, "I heard too in these days for the first time the Negro folk songs. A Hampton Quartet had sung among them in the Congregational church. I was thrilled and moved to tears and seemed to recognize something inherently and deeply my own. I was glad to go to Fisk."[51] After graduation, while teaching at a tiny rural black school in the hills of Tennessee, Du Bois finally heard the real thing:

> I now heard the Negro songs by those who made them, and in the land of their American birth. It was in the village into which my country school district filtered on Saturdays and Sundays. The road wandered from our rambling log-house up the stony bed of a creek, past wheat and corn, until we could hear dimly across the fields a rhythmic cadence of song—soft, thrilling, powerful—that swelled and died sorrowfully in our ears.[52]

Approaching the performed spirituals from another point of view was James M. Trotter, author of *Music and Some Highly Musical People: Remarkable Musicians of the Colored Race, With Portraits* in 1878. While admitting that the performances of the Jubilee Singers were not always sung "strictly in accordance with artistic forms," Trotter waxes poetic on the inherent power of the Fisk spirituals:

> [T]hey possessed in themselves a peculiar power, a plaintive, emotional beauty, and other characteristics which seemed entirely independent of artistic embellishment. These characteristics were, with a most refreshing originality, naturalness, and soulfulness of voice and method, fully developed by the singers, who sang with all their might, yet with most pleasing sweetness of tone.[53]

With the success of the Jubilee Singers, numerous songbooks followed, including Seward's, then editor of the New York *Musical Gazette*. His twenty-eight-page booklet featured sixty-one songs and an introduction that both explained the goals of the Singers and offered an analysis of the spirituals they sang.[54] Interestingly, there is little duplication between Seward's *The Jubilee Songs: As Sung by the Jubilee Singers* and either *Slave Songs of the United States* or Higginson's original "Negro Spirituals" article in *Atlantic Monthly*. Other popular collections, such as *Religious Folk-Songs of the Negro as sung at Hampton Institution*, issued by Hampton Normal and Agricultural Institute, and Marshall W. Taylor's *Plantation Melodies, Book of Negro Folk Songs*, went through several editions and reached thousands as well.

But what was contained in the books and sung by the groups from Fisk and Hampton and the others—again—were not the spirituals still being sung by African Americans in churches throughout the United States. The high-profile Jubilee Singers may have helped keep the average American aware that the spirituals existed and they did much to preserve the original words and melodies of certain spirituals captured at that moment in time. They also helped spawn a wonderful subgenre, the classically arranged spiritual, which provided the impetus for important careers for composers such as R. Nathaniel Dett, John Wesley Work, Clarence Cameron White, J. Rosamund Johnson, William Dawson, Samuel Coleridge-Taylor, and Harry Burleigh, and—in time—for classically trained singers such as Paul Robeson and Marian Anderson. But what these singers performed were not spirituals.[55] In fact, an unknown reporter for the *Peoria Journal* wrote in 1881 after a Fisk Jubilee Singers concert that "They have lost the wild rhythms, the barbaric melody, the passion . . . [T]hey smack of the North . . .".[56]

The Fisk Jubilee Singers are responsible for coining a name for this new music, which included spiritual-like lyrics, but was almost always upbeat and "more lively" in tempo than the original spiritual: the jubilee song.[57] In time, the distinctions between the words *spiritual* and *jubilee* would become blurred in the minds of many musicians.[58] But to those who study and love African-American music, the distinctions are worth preserving.

One who felt strongly about "losing" spirituals was noted author Zora Neale Hurston. Her book, *The Sanctified Church*, was assembled from a collection of articles commissioned by the Works Progress Administration in 1938 for a proposed guidebook titled *The Negro of Florida*. Hurston, who also wrote *Their Eyes Were Watching God, Mules and Men*, and other works, died in 1960.[59] Hurston said that by allowing the misperception of what the term *spirituals* eventually came to represent to persist, even the African Americans themselves had "sinned" because "no genuine presentation" of the spirituals had yet been made to a white audience:

> The spirituals that have been sung around the world are Negroid to be sure, but so full of musicians' tricks that Negro congregations are highly entertained when they hear these old songs so changed. They never use the new style songs, and these are never heard unless perchance some daughter or son has been off to college and returns with one of the old songs with its face lifted, so to speak.

I am of the opinion that this trick style of delivery was originated by the Fisk Singers; Tuskegee and Hampton followed suit and have helped spread this misconception of Negro spirituals. This Glee Club style has gone on so long and become so fixed among concert singers that it is considered quite authentic. But I say again, that not one concert singer in the world is singing the songs as the Negro songmakers sing them.

If anyone wishes to prove the truth of this let him step into some unfashionable Negro church and hear for himself.[60]

Minstrelsy

A second cultural phenomenon that directly affected the survival of the spiritual as an art form came from a less quantifiable, but no less potent, source: the blackface minstrel tradition. Few topics have generated more scholarly heat in recent decades, and numerous excellent books have examined various aspects of the long history of minstrelsy in America, including Eric Lott's 1993 reexamination of the racism in antebellum minstrel shows, *Love and Theft: Blackface Minstrelsy and the American Working Class.*[61] As for the minstrel tradition's relationship to the promulgation of spirituals, it is also an important, if slippery, connection.

There is, for instance, no real consensus as to when the first minstrel troupes began performing in the United States. Reasonable arguments have been made for 1815,[62] 1829,[63] or 1832,[64] while the term *minstrelsy* itself doesn't even become tied to the various forms of blackface entertainment until 1842.[65]

But as important as the cultural impact of the Jubilee Singers was on the young country, black minstrelsy was perhaps more so. It was, after all, America's first successful cultural export,[66] flourishing throughout Europe even before the Civil War. How popular was it? Eric Lott speculates that the Fisk Jubilee Singers added "jubilee" to their name, in part, because they had been mistaken for a minstrel troupe.[67]

Somewhere in the late eighteenth and early nineteenth centuries, groups of mostly white men, their faces painted (or "corked") black, began staging concerts featuring "authentic" African-American music from the South. Early performers, especially in the North, originally sang generally sympathetic songs about blacks, but somewhere between 1810 and 1820, the songs and performances twisted into abusive performances, savagely ridiculing and caricaturing African Americans.[68] Tuskegee President Dr. Robert Moten once described seeing a white minstrel company as a child:

I felt that these white men were making fun, not only of our color and our songs, but of our religion. . . . White minstrels with black faces have done more than any other single agency to lower the tone of Negro music and cause the Negro to despise his own songs.[69]

Dan "Daddy" Rice is credited as the father of "Ethiopian Ministrelsy" for popularizing the nonsense song "Jim Crow," although the first full-length blackface minstrel performance is generally acknowledged to be by the Virginia Minstrels in January 1843.[70] Blackface minstrelsy quickly became the most popular form of entertainment in the United States and remained that way until nearly the dawn of the twentieth century. Free blacks and former slaves began forming their own troupes shortly after the Civil War, most notably the Georgia Minstrels, first under Charles "Barney" Hicks, then under Charles Callender.[71]

The pervasive nature of blackface minstrelsy was such that in a mostly preliterate, pre-radio, pre-television era, many nineteenth-century Americans may have received their first exposure to the America beyond their city block—"plantations, cities, Negroes, Irishmen, or Germans"—from minstrel troupes that helped codify a "national folklore" for poor white Americans.[72] For the first time, northern audiences without access to the legitimate stage had a rousing entertainment they could afford. For the first time, marginally educated audiences hungry for entertainment saw the extraordinarily rich culture of African Americans. "The enthralling vitality of this material, even as adapted by white performers, accounted in large part for minstrelsy's great initial impact," writes Robert C. Toll. "Although minstrel use of black culture declined in the late 1850s as white minstrels concentrated on caricatures of blacks, when Negroes themselves became minstrels after the Civil War, they brought a transfusion of their culture with them."[73]

The success of the Fisk Jubilee Singers and the other jubilee groups prompted a shift in the long-standing performance format employed by the minstrels in the 1870s. Different troupes, both white and black, began adding spirituals and quasi-spirituals, usually sung in dialect. By the mid-1870s, however, religious songs became more prevalent with the African-American minstrel groups, already acknowledged by the public and most newspaper "critics" as the "true" experts on slave and plantation life. When Toll compared songbooks published during this era, he found that the black minstrel songbooks contained many more religious songs than their white counterparts.[74] Likewise, when he compared concert playbills by the popular Callender's Georgia Minstrels, he found that while the Georgia Minstrels featured no religious songs or jubilee groups in the program prior to February 1875, just fourteen months later the program boasted numerous religious songs (including "Oh, Rock o' My Soul") and a separate section on the bill just for a jubilee group.[75]

Soon, spirituals, other religious songs, and a jubilee group became a mandatory part of any touring minstrel group. Several popular troupes even added the word *jubilee* to their name—i.e., the Alabama Colored Minstrels and Plantation Jubilee Singers—to capitalize on the success of the Fisk University group.[76] Additionally, according to Toll and others, the black minstrels in particular performed the spirituals in the "classic" manner, employing a call-and-response format, alternating soloist and chorus, and using extended repeated phrases. "With the introduction of Afro-American religious music," he notes, "black culture revitalized minstrelsy."[77]

Not surprisingly, the better minstrel groups and the Fisk Jubilee Singers eventually came to share some of the same spirituals, including "I'm A-Rolling."[78] Most of the African-American minstrels strived to present both the spirituals and jubilee songs as authentically as possible. Toll maintains that neither the white minstrels (such as the various Hamtown Students groups) nor the black university groups (such as the Fisk Jubilee Singers) performed authentic spirituals to their audiences. The Fisk groups, he writes, "cleaned up" their music to make it palatable to their white audiences' preconceived notions of religion and music.[79] "Black minstrels found that their audiences responded positively to genuine, or at least only moderately adapted, Afro-American religious music," Toll writes. "Certainly the black people in the audience would have been knowledgeable critics as well as enthusiastic supporters."[80]

As John Rublowsky points out, it is possible to attribute at least some of the popularity of the minstrel shows to a pervasive white guilt. "It must have been comforting, then, to go to the theater and watch the fake blacks project an image of 'happy,' 'shiftless' darkies," he writes. "See how they sing and dance and laugh. They don't mind slavery, not really. Everything is all right. Besides, the music was nice. It set your feet to tapping and your voice to singing."[81] But the fact that minstrelsy—black and white—survived more than seventy years implies that the music must have had *something* compelling about it. "It represented the first great wave of music that flowed out of the black experience into the mainstream of American cultural life," Rublowsky notes.[82] And a significant part of that "black experience," at least from the 1870s onward, made heavy use of the spirituals.

The controversy, of course, revolves around the question, "Could *anything* good come out of something so blatantly racist, especially a racism that features such demeaning stereotyping and caricature of another race?" It is possible to posit certain aspects of blackface minstrelsy as being transformed into something useful for African Americans (See *Where Dead Voices Gather* by Nick Tosches for a lively discussion of the topic.[83]), a concept inconceivable even a few years ago, but one that seems less unthinkable when the ability of African Americans to convert something meant for evil into something usable is taken into consideration. Even W. C. Handy defended minstrelsy to the administration while on the faculty at Alabama Agricultural and Mechanical College:

> The minstrel show at that time was one of the greatest outlets for talented musicians and artists. Some of them were paying for education of brothers and sisters, some taking care of aged parents, others supporting their own families, but all contributing to a greater degree of happiness in the entertainment world.[84]

Interestingly enough, the first revisionist look at minstrelsy dates from the groundbreaking *Music and Some Highly Musical People: Remarkable Musicians of the Colored Race, With Portraits,* from 1881. James M. Trotter's noble aim was to provide the first chronicle of the extraordinary breadth of black musicianship extant in the 1870s and 1880s. Each chapter is a breathless account of the greatest classical artists of the day: Elizabeth Taylor Greenfield ("The Black Swan"), Henry F. Williams, Thomas J. Bowers ("The American Mario"), Thomas "Blind Tom" Greene Bethune, Rachel M. Washington, Sarah Sedgewick Bowers ("The Colored Nightingale"), the Jubilee Singers of Fisk University, the Georgia Minstrels, and dozens—perhaps hundreds—of others. It is a valuable, if subjective, document of an era, even if Trotter's single-minded emphasis is on performers of European-styled classical music.[85]

But when it came to detailing the prevalent blackface minstrelsy of the day, Trotter admitted that he hated the idea of African Americans reinforcing stereotypes, writing that he'd always heard that these performances consisted, for the most part, of "disgusting . . . buffoonery" and "malicious caricaturing" of blacks.[86] Still, in an effort to make his book comprehensive, he reluctantly attended a performance by the famed Georgia Minstrels, who were composed of "the genuine article"—actual African Americans.[87] Afterward, Trotter confessed that he was appalled by the racial stereotyping but delighted by the caliber of the musicianship of the rest of the program: "And so (I) came away thinking, on the whole, that there were, to say the least, two sides to the minstrel question."[88]

Under the direction of Charles Callender, the "Georgias" in 1877 featured twenty-one topflight musicians and singers, including a religious quartet, which Trotter says had been invited to sing—presumably spirituals or other similar religious songs—"in one of the most fashionable churches" in an unnamed western city.[89] Trotter buttressed his praise of the Georgia Minstrels with several pages of rave reviews from various newspapers following their recent tour of Europe (including a command performance for the Queen of England) and a glowing note from the legendary P. T. Barnum, who called them "extraordinary."[90] (Barnum—a keen observer of popular taste—added a "jubilee group" to his circus in 1873, billing himself as "The first man who has ever engaged a full Band of Southern Negroes . . . for a Menagerie and Circus in this Country."[91]) Trotter's commentary includes a listing of former members of the Georgia Minstrels who went on to join more serious classical orchestras and opera companies.[92] (*Music and Some Highly Musical People* also includes an invaluable listing of African-American pastors whose choirs performed primarily classical sacred music in his extensive, city-by-city chronicle of African-American musicians in the United States.)

According to Trotter, much of the appeal of the Georgia Minstrels, besides Callender's insistence on musical excellence, is that they provided opportunities for first-rate African-American musicians to perform for both black and white audiences, just as the Fisk Jubilee Singers continued to sing for both audiences in the United States and abroad. In the same manner that the spirituals employed "double-voicedness," so do some writers, including Dale Cockrell and W. T.

Lhamon, Jr., believe that the African-American minstrels—even within the demeaning stereotyping of the minstrel shows—were able to provide an alternative
voice for those with discerning ears. Although Cockrell primarily notes the sub-
versive attack minstrelsy makes on the industrialization of the country, might
not this "Signifyin(g)" also be applied to racism? "Minstrelsy attacked these institutions," Cockrell maintains, "and did so using a technique that shows up in
the cultural expressions of nearly all enslaved or colonized societies: seeming
accommodation to the tropes and values of the powerful, but with underlying
subversion of them and affirmation of traditional modes of understanding."[93]
African-American historian Alain Locke puts it this way: "We might say that
Negro musical comedy made its way luring its audience with comedy farce and
then ambushing and conquering them with music."[94]

Another interesting twist to the spiritual/ministrel connection is that as early
as 1875, African-American songwriters such as Sam Lucas and James Bland
began composing imitation spirituals for the minstrel groups to perform. These
imitations were often based, in part, on actual spirituals and—as Sandra Graham
notes—"sometimes asserted black pride."[95]

At the advent of the twentieth century, the minstrel show was dead everywhere save for rural areas in the Deep South, replaced by the emerging musical
comedies of Tin Pan Alley and vaudeville.[96] It never quite disappeared though,
bubbling just under the country's corporate consciousness for decades. It's worth
mentioning, as Lhamon does, that America's first "talkie" motion picture—*The
Jazz Singer*—featured Al Jolsen in blackface.[97] But for all of the psychic damage
of cork-blacked faces and plantation ditties, the long reign of minstrelsy gave,
for the first time, a stage to African Americans, something close to a living wage,
and the opportunity to perform before a variety of audiences.

Likewise, the jubilee phenomenon continued and eventually evolved and
splintered into several musical traditions, both classical and popular. It, too,
offered African Americans a way out of the serf-like conditions in the South and
tenements of the North.

As for the spirituals themselves, both minstrelsy and jubilee, in their own
ways, both preserved and subtly changed them, paving the way, in time, for
gospel music.

Not that the spirituals, in their most basic form, ever truly died. Over the
remainder of the century, various writers and researchers sadly pronounced the
spirituals dead—at the same time other writers and researchers published newly
discovered spirituals still being sung throughout the country. Elizabeth Kilham's
article "Sketches in Color IV" from the March 1870 *Putnam's Monthly* closes by
bemoaning the fact that the distinctive features of African-American spirituals
are disappearing, especially in the cities, where young African Americans are
forming choirs and singing the same hymns used in white churches. She admits,
however, in the rural areas African Americans still sing a favorite hymn several
times with different music each time and add choruses to hymns that don't have

them. In fact, the bulk of the article details how she listened to a host of wonderful spirituals sung following a lecture by Gen. O. O. Howard, commander of the Army of Tennessee and founder and first president of Howard University![98]

Perhaps the first collection of spirituals by an African-American author was the Reverend Marshall W. Taylor's *Plantation Melodies, Book of Negro Folk Songs* (with W. C. Echols), published in 1882.[99] Authentic spirituals are interspersed with a few white camp meeting songs that had also made their way into black churches, particularly in the Midwest.

A few years later, another author, in an article in *New England Magazine*, declares that "The old-time melodies are fast disappearing and a new order of things is beginning to supplant them . . ."[100] only to spend four pages describing in great detail the performance of spirituals at a camp meeting attended solely by African Americans.[101]

Just before the turn of the century, William E. Barton, a Congregational minister who taught school in Tennessee (and later served as biographer for his sister Clara Barton) published another series of articles in *New England Magazine* that eventually comprised the bulk of his book *Old Plantation Hymns*. The book features a number of fine additions to the spiritual canon, all collected in the 1880s and 1890s.[102]

In late 1899, author Marion Alexander Haskell wrote yet another article pronouncing the imminent doom of spirituals in the *Century Magazine,* stating,

> The education of the Negro in the South is gradually abolishing a species of folk-song as interesting as it is unique—the Negro "spirituals," the most truly characteristic music that the race has as yet produced.
>
> Spirituals are the religious songs composed by the Negroes themselves, never written or printed, but passing from one generation to another with such additions and variations as circumstances may suggest.[103]

Haskell bemoans the passing of the spirituals as the former slaves became literate, replacing them with the hymns of the white denominational churches. "But among those who are as yet innocent of any educational aspirations," she adds, "especially among the coast Negroes, upon whom the yoke of civilization rests but lightly, spirituals still hold undisputed sway, and hymns are regarded as the sacred property of city churches and those who have attained greatness through knowledge of reading, writing, and 'figgahs.'"[104] And despite her prophecy of a systematic end to the spirituals, she too steals away to an African-American religious service in Columbia, South Carolina, in 1897 and reports on the spirituals she hears sung there![105]

Obviously, the spirituals endured because they continued to provide comfort to that portion of the population suffering the most in the Jim Crow South. Likewise, the African-American church continued to grow during this dark period, much as the early Christian faith originally flourished during the Roman purges and the Chinese church boomed during the height of communism. "Much about postbellum black religion and religious song remained familiar," writes Lawrence Levine. "The war and emancipation . . . initially tended to reaffirm the validity of the slaves' religion. For three quarters of a century after emancipation, folklorists, travelers, and local residents were to collect songs of the type the slaves had sung and to describe religious meetings which differed little from those the slaves had participated in."[106]

Like their prewar counterparts, postbellum spirituals were layered with double-voiced meanings, speaking to the listeners on multiple levels. Alan Lomax and Joan Halifax maintain that such music serves as a "cultural indicator,"[107] while Levine offers this transcription of a turn-of-the-century spiritual that provides a penetrating commentary on African-American life in the United States:

> *Ef salvation wuz a thing money could buy*
> *Den de rich would live an' de po' would die*
>
> *But Ah'm so glad God fix it so*
> *Dat de rich mus' die jes' as well as de po'!*[108]

In 1916, Alabama blacks gave the song an even more contemporary twist:

> *If-a 'ligion wuz er thing that money could buy*
> *The rich would live and the po' would die*
> *I'm so glad things je' like dis*
> *Dere's 'nother good chance for the po' coon yet.*[109]

"In freedom as in slavery, the Devil—over whom blacks generally triumphed in their songs—often looked suspiciously like a surrogate for the white man," adds Levine.

> Similarly, while Negroes had long sung of "letters from the Lord" and "trains to glory" and while there can be no doubt that these phrases were frequently meant literally, during the late nineteenth- and early twentieth-century migrations of blacks from the South to the North, which many southern states desperately tried to stop, it is difficult to imagine that these metaphors did not assume contemporary connotations. One spiritual after another during these years contained such lines as: "I am huntin' fo' a city fo' to stay a while," "You better run to de City of Refuge/You better run!"[110]

Instead of avoiding the "pater-rollers," poor African Americans were now obliged to stay one step ahead of the country sheriff. And the best way north was the railroad. Barton's collection, *Old Plantation Hymns*, contains an entire section on railroad-related songs.[111] And, for the many blacks who died building America's ribbons of steel, he includes the poignant spiritual "The New Burying

Ground," which he heard sung both by railroad work gangs *and* by worshippers in a local African-American church.[112]

Another important collection of spirituals from this era was Charles L. Edwards's *Bahama Songs and Stories,* first published in 1895. The population in the Bahamas is particularly noteworthy as it relates to spirituals. At the time of Edwards's collection, the majority of the people were either former slaves of "direct" African descent imported to the islands or the descendents of the slaves of the Loyalists who fled the United States following the Revolutionary War. A few, like "Unc' Yawk" of Green Turtle Cay, still had vivid memories of Africa.[113] The striking similarity of many of the spirituals (still called "anthems" on the Bahamas)[114] reinforced the theory of a vibrant body of spirituals already in existence before the American Revolution.

Edwards collected numerous Bahamian folktales, many directly descended, he believes, from Africa, including the "B'Rabby" stories, which parallel those of the more familiar "Brer Rabbit" stories in the United States—including one popular tale about a tar baby.[115]

In all, Edwards assembled a set of forty "anthems," among them several not collected in major U.S. collections, but including such familiar titles as "Go Down, Moses," "Death was Little T'ing," and "Lord, I Wish I Could Pray." One of the more interesting spirituals in *Bahama Songs and Stories* is "Git on Board." A stateside version of the same spiritual features various railroad themes and allusions, but in the Bahamas it had taken on a number of nautical verses:

> *No second class on bo'd de train*
> *No diffren' in de fa-are*
>
> *The Gospel sails are histed*
> *King Jesus is de crew*
> *Bright angels is de captain, Lawd*[116]

Perhaps the most beautiful spiritual in Edwards's collection is titled "When de Moon Went Down":

> *When de moon went down in purple stream, purple stream*
> *When de sta's refused to shine*
> *When ev'ry sta' dat disappeah*
> *King Jesus will be mine*
> *King Jesus will be mine*
>
> *When de sun went down in purple stream, purple stream*
> *When de sta's refused to shine*
> *When ev'ry sta' dat disappeah*
> *King Jesus will be mine*
> *King Jesus will be mine*[117]

As the century turned, spirituals were changing—or at least the spirituals as they were sung in the new urban cities, both North and South, were changing. While the true spiritual continued to be sung in the small rural churches, they were in the early stages of evolving into gospel music in the cities. They changed because the needs of the people who sang them changed.

In time, Lynn Abbott and Doug Seroff note, all African-American performers fell under the broad category of "authentic Negro minstrelsy," and Americans in general did not distinguish between true jubilee singing or minstrel imitations or parodies. Instead, more than ever before, the great mass of their country preferred to ignore the hideous treatment of African Americans in the South, treatment that only accelerated after the Plessy v. Ferguson decision in 1896, which sanctioned Jim Crow exclusionary laws. "In that low spirit," Abbott and Seroff write, "the general public retained a taste for jubilee singing while emphatically rejecting its spiritual and cultural implications. Widespread corruption of the spiritual with derisive satire allowed white listeners to enjoy the music from an emotionally detached distance, without brotherly empathy."[118]

Consequently, many African-American musicians drifted away from both religious performance and minstrelsy and into the emerging light musical comedy of vaudeville. "The late-nineteenth-century assault on the dignity of the spiritual unwittingly built a fire under twentieth-century black popular music," state Abbott and Seroff.[119] In other words, once again, the African American took something that had evil intentions and creatively transformed it into something usable and positive.

And in the midst of that change, it took a Bohemian composer to remind Americans what a treasure they had in the spirituals. Antonín Dvořák's "Symphony No. 5 in E Minor, Op. 95—"From the New World"—employed several folk music motifs, including spirituals, when it premiered in the spring of 1893. Writing in *Harper's New Monthly Magazine* a couple of years later, Dvořák dared suggest that America's only true indigenous music forms—African-American spirituals and native-American chants—"are indeed the most striking and appealing melodies that have yet been found on this side of the water."[120]

"The most potent as well as the most beautiful among them," he adds, "according to my estimation, are certain of the so-called plantation melodies and slave songs, all of which are distinguished by unusual and subtle harmonies, the like of which I have found in no other songs but those of old Scotland and Ireland."[121]

Unmistakable, unshakable, unbroken, the African-American spiritual entered the twentieth century as it would ultimately enter the twenty-first century, "with remarkable resilience and continuing popular resonance."[122]

Chapter Seven

The Foundations of Gospel: the Black Exodus, Barbershop Quartets, the Pentecostals, and Jack-Leg Preachers

I do remember I was always singin', "I cain't be satisfied, I be all troubled in mind." Seems to me like I was always singin' that because I was always singin' jest the way I felt, and maybe I didn't exactly know it, but I jest didn't like the way things were down there—in Mississippi.

—Muddy Waters, on growing up in Mississippi in the 1920s[1]

Lord in Heaven! Good God Almighty! Great Day in the Morning! It's here! Our time has come! We are leaving!

—Richard Wright, 1941[2]

The wash and rush of this human tide on the beach line of northern city centers is to be explained primarily in terms of a new vision of opportunity, of social and economic freedom, of a spirit to seize, even in the face of an extortionate and heavy toll, a change for the improvement of condition.

—Alain Locke, 1925[3]

Why is our music so contagious? Why is it that those who deny us are willing to sing our songs? Perhaps it is because so many of those who live in cities feel deep down just as we feel.

—Richard Wright, 1941[4]

Every opportunity to introduce a new rhythm is eagerly seized upon. The whole movement of the Sanctified Church is a rebirth of song-making! It has brought in a new era of spiritual-making.

—Zora Neale Hurston, 1938[5]

The Black Exodus

For twenty years on either side of the turn of the century (1800 to 1900), the forces that led to the creation of black gospel music gathered steam and momentum. In retrospect, the outcome was inevitable, though the cosmic alignment of these disparate—and sometimes apparently contradictory—forces was probably invisible at the time to the most significant players in this drama.

In terms of sheer numbers, the African diaspora pales by comparison to what came to be called the Great Migration of African Americans from South to North. What began as a trickle in the latter years of the nineteenth century became a flood by World War I. One estimate puts the total migration at five million—five million rural southern African Americans making the dangerous trek by rail, on horseback, on foot, and by any other means possible.[6] The two most commonly given reasons for this mass exodus have been the intensifying oppression of blacks in the South and the increasing employment opportunities for blacks in the North. But as that migration relates to the birth of gospel music, within that twin continuum is a complex set of interrelated factors. The shape of gospel music might have been greatly altered had not cities such as Chicago and Detroit been the favored destinations of some of the South's most musical refugees.

Following the collapse of Reconstruction, conditions degenerated rapidly for African Americans in the South. At the beginning of the twentieth century, the overall African-American population had doubled from the year 1860 to about nine million. About eight million of these lived in the South—and four fifths of them lived in rural settings. And virtually all of them lived in abject poverty, punctuated only by moments of abject fear.[7]

In addition to the Black Codes, Jim Crow laws, the Ku Klux Klan, systematic lynchings, and daily humiliation on the streets of every southern town, African Americans had reasons aplenty to leave their homes at the turn of the century and flee northward. Southern blacks faced the boll weevil infestations (the years 1892 and 1915–1916), a series of devastating floods (1915–1916), a virtual lack of justice in the southern states, atrocious to barely adequate educational opportunities, atrocious to barely adequate access to quality health care, and almost complete disenfranchisement at the polls. Between 1870 and 1910 virtually every southern state took away the right of African Americans to vote, either through legislation, the Poll Tax, the grandfather clause, or outright terrorism.[8] When Booker T. Washington and a few other guests dined informally with President Theodore Roosevelt at the White House on October 16, 1901, the event sparked riots and much of the southern press was ferocious in its attacks, venomously slandering Washington for another six decades.[9]

But a simple list of grievances isn't enough to personalize these tragedies. Richard Wright tells of textbooks designed for African Americans that omitted

all references to "government, voting, citizenship, and civil rights"—when textbooks were available at all.[10] Leon Litwack notes that by conservative estimates,
"two or three" African Americans were "hanged, burned at the stake, or quietly
murdered every week" in the South between 1890 and 1917:

> Even an accurate body count of black lynching victims could not possibly reveal
> how hate and fear transformed ordinary white men and women into mindless
> murderers and sadistic torturers, or the savagery that, with increasing regularity,
> characterized assaults on black men and women in the name of restraining their
> savagery and depravity.[11]

Charles Evers states it even more starkly in his book, *Evers:* ". . . [B]ack in
those days to kill a Negro man wasn't nothing. It was like killing a chicken or
killing a snake. The whites would say, 'Niggers jest supposed to die, ain't no
damn good anyway—so jest go on an' kill 'em.' "[12]

Tenant farming, the occupation of the majority of African Americans, had
degenerated into perpetual serfdom, different only in the cruel fact that at least
slaves once had value to slave owners, while tenant farmers had virtually no
value to most landowners. They were cheap, disposable, and faceless. The end
result—codified by the 1896 Plessy v. Ferguson Supreme Court decision—was a
caste system, not unlike what existed in India with the untouchables, an entire
class of people slowly starving to death. Representative studies by Charles S.
Johnson and Carter Woodson of rural black Southerners in the 1920s and 1930s
(and presumably similar to conditions from 1880 to 1920) confirmed that the
horrifying mortality rates among African-American children were due in a great
part to "deficient diets born of restrictions imposed on tenant farmers by landowners who feared reduced cotton acreage if food crops were allowed to be
cultivated and livestock kept."[13] A later U.S. Department of Agriculture survey
of African-American families in the mid-1930s showed eight out of ten families
"subsisted on diets not meeting even minimum nutritional recommendations."[14]
Other factors, including several misguided (or mismanaged) government subsidy
programs, only exacerbated the problems.

Meanwhile, particularly in the states north of the Ohio River and east of the
Mississippi, increased industrialization, fueled by a war economy beginning in
1915, provided oppressed African Americans with an attractive alternative. The
onset of World War I in Europe virtually halted the continual waves of European
emigration to the United States. This occurred "precisely at a moment when
northern captains of industry and finance, recipients of huge contracts to supply
their favored combatants with munitions and other emergency requirements for
nations involved in modern war, experienced a need to quickly expand a labor
force."[15] That labor force streamed from the South to toil in the burgeoning
industrial, military, transportation, and communications complexes in Chicago,
Detroit, Cleveland, Philadelphia, and elsewhere. The greatest numbers fled from
Mississippi, Alabama, Georgia, and South Carolina.[16]

The migration patterns are interesting and are still the subject of lively research and inquiry. But the focus of the movement appears to be proximity- or transportation- (along major north-south highways and railroad lines) related. For example, the bulk of migration from Mississippi was to Chicago, with lesser numbers of migrants stopping in Memphis and (later) Birmingham or even trekking west to southern California. In Virginia, the exodus was primarily toward Washington, D.C., with lesser patterns first to New York City and Philadelphia, and then to Richmond and the ship-building cities such as Norfolk along the Atlantic coast.[17]

The clear winners in this migration, of course, were the northern industrialists who found an inexhaustible supply of cheap, reliable workers, grateful to fill the worst jobs. But even the most rabidly racist Southerner soon felt the loss of a significant percentage of his available workforce. According to Carole Marks, "Mississippi in particular lost more than it gained in this struggle, for in casting off its orphans, it discarded not only a valuable labor supply but its most useful natural resource."[18] The industrialists recruited widely in the South, but soon glowing letters home from the new immigrants and the work of activist African-American newspapers, especially the *Chicago Defender* (which encouraged migration both editorially and in its famed classified advertising "job opportunities" sections), lessened the need for hired agents.[19] The South Side of Chicago (often called Bronzeville), the Near East Side in Cleveland, Harlem in New York, Paradise Valley in Detroit, and other black enclaves filled with eager newcomers looking for work.

Eventually, many Southerners became alarmed at the great exodus and—predictably—began to search for ways to slow or end it completely. Some chose coercion, some chose persuasion, some chose both, but still the African Americans marched northward from the Deep South. "Repressive responses involved impediments either to the transmission of information about opportunities in the North or to departure itself," writes James R. Grossman.

> Like their antebellum forebears, who had banned abolitionist literature and had forbidden slaves to play drums or trumpets because they might be used to pass signals, white southerners during the Great Migration thought they could control communications sufficiently to prevent the spread of knowledge that threatened the labor system. *The Chicago Defender*, incessant critic of the South and cheerleader of northward migration, posed an obvious target.[20]

Some white authorities in Mississippi confiscated copies of the *Defender*, while a black minister was fined $400 and sentenced to five months on a county farm for selling the NCAAP's *Crisis* in one Mississippi city.[21] Legendary bluesman W. C. Handy augmented his salary playing for bawdy houses outside Clarksdale, Mississippi, by covertly distributing copies of the *Defender*, the *Indianapolis Freeman*, and the *Voice of the Negro* at great personal risk.[22]

Elsewhere, Southerners enforced or created laws banning "enticement" by outside labor agents, refused to honor prepaid tickets on northern railroad carriers, and some landlords simply had "suspicious" tenant farmers jailed or refused to pay for their crops in a timely manner.[23] Northern factory and mill owners responded by sending special trains south to pick up prospective employees.[24]

New Orleans jazz musician Danny Barker remembers that Chicago by train was the destination of choice for African-American residents of the Big Easy in the 1920s. Even mentioning the name "Mississippi" would cause conversation to abruptly cease in some circles, especially within his family. "The word was so powerful that it carried the impact of catastrophes," he writes in *A Life in Jazz*. In fact, "the states of Alabama, Florida, Texas and Georgia were equally fearsome concerning their treatment of Negroes when the least bit of friction with white folks occurred." When the unthinkable happened, New Orleans residents immediately thought of Chicago via the Illinois Central Railroad (ICR). While the Southern or L&N lines passed through portions of the Deep South, "the ICR track ran virtually straight up north to Chicago—not one slight bend or turn along the whole route."[25]

As crucial as the rail connections were, fares were often out of reach of tenant farmers living on pennies, and the odd-numbered highways (north-south) became even more important to potential migrants. Old blues songs tout the value of "Highway 49" (Big Joe Williams) and "Highway 51" (Tommy McClennan),[26] while Sunnyland Slim's "Highway 61" features what may be the most famous "blues" highway of all. One musicologist combined a study of lyrics with interviews with blues artists in *Living Blues* magazine and *Blues Unlimited* to determine the actual number (and names) of blues singers who left which southern states for which northern states—and the specific routes they used.[27] Douglas Langille found that highways 51 and 61 and the Atlantic Central, Illinois Central, and Missouri-Kansas-Texas Southern rail lines were the primary linkages.[28]

What these new immigrants found, whether it was in Bronzeville or in the shotgun houses along the tracks in Birmingham, was nothing less than an alien world.

The African-American communities within the urban centers were radically different than what southern blacks had experienced before—socially, culturally, and even spiritually. Members of many of the established northern African-American churches often regarded the migrants as a "threat" and either ignored or ridiculed the newcomers. The older Baptist churches in particular resembled their urban white counterparts more than the migrants' more modest country churches. Even their music was more white than black.[29] Or, as one former South Carolina native complained to a writer following her move north in the 1890s, northern blacks, she said, "ain't got no Holy Spirit and dey is singing no 'count songs—dese white songs from books."[30]

Fifty years of (relative) freedom in the urban North had also seen the rise of the great African-American classical composers. In 1914, R. Nathaniel Dett composed and published one of the first "anthemized" versions of a spiritual, "Listen to the Lambs." Harry T. Burleigh produced a series of artistically arranged spirituals for solo voice in 1916, followed by James Weldon and J. Rosamund Johnson and several others, all transforming the spiritual into Western European-styled arias and hymns. The words may have been the same, but for the poor black sharecropper from Waycross, Georgia, or Waco, Texas, the music and performance style was all but unrecognizable.[31]

Consequently, when these American refugees moved into neighborhoods populated by friends, family members, and people from the same parts of the Old South—like the Irish before them—they sought to recreate the villages of home:

> There are two blocks in Chicago made up largely of Mississippians from Holmes County. Social life revolved around the folks from downhome as counties and small towns were contracted and re-formed on Chicago's South Side. Like most immigrant groups, black Chicagoans recreated, in a modified form, the institutions from back home. Store-front churches and blues bars and clubs sprang up as refuges from the strange and bewildering environment of a metropolitan city. The importance of these institutions was the creation of something familiar and therefore secular, giving life at least a superficial continuity after the break in lifestyle, customs and climate.[32]

Barbership Quartets

Simultaneously with this mass movement, a new form of quartet singing experienced a remarkable rise in popularity in the United States during the last decades of the nineteenth century: "barbershop" quartet singing, although that term wouldn't become universally applied until the song "Mr. Jefferson, Lord, Play That Barbershop Chord" became popular in 1911.[33] As Eileen Southern notes, the barbershop held a pivotal place in the musical life of both small southern towns and large urban neighborhoods. "Owned and operated by black men, open from early morn until late at night," she notes, "barbershops provided congenial meeting places where the musically inclined could discourse on music or practice in a back room without interruption. It is no accident that many of the early musicians were barbers . . .".[34] Like their ancestors, young African Americans without the financial resources of their white counterparts utilized the gifts they had—their voices—and in ten thousand barbershops and on the steps of uncounted tenement stoops rehearsed both the sacred and the profane.

James Weldon Johnson's *Book of Negro Spirituals*, first published in 1925, contains valuable clues about how long and how pervasive the penchant for harmonizing was among African Americans. Johnson writes that part of the attraction for slave singing in the Big Houses of southern plantations was not necessarily the quality of the untrained voices but, instead, the quality of their natural inclination toward harmonizing:

Nᴼ I ɪɴ C   Nᴼ 2 ɪɴ Db   Nᴼ 3 ɪɴ F
116006   116040   116059

Respectfully dedicated to
Mɪss Mᴀʀʏ Jᴏʀᴅᴀɴ

DEEP RIVER

Sᴏɴɢ

Oʟᴅ Nᴇɢʀᴏ Mᴇʟᴏᴅʏ

Arranged by

H.T.Bᴜʀʟᴇɪɢʜ

Price 60 cents

COPYRIGHT MCMXVII,
BY G. RICORDI & CO., INC.

G.Rɪᴄᴏʀᴅɪ & Cᴏ.,
14 Eᴀsᴛ 43ᴿᴰ Sᴛʀᴇᴇᴛ
Nᴇᴡ Yᴏʀᴋ

AND AT
LONDON, PARIS, LEIPZIG,
ROME, PALERMO, NAPLES,
BUENOS-AYRES AND MILAN.

African-American composer H. T. Burleigh's arrangement of the spiritual "Deep
River" remains popular even today. (author's collection)

Pick up four colored boys or young men anywhere and the chances are ninety out of a hundred that you will have a quartet. Let one of them sing the melody and the others will naturally find the parts. Indeed, it may be said that all male Negro youth of the United States is divided into quartets.[35]

Johnson, who was born in 1871, spent much of his youth in Florida listening to the "crack quartets" made up of waiters at top Jacksonville resort hotels.[36] The hotels often had both a "first" and "second" quartet, and by age fifteen, Johnson and his brother, composer Rosamund Johnson, then thirteen, both competed in such a quartet. Johnson also spent much of his spare time in barbershops, at a time when, in the South at least, white barbers were unknown:

. . . [E]very barber shop had its quartet, and the men spent their leisure times playing on the guitar—not banjo, mind you—and "harmonizing." I have witnessed some of these explorations in the field of harmony and the scenes of hilarity and back-slapping when a new and peculiarly rich chord was discovered. There would be demands for repetitions, and cries of "Hold it! Hold it!" until it was firmly mastered. And well it was, for some of these chords were so new and strange for voices that, like Sullivan's Lost Chord, they would never have been found again except for the celerity with which they were recaptured. In this way was born the famous but much abused "barber-shop chord."[37]

To Johnson, who himself later joined the popular Atlanta University Quartette, the "barber-shop chord" is the foundation of the close harmonies later used by composers arranging songs for male voices. "'Barber-shop harmonies' gave a tremendous vogue to male quartet singing, first on the minstrel stage, then in vaudeville," he writes, "and soon white young men, wherever four or more were gathered together, tried themselves at 'harmonizing.'"[38] As with previous African-American musical trends, the white community wholeheartedly embraced the new musical style to the extent that thousands of "clubs, fraternal organizations, churches, and companies like Westinghouse and 7-Up" sponsored quartets.[39] In his memoirs, minstrel performer Ike Simond identifies a number of black quartets that were popular in the 1880s and 1890s, including groups with such colorful names as Black Diamond, the Dark Town Quartette, Eclipse, Buckeye, Beethoven, Mountain Pink, Garden City, Twilight, Climax, Olympic, and the elegant-sounding Sans Souci Quartet.[40]

The fad swept from vaudeville to the early recording companies and many of the top-selling artists of the day were barbershop quartets, including the Peerless Quartet and the influential Revelers. But as the new century dawned, changes were occurring in the music. African-American groups catering to mostly white audiences performed in a manner more acceptable to Western European-styled concert tastes. But within their own communities, the harmonies of the barbershop quartets were evolving, and groups that sang exclusively for black audiences slowly began to incorporate more African-American influences.[41] Barbershop finally faded with the advent of the Great Depression in 1929 and the rise of radio in 1930 when the new songs, with their minor seventh chords, proved difficult to harmonize.[42]

Eventually, barbershop singing became firmly established in the public's mind with white college boys and the Gay Nineties, or as a movement somehow attached to the obviously unrelated "barber's music" from the continent. But as Lynn Abbott in " 'Play That Barber Shop Chord': A Case for the African American Origin of Barbershop Harmony" and others have argued, it more likely first arose from the black community.[43] And it was only after his "little quartet" of barbershop singers folded with the closing of Storyville in 1917 that a young Louis Armstrong turned to jazz full time.[44]

The Pentecostals

The new urban African-American world brought about almost immediate changes in the economic, social, and musical lives of original city resident and wide-eyed immigrant alike. It is not surprising, then, that this new world would need a new religion as well. Many former Southerners soon found themselves more comfortable—and more accepted—in the hundreds of smaller, more intimate storefront Sanctified churches springing up throughout the inner cities of America.[45] In these new churches, refugees working twelve-hour days, six days a week in the jobs that white America refused to do, found something else:

> Beyond the gospel shouts and jubilant cries heralding an imminent salvation, it was the only place where a weekday maid called "Mary," or some other disrespectful first name, might wear some weekend dignity by ushering others, just as proud and poverty-stricken as she, to their seats. It was the sole arena where a chauffeur or a handyman, reduced to facelessness and namelessness by his employers and often mute within his own home, might speak with some seldom exercised authority as a deacon of the congregation.[46]

The seeds of the Holiness/Pentecostal religious traditions began in the eighteenth century with John Wesley, the founder of Methodism, and his desire to follow Matthew 5:48, "Be ye therefore perfect ever as your Father which is in heaven is perfect." To followers of what would become the Holiness movement, terms like *sanctification* and *justification* are part of the process of becoming "perfected" through a "born-again" experience and—later—when "the Holy Spirit cleanses the heart from sin and imparts his indwelling presence, giving power for living the Christian life."[47] The movement became a part of the American religious experience in 1839, mostly through the work of one of the country's most famous evangelists, Charles G. Finney. This was followed by another strain of the Holiness movement that originated a few years later by Phoebe Palmer, a member of the Allen Street Methodist Church in New York City.[48] After an

African-American women opened a club in Newark, New Jersey, for the soldiers about to leave for army camp, ca. 1918 (photo: the National Archives)

explosive period of growth, the new movement began to splinter in the 1880s, dividing into numerous smaller Holiness-related denominations.[49]

Pentecostalism, with its emphasis on "speaking in tongues" (or *glossolalia*) and healing, also sprang from the Holiness tradition. Two revivals provided the foundations for Pentecostals: Topeka, Kansas, in 1901 (with Charles Parham) and Azusa Street, Los Angeles, California (with William J. Seymour).[50] The movement separated itself from the parent Holiness movement with a defining convention in Hot Springs, Arkansas, in 1914, and eventually evolved into the Assemblies of God. This movement continued to split until the Church of God (Cleveland, Tennessee) and the Church of God of Our Lord Jesus Christ of the Apostolic Faith emerged, along with the older Assemblies of God, as the three main components of modern Pentecostalism.[51]

Both the Holiness and Pentecostal (also called "Sanctified") traditions "swept through black communities." Seymour, an African American, was one of the first major Pentecostals. And the famed "Azusa Street Revival" was remarkably integrated in the beginning, although the denomination eventually split along racial lines.[52] But even more attractive to blacks was the "emotional nature of Pentecostal worship" that almost immediately "held a strong appeal to African

American Christians already accustomed to highly charged modes of worship."[53] Where the Baptist and Methodist denominations had once catered to the oppressed, the new Pentecostal churches were "essentially a religion of the socially underprivileged" and "African Americans naturally gravitated into it, feeling themselves to be truly at home in the Pentecostal environment."[54] Soon, the largest congregations of Pentecostal denominations, such as the Church of God in Christ (COGIC), the United Holy Church, and the Fire-Baptized Holiness Church were located in the large urban centers of New York, Chicago, Detroit, and Philadelphia.[55]

The Pentecostal/Holiness churches had one more advantage for many African Americans over virtually all other mainstream Protestant denominations: They not only allowed the use of musical instruments in their services, they *encouraged* their use. The key verses that guided the different Pentecostal churches and separated them from sister denominations, which required either a cappella singing or muted piano and/or organ accompaniment, are the final verses of the Old Testament Book of Psalms 150: 3–6[56]: "Praise him with the sound of the trumpet; praise him with the psaltery and harp; praise him with the timbrel and dance; praise him with stringed instruments and organs; praise him upon the loud cymbals; praise him upon the high-sounding cymbals. Let everything that hath breath praise the Lord. Praise ye the Lord." Consequently, "the Sanctified and Pentecostal churches made extensive use of the hand clapping and foot stamping that descended from the shout; they also used drums and tambourines, and their own distinctive songs were heavily laced with or based on call-and-responses figures."[57]

The "Pentecostal fervor" of the Holiness churches meant that enraptured congregations whirled in holy dances, spurred on by a variety of "worldly" instruments—including guitars.[58] Caught in the ecstasy, congregants quickly integrated ragtime, jazz, even blues motifs and melodies to sing their praises to God. The wide choice of musical instruments in the independent Sanctified churches spurred a "musical renaissance" among African-American believers, notes Glenn D. Hinson. "Congregations were quick to incorporate the instruments of 'the world' into worship, restoring them—in the eyes of many believers—to their 'legitimate' roles as tools of praise."[59]

"Whatever the absence of decorum in the folk of Holiness churches," Leon Litwack writes, "they were places of refuge that filled an emptiness in black lives, that raised people out of despair. The shouts, the rhythmic chanting, the foot stomps, the preaching, the singing, the hand claps, the degree of personal participation made for an intense emotional experience."[60] In basement and storefront churches, the exhausted workers from the South found the counterparts of the mystic brush arbor ring shouts and ecstatic musical release from backbreaking labor in a strange land. They found a piece of home.

Exactly when guitars and pianos were introduced into Sanctified and COGIC services is still uncertain, although Mattie Moss Clark, once International President of the Music Department of COGIC, recalls that those instruments were "always" present in the COGIC services: "My mother, Mattie Moss Ramsey, played piano and guitar in her Sanctified church in the 1890s. The saxophone and other instruments came much later, in the 1920s and 1930s, while the organ was [used] even later than that—1940s."[61]

The statement "The devil should not have all of the best tunes," often attributed to Martin Luther, is actually credited to English cleric Rev. Rowland Hill.[62] In that vein, John W. Work writes that an elder of the Holiness church once told him, "The devil should not be allowed to keep all of the good rhythms." Work's response:

> And, he has not. He is in danger of losing it to the musicians of the Holiness Church. Both instrumentalists and congregational participants have developed a rhythmic intensity possibly unequalled in any prior musical performance. These combined forces under prolonged religious excitation frequently extend the length of a song by as much as six minutes, and even more beyond its normal singing time. The active participation of hundreds of church members together with the instrumentalists develops a degree of rhythmic intensity which cannot be matched by any dance band.[63]

While the advent of musical instruments opened Sanctified believers to avenues of musical expression previously restricted to the secular world, it did not lead to the wholesale embracing of "worldly phrasing, forms and rhythms," Hinson adds. Instead it led to the "inventive reinstatement of musical ideas and stylistic propensities common to all Black American music." The end result was that "sanctified music emerged with a power distinctively its own, a power steeped in passion and bolstered by faith."[64]

Poet Langston Hughes, then a young teenager in Chicago during World War I, never forgot entering an instrument-fueled Holiness service for the first time:

> I was entranced by their stepped-up rhythms, tambourines, hand-clapping, and uninhibited dynamics, rivaled only by Ma Rainey singing the blues at the old Monogram Theatre. . . . The music of these less formal Negro churches early took hold of me, moved me and thrilled me.[65]

It was from this rapturous convention that the singing preachers of the Sanctified tradition "emerged."[66]

Eager factory workers weren't all that migrated northward. America continued its fascination with African-American music and—following the spirituals and minstrel music—successive waves of music flowed northward from the Deep South: ragtime, the blues, and jazz. And, each time, white audiences quickly embraced this new music as well—a tradition that continues into the twenty-first century because, as George Lipsitz notes, "White Americans may have turned to black culture for guidance because black culture contains the most sophisticated strategies of signification and the richest grammar of opposition available to aggrieved populations."[67]

Jack-Leg Preachers

Black musicians took the sounds of New Orleans and the Mississippi Delta with them to the tenements of Chicago and Kansas City. Among the most intriguing of those musical missionaries were the singing street preachers, a particularly American phenomenon that—while only sporadically documented and re-searched—provides yet another musical link in gospel's chain.

Eileen Southern writes that at around the turn of the century itinerant singers emerged on the scene—some singing the blues, some singing a rough-hewn ver-sion of the spirituals, and some singing both (which she dubs "blues-spirituals").[68] Richard Raichelson argues that the phrasings employed by early blues and spiri-tuals artists and groups were part of a "common stock in black music at that time." The lines of demarcation are certainly not well drawn. And while the man many consider the greatest of the religious street performers, Blind Willie John-son, may have shared guitar phrasings with his blues counterparts, there is no indication that he ever shared their sometimes rowdy lifestyles.[69]

The term "jack-leg preachers"—referring to someone with little or no educa-tion and no regular church—soon came to refer to all such musical evangelists. Some would remain on the streets their entire lives, others would find a sympa-thetic group of listeners and form a storefront church, particularly in the larger northern cities.[70]

In his autobiography, W. C. Handy recalls seeing "blind singers and footloose bards" throughout the Mississippi Delta near Clarksdale just after the turn of the century. They often rode the rails and sometimes performed near the railroad station, singing to the passing crowds. "They earned their living by selling their own songs—'ballats,' as they called them," he writes, "and I'm ready to say in their behalf that seldom did their creations lack imagination."[71] While some sang strictly secular songs, others preached and sang their songs for religious pur-poses. "I remember buying such a ballat [ballad] entitled 'I've Heard of a City Called Heaven,'" he adds. "It was printed on a slip of paper about the size of a postcard." Handy writes that he later published a choral arrangement of the song and that years later the Hall Johnson Singers performed it in the film *The Green Pastures*.[72]

The term *ballads* (or *ballats* or *ballots*) serves as an interesting bridge between spirituals and the emerging music of the African-American church. Jeanette Murphy Robinson quotes an elderly former slave in the 1890s making a very clear distinction between the terms:

Us ole heads use ter make 'em up on de spurn of de moment, arter we wrassle wid de Sperit and come thoo. But the tunes was brung from Africa by our granddaddies. Dey was jis 'miliar songs. Dese days dey calls 'em ballots, but in de ole days dey call 'em spirituals, case de Holy Spirit done revealed 'em to 'em.[73]

Although the recording industry was in its infancy during these years, a number of jack-leg preachers and street-corner singers were recorded in the first decades of the twentieth century and some of these recordings survive. They comprised a small but vital segment of the seminal industry, and their recordings fell under the general category of "race records" (a phrase coined by early recording executives), music created for release exclusively in the African-American marketplace.[74] In addition to Blind Willie Johnson, fascinating records exist by the mysterious Washington Phillips (who performed on a strange zitherlike instrument that's still the subject of heated debate among musicologists), Sam Jones, Julius Daniels, "The Guitar Evangelist" (the Reverend Edward Clayborn), A. C. and Mamie Forehand, and others. An inordinate number of these artists were blind (music and religion being two of the few avenues open for blind African Americans to earn a living), but the constant singing in all kinds of weather took an awful toll on the vocal cords and gave many jack-leg preachers and songsters rough, raspy voices that even today convey a thrilling urgency and conviction.[75] That "rough" sound soon became both the accepted norm and a much-admired standard among gospel singers of succeeding generations.

Perhaps more important, these artists' practice of selling printed versions of their songs, often about contemporary events, helped change the perceptions of religious music. A. E. Perkins writes that within a week of the sinking of the *Titanic* on April 14, 1912, he heard a "blind preacher" on a train selling a ballad he had composed, based on the disaster. Perkins even remembered the refrain to the song "Didn't That Ship Go Down?" a decade after the incident:

> *God Almighty talked like a natural man*
> *Spoke so the people could understand*[76]

These songs would help pave the way for Thomas Dorsey and others to sell printed versions of their music and make it much more accessible to blue-collar families and storefront church congregations. Printed hymnals, after all, cost much more than a few printed broadsides.

The first of many African-American preachers to be recorded was Calvin P. Dixon, "the Black Billy Sunday" (after the white revivalist) in 1925. While his recording of "As an Eagle Stirs Her Nest" for Columbia didn't set any sales marks, it opened the door for others, most notably the Reverend J. C. Burnett. Burnett's "The Downfall of Nebuchadnezzer"—featuring an opening "long meter spiritual sung by Sisters Lucille Smith and Fannie Cox"—sold nearly 100,000 copies, an astonishing number at the time.[77] Paul Oliver's transcription of Burnett's wonderfully hoarse delivery places the most heavily stressed words in italics:

> And when Nebuchadnezzar had went out and eat grass seven long years,
> Finger*nails* growing out like bird claws,
> And his body washed with the dew of Heaven,
> *Lo-rd* when seven *years* passed over him
> He lifted up his eyes and declared: "The Heaven do rule." (Yes sir!)
> Now friends let me tell you, *God rules* in this *kingdom of men*
> And he can take the kingdom from whomsoever he *will*
> And give it to the one he want to give it to.
> *Now* you liars, *now* you backsliders, *now* you rich men—
> Let me tell you that *God* is able to bring you down, my friends. . . .[78]

Alas, the primitive early recording devices of the day could only record three minutes or so at a time, so these surviving sermons may not be a true reflection of the power of those early preachers. Cutting through the static, however, is the impressive command of rhythm displayed by Burnett and virtually all of his contemporaries. Jon Michael Spencer says it is the rhythm that has always endowed African-American preaching with "locomotion and momentum." "Without it," he notes, "preaching would not only be static, it would hardly have an audience."[79] Even today, these scratchy recordings have a palpable, straining urgency. Burnett's rhythmic delivery and musicality drew on a long tradition in African-American preaching and music: "[t]hrough his growls, gasps and constricted utterances he communicated much of his message by the techniques that had often been noted in the past."[80] The Reverend J. M. Gates (best known for the apocalyptic "Death's Black Train Is Coming") recorded a mind-boggling forty-two sides of these heavily cadenced sermons in just three weeks for six different record labels![81]

Another significant jack-leg preacher of the era was the Reverend Ford Washington (F. W.) McGee, a faith healer and tent evangelist, who began his career in Oklahoma City where he was accompanied by the extraordinary blind pianist, Arizona Dranes. After World War I, Rice accepted the pulpit at a COGIC church in Chicago. McGee recorded a series of popular sermons for Victor, usually with musical accompaniment, including "Lion of the Tribe of Judah" (1927, which included Dranes on piano), "Holes in Your Pockets" (1930), "Death May Be Your Pay Check" (1928), and "The Light of the World" (1929). The two-sided 78 "Jonah in the Belly of the Whale" and "With His Stripes We Are Healed" sold more than 100,000 copies.[82] "Fifty Miles of Elbow Room" (1930) features not only Rice's powerhouse preaching style but also "trumpet, guitar and piano accompaniment to strong, rhythmic congregational singing."[83]

McGee's most important contribution to African-American sacred music, however, may have been introducing Dranes to the religious public. Little is known definitively about Juanita Arizona Dranes, although in a few years she would work with some of the most powerful young preachers in the rising new denomination, the Church of God in Christ. After accompanying a number of preachers in Texas, she gained attention for her work with Samuel M. Crouch, Jr., later a bishop with the COGIC. She was discovered in Dallas by OKeh talent scout Richard M. Jones and traveled from Texas to Chicago with a note that read, "[s]ince she is Deprived Of Her Natural Sight, the Lord Has Given Her a Spiritual Sight that Churches Enjoy. She is loyal and Obedient, Our Prayers Assend for her."[84] And while she only recorded thirty sides for the OKeh label between 1924 and 1928, the combination of her electrifying singing and her thumping, rhythm-fused piano playing made her a much-in-demand artist at black churches and revivals throughout the country.[85] One contemporary recalls that the "gifted" Dranes was a consummate performer as well: "she would get up off that piano and turn all around and sit back down and start."[86]

Horace Boyer describes her piano playing as a "combination of ragtime, with its two beats to the bar feel, octave passages in the left hand, exaggerated syncopation in the right hand, and [the] heavy, full and ragged [syncopated] chords of barrelhouse piano, and the more traditional chords of the standard Protestant hymn." Boyer also notes her voice, which was "remarkable for its piercing quality," which enabled her to "cut through the clapping and stamping of church services." Dranes often sang with a true backup group and was one of the first to introduce songs in three-quarter time, which would become the widely imitated 12/8 rhythm favored by a host of gospel artists in the 1950s.[87] Jerma A. Jackson adds that Dranes "embellished the melody with improvisational run" while at the same time "executing a driving rhythm in the bass." In short, she played an early form of boogie-woogie.[88]

What little is known about Dranes answers none of the questions about this astonishing talent. It's possible that she learned the highly infectious style of playing from the legions of "fast Texas boogie-woogie pianists who played in Dallas' Deep Ellum, not far from Dranes' State-Thomas neighborhood."[89] But where did her razor-sharp mezzo-soprano, with its "remarkable thrust," come from? Paul Oliver notes that it was the blind pianist who was "instrumental" in convincing McGee to initially record, and it is her performance that elevates his recordings of "Bye and Bye We're Going to See the King" and "Lamb's Blood Has Washed Me Clean."[90] Despite continued ill health (perhaps from repeated bouts of influenza), Dranes was an indefatigable performer and her unique combination of barrelhouse piano and modified spirituals sold thousands of records. "Arizona Dranes . . . set a model for lusty, committed singing," Oliver notes, with "clear, sharp vocals" that provided obvious inspiration for a number of other pre-gospel artists, including Jessie Mae Hill and Laura Henton.[91] Dranes never recorded again after the 1928 sessions.

A few letters between Dranes and OKeh executives surfaced in 1970 and, on the eve of the Depression, paint a portrait of an inveterate nomad, a woman frequently wracked with debilitating illnesses, who dictated short, plaintive letters asking for small advances of $25 from her nonresponsive record company.[92] Arizona Dranes was soon lost to history, leaving a handful of tracks, virtually no written record or known interviews, but an influential musical legacy. She spent her final years in southern California, often performing at the church of the Reverend Crouch, the Emmanuel Church of God in Christ in South Central Los Angeles. (Crouch is the great-uncle of gospel superstar Andrae Crouch.) The first sacred-music-singing female piano player died in obscurity of cerebral arteriosclerosis in 1963, virtually unknown save to the musicians who were profoundly influenced by her playing, including Roberta Martin, Jerry Lee Lewis, Fats Domino, and a thousand more besides.[93]

The success of the recorded music and sermons of jack-leg preachers (and their "chair-backer" counterparts who had established churches) even induced many blues singers to record religious songs as well, including Blind Lemon Jefferson (as Deacon L. J. Bates), Charley Patton (sometimes under the name of Elder J. J. Hadley), Barbecue Bob, Leola Manning, Blind Roosevelt Graves, and Blind Joel Taggart.[94] As a boy, blues artist Josh White earned several dollars a week guiding blind jack-leg preachers and blues men (including Taggart) from street to street and town to town.[95]

Among the haunting performances on *Afro-American Spirituals, Work Songs, and Ballads* is "The Blood-Stained Banders" (probably "Blood-Stained Bandits") by Jimmie Strothers, recorded at the Virginia State Prison Farms in 1936. In their book *Our Singing Country*, John A. and Alan Lomax write that "itinerant street singers" like Strothers have played a vital role in the preservation and dissemination of African-American religious music:

> Usually blind, piloted by his wife or by some little boy, he inches along through the streets and down the alleys of Negro working-class neighborhoods, shouting and groaning out a spiritual in his hoarse, twelve-hours-a-day voice, reminding saints and sinners that the blind must eat. The comrade of his dark, slow journeys is the battered guitar he plays. It provides his drum and tambourine accompaniment, it hums his background harmony, it comes in strong on the chorus, it stomps his two-four rhythm and claps a counter-rhythm against itself. And when his breath is gone, "Talk it for me now," says the blind singer, and his old box sings the words of the chorus, plaintively and high on little E.[96]

But few artists of any generation, in any style, can compare with Blind Willie Johnson, "a slide guitarist without parallel, a player so perfect he's impossible to adequately imitate," a street-corner evangelist with a "scary, emotion-charged voice."[97] Born in poverty, accidentally blinded in a domestic dispute between his father and stepmother, Johnson taught himself to play a handmade guitar with a pocketknife. When not singing in small Church of God in Christ congregations in central Texas, he would stand on street corners and play and sing, a tin cup around his neck for tips. At one point, Johnson and Blind Lemon Jefferson sang on competing street corners in tiny Marlin, Texas, outside Waco.[98] Somehow, word of Johnson's prowess reached an early talent scout and beginning in 1927 he recorded a mere thirty sides in the next few years, a mixture of haunting originals and electrifying covers of spirituals and old hymns, all sung "in a rasping, false bass that could freeze the blood."[99] At least one writer links Johnson's "deep and deliberately gravelly" voice to the "possession voices" of priests in certain African religions, including the Serer songs of Senegal.[100]

The Depression ended Johnson's career—along with that of many other artists, including Arizona Dranes—and he died in the winter of 1949, apparently from sleeping on wet sheets following a house fire, then trudging to the streets to sing in the cold wind. Dying of pneumonia, no hospital would accept him.[101] But those thirty incomparable 78s are "the work of a pained believer seeking street-corner redemption with a guitar and a tin cup." Master guitarist Ry Cooder once described Johnson's chilling, wordless moan "Dark Was the Night, Cold Was the Ground" as "the most transcendent piece in all American music."[102] Cooder may be understating the scope of this music. When Carl Sagan and his staff selected the music to include on *Voyager I* in 1977, they chose both the sounds of a human heart and falling rain and the most revered music known to humanity: ancient chants, Beethoven, Bach . . . and Blind Willie Johnson's "Dark Was the Night."[103]

Early Recording Artists

While scores of titles by jack-leg preachers were available to the public, another African-American vocal tradition was also being recorded and released by the major record labels of the day. "Groups that sang spirituals in the manner of the nineteenth-century Fisk Jubilee Singers, like the Pace Jubilee Singers or the Elkins Payne Jubilee Singers, were prolific," Paul Oliver adds, "though they were challenged by the newer harmonizing quartets such as the Birmingham Jubilee Singers or the Excelsior Quartet." Their carefully rehearsed techniques contrasted mightily with the gospel songs of guitar-playing street evangelists such as Reverend Edward Clayborn or Blind Willie Johnson.[104] Only a few of the jack-leg preachers (most notably the Reverend J. M. Gates) continued to record into the 1930s. Their short recording careers fell victim to the Depression, although some were assimilated into the various denominations. The rising accessibility and popularity of radio and the new musical crazes, such as hokum, also served to curtail the demand for their recordings. Still, "[t]he sermons and the congregational singing, the Sanctified churches with their music, and the street evangelists with their self-accompanied songs in the first phase of Race records revealed the richness, variety, energy and conviction of the black churches," Oliver writes, "qualities that were to carry them through the years of stress which were to come."[105]

The religious quartets, however, flourished. Even as the jubilee music era was ending, Fisk University was finding unexpected success spinning off a series of smaller (and cheaper to maintain) quartets. Other successful spiritual and minstrel groups spun off quartets of their own.[106] One of the earliest known quartets was the Lew Male Quartet, which toured throughout New England in the 1880s.[107] The first known commercial recordings by an African-American quartet are twenty cylinders recorded by the Standard Quartette of Chicago in 1894. The group, then part of the "South Before the War" touring company, recorded for the Columbia Phonograph Company but, alas, none of these recordings are known to still exist.[108]

The Hampton University Archives contain a number of cylinders and photographs of the Hampton University Quartet from the middle 1880s and cylinder recordings of the group from 1898.[109] Six sides featuring the Dinwiddie Colored Quartet, recorded in Philadelphia in 1902, are known to have been recorded.[110] Like their predecessors from the Reconstruction South, these groups worked hard, touring relentlessly and sometimes singing several times a day. (A teacher/ escort for the Utica Institute Jubilee Singers from Utica Normal and Industrial Institute in Utica, Mississippi, died of exposure when no one would house the group in a New Hampshire town[111].) And an edition of the *Chicago Defender* on August 12, 1911, contains a reference to the Clafin (Texas) University Jubilee Singers, who *after being on the road the previous nine years* would be performing the following week in Chicago.[112]

Still, the best known of the very earliest black recording groups was the Fisk Jubilee Quartet, led by John Wesley Work, Jr. Work, who would become a noted author and composer, almost single-handedly revived the Fisk singing tradition after twenty years of inactivity with a popular quartet at the turn of the century. "It has been goading to hear the slight remarks made about Jubilee music," he once wrote in the Fisk University journal. "What the best critics have pronounced 'excellent,' and the world has approved and wept over, let *us* not despise."[113] His clear, bright tenor can be heard on the group's early recordings for Victor Records (1910), Edison cylinder records (c. 1913), and on Columbia (beginning in 1914). Work continued Fisk's tradition of singing mostly spirituals, arranged in the classic Western European SATB style.[114]

A number of other early jubilee quartets recorded during World War I and the early years of the 1920s, including the Four Harmony Kings, Harrod's Jubilee Singers, the Double Quartet (from Tuskegee Institute), and the Pace Jubilee Singers.[115]

The Pace Jubilee Singers serve as a significant bridge between the old style of religious quartet singing and the emerging new styles. Founder and director Charles Henry Pace was a musician, composer, publisher, and conductor in the early 1920s, first in Chicago, then in Pittsburgh. Pace, who studied the European masters in his piano lessons, composed more than a hundred songs (variously called "spiritual anthems," "spiritual medleys," and "gospel songs"[116]) in his lifetime, including such well-known numbers as "Bread of Heaven," "Hide My Soul," "Rockin' in My Jesus' Arms," "We Will Shout Hallelujah, Afterwhile,"

"Amen," and "Nobody But You, Lord," along with many arrangements of spirituals and other early gospel songs.

In 1925, Pace organized the Pace Jubilee Singers at Beth Eden Baptist Church in the Morgan Park section of Chicago. The Jubilee Singers were among the first not only to record his songs but to record the early works of Charles Albert Tindley (see next chapter) as well. The group recorded for a number of labels, including Victor, Black Patti, Paramount, and Brunswick. One of the singers in the group, Hattie Parker, even achieved some measure of national recognition. According to musicologist Samuel B. Charters, "The singing of Hattie Parker, soloist with the Pace Jubilee Singers on their 1927 recording of 'Leave It There' . . . shows already a greater expressiveness in her use of rhythm and vocal phrase, and represents the fullest use of the materials of the more Negroid tradition while retaining the quality of the trained choir group."[117] The Jubilee Singers also performed regularly on radio stations WLS and WGN in Chicago.

Pace left Chicago for Pittsburgh in 1936 where he founded the successful Ole Ship of Zion Music Company and Charles H. Pace Music Publishers. It was in Pittsburgh that Pace wrote many of his best-loved numbers. But despite the popularity of the Jubilee Singers and their recordings and Pace's own compositions, he remains overshadowed by his contemporary Thomas Dorsey. This may be due to Pace's departure from the gospel music hotbed of Chicago for the relatively quieter Pittsburgh, or it may be because his charming, often very melodic work is still more rooted in an older choir tradition than Dorsey's loosely notated, more rhythmic early gospel songs. As Mary Ann Lancaster Tyler notes, "the Pace Jubilee Singers' recordings of the late 1920s are barely a subtle hint of what was to be."[118] But at his peak, Pace's publishing companies employed more than 300 agents "committed" to selling his music[119] and he remained an active songwriter into the 1950s. Still, as composer/publisher Kenneth Morris once told Horace Boyer, "Pace . . . never got the same note that Dorsey got, but he certainly was by far the better musician of the two."[120]

Among the Pace Jubilee Singers' contemporaries, the Four Harmony Kings were so popular that they were cast in the Broadway musical *Shuffle Along*, which had a long run in New York in 1922. During their performance, they sang an updated version of a spiritual titled "Ain't It a Shame to Steal on Sunday" that prompted a writer for the *Journal of American Folk-Lore* to track down its origins. According to an account offered by an unnamed member of the Four Harmony Kings, the ensemble first heard the song performed by a "jubilee group" in St. Louis and quickly added it to their "jubilee work" before introducing it in *Shuffle Along*:

> It is the biggest number we use now. We had several offers from publishers who wanted to put the song into a jubilee catalogue; but before this could be done, J. S. B. and W. H., hearing us sing the song, slipped away and had it published. But they added a whole lot to it, which has spoiled it, and is not the way we sing

it at all. Now the Black Swan Record Company have put it out, with us singing it. It is a wonderful song that not only expresses the religious feeling of older days, but fits into this day and time.[121]

Not surprisingly, with this kind of regular "crossover" of styles, the vogue for close harmonies influenced those who sang strictly spiritual songs as well as those who sang in secular venues or just for fun. As a result, the style spread to the African-American houses of worship as well—both the emotion-fueled Pentecostal/Holiness churches and their somewhat more sedate siblings, the Baptist and Methodist congregations. And, of course, the denominations exerted their own influences in return. "It was not long before these quartets began borrowing from the singing style of the Pentecostal/Holiness singers," Boyer adds.[122] While their secular counterparts were finding plentiful work singing in cafes, restaurants, fairs, theaters, private parties, street corners, barrooms, company picnics, and the remaining minstrel shows,[123] other quartets—almost universally called "jubilee quartets" regardless of the number of singers—preferred to stick with religious numbers and sing solely in religious venues or as part of fund-raising events for church or community organizations.[124]

One commonality among all of the new immigrants was a tradition in singing spirituals. The singing of spirituals did not die with the new century. In an issue of the *Journal of American Folk-Lore* from 1922, A. E. Perkins presents an extraordinary array of spirituals, many not available in previous collections. Though Perkins only provides the lyrics, some of these latter-day spirituals have a haunting beauty that allows the reader to imagine the music:

> "In Some Lonesome Graveyard"
>
> *This time another year*
> *I may be gone in some lonesome graveyard*
> *O Lord! How long?*
>
> "King Jesus Come Er Ridin' 'Long"
>
> *Dark clouds is er risin'*
> *Thunder-balls er burstin'*
> *King Jesus come er ridin' 'long*
> *Wid er rainbow 'cross his shoulders*[125]

Unfortunately, Perkins, who was from New Orleans, does not state when or where (other than obliquely in the title of the article, "Negro Spirituals from the Far South"—which presumably means he heard them in Louisiana) he collected the forty-eight spirituals in his article, but other writers from the era continued to stumble on rural churches were the spirituals were a continuing tradition. And as the Great Migration continued, rural African Americans carried those traditions with them. When the new religious quartets were being formed, spirituals provided logical starting points for material.

According to Doug Seroff, African-American quartets were quickly organized in the mostly Baptist churches, schools, and places of employment—whatever was available to them, since much of the country still operated under overt or tacit Jim Crow laws. "Denied access to other forms of popular entertainment and diversion, quartet singing became a general pastime for Jefferson County's black youth."[126]

In the new close-knit African-American communities, jubilee quartet singing was "respectable"—unlike minstrel, jazz, blues, or ragtime—because it was identified with the "positive aspects of culture," Kip Lornell writes, providing an "important, acceptable social and musical outlet."[127] Boyer adds, "Quartet singers found another opportunity to express their belief in God and their Christianity in public. This was inspired by a desire—not to become famous but—to be another 'witness' for the Lord."[128]

In a day when travel for African Americans was difficult and the few national radio networks rarely played the new religious music, isolated pockets of singers soon created their own performance styles within the religious quartet tradition. This is what happened in two of the most popular destinations during the Great Migration, Jefferson County, Alabama (beginning in 1871, the site of the South's lone significant coal-and-iron industrial complex) and the Virginia Tidewater region (shipbuilding). Consequently, the two most important early schools of African-American religious quartet singing were the "folk style" of Jefferson County, Alabama (including the cities of Bessemer, Birmingham, and Fairfield) and the "jubilee style," best typified by quartets from the Tidewater area of Virginia and North Carolina.[129] These different styles of gospel singing quickly dominated each region. (Just how they may have been nurtured or influenced by the radically different management techniques of the principal industries of the two regions is a subject for further study—how much a prevailing work environment impacts religious music *anywhere,* not just in the American South.) Cedric Dent dubs these two forms of quartet singing "folk" and "jubilee":

> Characteristics of the folk style include part-singing that is less developed than in the jubilee style, often exhibiting chord structures that lack thirds, roots or both. Generally, the bass voice moves rhythmically with the other voice parts but is often nonfunctional. Authentic cadences are often incomplete or avoided. Added dissonance is generally limited to seventh chords, and there is generous use of blue notes, which creates melodic variety in repeated sections of music within individual voice parts. Also, a two-beat per measure rhythmic feel is commonplace in folk-style quartet singing.[130]

One example of this style of quartet singing is Mitchell's Christian Singers, originally from Kinston, North Carolina, in the late 1920s. Founded by four unschooled day laborers, Mitchell's Christian Singers tenaciously held to the oldest, "most primitive" folk style of jubilee quartet singing. Among their many fans was talent scout John Hammond, who championed their "pure" harmonies at the legendary "From Spirituals to Swing" concerts at Carnegie Hall in 1938 and 1939.[131] When the young men, still slightly in shock from their first visit to a big city, were led into a New York recording studio, they recorded for eighteen and a half hours, then immediately returned to Kinston. Their recordings, which appeared on the Banner, Top Rank, Vocalion, Brunswick, OKeh, and Columbia labels, included mostly spirituals. Mitchell's Christian Singers never toured, although they occasionally performed in churches in nearby North Carolina towns.[132]

In his liner notes for the *From Spirituals to Swing* records, Charles Edward Smith notes that "My Poor Mother Died A' Shouting" features the "charged simplicity of great gospel music."[133] Jazz historian Marshall Sterns calls them a "fascinating transitional stage" in the history of harmony:

> Whether or not the legend that they never heard a piano is true, the group sings . . . as if they had just discovered the three simplest chords in our music. Here is a European harmony—the harmony of the hymn—with the dew still on it. The transitions to the final chord with what Fanny Kemble would have described as their "extraordinarily wild and unaccountable" slurs, dips, slides and loops, bring exclamations of delight from modern academic musicians who have tried—and failed—to notate them.[134]

But it is Hammond—who spent his life chasing authentic music of the heart, much to the dismay of his wealthy parents—who has the final word on Mitchell's Christian Singers:

> They were so good, so pure, so non-commercial. There was no hype, no show business tricks, like side-slapping. When Goddard and I heard them in Willie Brown's house in Kinston, Goddard started to cry. I think I did, too. At the Carnegie Hall concert, my mother and father attended and they suddenly realized what I have been working at all these years. They appreciated it for the first time.[135]

By contrast, the more polished jubilee style is more musically "correct," with fewer "blue notes," and more of an emphasis on group vocal blend. Additionally, jubilee songs often have a more pronounced rhythmic feel than the folk-style counterparts.[136] According to Cedric Dent, it was the Silver Leaf Quartette of Norfolk that first introduced a significant variation of the spiritual call-and-response technique to African-American quartet singing in 1928 with "Sleep On, Mother." "This technique," he writes, "set a lead vocalist (usually the second tenor) apart from the remaining voices, which supplied a repeating rhythmic pattern or riff as accompaniment."[137] This development was instrumental for the Silver Leaf Quartette to then introduce the singing of nonsense syllables behind the lead singers as a rhythmic device—the so-called "clanka-lanka" technique.[138]

Other groups would quickly emulate the sound, including the Famous Blue Jay Singers' "Clanka-a-lanka" from 1932, but few could match the extraordinary falsetto of the Leaf's William Thatch.

While there was much content overlap in the early days of quartet singing, different groups eventually began to specialize in either religious or secular venues. Dent identifies five characteristics that help distinguish black religious quartet singing from barbershop, male chorus, doo-wop, jubilee-style chorus, and vocal jazz:

1. A common source for song selection—primarily spirituals and gospel songs
2. Vocal arrangements which stand rhythmically and harmonically independent of the instrumental accompaniment
3. A vocal group of four to six singers
4. Vocal arrangements based harmonically on prior performances (when using songs previously performed by other groups)
5. Individual voice parts that are free to perform melodic variations in repeated sections of a song.[139]

"All jubilee quartets specialized in singing spirituals in harmonized verse-chorus arrangements, although many groups also sang secular love, novelty or patriotic songs," writes Kerill Rubman. "Songs with verses recounting Bible stories in couplets were special quartet favorites."[140] The majority of the narrative or humorous songs were performed up-tempo, using off-beat phrasing, syncopation, and a heavy accent on rhythm, with the emphasis on the second and fourth beats of most measures. And, as Rubman notes, some of the groups continued to employ "'blue notes,' slides, melismas," and other traditional Afro-American vocal traits to their arrangements, continuing traditions begun in black sacred music hundreds of years earlier.[141] The focus in nearly all of these quartets was tight, beautifully blended harmonies, usually two tenors, a baritone, and a bass, with minimal or no musical accompaniment. The jubilee quartets—at least judging from early recordings—generally combined "the harmonized ensemble singing of barbershop quartets and jubilee choirs" with the "leader-chorus forms of black folk spirituals and work songs."[142]

"Jubilee quartets depended on a strong bass singer to give fullness to chords," writes Rubman. "In many arrangements basses sang distinctive parts that filled in group rests and moved against the rhythms and tonal direction of the other parts. Some quartets used falsetto singers on lead or group parts. Lead singing was usually smooth, sweet, and undifferentiated in vocal tone from the group's sound, although it would become more expressive and creative in later groups."[143]

There are, of course, other methods of categorizing the styles of jubilee music, including one proposed by William H. Tallmadge that separates the different quartets into "hot" and "cool" and "trained" and "folk-style."[144]

Certain southern cities became noted for their jubilee groups, including Jacksonville, Florida; Richmond, Virginia; and Memphis, Tennessee. Despite the almost exclusively religious focus of most of these groups, some began to attract regional and even national followings. After World War I, the focus shifted to the larger northern cities, especially Detroit, Chicago, New York, and Cleveland, but the quartet tradition never died in Norfolk, Birmingham, and Memphis. As Thurmon Ruth of the Selah Jubilee Singers once told Kip Lornell, "Norfolk, Virginia, that used to be a quartet town! I used to want to go to Norfolk because they told me that you could just be in bed at night and put your head out the window and guys would be on the corner blending, harmonizing."[145]

Norfolk and the entire Tidewater region (generally including Charles City, Middlesex, Mathews, King and Queen, and King William counties) was a magnet for African Americans with shipyards, munitions dumps, army bases, three historically black colleges (Virginia State, Hampton Institute, and Virginia Union), and a long tradition of quartet singing. Alton Griffin, once a member of the Golden Crown Quartet and later a widely respected Baptist preacher, fondly recalled his days in Norfolk: "That Tidewater crowd was something else. They came from the place where singers were really born. It was a place where singing went over big and it was the first thing folk learned when they got so they could walk good."[146]

One of the earliest and most popular groups to emerge from this fertile setting was the Norfolk Jazz Quartet/Norfolk Jubilee Quartette—two names for the same group of singers, who formed a group during World War I as a latter-day vaudeville/minstrel organization. (The group also recorded under various other names between 1921 and 1940.) The Norfolks began recording for OKeh in 1921, but switched to Paramount two years later where their recording "Father Prepare Me"/"My Lord's Gonna Move This Wicked Race" stayed in the catalog until Paramount went out of business in 1932. Other hits included "Who Built the Ark," "I Hope I May Join the Band," and beloved spirituals such as "Roll Jordan Roll," "Swing Low, Sweet Chariot," and "Every Time I Feel the Spirit." The dichotomy of the group was such that one week-long recording session in New York in the 1930s yielded both jubilee songs like "Believe in Jesus" and "King Jesus Stand by Me" and secular songs like "Shim Sham Shimmie at the Cricket's Ball" and "Beedle De Beedle De Bop Bop (Adi Aedi Idio)."[147]

Also from Norfolk, the Silver Leaf Quartette was so popular in the late 1920s that they toured New York City on a regular basis and performed on New York radio stations. At one point, over the summer of 1929, the Silver Leaf Quartette sang for twenty-one straight nights at the Metropolitan Baptist Church and began a successful relationship with OKeh Records.[148]

Both the Norfolk Jubilee Quartette and the Silver Leaf Quartet began performing live on Norfolk radio about 1928, which quickly increased their popularity in the Tidewater region. When most recording labels went bankrupt during the Great Depression, Lornell notes, local radio survived, providing an outlet for dozens, perhaps hundreds, of early jubilee groups. "Thus black gospel quartet singing began its rapid transformation from a religious, regional genre to a form of popular entertainment that was being heard across the United States."[149]

The African-American populations of Birmingham, Fairfield, and Bessemer increased more than fourfold between 1890 and 1920. "Sprawling settlements of industrial workers and their families broadened out from the coal and ore mines and the steel mills," Doug Seroff writes. "Community life within the mining camps, company quarters and other segregated black settlements around Bessemer were unusually rich in fellowship."[150]

Jefferson County's vibrant combination of strong union activities and quartet-singing tradition has been the subject of numerous studies, including Brenda McCallum's "Songs of Work and Songs of Worship: Sanctifying Black Unionism in the Southern City of Steel." Because the unique set of circumstances in the Birmingham district (the largest employer, Tennessee Coal, Iron and Railroad, once operated twenty-two separate company towns), TCIR regulated and dominated every facet of life for employees, including religion, recreation, and entertainment. This generally meant fewer opportunities and more restrictions for African Americans.[151] Still, despite widespread prejudice and segregation, TCIR's black workers formed "a special camaraderie" that grew out of "camaraderie on the job, solidarity in the union and fellowship in the church." Hemmed in on every side, their "expressive culture" was channeled through music.[152] "The formative period of the jubilee gospel quartet tradition in Birmingham," McCallum writes, "coincided with the period of greatest industrialization and unionism and the largest migration of rural blacks to the District."[153] In time, every major African-American community in Jefferson County seemed to have one or more quartets associated with it, including particular churches, mine sites, industrial plants, company towns, and union halls.[154] And all were striving to out-do one another. Since TCIR often used the groups for its (segregated) social activities, such as company-sponsored picnics and baseball games, the company even provided musical training at company-sponsored music schools.[155]

Group singing so permeated the culture in the Birmingham District that old-time singers recalled groups spontaneously formed even in bathhouses. McCallum located some of the original singers, including Alfred Rutledge, Jr., once of the Delta-Aires, who said that harmony singing helped the difficult, back-breaking labor pass: "Somebody would be always wanting to hit a song. You know, we'd be sitting around and when you love singing—and me, I was just a boy considered to them—and they would go to singing . . . I'd find me a tune, too, and we'd just go to singing."[156]

Eventually, an egalitarian Birmingham sound emerged in the gospel quartet singing, one marked by "broad, extended chords of deep four-part harmony," McCallum writes. "Rather than spotlighting the individualistic lead singer . . . emphasis was placed on the evenness and equality of all voices collectively striving for a cohesive, blended sound."[157] Or, as one fifty-year veteran of Jefferson

County gospel quartets put it, in the face of a stressful, unfair world, "Peace and harmonizing kind of holds you together. If you're harmonizing, why, it sounds like one."[158]

Another city where religious quartets proliferated was New York. As the home of one of the oldest and largest African-American urban communities, it has a long history of public performances by black singing groups, including the breakthrough performances by the Fisk Jubilee Singers in the 1870s. One well-documented performance was the "Black America" extravaganza of 1894, an outdoor concert that featured sixty-three groups, including the Old South Quartette and the Four Harmony Kings.[159] One of the many college-based quartets to perform in New York City, the Utica Institute Jubilee Singers were so well received that they permanently relocated to the city where they were featured performers on NBC radio stations WJZ and WEAF.[160] The radio columnist for the *New York Telegram* wrote this curious backhanded, if mostly positive, review of one of their shows on November 21, 1927: "Here were Negro spirituals given in the way in which they were intended to be, with all the sonorous beauty of phrasing, all the depth of feeling and all the barbaric pagan beauty that the Negro brings to white men's religion."[161] The Uticas, founded in 1910, would eventually record for the Vitaphone, U.F.A., Germany, and Victor labels, and tour Europe, the Middle East, Russia, Australia, China, and Japan in the late 1920s and early 1930s. The group, noted for their barbershop-style close harmonies and performances of spirituals, once performed with Marian Foster Welch, daughter of legendary American songwriter Stephen Foster, who traveled from Kentucky to sing with the Uticas.[162]

Also popular in the 1920s were two more college-trained groups that specialized in barbershop harmonies and semiclassical arrangements of spirituals: the Original Dixie Jubilee Singers (later known as the famed Eva Jessye Choir) and the Southernaires.[163] The Southernaires were so popular in New York that even their regular rehearsals at Williams Institutional Colored Methodist Episcopal Church (CME) in Harlem were well attended. By 1933, they were broadcast regularly over NBC's Blue network under the title of "The Little Weather-Beaten Whitewashed Church," a series that lasted more than ten years.[164]

Kip Lornell's definitive *Happy in the Service of the Lord: Afro-American Gospel Quartets in Memphis* details still another city that provided a "tenacious, influential hearth" for gospel quartets. Lornell's research has uncovered a host of quartets from pre-Depression days, including the I.C. (Illinois Central Railroad) Glee Club, an a cappella group that recorded in the 1920s. Other popular quartets included the I.C. Hummingbirds, the Harmony Four, the Old Red Rose Quartet, the L. and N. (Louisville and Nashville Railroad) Quartet, the Hollywood Specials, the Gospel Writers, the Mount Olive Wonder, and the best-known group to come from Memphis, the Spirit of Memphis Quartette.[165]

The railroads, particularly the Illinois Central, believed that sponsoring obviously Christian groups, like the quartets, could help their sagging economic fortunes in the late 1920s and 1930s and had the groups sing at public parties, dances, picnics, and sporting events. Other quartets, such as the I.C. Humming-birds, rode in special cars, and traveled up and down the I.C.'s lines from Chi-cago to New Orleans, entertaining passengers.[166]

The Spirit of Memphis (the group dropped the "Quartette" part of its name in the late 1940s) was the most commercially successful of the city's many jubilee groups. Founded in 1926 or 1927 as the T.M. and S. Quartet, the group changed its name to honor Charles Lindbergh's Atlantic crossing in 1927.[167] The Spirit of Memphis rehearsed faithfully and toured relentlessly throughout the Midwest, mostly on the weekend since the members kept their full-time jobs during the week. The group finally recorded in the late 1940s and had a hit with its first release, "Happy in the Service of the Lord," featuring sizzling leads by Wilbur "Little Axe" Brodnax, Silas Steele, and Jethroe Bledsoe.[168]

Other popular American jubilee groups in the late 1920s and early 1930s included the Bright Moon Quartet, the Heavenly Gospel Singers, Birmingham Jubilee Singers, the Charioteers, the Mobile Four, and the Richmond Harmoniz-ing Four. Surviving recordings by the Southern Negro Quartet (Columbia, early 1920s) and the Silver Leaf Quartet reveal a startling mixture of styles, including eerie early echoes of rhythm and blues.[169]

But for the quartets, the coming of the Mills Brothers into the popular mar-ketplace changed everything. In 1931, the four brothers from Piqua, Ohio, were among the first to record songs incorporating jazz instruments and orchestra-tions. They were heavily influenced by both Duke Ellington and Louis Armstrong and often featured solos with their voices imitating wind instruments and trum-pets set to their smooth harmonies. The Mills Brothers, and to a lesser degree the Ink Spots, attracted both black and white audiences.[170] Among the 2,500 songs recorded by the Mills Brothers are a number of hits from their early days: "Tiger Rag," "Paper Doll," "You Always Hurt the One You Love," and "Glow Worm." Singers from Bing Crosby to Dean Martin acknowledged their debt to Harry Mills through the years.[171]

One lasting innovation the Mills Brothers brought into both popular and gospel music was the introduction of a bass singer singing in a heavily rhythmic "pump bass," a technique derived from Chicago-style Dixieland music where the bass voice pulses like a washtub or string bass on the strong beats of the measure. (This would eventually become a mandatory element of all gospel groups until the widespread acceptance of the electric Fender bass guitar more than thirty years later.)[172]

No one understood—or replicated—the Mills Brothers' innovations better than the Golden Gate Jubilee Quartet (they would drop the "Jubilee" from their name in 1940). The group was founded in Eddie Griffin's barbershop, and the four friends from Norfolk's Booker T. Washington High School originally sounded like most of the barbershop-tinged jubilee groups, "emphasizing close harmony with precise attacks and releases," but soon they began singing spirituals with a more pronounced beat, almost a sanctified feel.[173] "The Gates" offered a unique blend of "sophisticated" harmonies, heavily laced with jazz, and only the Mills Brothers were better at sounding like saxophones.[174] The Gates were more than pale imitations, however; they "aren't simply playing jazz, they're also moaning," notes Anthony Heilbut, and "the momentum bespeaks 'spirit-feel' more than technique."[175]

Thus began in the mid-1930s a long and rewarding career, one that took the Gates both to churches and national mainstream audiences. Beginning in 1935, the Gates began broadcasting on Charlotte's powerful WBT, a 50,000-watt station that reached much of the East Coast. Audiences black and white with no particular religious affiliation tuned in as much for the Gates' finger-popping rhythms as for their lush harmonies. "We were singing in every church that let a quartet sing in it," bass singer Orlandus Wilson once said. "The main churches that got to me were the Holiness churches, because they sang with a beat. And whenever I got around to training the group, I'd give our things a beat."[176]

What the Gates and their counterparts were creating featured harmonies honed from hours of rehearsal—emotional, accessible spirituals and songs in the time-honored spiritual format (call and response; simple, direct storytelling and lyrics; rhythmic emphasis; free improvisation; and African vocal survivals), fueled by a "pumping bass," the emotionalism of Holiness/Pentecostal church services, and a vibrant showmanship based on the exacting professionalism of the new jazz artists of the day.

In short, they were assembling something new. And they needed new songs to sing.

Chapter Eight

The Fathers of Gospel: William H. Sherwood, Charles A. Tindley, and Thomas A. Dorsey

I been drug about and put through the shackles, till I done forgot some my children's names. My husband died and left me with nine children, and none of 'em could pull the others out of the fire iffen they fell in. I had mo'n that, but some come here dead and some didn't. Dey ain't a graveyard in this here settlement where I ain't got children buried, and I got children dead in Birmingham and Bessemer.

I mos' blind now and I can't hear good and I ain't never read no verse in no Bible in my life 'cause I can't read. I sets 'cross the road here from the church and can't go 'cause I'm cripple and blin'—but I hear 'em singin'.

—Vera Hall, recorded outside Livingston, Alabama,
by John A. and Alan Lomax, 1937[1]

The gospel song expresses theology. Not the theology of the academy or the university, not formalistic theology or the theology of the seminary, but a *theology of experience*—the theology of a God who sends the sunshine and the rain, the theology of a God who is very much alive and active and who has not forsaken those who are poor and oppressed and unemployed. It is a *theology of imagination*—it grew out of the fire shut up in the bones, of words painted on the canvas of the mind. Fear is turned to hope in the sanctuaries and storefronts, and bursts forth in songs of celebration. It is *a theology of grace* that allows the faithful to see the sunshine of His face—even through their tears. Even the words of an ex-slave trader became a song of liberation and an expression of God's amazing grace. It is a *theology of survival* that allows a people to celebrate the ability to continue the journey in spite of the insidious tentacles of racism and oppression and to sing, "It's another day's journey, and I'm glad about it!"

—William B. McClain's preface to *Songs of Zion*[2]

I always had rhythm in my bones. I like the solid beat. I like the long, moaning, groaning tone. I like the rock. You know how they rock and shout in the church. I like it. It's a thing people look for now. Don't let your singing group die, don't let the movement go out of the music. Black music calls for movement! It calls for feeling. Don't let it get away.

—Thomas Dorsey, 1973[3]

William H. Sherwood

William Henry Sherwood is a shadowy but influential figure in the history of African-American religious music. Apparently rarely leaving his Petersburg, Virginia, home, he served as superintendent of Sherwood's Orphan School, an orphanage for black children. He was both an evangelist and a composer and led local choirs and bands. Most important, Sherwood published the *Soothing Songs Hymnal* in 1891.[4] It was followed, in 1893, by another hymnal, *Harp of Zion*. *Harp of Zion* features a collection of gospel songs and spirituals by a variety of authors, including Sherwood. It is important, as Horace Boyer writes, because Sherwood was "the first African American to publish songs that were decidedly cast in the Negro spiritual, pre-gospel mode. The melodies, harmonies, and, to an extent, the rhythm, all forecast music that in less than thirty years would be called gospel."[5]

The National Baptist Convention Publishing Board (NBCPB) heard about Sherwood's planned hymnal and contracted to release it later that same year, with some changes, as *Baptist Young People's Union National Harp of Zion*.[6]

Sherwood's songs are simple and repetitive, easy to sing and catchy. His compositions "Happy Hosts of Zion," "Mountain Top Dwelling," and "Take It to the Lord" are "uplifting, confident, and encouraging" and focus on the daily lives of churchgoers. They stand in marked contrast to the intense, otherworldly demeanor of many spirituals.[7] The quick adoption of Sherwood's "lively arrangements" by the NBCPB indicates that even the more traditional African-American Baptist churches were in the early stages of recognizing the power of "the new wave of what were now being termed 'gospel songs.'"[8]

Charles Albert Tindley

Better known today is the Reverend Charles Albert Tindley, born circa 1851 on the Eastern Shore in Maryland. Tindley was the son of slaves and mostly self-educated, and his rural upbringing meant he had access to both spirituals and camp-meeting songs. He became a minister and pastored several enormously successful congregations, culminating with a long stint at Bainbridge Street Methodist Episcopal in Philadelphia (later renamed Tindley Temple), which eventually grew to ten thousand members and became renowned for its large and successful social services to Philadelphia's poor and hurting, especially during the Great Depression.[9] But Tindley, who died in 1933, was even more influential as a songwriter.

Despite the inroads made by the Holiness/Pentecostal churches, more African Americans were still Baptists than any other denomination, with sixty-one percent of the 5.2 million black church members in the mid-1920s calling themselves Baptist,[10] followed by the Methodists in distant second. Until Sherwood and Tindley, black Baptist and Methodist churches generally sang modified spirituals and camp-meeting songs, along with "hymn-like compositions," similar to those sung in mainstream white churches. According to Boyer, these songs almost always featured a salvation-based message, a standard verse/chorus format (eight bars each), rhythms dominated by quarter and dotted eighth notes, and an antiphonal chorus.[11] But the songs of C. A. Tindley—and only about fifty are known to exist—differ significantly from the hymns of popular white composers such as William B. Bradbury, Fanny J. Crosby, and William Howard Doane. Tindley's lyrics focused instead on specific concerns of African-American Christians, including "worldly sorrows, blessings, and woes, as well as the joys of the afterlife." Furthermore, most of his songs were placed in the pentatonic scale and allowed ample room for rhythmic, melodic, and even lyric improvisations.[12]

In addition to occasionally singing his songs with his large (and loyal) congregation, Tindley oversaw the formation of the seven-member Tindley Gospel Singers (also called the Tindley Seven) in 1922—an exceptional group that took his songs throughout the country.[13] The Tindley Gospel Singers were influential in other ways. Boyer says they were among the first groups to come from the predominant Baptist tradition who were attracted to the new, more emotional music emanating from the Sanctified tradition, "but found no way to participate, given their sense of moderate vocal and physical indulgence." The group was also among the first from this tradition to be accompanied by a piano (although, as Boyer notes, the piano accompaniment was "much more like hymn playing than gospel singing"), and they sang some of the earliest gospel songs, including those of their founder.[14]

Tindley, who was apparently not a trained musician, composed the songs in his head and several different musicians transcribed them for him through the course of his career. Beginning in 1901, he began publishing a remarkable series of enduring songs, including "What Are They Doing in Heaven?" (1901), "I'll Overcome Someday" (1901), "When the Storms of Life Are Raging, Stand by Me" (1905), "We'll Understand It Better By and By" (1905), "Nothing Between" (1905), "The Storm Is Passing Over" (1905), "Some Day/Beams of Heaven" (1905), "Here Am I, Send Me" (1911), "Take Your Burden to the Lord, Leave It There" (1918), and others.[15] Among the artists who would record his songs include such names as Blind Willie Johnson, Sister Rosetta Tharpe, the Pace Jubilee Singers, the Caravans, Roberta Martin, Donald Vail and the Choraleers, the Fairfield Four, Sweet Honey in the Rock, and Marion Williams.

Tindley had a rare gift for both creating Bible-based images and imminently singable choruses:

> "Stand by Me" (Charles Albert Tindley, originally copyrighted 1905)
>
> *When the storms of life are raging, Stand by me*
> *When the storms of life are raging, Stand by me*
> *When the world is tossing me, Like a ship upon the sea*
> *Thou who rulest wind and sea, Stand by me*[16]
>
> "We'll Understand It Better By and By" (Charles Albert Tindley, originally copyrighted 1905)
>
> *We are tossed and driven on the restless sea of time*
> *Somber skies and howling tempests oft succeed bright sunshine*
> *In the land of perfect day, When the mists have rolled away*
> *We will understand it better by and by*
>
> *CHORUS*
> *By and by, when the morning comes*
> *When the saints of God are gathered home*
> *We'll tell the story how we've overcome*
> *For we'll understand it better by and by (by and by)*[17]

Few of his songs, however, have had the lasting impact of "I'll Overcome Someday" ("I'll overcome someday, I'll overcome someday, If in my heart I do not yield, I'll overcome someday"), which became the adopted anthem of the civil rights movement of the 1960s as "We Shall Overcome." Of more than passing interest to musicologists and musicians alike is blues artist Blind Joe Taggart's sizzling rendition of "The Storm Is Passing Over" from 1927, which Samuel Floyd says is more "demonstrative" of Tindley's gifts than simply reading the music and words on the printed page.[18] Even more than Sherwood, Tindley's songs were crafted to be "hospitable to African American performance practices"[19] and singers almost immediately exploited the "spaces" in them to exercise their gifts for improvisation. Even the more conservative older gospel groups, such as the Pace Jubilee Singers, found his songs too singable to ignore—their version of Tindley's "Stand by Me" was a hit in 1930.[20]

"The hymns written by Tindley carried a camp-meeting intensity and fervor that would inspire the later development and crystallization of the black gospel style," Floyd adds.[21] "Tindley had smoothed the path for the development of African-American gospel music and the later crystallization of its style. He had created space in his songs to accommodate the call and response figures and improvisations that, together with flatted thirds and sevenths and other core-culture performance practices, would come to make the style."[22] And as Anthony Heilbut notes, "Neither spirituals nor hymns, Tindley's songs comprised a whole new genre. Amidst the most banal sentiments, Tindley incorporated folk images, proverbs, and Biblical allusions familiar to black churchgoers for over a hundred years."[23]

The first African American to publish an original song collection in 1901, Tindley remains a pivotal figure in the history of black church music. In a later hymnal, the editors write that Tindley "bequeathed to all Methodism and Christianity a legacy that will live on through his hymns."[24]

Lucie Campbell

One of Tindley's contemporaries was a woman whose life would have been remarkable at any point in American history, but which was more amazing for having been lived in a day when Ku Klux Klan members openly celebrated segregation in the streets of a thousand towns and the lot of African-American women was little improved in a century. Lucie (sometimes spelled Lucy) Campbell was the seventh and youngest child of a poor Mississippi family. After her father, a railroad man, was killed en route to be present for Lucie's birth, her mother moved the family to Memphis. When the family scraped together enough money for her older sister Lora to take piano lessons, Lucie hid nearby and listened, then practiced what she'd heard in secret. In time, she became an accomplished pianist and a famed educator—teaching history and English for forty-three years at Booker T. Washington High School in Memphis.[25]

But Campbell's influence was even more significant in the National Baptist Convention U.S.A., Inc. (NBC), the largest black organization in the world at the time. By 1916, she'd been named as music director of the NBC's Sunday School and Baptist Young People's Union Congress. As director, she organized thousand-voice choirs to sing at the annual conventions, wrote songs and elaborate musicales and pageants. Her best-loved songs from this era include "Something Within," "He Understands, He'll Say, 'Well Done,'" "Heavenly Sunshine," and "The King's Highway," all well-crafted, traditional hymns. As a member of the Music Committee for the NBC, she was on the selection committee for the denomination's new series of hymnals and songbooks, including *Golden Gems, Inspirational Melodies, Spirituals Triumphant* and *Gospel Pearls (GP)*—all of which, incidentally, included her compositions.[26]

Campbell's impact on the NBC conventions was significant from the beginning. At the conventions, "she used her music to set a tone and atmosphere of exuberant yet controlled joy and spiritual fervor."[27] Unlike some of her contemporaries, she actively campaigned to include new music and new artists in the giant annual conventions, even though her classically trained tastes originally leaned toward the conservative (one of her best-known compositions is the religious operetta *Ethiopia at the Bar of Justice*). "She was beautiful," Sallie Martin would write later, "she had 'grace' enough to bring Black music out of the hymn writing tradition."[28]

Gospel Pearls included the older, more familiar hymns of Isaac Watts, Charles Wesley, and Fanny J. Crosby, the revival songs of Ira D. Sankey and Homer A. Rodeheaver, and a section of songs and arrangements of spirituals by Campbell, Tindley, John W. Work, and others.[29] It's hard to overstate the impact of *GP*—as it is commonly called in the denomination—both on Baptists and African-American Christians as a whole. In addition to being the first publication by a black congregation to include the word *gospel* in the title, it was the first to include examples of the kinds of songs that would someday be called by that name, "a new and different style of singing that sought to capture the ecstasy of the Holiness church singers but without the excesses."[30] While the bulk of the songs were standard Protestant hymns of the previous 200 years, the twenty "gospel" songs meant that members of the world's largest black denomination "no longer had to attend Pentecostal, Holiness or sanctified churches to hear this music."[31]

In fact, the second edition of *GP,* released in late 1921, was so popular that the NBC's Publishing Board decided to use the original plates for all subsequent editions through the 1990s![32] *Gospel Pearls* debuted at the NBC's forty-first annual convention in Chicago in September 1921.

Another influential figure in Baptist circles, and one of Campbell's coeditors of *Gospel Pearls* in 1921, was the popular evangelist "Professor" W. M. Nix from Birmingham, Alabama. Nix was invited to preach the Sunday sermon at the convention and, according to Michael W. Harris, was compelled to "sell" the new hymnal to "demonstrate its effectiveness" in soul-winning. Nix gave his personal testimony and sang E. O. Excell's song, "I Do, Don't You?" The otherwise dry minutes of the meeting say that his performance "thrilled" the convention.[33] Nix apparently improvised sections of both his message and, during the performance, the song itself. In fact, "melodic embellishment seems to have assumed a crucial significance for achieving expression."[34]

Thomas Andrew Dorsey

Sitting in the congregation that day was a whippet-thin recent convert, a former blues/jazz performer named Thomas Andrew Dorsey. Dorsey was mesmerized. While "embellishments" were certainly not unknown in African-American Baptist circles, Dorsey told Harris in an interview in 1977 that "These turns and trills, he [Nix] and a few others brought into church music. Hymns singers, they couldn't put this stuff in it. What he did, I wouldn't call blues, but it had a touch of the blue note there. Now that's the turn and the feeling that really made the gospel singers."[35]

Born in rural Georgia in July 1899, Dorsey was heir to two rich sacred music traditions, the "moaning" of early spirituals and improvised sorrow songs, and shape-note singing. At Mount Prospect Baptist Church in tiny Villa Rica, the

Pianist/songwriter Thomas A. Dorsey is considered the "Father of Gospel Music."
Here he accompanies Mahalia Jackson on one of his own compositions. (photo: Hogan
Jazz Archive, Howard-Tilton Memorial Library, Tulane University)

"moaning" (an intensely personal, almost inarticulate interpretation of existing songs) sounds much like a musical version of glossolalia (speaking in tongues)—music that is better felt than said or sung. Of moaning, Dorsey once said, "people sang from their very hearts."[36]

At the other end of the spectrum, the shape-note, or sacred harp, musical tradition is nearly as old as the United States itself, beginning in New England in the 1700s as an effort to teach both music and text to a mostly illiterate population. The shape of the individual notes—triangle, oval, square, and diamond—indicated to the singers both the tune and the pitch. Dorsey loved the structure that came with the keening sounds of shape-note singing: "every man and every woman knew their place. It was beautiful singing. You wouldn't hear any better singing now than those folks did in those days."[37]

Dorsey's religious upbringing was equally divided. In later interviews, he talked of his mother, Etta Plant Dorsey, and her intense devotion and how it was manifest from feeding the hungry to faithfully conducting the family Bible studies. His father, Thomas Madison Dorsey, was the child of former slaves and one of the first to attend Atlanta Baptist (later Morehead) College. He was a flamboyant evangelist and often preached at area churches but apparently neither wanted nor held a full-time pastorate.[38] As part of his ministry, he purchased a portable organ, which his wife quickly mastered. Young Thomas was "fascinated" with the instrument and later said that his musical development "sprang" from playing it.[39]

The rest of his musical training was just as wide ranging. When the family's farm failed, they were forced to move from quiet Villa Rica to Atlanta. Dorsey dropped out of school at age eleven. A natural musician, he scraped up enough money to study piano from a piano teacher and soon informally apprenticed himself to the pianist at the local theater, where he began a lifelong fascination with "barrelhouse piano" styles. Another influence was Dorsey's uncle Phil, a popular blues guitarist (and bootlegger). Eventually, Dorsey drifted to playing piano in brothels and for rent parties. By the onset of World War I, he was considered the top "party pianist" in Atlanta.[40] Three great tragedies, however, would ultimately shape Dorsey's future in music.

In 1916, Dorsey joined the Great Migration and moved to Chicago in hopes of larger paychecks and greater prestige. He resumed playing bars and small nightclubs but eventually buckled under the strain and returned to Atlanta in 1920 to recover from a bout of depression and what may have been a nervous breakdown. He returned to Chicago in 1921, eager to rejoin the burgeoning blues and jazz (still called "jass") scenes on the South Side and only reluctantly attended the NBC convention that September at the urging of another uncle, a Chicago druggist and committed believer.[41] Like the rest of the convention, he was elated by Professor Nix's singing: "My inner being was thrilled. My soul was a deluge of divine rapture, my emotions were aroused; my heart was inspired to become a great singer and worker in the Kingdom of the Lord—and impress people just as this great singer did that Sunday morning."[42]

It was a watershed moment in the history of not just African-American sacred music but American popular music in general. "Though the history of African-American music, the genres of the tradition have been created and developed through the synthesizing of their various elements by makers of black music," Samuel Floyd observes in *The Power of Black Music*. "It was in Chicago that one of the most notable of these syntheses occurred: Thomas A. Dorsey's melding of blues elements with those of the religious hymn to make the gospel blues, spawning both what came to be known as the 'Dorsey Song' and the choral gospel-blues style."[43] Michael W. Harris, Dorsey's primary biographer, believes that Nix's performance that morning, in its own way, may have been as significant to black Baptists—and black Americans in general—as the successful introduction of southern blues artist Mamie Smith was at the time to mainstream popular music. Nix's inspiration of Dorsey introduced and influenced the eventual acceptance of an "indigenous style of black music" into the powerful, musically conservative northern urban churches—enabling African-American Baptists to finally "rejoin that part of themselves they had sacrificed for another religion."[44]

Financial pressures soon forced Dorsey to resume playing in the clubs, but not before he'd written his first gospel song, "If I Don't Get There," for the second edition of *Gospel Pearls*, published at the tail end of 1921. It's a tribute to the editorial board of *Gospel Pearls* that not only would they include a very new song in a different mold than the bulk of the material in *GP*, they would include a song by someone so recently involved in secular music. It is another telling example of the "compassion and tolerance of individual musical style" that marked the otherwise officious, sometimes imperious Lucie Campbell.[45] Boyer notes that "If I Don't Get There" is a fine prototype of not just the music Dorsey would write in the years to come but the overall shape of what would be called *gospel music* itself, featuring "the sonorous language of the common folk set to a melody of only six [scale] notes, four chords [one more than in the blues of the 1920s] and a refrain of repeated lines" that include:

> *If I don't get there, if I don't get there*
> *They'll be disappointed with hearts in despair*
> *Dear father and mother, sweet sister and brother*
> *Kind kindred and others, if I don't get there*[46]

Dorsey joined Will Walker's Whispering Syncopators (which, for a time, included Lionel Hampton) for $40 a week, playing a variety of dance music styles. He met W. C. Handy and began composing (and copyrighting) his own music in earnest, including several songs that were eventually recorded by other artists: "I Just Want a Daddy I Can Call My Own," "Muddy Water Blues" (Monette Moore), and "Riverside Blues" (Joe "King" Oliver).[47] Their success brought Dorsey to the attention of "the Mother of the Blues," Ma Rainey. Dorsey was a talented pianist/arranger/composer, one of the few comfortable in both northern and southern blues styles, and thus the logical choice to direct Rainey's Jazz Wild Cats when she took the country by storm in 1924.[48] Another Jazz Wild Cat was Hudson Whittaker (or Whitaker), who would later become an important figure in Dorsey's life.[49] Dorsey also worked as an arranger for both the Chicago Music Publishing, Inc. and Vocalion Records, where he once met African-American composer and author J. Rosamund Johnson.[50]

Despite great personal success and his marriage in August 1925 to Nettie Harper, Dorsey again lapsed into a debilitating two-year depression, unable to work, eat, or find peace. At one point he considered suicide before returning to the church a second time.[51] Bishop H. H. Haley took Dorsey aside and whispered, "Brother Dorsey, there is no reason for you to be looking so poorly and feeling so badly. The Lord has too much work for you to do to let you die." Haley then pulled a "live serpent" from Dorsey's throat. Dorsey claimed to be never afflicted by depression again following this supernatural event.[52]

Shortly thereafter, a dear friend died unexpectedly. Dorsey meditated on the minister's words, found solace, and "from that day I took on new faith, consecrated myself fully to God and grew stronger and stronger physically, mentally and spiritually." From this incident he composed "If You See My Savior, Tell Him That You Saw Me," the song Michael Harris calls Dorsey's "first gospel blues."[53] It was followed shortly by "How About You?" Both, incidentally, were published through Dr. Charles H. Pace in Pittsburgh.[54]

There is no indication that Dorsey was trying to create—or even to codify—what came to be called "gospel music"; instead he was attempting to find the most effective vehicle to convey the anguish he felt inside. According to Harris, Dorsey believed that both gospel and the blues prompted "the same feeling" from listeners: "Music is a universal something. It was here when we come here and it was here when other generations came."[55] Dorsey instinctively tapped into the commonality between the two music forms, something verified by later researchers. Dorsey called it the same "grasping of the heart,"[56] but other writers talk about the "ritualistic quality" of the performance:

> . . . [It is] a situation in which all participants are aware of what will transpire but are unaware of how a particular performer will realize the predetermined plan. Within the gospel and blues traditions, people familiar with these art forms know that the expected goal is a point in the performance when the expressive power of the performer is so overwhelming that it demands a spontaneous response from the audience. That moment of collective catharsis is extremely important in reinforcing a sense of cultural solidarity.
>
> Within the black performance tradition, there is a communion of participants, not isolation between performer and audience.[57]

Dorsey's beliefs about the music behind the unabashedly Christian message differed sharply from the prevailing sentiments in Chicago's powerful African-

American Protestant (mostly Baptist) churches at the time. Harris writes that their musical practices were "virtual mirrors" of their white denominational counterparts as "choirs sang the Western European-style anthems and sacred compositions of composers such as Mendelssohn, Mozart, Beethoven, Bach, and Rossini."[58] Dorsey attempted to make a living writing, copyrighting, and selling his new religious music—as he'd successfully done in the past with secular music—but was rebuffed repeatedly. Despite the fact that "If I Don't Get There" had appeared in a second edition of *Gospel Pearls*, choir directors called his songs "that stuff" and "that mess."[59] Between 1928 and 1931, Dorsey says that while trying to sell his sheet music, he was "thrown out of some of the best churches" in Chicago. Once, when one of his songs was scheduled in the printed order of worship to be sung at a noted African-American church, the pastor simply chose instead to ignore it—along with the singer Dorsey had asked to perform the number—and continue the service.[60] Dorsey mailed a thousand copies of his songs to choir directors and pastors and the few orders he received didn't begin to cover expenses.[61]

Dorsey had the right idea—publishing gospel music for profit—it was just premature. To make money selling something as relatively inexpensive as sheet music requires not only full-time gospel music publishing houses but a small army of salespersons selling it in record shops, churches, and furniture and department stores across the country, not just on the South Side of Chicago. Dorsey, who was never interested in finances, also needed a business manager.[62]

Unable to provide for his family, Dorsey in desperation once again returned to secular music—and was an immediate, almost uncanny, success. Working again with lyricist/guitarist Hudson Whittaker, he co-wrote "It's Tight Like That"—a sexually suggestive combination of blues, vaudeville, early jazz, and ragtime that merged "sly urban sophistication and rural humour."[63] The public ate it up. Tampa Red (Whittaker) and Georgia Tom (Dorsey) became the Hokum Boys, Tampa Red on guitar, Dorsey on piano. Even that particular musical configuration was something new in the music industry, but it was the double-voicedness of lyrics that brought to the forefront something that had apparently long existed in the unrecorded folk music of African Americans.[64] The Famous Hokum Boys (which sometimes included Big Bill Broonzy and other artists) would eventually record more than sixty Dorsey compositions through 1932 for Vocalion and Columbia, including "Pat That Bread" and "Somebody's Been Using That Thing."[65]

Even his gospel music career finally began to pay off when, at the August 1930 National Baptist Convention in Chicago, Dorsey's "If You See My Savior" was performed at the morning session of the annual meeting. Like "It's Tight Like That," the song was an immediate hit.[66] The organizers, including Lucie Campbell, invited him to set up a booth in a corner and Dorsey claimed to have sold more than four thousand copies at the convention alone. "And I been in the music business ever since," Dorsey later told Harris. "That was the big moment right there."[67] Not that the acceptance was automatic by Chicago's dominant African-American church establishment—some held out against the new sound for years—but for Dorsey, there was no turning back. Years later, one gospel superstar recalled that Dorsey's songs "swept the convention" and infused it with renewed vigor: "[T]here was frantic expression all over the place the whole week and then it swept the Nation. The style started from Chicago with the bounce . . . true, honest, sincere expression in gospel music."[68]

In 1931, Dorsey was asked to organize a gospel chorus at Ebenezer Baptist Church in Chicago to complement Ebenezer's highly regarded—and more musically conservative—Senior Choir. Fiery new pastor (and former Southerner) the Reverend Dr. J. H. L. Smith wanted to broaden his church's constituency and believed that music could reach Chicago's booming population of recent southern immigrants. Dorsey joined charismatic singer Theodore Frye and quickly had every service packed—even the august *Chicago Defender* took notice.[69] Soon the new chorus was touring throughout the city.

In February 1932, the chorus was invited to perform at Pilgrim Baptist Church at 3301 South Indiana at East 33rd Street. The group's performance overwhelmed the church's congregation and pastor, the Reverend Junius C. Austin, who promptly recruited Dorsey and Frye to form and direct just such a choir at Pilgrim, despite the objections of his choir director.[70] Since Dorsey had only written four "gospel" songs by this point, the new choir transformed older songs like "I'm on the Battlefield for My Lord" while employing many of the qualities that would later be generally associated with gospel concerts: improvisation, theatrical movements by the participants, audience interaction, emotional responses by all involved—all set to rhythm-heavy arrangements. In short, Michael Harris notes, "Dorsey helped to spawn the choral gospel blues style before he actually composed for it."[71] Dorsey's deep roots in showmanship, from his flamboyant father the evangelist to his days first with Ma Rainey and later with the Hokum Boys, soon paid off. "Everything is a show," Dorsey once said, "but you got to know how to do your show." Other similar gospel choirs soon sprang up throughout Chicago.[72]

By August 1932, a number of the choruses met at the Metropolitan Community Church in Chicago for an informal convocation or musicale. Once again, Dorsey's Pilgrim Baptist choir, already known for its "histrionics," was the star attraction. Afterward, a group of the choir directors informally elected him "president," over his objections, of what would become the powerful National Convention of Gospel Choirs and Choruses. Years later, Dorsey would say ruefully, "I've been president ever since."[73]

But while at his first subsequent convention in St. Louis, a third tragedy interrupted Dorsey's period of greatest success and happiness. Dorsey's beloved wife, Nettie, died in childbirth; the child died the following day. Dorsey's religious faith was profoundly tested. But instead of helplessly careening into another depression, Dorsey articulated his grief—and newfound resolve—in what is considered by many to be the greatest gospel song ever written: "Take My Hand, Precious Lord." Loosely based on the melody of "Must Jesus Bear the Cross Alone," Dorsey wrote the first bars of "Precious Lord" at the urging of Frye, who also suggested the title change from the original "Blessed Lord" to "Precious Lord"[74]:

> *Precious Lord, take my hand*
> *Lead me on, let me stand*
> *I am tired, I am weak, I am worn*
> *Through the storm, through the night*
> *Lead me on, to the light*
> *Take my hand, Precious Lord, lead me home*[75]

According to Harris, "Dorsey's moment of catharsis pivoted on that turn of phrase from 'blessed' to 'precious' Lord—from a Lord whose holiness he proclaimed to one whose worthiness he cherished."[76] The result is an intensely personal and—at the same time—completely universal heart-cry, an exhilarating combination of helplessness and trust that has inspired performers and moved untold millions of listeners: "With 'Take My Hand, Precious Lord,' Dorsey allowed himself to wail, to get 'lowdown,' to purge—rather than soothe—his grief. Thus that moment in which he joined his divine pleadings to his lowdown blues assumed a near mystical aura."[77]

What would be called *gospel music* existed before "Precious Lord." But like no song before it, "Precious Lord" melded the "sorrow songs," spirituals, jubilee, and camp-meeting songs into the intimate wail of the blues. And his listeners knew it at once. When Frye and Dorsey introduced the finished song at Ebenezer the following week, a befuddled Dorsey recalled, "The folk went wild. They went wild. They broke up the church. Folk were shouting everywhere."[78] "Precious Lord" wasn't an immediate success as sheet music, although the grief-stricken Dorsey threw himself into songwriting and organizing the new gospel music in the years following Nettie's death.

Dorsey would eventually write a number of now-classic songs, including "My Desire," "When I've Done My Best," "I Will Trust in the Lord," "I'm Going to Live the Life I Sing About in My Song," and others. Decades later, his place in gospel music history secure, Dorsey talked about the man whose music paved the way for "Precious Lord" and the rest, Charles A. Tindley:

He was the greatest gospel songwriter—and this is not boasting—until I came along. I tried to do what Tindley did and that went along nicely, but it began to break off. I started putting a little of the beat into gospel that we had in Jazz. I also put in what we called the riff, or repetitive [rhythmic] phrases. These songs sold three times as fast as those that went straight along on paper without riffs or repetition.[79]

While Tindley's compositions had the "space/time" that encouraged impro-visation, Dorsey's songs (and piano accompaniment) also featured identifiable blues elements from his days as Georgia Tom. For his part, Dorsey credited the barrelhouse piano elements of his playing to hearing Arizona Dranes, then combining it with his own immersion in the blues. The result was the beginnings of something altogether new, although it didn't yet have a name.[80] With the popular songs, came a measure of financial security. Thomas A. Dorsey Gospel Songs, Publishing, soon was "a thousand times more lucrative than the blues," he once said. "For I was the only one in this business when I started."[81]

Chicago by the 1920s and 1930s rivaled the Harlem Renaissance as a hotbed of African-American creativity and energy. The Chicago Renaissance, which in-cluded literature (Richard Wright), jazz (Louis Armstrong), and blues (Big Bill Broonzy), fueled the fires, attracting more gifted black artists from across the country, not just from the rural South. Many arrived to capitalize on the city's Century of Progress (sometimes called Chicago's World's Fair) between 1933 and 1934.[82] Because of widespread housing discrimination, most settled on the South Side, in an area called "Bronzeville" or "Black Metropolis."[83] By 1928, the South Side was the second largest African-American city in the United States with 300,000 residents, second only to New York's Harlem. And as a frightened teenager from New Orleans once recalled, every inch of it was sheer magic:

> Chicago still had all the jazz musicians that had come up from New Orleans and Memphis and St. Louis; they hadn't moved on yet to New York City. There were black and tan music halls and cabarets. White people used to come out in crowds to the South Side to hear Louis Armstrong and Earl "Fatha" Hines at the Grand Terrace Ballroom. At the Royal Gardens and Grande Theater there was vaudeville every night with star performers like Ethel Waters and the Mills Brothers and the Whitman Sisters. I stood in line to hear Bessie Smith at the Avenue Theater and sat in my seat so thrilled to hear her as she filled the whole place with her voice that I never went home until they put us out and closed up for the night.[84]

As word of Dorsey's popular new choirs spread throughout this teeming, vibrant city, talented musicians began to seek him out. Soon a "school" of artists coalesced around Dorsey, beginning with Sallie Martin, the young woman who would enable him to write more gospel songs—and finally leave secular music forever.

Another poor refugee from the Deep South, Sallie Martin left school at a young age and soon joined the Fire Baptized Holiness Church. Despite her rough, untutored voice, she became a mainstay in Sanctified singing circles. At some point in the 1920s, Martin married and moved to Chicago. The couple divorced in 1929 and she supported herself and her young son by working in a hospital. By now, every Pentecostal in Chicago had heard of Dorsey's electrifying Ebenzer gospel choir. Despite Martin's "unrefined" style, "complete with whooping, groaning and a great deal of physical movement"—and the fact that she couldn't read music—Dorsey reluctantly allowed her to join his choir in 1932. It was more than a year before she sang her first solo, but it riveted the church audience in Danville, Illinois. Dorsey, always the canny entrepreneur, immediately took note.[85] Since he had hit his stride writing songs in "his strongly homiletical voice," he needed a "new old-line caller . . . the classic blues caller, the communal moaner." He needed someone who could combine blues technique *and* passionate religion. When he heard her, Dorsey knew he needed Sallie Martin.[86]

"Sallie can't sing a lick, but she can get over anywhere in the world," Dorsey once told Harris. At first he tried to "refine" that style, but the husky voice and commanding presence soon overwhelmed Dorsey's best efforts. The duo subsequently hit the road, assembling choirs and selling Dorsey's songs. Martin's greatest gift may have been that of organization. Dorsey frequently credited her as "being responsible for much of the success of gospel songs and singing."[87] Between 1931 and 1944, it is said that Martin established more than 100 choirs to sing this new music.[88]

Slowly, Martin transformed Dorsey's casual operation—which, until that time, had been fueled by word of mouth, gospel choir sales, and the occasional walk-in business to his house or his uncle's drugstore. "You know, you have something here but you don't know what to do with it," she told him plainly.[89] Martin became Dorsey's business partner and was even elected assistant secretary of the National Convention of Gospel Choirs and Choruses, where she assumed responsibilities of national organizer.[90] Martin sang the songs Dorsey wrote, helped organize the new gospel choirs that sang his songs, and built his sheet music operation into a thriving business. For the next few years, they traveled throughout the Midwest and South—even as far as California—successfully sharing and teaching this new music.[91] Together, the young woman with the "wrong, rough, gnarled" voice and the still-grieving Dorsey created what was for many years the largest African-American-owned gospel publishing company in America. "I've never been the greatest, nobody ever called me the greatest, never claimed to be the greatest, yet and still I've been everywhere the greatest have *been,*" she once told Anthony Heilbut, "and that's just the way it go."[92]

Dorsey's and Martin's nascent publishing empire helped jump-start the sluggish religious publishing industry, which had previously depended on expensive hymnbooks. Most hymnals, naturally, contained the older hymns exclusively. Individual sheet music was already a popular commodity in the world of popular music, and Dorsey worked hard to create a distinctiveness about his music. Beginning with "If I Don't Get There," the slogan "A Dorsey Song" appeared above the title. Elsewhere on the page was the tag-line "Organize a Gospel Chorus and sing."[93] These songs proved so popular that this kind of song became known as a "Dorsey" in African-American musical and religious circles and the name stuck for many years.[94] To the original four songs he had published when he began directing the gospel chorus in 1932, Dorsey added twenty-seven songs to his catalog by 1935 and "at least" 168 new songs by 1943.[95]

But Martin soon felt she was underappreciated for her Herculean efforts, and her complex, sometimes prickly, personality—vividly displayed in the brilliant gospel documentary *Say Amen, Somebody*[96]—soon put her at odds with Dorsey, who did not believe she accorded him the proper respect he believed he was due.

The friction came to a head in 1940 when Dorsey confronted Martin with various complaints from people within his entourage. The following dialogue is reported in *The Gospel Sound*:

> "I'll tell you the truth, brother, I wouldn't care to hear nothin' that anyone said," she retorted.
>
> "Well, that's what you always say," Dorsey answered. "Why don't you prove it?"
>
> "OK, here's your dawn—I'm gone."
>
> And with that, Martin recalls, she walked out and stood at a nearby bus stop.
>
> "Lord, liveordie, sinkorswim, I'll never go back there."

Martin's first collaboration was with Ruth Brown, who later changed her name to Dinah Washington and enjoyed a long career in popular music. This was followed by an equally brief partnership with rising young composer/pianist Roberta Evelyn Martin. Finally, she formed her own Sallie Martin Singers, one of the first all-female gospel groups.[97] Meanwhile, needing a steady source of income, she aligned herself with former jazz pianist and prolific composer Kenneth Morris.

Morris arrived in Chicago in 1934 as a teenager seeking work. Already an accomplished musician (he had attended both college and a music conservatory in his hometown of New York City), he followed Thomas Dorsey's lead and nearly worked himself to death playing nightclubs. On doctor's orders, he quit playing jazz and went to work for Lillian Bowles, a printer with no musical experience who was interested in entering gospel music publishing. Morris worked as an arranger and songwriter for Bowles from 1937 until 1940, replacing Charles Pace, who left to form his own company. Most of Bowles's work was on-demand—a songwriter would wander in and Morris would arrange the basic melody so that it could be sung by a chorus, although the occasional gospel quartet song would come his way as well. But unlike Dorsey, Bowles did not have a singing group that championed her copyrights. In time, like Martin, Morris felt that he was not receiving appropriate compensation for his work.[98] The two came together at the urging of Chicago's famed "Spiritualist" preacher Rev. Clarence Cobbs, who told Martin, "Sallie, why don't you go into business? I've got a man named Kenneth Morris at church and he's not doing anything but throw[-ing] his talent away, selling his songs for three dollars."[99] While serving as a music director for Cobbs's First Church of Deliverance, Morris is credited with introducing the Hammond organ into gospel music in 1937. Cobbs returned the favor by bankrolling the new partnership.[100]

Unsure at first whether there was any money in this new publishing venture, they named their company "Martin and Morris Music Studio; Teaching School" in 1940. "She was singer and I was a composer," Morris said in 1987; "she stuck to what she knew best and I stuck to what I knew best."[101] And what Morris knew how to do was write great, instantly memorable songs, including "Just a Closer Walk With Thee" (1940), which became one of the Sallie Martin Singers' first hits. Not wanting to repeat the mistakes he had seen made while working with Lillian Bowles, Martin and Morris turned to Ebenezer Baptist Church's Junior Gospel Chorus, directed by Dorsey's old friend Theodore Frye and their dazzling young pianist Roberta Evelyn Martin, to further promote their music.

As a young girl Roberta Martin (no relation to Sallie) moved with her family from Arkansas to Chicago. Something of a prodigy, she studied music at Northwestern and became well known at an early age for her gifts of writing and arranging music.[102] In 1933—the year she heard gospel music for the first time—Martin transformed the "Self-Organizers" into the Roberta Martin Singers. From that moment forward, there would be no stopping the beautiful young woman with the piercing eyes. "The Roberta Martin sound defined an entire musical era," writes Pearl Williams-Jones.[103]

There were, of course, other religious songwriters active in the 1930s. None had a more lasting impact than William Herbert Brewster. Like Lucie Campbell, he spent most of his life in Memphis. Brewster, though the son of sharecroppers, became one of the most revered and powerful African Americans in America. Only intermittently educated, he studied theology, Shakespeare, Greek, Latin, Hebrew, and law. And while mostly self-taught as a musician, he wrote some of the grandest, most beautiful songs of the twentieth century.[104] No less an authority than gospel music historian Anthony Heilbut calls Brewster "the greatest of all American religious composers" in a tribute book assembled a few years before his death:

> His songs have the great virtue of taking their audience seriously. Unlike so many evangelical hymns, his songs feature literate, innovative, witty lyrics, many including subtle but emphatic political and social messages. His melodies draw from blues, ballads, and plaintive waltzes. His rhythms are more innovative and reflect all the great musical changes that have occurred in Memphis itself.[105]

But in Memphis, Brewster was best known as the pastor of the East Trigg Baptist Church and founder of the Brewster Theological School of Religion. The Reverend C. L. Franklin, father of Aretha Franklin, is perhaps the most famous of the institute's many graduates. "He is not only a master preacher," notes Dr. William H. Wiggins, Jr., "but he has the even rarer gift of teaching other ministers how to preach."[106] Among those who repeatedly came to East Trigg to hear

When I Reach That City Over There

Kenneth Morris originally joined with Sallie Martin to form the most influential music publishing house in gospel music. (author's collection)

When I Reach That City Over There -2

TELL THE ANGELS

2

Arr. by
Virginia Davis.

Featured by: The Brewster Singers
The Ward Singers and
The Brewster-Aires

Words and Music by
Rev. W. Herbert Brewster, Jr.

VERSE Very Fast

1. My road is rough and rock - y,_ My cross is heav - y to
2. In this world I'm op - pressed I can't find hap - pi -
3. In a few more days my work will be done In a few more days my

bear._ My_ friends talk a - bout me_ I_ can't find peace an - y
ness;_ Here I'm so dis - tressed, My soul can't find an - y
race'll be won. In a few more days my bat - tle's o'er. I'll go march-ing to that Ce-

where, I'm tired,_ wor - ried, sick and sad, My
rest. Sin, and sor - row, oft be - tide.
lestial shore. I'll wave_ fare - well, say good - bye. In a

heart's heav - y la - den and I'm feel - ing bad. but I
En - e - mies_ stand-ing on_ ev - ery side. There is
few_ more_ days I'll wipe my weep - ing eyes. In a

know some day, I'm go-ing a-way. I'm go-ing to heav-en to stay.
joy for me I know in store In the land to which I go.
few more days I'll lay my bur - dens down. Tell the an-gels to get my crown.

The Reverend W. Herbert Brewster's eloquent gospel songs were much favored by the Clara Ward Singers. (author's collection)

Tell The Angels - 2

Brewster's booming voice and the famed choir was a young truck driver, Elvis Presley.[107]

Originally, like Campbell, Brewster wrote exclusively for the church's elaborate gospel-drama extravaganzas and pageants commemorating special events at East Trigg; his first songs would not be published until 1941. But for the next twenty years, few writers in any genre could compare with the breadth and scope of music flowing from Brewster's fertile imagination, beginning with "I'm Leaning and Depending on the Lord" (1941).[108]

And as for the man credited with starting it all? Thomas A. Dorsey had been busy as well. With the departure of Sallie Martin, he needed someone to sing his songs. He took a chance on a commanding young singer, still in her teens, from New Orleans: Mahalia Jackson.

So, on the cusp of the 1940s, all of the players, all of the influences, all of the music was, at last, finally in place. Or, perhaps, it had been there all along and nobody knew what to call it. Until now.

Chapter Nine

Chicago and the Rise of Gospel Music

I don't care where anybody else comes from or what anybody else does, Chicago is the capital of gospel and always will be. This is where the great talents come to learn, this is where the great singers live. Gospel music, you know, can't really be written down. You have to hear it and feel it, and you can do that best here in Chicago.

—Albertina Walker, 1990[1]

I suppose gospel music came into being because we black people, as a race, had been crushed so much, and so cruelly. So these gospel songs of ours were comforting to us. I believe that the people who wrote the first gospel songs were inspired by God to write, to give our people something to feed on, or to live on.

—Delois Barrett Campbell, 1990[2]

There is no music like that music, no drama like the drama of the saints rejoicing, the sinners moaning, the tambourines racing, and all those voices coming together and crying holy unto the Lord. There is still, for me, no pathos quite like the pathos of those multi-colored, worn, somehow triumphant and transfigured faces, speaking from the depths of a visible, tangible, continuing despair of the goodness of the Lord. I have never seen anything equal the fire and excitement that sometimes, without warning, fill a church, causing the church, as Leadbelly and so many others have testified, to "rock."

—James Baldwin, 1963[3]

Gospel

In the late 1930s, the term *gospel* eventually came to identify contemporary religious music of the sort Thomas Dorsey and his friends were performing in Chicago. The term's acceptance was not immediate, nor was it universal.

Some still called this music "spirituals"—such as John Hammond's "From Spirituals to Swing" concerts in New York City in 1938 and 1939. And, in fact, antebellum spirituals were still being performed throughout the rural South. Others called these songs "Dorseys" or "evangelistic songs." But eventually, *gospel music* or *black gospel music* became the defining words of choice.

The term *gospel music,* of course, predates Thomas Dorsey. The exact origin is uncertain, although it may have been inspired by British evangelist Henry Morehouse, who preached a series of sermons on John 3:16 at a Chicago mission in 1869. Among those in attendance was songwriter Philip Bliss, who shortly thereafter turned solely to writing upbeat, accessible religious songs.[4] The specific term *gospel song* appears in Bliss's landmark collection *Gospel Songs* in 1874, which also features this intriguing acrostic, a recasting of John 3:16:

God so loved the world that He gave His
Only begotten
Son, that whosoever believeth in Him should not
Perish, but have
Everlasting
Life.[5]

It is not insignificant that Bliss first heard the term in Chicago. The term *gospel song* was adopted by both races to help differentiate the songs from more formal—and older—hymns. When the National Baptist Convention assembled its latest collection of religious songs, *Gospel Pearls,* in 1921, the term *gospel* must have been in such widespread usage that the editors felt no need to explain their choice of title. The phrase *gospel singer* is also mentioned in the preface—again without explanation.[6]

Still, while the older jubilee style still dominated into the 1930s and 1940s, the music that Campbell, Dorsey, Brewster, Morris, and others were writing would eventually win the day, with only a few of the original quartets still performing jubilee by the 1950s. Differentiating between jubilee and gospel, however, is complicated because many groups (and churches) continued to perform *both* styles of songs, even as new hybrids of the two appeared and disappeared. Just as some older spirituals were transformed into jubilee songs, so were some spirituals transformed into gospel songs. For instance, the spiritual "Every Time I Feel the Spirit" was recorded both by the Golden Gate Jubilee Quartet in 1939 as a jubilee and by the Pilgrim Travelers as a straight-ahead gospel song in 1971.

Doug Seroff claims that while Dorsey is commonly considered the "father" of African-American choral singing and religious soloists, no single songwriter can claim to have created gospel quartet music, since this unique sound is as much a function of arrangement and performance as it is of melody or beat:

As interpreted by the Golden Gate Quartet, gospel compositions "Precious Lord" and "Bedside of a Neighbor" become rhythmic spirituals, stylistically quite a different thing. Conversely, in the hands of community quartets, nineteenth-century spirituals "Old Ship of Zion," "Inching Along" and "Nobody Knows the Trouble I've Seen" were readily accessible to gospel arrangement.[7]

As we have seen, however, gospel is first and foremost a direct descendent of spirituals. What Dorsey and his friends kept as the defining attributes of gospel music—the call and response format, ample room for improvisation, rhythm, frequent use of the flatted seventh and third in melodies—remain true even today. The elements introduced by later musical forms, such as close harmonies (barbershop quartets), a sense of professionalism (jubilee quartets), showman-ship (minstrelsy), the regular use of an *aab* rhyming scheme, and a pronounced beat (the blues) all endure, but are tacked on the spine of the original spirituals, which are for the most part irrevocably linked to their African forebears. Like the spirituals, gospel songs "are emotionally inspired—by visions, trouble, sorrow, thanksgiving, and joy," notes George Ricks. He also points out that both spiritu-als and gospel not only foster innovation during performance—the two art forms *demand* it. "A song is rarely, if ever, sung 'straight,'" he notes, "and the same may be said of accompaniment, and an unusually high premium is placed upon individual ability in improvisation."[8]

It is this distinction that may ultimately account for the eventual ascendancy of gospel over jubilee. While jubilee continued to flourish into the late 1940s and, through the voices and imagination of groups such as the Gates, became a rich and rewarding genre, the emphasis on close harmony was always at odds with the need for individual expression and improvisation inherent in the spiri-tuals from the beginning. Quartets like the Dixie Hummingbirds and the Soul Stirrers understood this and began the slow evolution to one or more "lead" vocalists, vocalists able to "riff"—improvise and preach—over the heavily rhyth-mic backing provided by the rest of the group. "Gospel music seems to have gained prominence," Ricks adds, "because its producers have been successful in absorbing and reflecting the admiration of their public for innovation."[9]

The most profound differences between spirituals and gospel can be identi-fied through their composition and content. Whereas the spirituals were primar-ily congregational, created and continued orally from worship service to worship service, gospel music "encouraged self-conscious artistry and creative perform-ance," writes Glenn Hinson. This broadened "the musical scope of worship while changing [the] performative contours" of the music. It was still worship music, but it was music performed *by* an artist *to* a congregation (or audience), rather than the spontaneous creation *of* an audience.[10]

Dorsey himself made the same distinction, saying that while "spirituals are mostly a spontaneous outburst," gospel songs are composed with a goal—"an expoundation [sic] of that something good" that will "help somebody else."[11] Dorsey and others also emphasized the emotional content of gospel music—the joyful, upbeat retelling of the "good news" to contrast it with the often "sad and sorrowful" spirituals and blues.[12] In the heart of economically devastated Chicago in the 1930s, Dorsey continued to compose songs: "I wrote to give them something to lift them out of that Depression," he once said. "They could sing at church but the singing had no life, no spirit. The preacher would preach till his collar would melt down around his neck but there wouldn't be no money in the oblations."[13] Indeed, some of Dorsey's songs seem to celebrate the opportunity just to be able to sing gospel songs: "Singing in My Soul," "If You Sing a Gospel Song," "I Thank God for My Song," among others.

The final point of difference between jubilee and gospel is the beat. Most jubilee songs, to be sure, had a bouncy, toe-tapping feel. Marshall Stearns cites the original "When the Saints Go Marching In" as the prototypical example. "Jubilees are both cheerful and rhythmic," he writes, "usually announcing some sort of good news."[14] But Dorsey and Morris lived in Chicago's music-laden Bronzeville, while Campbell and Brewster lived and worked near the musical hotbed of Beale Street in Memphis. Jazz and the blues were everywhere. And when the blues is added to first the spirituals and then jubilee, it becomes gospel.[15] Or, as blues great T-Bone Walker recalled, "The first time I ever heard a boogie-woogie piano was the first time I went to church. That was the Holy Ghost Church in Dallas, Texas."[16]

The barrelhouse piano of Arizona Dranes, the haunting, propulsive slide work of Blind Willie Johnson, the proto-blues and jazz of both the Whispering Syncopators and the Jazz Wildcats together combined to give Dorsey's songs a definite beat—even a *danceable* beat. The word *dance*, while anathema to Baptists, was embraced by Pentecostals: "One defining feature is [gospel's] heavily accented beat and rhythm, the source of which was the sanctified church."[17] The Reverend Dr. Wyatt Tee Walker, of New York's famed Canaan Baptist Church, is even more direct: "The same beat that Black folks dance to on Saturday night is the same beat that they shout to on Sunday morning. If you hear the beat and do not know what the program is, watch the direction of the shout; if the shout is up and down, it is religious; if it is from side to side, it is probably secular."[18]

Slowly, church by church, choir by choir, singer by singer, gospel spread through America's black churches. Dorsey compared gospel's gradual, grudging acceptance to that experienced by the blues:

> Now blues, they kept hammering on the blues and everybody liked to listen to the blues. There was nothing wrong with the blues, it was good music.[19]
>
> But the times just wasn't right, until the time of acception [sic] of the blues and so many people singing the blues, it was something that people liked, it was something that kind of touched them. Like gospel songs, kind of touched them inside, and they accepted it.[20]

In time, Dorsey became known as "the Father of Gospel," although it may have been, at first, a self-appointed title and one that Dorsey shrewdly marketed.

"I'm too truthful to pretend to be over-modest," he said on his seventy-fifth birthday. "As far as gospel is concerned, I did begin popularizing the whole thing. And I gave it its name—gospel music. I'm proud of that."[21] It's certainly quite clear today that Dorsey did not coin the term *gospel*. Still, the term *Father* is appropriate. The recognition due Dorsey—and Sallie Martin—derives from their success in disseminating gospel music, taking it first from Holiness to Baptists churches in Chicago in the 1930s and, by the late 1940s and early 1950s, to all of America's black denominations.[22]

But in the late 1930s, despite their success in the Midwest, the possibility of that level of penetration and acceptance must have looked awfully remote to Dorsey, Morris, and the other creators and publishers of gospel music. No matter how systematically they traveled and trained choirs, they were still only making converts one church at a time. Additionally, the advent of commercial radio and phonograph records, coupled with the demise of vaudeville, sent sheet music sales plummeting. In the 1920s, a popular piece of sheet music could expect to sell 500,000 copies. A "good seller" (as they were then called in the industry) in the 1930s moved 50,000 copies.[23] The great majority of African Americans simply had not yet heard this music. Nor was there much opportunity to do so. Dorsey rarely recorded and, if he had, his thin voice and new music probably wouldn't have caused much of a stir. The number of radio stations featuring black religious music of any kind was still relatively small.

Only one area of popular religious music was experiencing growth: the quartets. In 1934, only eight jubilee quartets were recording. By 1938, that number had climbed to more than fifty. Every major label—Vocalion (Mitchell's Christian Singers), Blue Bird (the Heavenly Gospel Singers), and Decca (the Norfolk Jubilee Quartet)—featured at least one quartet.[24]

The undisputed kings of the quartet scene were still the Golden Gate Quartet. The Gates continued to be musical trailblazers, introducing rich, complex harmonies, some improvisation, and strong falsetto singing into the older spirituals and hymns. They were among the earliest of the quartets to record the songs of Dorsey, Campbell, and Brewster. Their widespread acceptance also meant that the Gates were also among the first quartets to aspire to full-time professional status. "While groups from Texas, such as the Soul Stirrers, Birmingham's Famous Blue Jay Singers and the Kings of Harmony were key quartets during this transition," Kip Lornell writes, "it was Norfolk's Gold Gate Quartet that was the single most influential group to take this major step."[25]

Their regular broadcasts on WBT soon caught the ears of Victor Records A&R scouts. Their first recording session in 1937 resulted in a giant hit, a rhythmic retelling of the spiritual "Jonah."[26] One legendary two-hour recording session in a Charlotte, North Carolina, hotel resulted in fourteen classic sides for Victor's Blue Bird label, including "Go Where I Send Thee," "The Preacher and the Bear," and "When the Saints Go Marchin' In." Their success led to a rare performance by African Americans on NBC's "Magic Key Hour" in 1937.[27]

The Golden Gate Quartet is credited with revitalizing jubilee singing by emphasizing the rhythmic aspects of singing. Willie Johnson, one of the founders of the Gates, called it "vocal percussion" and said that one of the group's goals was to get listeners to tap their feet to the beat:

> It was a joyous sort of thing . . . it was a thing you patted your foot by. It wasn't a thing that made you want to cry, like "my mama's dead and gone" . . . It was all light, really entertaining. And it had some merit, like in the narrative tunes, a lot of people had never heard about all the Biblical heroes. They could hear the story start and they'd see when it reached the middle and they'd see it reach the apex and then quit.[28]

The story songs like "Jonah" and "Noah" quickly became a staple of all jubilee groups, just as narrative songs from the Old Testament had been popular in the spirituals. "The Gold Gate Quartet in particular became the model for innumerable quartets in the Carolinas, Virginia, Maryland, and the urban corridor between Washington D.C. and New York City," notes Lornell. In addition to imitating the Gates' use of biblical narratives, other groups copied bass singer Willie Johnson's "syncopated bass arrangements,"[29] but he had few peers as a songwriter.

By the late 1930s, the Gates were featured regularly on NBC radio and had moved to New York where they were tapped by John Hammond to perform in the influential "From Spirituals to Swing" concert with the likes of Count Basie, Benny Goodman, Lester Young, Charlie Christian, Sonny Terry, Joe Turner, and Sister Rosetta Tharpe (see below). This was followed by a stint at New York's groundbreaking racially integrated venue, Café Society. As Barney Josephson, Café Society's owner, later recalled, the Golden Gate Quartet "made the blood rush up my arms, which brought the goose pimples out, when they sang—and here I was a disbeliever—'As they were driving nails in His feet, You could hear the hammer ringing in Jerusalem's streets.'"[30]

This exposure may have also provided the impetus for two albums with other emerging celebrities: *The Midnight Special and Other Prison Songs,* with folksinger Leadbelly (for Victor Records), and *Freedom: The Golden Gate Quartet with Josh White in Concert.* The latter, with commentary by Sterling Brown, Alain Locke, and Alan Lomax, was recorded and released by the Library of Congress to mark the seventy-fifth anniversary of the Thirteenth Amendment to the Constitution.

That popularity eventually placed the Gates at the center of a minor firestorm on the eve of World War II. Among their fans was Eleanor Roosevelt, wife of President Franklin Roosevelt. In 1937, Eleanor Roosevelt had requested that African-American opera star Marian Anderson perform at Constitution Hall, traditionally operated by the Daughters of the American Revolution, but the request had been rejected by the DAR. In response, a group of supporters in the

administration, led by Secretary of the Interior Harold L. Ickes, scheduled Anderson to perform on the steps of the Lincoln Monument on Easter 1939. An
estimated 75,000 people showed up to hear Anderson sing spirituals in the brisk
weather. Roosevelt later scheduled Anderson to sing in the White House for the
king and queen of England.[31] Roosevelt then scheduled the Gates to perform at
her husband's inaugural gala (along with actors Charlie Chaplin, Mickey Rooney,
Ethel Barrymore, singer Nelson Eddy, and the National Symphony Orchestra) in
January 1941, again at Constitution Hall. According to *Time,* the DAR "moodily
approved" the booking.[32] The quartet would subsequently appear at the White
House on several more occasions at the request of the Roosevelts.[33]

The Golden Gate Quartet broke through a number of barriers in those years,
including performances in the films *Star-Spangled Rhythm* (with Betty Hutton
in 1943), *Hollywood Canteen* (with Bette Davis in 1944), and *A Song Is Born*
(with Danny Kaye in 1948). They even recorded a couple of secular 78s: "Stormy
Weather" and "My Prayer." In 1941, the group moved to Columbia Records'
OKeh label, where they produced two of their greatest successes: "Stalin Wasn't
Stallin'" and "Coming in on a Wing and a Prayer" in 1943.[34]

The Golden Gates would remain the premiere close-harmony jubilee group
until the public's tastes changed in the mid-1950s, when they subsequently
moved to France and successfully rejuvenated their careers on the Continent.

There were, of course, numerous other first-rate quartets, some content to
remain firmly in the jubilee camp, some already moving toward gospel and away
from jubilee. The Alphabetical Four were among the first to use a guitar behind
Dorsey's "Precious Lord" in 1938, and the Golden Eagle Gospel Singers' "Tone
the Bell" was accompanied not just by a full band but an entire congregation.
But even the Gates must have been taken aback by the first recordings of a
new quartet, the Dixie Hummingbirds, particularly the "extraordinary, sustained
falsettos" of "Soon Will Be Done with the Troubles of This World," recorded
for Decca in 1939.[35]

The use of falsetto, first popularized by the Silver Leaf Quartette, marked a
significant shift in the transformation of jubilee into gospel. Falsetto, another
remnant of gospel's African musical heritage, was the first step in breaking the
stranglehold of close-harmony barbershop-styled harmonies, allowing for more
freedom and improvisation by lead singers.[36]

Founded in 1928 in South Carolina, the Dixie Hummingbirds have enjoyed
an unusually long and productive career and were universally "renowned for
their imaginative arrangements, progressive harmonies, and all-around versatil-
ity."[37] Not that it came easy, as cofounder James Davis once said:

We picked the hardest field there is to try to make a living in by singing gospel.
If you start singing beautiful songs about some girlfriend of yours, the audience
starts thinking about their girlfriends or wives. But when you start singing about
Jesus, some of the people want to know what was his last name. You can be a

The Dixie Hummingbirds, founded in 1928 (courtesy of AIR Gospel)

very successful rock and roll singer without having a good voice, but you have to have some voices to make it singing gospel.[38]

The Birds (as they were affectionately called) scored several hits with their first recordings for Decca, including "Joshua Journeyed to Jericho," "Little Wooden Church," and "Soon Will Be Done with the Troubles of This World," but didn't record again until several years later. At the onset of World War II, rationing severely restricted the purchase of gasoline and automobile tires. This hampered both performer and audience. In 1942, the American Federation of Musicians reluctantly imposed a "300-mile jump limit"—the distance between performance sites. In the East, where gas supplies were especially tight, the Hummingbirds found that working out of South Carolina became increasingly difficult. So later that same year, they moved first to Washington, D.C., then to Philadelphia.[39] Once in Philadelphia, they joined a growing band of gospel musicians, including Margaret Wells Allison, the Angelics, Mary Johnson Davis, Ruth Davis, Kitty Parham, the Sensational Nightingales, Rosie Wallace, Clara Ward, Gertrude Ward, and Marion Williams. All enjoyed Philadelphia's vibrant church scene, including the famed Mount Zion Fire Baptized Holiness Church, the proximity of popular performance venues (including the Swan Club, the Earle Theater, and Kaliner's Rathskeller) along the Boston-New York-Baltimore-Washington, D.C. corridor, and the large expatriate population from South Carolina.[40]

The Dixie Hummingbirds replaced the Royal Harmony Singers as featured performers on 50,000-watt CBS radio affiliate WCAU (under the pseudonyms the Swanee Quartet—WCAU management thought "Dixie" was "too black" to appeal to the station's white listeners). The station also featured the nationally popular Wings Over Jordan Choir at 10:30 A.M. on Sundays. It was a performance on WCAU that brought the Birds to the attention of Barney Josephson and Café Society. This was the venue, incidentally, where Billie Holiday premiered her searing indictment of lynching, "Strange Fruit."[41] John Hammond, Café Society's booking agent, didn't like either of the names Dixie Hummingbirds or Swanee Quartet—so they went by the Jericho Quintet when their lengthy engagement began November 11, 1942.[42]

The size of the venue meant that the Birds also began introducing more instrumentation into what had originally been an a cappella act, although for certain songs they previously would include a pianist or guitarist. At Café Society, they were initially backed by the legendary saxophone artist Lester Young and his sextet. It was also during this time that the Hummingbirds' popular choreography took shape, including their opening "slide" into place in front of the microphones from offstage.[43]

Perhaps most important, however, it was during the Café Society run that one of the most influential lead singers in the history of gospel music, Ira Tucker, came of age. Tucker joined the Birds in 1938 as a thirteen-year-old prodigy. As his voice matured, he dazzled mainstream and religious audiences alike with his commanding stage presence. Tucker forever shattered the "flat-footed" image of the jubilee group, dancing energetically, dashing up the aisles, even hurling himself off the stage. It is in Tucker's theatrics that many believe that the roots of the showmanship of both R&B and rock and roll are found.[44] The rock and roll world would return the favor with the release of *Diamond Jubilation: 75th Anniversary* in 2003, featuring accompaniment by Stevie Wonder, Paul Simon, Levon Helm, and Garth Hudson (formerly of The Band), Dr. John, and others.

The Birds were not the only top-flight gospel group prospering during World War II. They had stiff competition from the likes of two more Philadelphia-based groups, the Clara Ward Singers and the Sensational Nightingales, along with the Soul Stirrers, the Swan Silvertones, the Pilgrim Travelers, and other quartets, all riding the newly paved "Gospel Highway."

Interestingly, real distinctions arose between gospel groups (mixed voices with backing instrumental accompaniment) and quartets (all male, no backing instrumentation). According to Daniel Wolff and others, the gender difference was significant:

> Gospel groups reflected the largely female church congregations. When someone like Roberta Martin came forward, the sisters heard one of their own; many found gospel groups more intensely religious—and more innovative. The quartets like the Soul Stirrers or their chief rivals the Famous Blue Jay Singers (whose office was right around the corner from the Cooks at 3609 Cottage Grove) functioned more like male preachers: cocks in the henhouse. They tended to dress sharp, turn a harmony till the church ladies squealed, and generally strut their stuff.[45]

Few singers, male or female, crossed easily between the two competing camps.

Back in Chicago, the group of artists who had originally coalesced around Dorsey were finding their wings as well. Roberta Martin built her own group, the Roberta Martin Singers, around her "dark, rich contralto," creating a group that complemented her stately, "refined" nature—in marked contrast to Sallie Martin's raucous Sanctified group. But it is as a pianist that Roberta Martin is remembered today. Horace Boyer notes that Martin, who was classically trained, "played mainly in the middle of the piano, introducing chords—magnificently voiced—that she borrowed from the Western European classic music she had studied and that were new to gospel."[46] Like Dorsey, however, she also was influenced by Arizona Dranes's barrelhouse piano styling. Merging these styles together, Martin created "classic gospel music" on the piano—a style so distinctive that an entire school of gospel musicians hail her as their founder. While Dorsey's piano may have made the gospel sound famous, Martin's piano accompaniment is "more classical and ensemble-oriented" in providing instrumental support for her crack group of singers both "chordally and melodically."[47]

Martin opened the Roberta Martin Studio of Music in 1939 and would eventually publish outstanding compositions by gospel artists ranging from Prof. Alex Bradford to James Cleveland. Her first composition, "Try Jesus, He Satisfies," was an immediate hit in 1943.

But if a measure of an artist is how she passes on her genius, then Martin founded and nurtured one of gospel's greatest dynasties, handpicking brilliant singers and coupling them with unforgettable songs in classic arrangements. "Miss Martin created a school," writes Irene V. Jackson, "a way of playing, singing and arranging the then-new music called gospel."[48] The Roberta Martin Singers were the first major gospel group featuring both male and female singers, which naturally created a distinctive sound in an industry dominated by all-male quartets and a lesser number of all-female groups. The Singers replaced the standard male bass singer with a second soprano. And, over it all, Martin's silky contralto, once described as "refined, subdued, achieving its greatest effects through timing and phrasing."[49] The group would enjoy its greatest successes from the mid-1940s through the early 1960s and received a gold record for "The Old Ship of Zion."

In 1945, Eugene Smith, a popular member of the Roberta Martin Singers and the first of the group's individual members to enjoy success on his or her own, had an even bigger hit with "I Know the Lord Will Make a Way, Oh Yes, He Will." Boyer calls this an "extremely important" composition, one that would provide still another "formal structure to composers of gospel and would continue to intrigue composers even into the 1980s": gospel blues. Boyer equates it with the structure of "secular blues" songs such as "Stormy Monday" and "Everyday I Have the Blues," with an *aaba* rhyme structure, as compared to the *aab* rhyme structure of classic blues. Despite repeated offers from other mainstream and gospel groups, Smith remained with the Roberta Martin Singers until it disbanded in 1969.[50]

Other notable Roberta Martin Singers alumni include Robert Anderson, Willie Webb, and Delois Barrett. Anderson studied piano with Martin but was best known for his husky, melodious baritone voice, which was often compared to Bing Crosby's. His most famous group, the Gospel Caravan, included the precocious teenager Albertina Walker, but Anderson was an accomplished "house-wrecker" himself, sending churches into a frenzy with his own theme song, "Something Within Me."[51] Another Anderson composition, "Prayer Changes Things," was an immediate hit when released in 1950, propelled by lines like these and repeated thrilling performances by Mahalia Jackson:

> *I've traveled through sorrow valley,*
> *So many times my heart's been made to bleed,*
> *By some friends whom I thought were with me,*
> *Through disappointment, I was knocked down to my knees.*
> *But I rose with faith and grace,*
> *I found nobody to take God's place,*
> *I know, yes I know, prayer changes things.*
> "Prayer Changes Things," Robert Anderson, 1947[52]

Another Roberta Martin Singers veteran was Willie Webb, a fine singer, better pianist, and first-rate composer—"I'm Bound for Higher Ground" (1945), "He's All I Need" (1947), and "Every Day and Every Hour" (1951). Webb was also the group's comedian. Delois Barrett tells how he would whisper to her during the most serious moments of a religious revival, "Sing mustard greens. Sing turnip greens."[53] But Webb is now best remembered for introducing Alex

Bradford to the gospel world in the late 1940s.[54] Still another famed alumni was "Little" Lucy Smith, who not only studied under Roberta Martin, she became her daughter-in-law. Smith was another accomplished writer ("I'll Never Let Go His Hand" and "Somebody Bigger Than You and I" for her own Lucy Smith Singers) and became the Roberta Martin Singers' pianist in the 1960s.[55]

Of all the gifted artists who passed through the Roberta Martin Singers, perhaps the most talented was Delois Barrett Campbell. Sisters Delois, Billie, and Rodessa Barrett began singing in Chicago's Morning Star Church in the mid-1940s, and Delois was recruited to join the Roberta Martin Singers while still a teenager. The sisters reformed their group in 1962 and enjoyed the admiration of their peers but only moderate commercial success.[56] But what elevated Delois and the Barretts to cult status were their electrifying performances on George Nierenberg's documentary *Say Amen, Somebody* in 1984. Song after song—"No Ways Tired," "The Storm is Passing Over," and "He Brought Us"—are among the most magical moments in gospel music history. In fact, *New Yorker* reviewer Pauline Kael says that the Barretts "sing so exhilaratingly" that they create a dramatic "problem" for the filmmaker in the second half of the documentary.[57] Nierenberg's unflinching insider's look into the gospel music life is all the more powerful when the viewer realizes how few such performances by any of gospel's greatest artists were ever captured on film.[58] "It's a profoundly joyous craziness," adds Kael, "this gospel music."[59]

Say Amen, Somebody is also a fitting coda to the lives of two other gospel giants. One—Thomas A. Dorsey—is justly celebrated for his accomplishments. His imperious, theatrical direction of a convention's mass choir in "Take My Hand, Precious Lord" is among his last known public appearances. But the other artist, Willie Mae Ford Smith, despite her early work as one of Dorsey's song-pluggers, toiled in relative obscurity most of her life. *Say Amen, Somebody* chronicles and rejoices in a life spent in service and song.

The All Music Guide to the Blues calls her the "greatest of the anointed singers" and hails her "incendiary live performances." Smith rarely recorded, but her influence extends to every phase of gospel music. Another Mississippi native, Willie Mae was one of fourteen children who relocated with her family first to Memphis, then to St. Louis. She formed a quartet with three of her sisters and performed at the 1922 National Baptist Convention where their versions of "Ezekiel Saw the Wheel" and "I'm in His Care" created a "sensation." She began performing solo a few years later and, after marrying St. Louis businessman James Peter Smith, toured "relentlessly, conducting musical revivals." It was during one of these tours that she met Dorsey, who invited her to help found the National Convention of Gospel Choirs and Choruses in 1932. She later returned to St. Louis and established an active chapter there.[60]

Possessed of a commanding, pliable contralto even in her later years, Smith was able to bend every song to her will. A thrilling performance of her composition "If You Just Keep Still" "tore up" the 1937 NBC.[61] An accomplished arranger and evangelist, Smith mentored Brother Joe May, Martha Bass (mother of singer Fontella Bass), the O'Neal Twins, and Myrtle Scott, among others. She joined the Church of God Apostolic in 1939 and embraced the rhythms she was hearing in the charismatic church services. In time, she became an ordained minister (a rarity for women in the late 1930s and early 1940s) and turned to evangelism almost exclusively, though she continued to sing in the services.[62]

Still, "Mother" Smith's influence, both musically and philosophically, extends through gospel's so-called "Golden Age" and into the present. Singer and radio announcer Zella Jackson Price (who also appears in *Say Amen, Somebody*) recalled seeing Smith repeatedly in the late 1940s:

> Mother Smith was dramatic and . . . Holy Ghost-filled . . . When she said she felt like flying away, in your mind's eye, you could visualize this . . . She had power in her voice [and] in her expression. She was a *singer,* I've seen her walk out singing . . . on the way to her next appearance . . . and folks is just shoutin' everywhere, hat's flyin' and carryin' on, just somethin' terrible. She'd come in and just wreck all them buildings. That was Mother Smith, and she loved it.[63]

Smith opened every service with "Lest I Forget" and closed each service with "God Be With You Till We Meet Again." But in between, she followed no song list, instead trusting her instincts—or the Holy Spirit—and taking written or spoken requests. Her performances were filled with impromptu prayers and sermonettes and physical recreations of the lyrics she sang. Chronically late, sweating profusely, and always draped in a dramatic cape—few who saw or heard Mother Smith ever forgot her.[64] "I always did have emotional gestures," she once said. "You move with the feeling, you sway with the feelings. I'll sing with my hands, with my feet—when I got saved, my feet got saved, too. I believe we should use everything we got."[65]

William Dargan and Kathy Bullock state that Smith's pervasive influence within gospel music stems from a number of factors, including the informal mentoring she did with many emerging gospel artists, her status as one of the first (if not the first) solo female gospel artists to tour extensively, her introduction of "worried notes, bends, scoops, growls, and melismas from the blues and spirituals" in gospel music's vocal tradition, and her position as an ordained minister and evangelist.[66] Anthony Heilbut calls her the "greatest" of the "sanctified singers" during the war years and quotes a frankly admiring Mahalia Jackson as saying, "Whew! She [Smith] could sing."[67] For herself, Smith modestly proclaimed, "The gospel song is the Christian blues. I'm like the blues singer, when something's rubbing me wrong, I sing out of my soul to settle me down."[68]

Mother Smith's belated canonization followed her extraordinarily moving interview and performances ("Singing in My Soul," "What Manner of Man," "Canaan," and particularly "I'll Never Turn Back") in *Say Amen, Somebody,* followed by an appearance in Washington, D.C., as one of the twelve National

Heritage Fellowships awarded by the National Endowment for the Arts in October 1988. Later that day, while still in a wheelchair, she brought the audience at Washington's Lisner Auditorium to its feet with a heartfelt "Amazing Grace." She died February 2, 1994, in her beloved St. Louis at the age of eighty-nine.[69]

Meanwhile, back in Chicago, the war years passed quietly for one Thomas A. Dorsey. Now happily remarried, unaffected by the shellac shortage (caused by the Japanese invasion of Singapore) that caused other artists to curtail their recording careers, Dorsey simply wrote and published some of his greatest, most enduring songs:

1938
"(There'll be) Peace in the Valley for Me"
"I'll Tell It Wherever I Go"

1939
"Wings Over Jordan!"
"Hide Me in Thy Bosom"

1940
"How Many Times?"

1941
"How About You"
"I'm Going to Live the Life I Sing About in My Song"
"When the Gates Swing Open"

1942
"I Don't Know Why I Have to Cry Sometime"

1943
"If We Needed the Lord Before, We Sure Do Need Him Now"
"The Lord Will Make a Way Somehow"

1944
("I'll) Never Turn Back"

1945
"I'm Waiting for Jesus, He's for Me"

. . . and two dozen more besides.[70] But at a time when the country needed it most, Dorsey knew what was in shortest supply: hope. And his best song from this period, "Peace in the Valley"— eventually recorded by everybody from Elvis to Red Foley—provided exactly that:

> *There the bears will be gentle and the wolves will be tame*
> *The lions will lie down by the lamb*
> *And the host from the wild*
> *Will be led by a child*
> *I'll be changed from the creature I am*

There'll be peace in the valley for me someday
There'll be peace in the valley for me, I pray
No more sadness, no sorrow, no trouble I'll see
There'll be peace in the valley for me.

"(There'll Be) Peace in the Valley"—Thomas A. Dorsey, 1938. Copyright Unichappel Music, Inc. All rights reserved.

Chapter Ten

Three Divas: Rosetta Tharpe, Clara Ward, and Mahalia Jackson

There's a lot more to gospel than just singing. It goes a whole lot deeper than that. 'Cause gospel is praising and praying and preaching all rolled into one. And when it's got the anointing, when God's pouring His holy blessings out on the singer then—good God Almighty!—gospel's got the power to pure move a church!

—Elder Lawrence Richardson[1]

In the Black Belts of the northern cities, our women are the most circumscribed and tragic objects to be found in our lives, and it is to the churches that our black women cling for emotional security and the release of their personalities.

So they keep thousands of Little Bethels and Pilgrims and Calvarys and White Rocks and Good Hopes and Mount Olives going with their nickels and dimes. Nurtured in the close and intimate folk culture of the South, where each person knew the others, where the basic emotions of life were shared by all, many of them sometimes feel that the elaborate ritual of our big churches is too cold and formal for them. To retain the ardent religious emotionalism of which they are so fond, many of them will group themselves about a lonely young black preacher and help him to establish what is called a "store front" church, in which they are still able to perform their religious rituals on the fervid levels of the plantation revival.

—Richard Wright[2]

In a day when it was still acceptable—and legal—to discriminate against women, the African-American woman was at the bottom of the social ladder. There were few opportunities for black women outside of marriage: she could be a maid, take in laundry, cook, waitress, or work in a beauty salon. A precious few were teachers and nurses, but they were generally limited to working with African Americans. There were virtually no black women in religion, politics, medicine, the military, or the unions. And with the end of World War II, Rosie the Riveter—who was usually white—was sent home to make way for the boys returning from Iwo Jima and the beach at Anzio.

Even the entertainment world was heavily dominated by males. Some of the big bands had female lead singers and a few African-American blues and jazz artists scuffled around, playing the smaller clubs in Paradise Valley and Harlem. Brilliant artists such as Billie Holiday, Lena Horne, and Bessie Smith usually sang for chump change or scrounged for small roles as maids in white films.

Into this lily-white boys-only club barged three strong black women, gifted, indefatigable, undeniable: Sister Rosetta Tharpe, Clara Ward, and Mahalia Jackson. Together, they changed not only gospel music but they helped transform American popular music as well. Gospel music was one of the few places an African-American female could command respect in the face of a double whammy: endemic male sexism and a Jim Crow world.

Sister Rosetta Tharpe

America had never seen—nor has it seen since—anyone quite like Rosetta Tharpe. She was the Madonna of her day—fearlessly challenging roles and costumes and social mores. She was the Dolly Parton of her day—irrepressible, unfazed by criticism, a sexy girl from the country. She was the Queen Latifah of her day— larger than life, lavishly talented, able to move between seemingly irreconcilable worlds with consummate ease. "Before Tharpe," notes Jerma A. Jackson, "gospel singers enjoyed mostly local reputations in the African American communities in which they were a part. Performing in New York nightclubs and theaters, Tharpe extended the music to new audiences: secular, middle-class, and white."[3]

Tharpe is all but unknown to the staunchest gospel and jazz fans today, and yet she was featured twice in Martin Scorsese's epic series of films on PBS, (*Martin Scorsese Presents) the Blues*. In 2003, MC Records released *Shout, Sister, Shout: A Tribute to Rosetta Tharpe*, featuring Maria Muldaur (MC Records MC-0050), Phoebe Snow, Sweet Honey in the Rock, Marie Knight, and others performing some of Tharpe's best songs. And in October 2003, a tribute concert to Tharpe at the Bottom Line Cabaret in New York City boasted a lineup that included Odetta, the Holmes Brothers, the Dixie Hummingbirds, and more.

Little is known about Tharpe's early life. It's believed she was born in rural Arkansas in 1915, the daughter (although some writers believe she was the granddaughter) of Holiness evangelist Katie Bell Nubin. In later life she told stories of life as a child prodigy, mastering the guitar before the age of six, performing for thousands as a child. Katie Bell Nubin and Rosetta performed extensively before moving to Chicago, perhaps in the late 1920s or early 1930s. Like so many artists in the Pentecostal tradition, it's known that she once heard Arizona Dranes—and her singing often resembles Dranes's. She married her first husband, another Holiness revival preacher, the Reverend Thomas J. Tharpe in 1934, and he joined the singing/performing trio, barnstorming across the country.[4]

Tharpe caught the ear of the potent Decca label in 1938 and released four sides, backed by Lucky Millinder's jazz orchestra. According to musicologist Horace Boyer, "The members of the sanctified church were shocked, but the record-buying public went into a frenzy for this new singer with the new sound."[5]

John Hammond then featured Tharpe in the first "From Spirituals to Swing" concert at the end of that year, performing "Rock Me" (a remake of Thomas Dorsey's "Hide Me in Thy Bosom") and "That's All" (recorded in an earlier incarnation by Washington Phillips as "Denomination Blues I and II"), backed by boogie-woogie pianist Albert Ammons. Hammond recalled that she was a "surprise smash" and that she "knocked the people out."[6] There were more outcries from the Holiness church, whose members objected to Tharpe taking sacred music out of the church.

Not all the comments about "Rock Me" were negative, however. A writer for the Illinois Writer's Project noted that when Cab Calloway heard "Hide Me in Thy Bosom" he was "deeply impressed and engaged her to sing with his band." Tharpe's "inflection in saying 'Rock me, rock me in thy love'" so "swayed" her listeners that they "could see a double meaning in the words [so] that her success was assured." In fact, the bouncy rhythms in the song touched "answering chords in the make-up of the people in whom a love for rhythm was born."[7]

A second Decca session in January 1939 yielded several more hit songs, including the novelty tune that became her trademark, "This Train," Charles A. Tindley's "Beams of Heaven," and "Bring Back Those Happy Days."[8] One fascinating keyhole into Tharpe's life at this time comes from the pages of *Life* magazine, when African Americans were rarely featured in any national magazine. In the April 28, 1939, issue (next to an advertisement for MGM's splashy new musical, *The Wizard of Oz*) is an article headlined "Singer Swings Same Songs in Church and Night Club." The top picture features Tharpe performing with a large orchestra at the Church of God in Christ in Harlem. The bottom picture shows Tharpe dressed in white singing at the Cotton Club in Harlem, surrounded by jitterbugging dancers. The article gives Tharpe's age as twenty-four and states that she'd already written forty-seven new songs for future releases. It also features a few lines of her song "God Don't Like It":

> *I know you don't like my song*
> *I just made it up in my mind*
> *I won't take back not a word I said*
> *'Cause I sure don't drink moonshine*
> *God don't like it—I know he don't like it*

I know, ain't you glad he don't like it
I know it's scandalous and a shame[9]

In the days that followed, Tharpe toured New England and performed in other New York City venues. She parlayed her "bouncy melodies, aggressive guitar playing and ebullient stage presentation into a stardom that reached beyond gospel."[10] Tharpe soon became the most successful of all the guitar evangelists, including Blind Gary Davis. Like Davis, Tharpe originally used a "powerful, metal-bodied National resonator guitar" and, like Davis, "her guitar-playing was aggressive and skillful, with strong blues overtones." But whereas Davis remained a street singer, Tharpe's career blossomed when she moved permanently from playing tent revivals and "love offerings" in Holiness churches to New York in the 1930s.[11] Only Memphis Minnie could match Tharpe's prowess on the guitar among the admittedly few women who played guitar.

Through the 1940s, Tharpe fronted bands lead by Millinder, Benny Goodman, and Cab Calloway, "combining the smooth, orchestrated rhythms of the bands with her syncopated phrase, Tharpe filled her songs with unequivocal rhythmic intensity," as cited by Jerma Jackson. Another review claimed Tharpe could "make a Republican Senator rock."[12] She also frequently performed on the same bill with the likes of Bill "Bojangles" Robinson and Louis Armstrong. A third session for Decca in March 1941 resulted in recordings of Lucie Campbell songs "The End of My Journey" and "In the Upper Room" (later a big hit for Mahalia Jackson) and another Tindley song, "There Is Something within Me." Two months later she joined Lucky Millinder's big band as featured vocalist. Millinder's electrifying swing band was composed of some of the top African-American musicians in the country and was revered by black audiences. At different times during the band's run it featured Wynonie Harris, Dizzy Gillespie, and drummer David "Panama" Francis, among others. Tharpe and the Millinder band recorded a number of early "soundies"—three-minute films featured in "video jukeboxes" around the country. Among those that survive are their recordings of "Shout, Sister, Shout," "Four or Five Times," and "The Lonesome Road." In September 1941, Tharpe and Millinder and the band recorded "Shout, Sister, Shout," which peaked at twenty-one on the Harlem Hit Parade, the bestseller list for "race" records, the following year.[13]

Tharpe continued to record with Millinder and even took time, perhaps because of growing criticism within Pentecostal circles, to record a number of gospel songs under her own name, including "Precious Lord." Back with Millinder in February 1942, they recorded a novelty blues tune, "Tall Skinny Papa," which hit number thirteen on the Hit Parade the following summer. She also spent a week at New York's Café Society and sang with the Benny Goodman Orchestra.[14]

But just as Tharpe's career was gathering momentum, it was interrupted by America's first music strike. Founded in 1914, the American Society of Composers, Authors and Publishers (ASCAP) collected royalties and issued licenses from the performance of songs by its members, sales of its members' records, and the sale of original music to publishers. Only ASCAP-licensed music could be "played in Broadway musicals, performed on the radio and incorporated in the movies."[15] When ASCAP raised its rates in 1937, the National Association of Broadcasters rebelled. In 1939, NAB founded a competing organization, Broadcast Music, Incorporated (BMI), and busily set about creating an alternative library of music. When ASCAP increased its rates in 1940, NAB ended its ASCAP contracts at the end of that year. ASCAP's leadership declared a strike on January 1, 1941, and suddenly music by its members could no longer be broadcast.[16] The ban lasted ten months and radio listeners were suddenly confronted with public domain music ("Jeannie with the Light Brown Hair" was an unlikely hit) and the few BMI artists who were available. By October, most of the networks had buckled under the pressure and ASCAP music was back on the air.[17]

The American Federation of Musicians (AFM), led by James Caesar Petrillo, also joined the fray, announcing in mid-1942 that the AFM would not pursue new contracts with any recording labels once their contracts ended in July 1942. The AFM contended that the growth of jukeboxes and radio was eliminating jobs for musicians who performed "live" concerts and dances.[18] Like the ASCAP ban, this action only nominally impacted gospel, jubilee, country, and blues artists—since the AFM never considered them "real musicians."[19] In fact, John Hajduk argues that the strike actually helped these "marginalized" artists, especially country singers, who suddenly found themselves topping the charts.[20] By the end of World War II, this discord led to the appearance of numerous small independent labels, many owned by African Americans, all eager to supply the market with gospel, blues, rhythm and blues, and folk artists. Still searching for composers, BMI moved quickly to sign and assist these artists.[21] By the 1940s, there were still relatively few African-American members of ASCAP and no gospel composers.[22] Gospel's best-known writer, Thomas A. Dorsey, was no fan of ASCAP: "And, of course, until BMI came along, see, they wouldn't let we small fellows get in ASCAP, and they come along and gathered up all the small fellows, and made BMI. So that gave us all a break. So, now they look out for us; they come up and send us a check."[23]

The ban was lifted in 1944 and, despite terrible losses suffered by musicians, the music union was "successfully integrated into the business structure of the industry."[24]

Not surprisingly, public opinion was vociferously against both the AFM and ASCAP. To counter the attacks, the AFM volunteered to perform for the new Armed Forces Radio Services, providing taped "V-Disc" records, usually in front of enthusiastic groups of servicemen, to be aired overseas. The "AFRS Jubilee" shows featured African-American artists, including Marian Anderson, the Charioteers, the Golden Gate Quartet, and Tharpe. She made a number of transcriptions, usually backed by the Lucky Millinder band, often rerecording some of her earlier hits but now with a swinging big band.[25]

As the war wore on, Tharpe continued to record on her own and perform in such high-profile venues as the Streets of Paris, a popular Hollywood nightspot. A second round of V-Discs included accompaniment by Louis Jordan's legendary Tympany Five. Other Jubilee transcriptions included recordings with Erskine Hawkins's big band and the Noble Sissle Orchestra. In late November 1943, Decca organized several illegal recording sessions for Tharpe. These resulted in several classic tracks, including "Let That Liar Alone," "The Devil Has Thrown Him Down," and a "brilliantly moaning" version of her own composition, "I Want to Live So God Can Use Me." These were followed by several more V-Disc sessions, again with Lucky Millinder.[26]

In 1944, Tharpe recorded extensively with boogie-woogie pianist Sammy Price and his trio and hit the race-record Top 10 again, this time with "Strange Things Happening Every Day." The following year, Alan Lomax asked her (and Roy Acuff) to produce a program warning about the perils of venereal disease—in part because they were "the folk entertainers the masses trusted the most." In 1946, Tharpe released a series of duets with Marie Knight, another Sanctified singer with a "magnificent contralto." Their interplay delighted audiences and spawned still another *Billboard* hit, "Up Above My Head."[27]

The following year, Tharpe, now at the top of her game, chose the Dixie Hummingbirds to open for her on a prestigious series of dates. The Birds, now headliners in their own right, had just signed with Apollo Records and had impeccable credentials in the religious-record-buyer marketplace. Tharpe, however, was under increasing attack for appearing in nightclubs and releasing secular tunes. Her decision may have also been influenced by the fact that she began a long-term relationship with Barney Parks, the Birds manager and booking agent (and a former singer with the group). Tharpe told the *New York Amsterdam News* that she was now singing gospel exclusively—though she still quietly went "out west" to perform "a few nightclub dates on the q-t." Parks recalled that the dates with Tharpe were wildly successful:

> And Rosetta really brought them out. I took over the business that's when the Birds got on their feet. I booked them by themselves and booked them on shows with Rosetta. Because of Rosetta, I got them in armories in the Carolinas that blacks hadn't been in . . . places like the Bell Auditorium in Raleigh.[28]

Tharpe continued to record with Price and Knight, remaking old favorites like "This Train" and "Beams of Heaven," and a lovely version of "Precious Memories," which rose to number thirteen on the race chart in July 1948. But postwar American music tastes were changing and Tharpe never charted again.[29] Still, it hardly changed the gregarious, irrepressible Tharpe. Abner Jay, Tharpe's manager during the early 1950s, recalled that she was almost preternaturally generous. "And money, money, money, money, money she gave away more than anybody," he told Jerma Jackson. Whether traveling or simply shopping in town, Tharpe impulsively shared her wealth:

> Street corners, stop on the street corners start throwing it out the window. "It's sister Rosetta Tharpe." Stop in front of the schools and children be turning out. Stop on the street corner. "Come here, mama. You need a new dress. Here's fifty dollars. Sister Rosetta Tharpe gave it to you." And she—like we stayed in them homes, they's the places where we stayed. Like Spartanburg, South Carolina, for instance, told this woman, say, "Mama, you need a new stove and refrigerator. Come on, let's go downtown." Bought that woman a new stove and refrigerator.[30]

Sister Rosetta Tharpe had one more surprise. Only July 3, 1951, she married Russell Morrison, former manager of the Ink Spots, in an extraordinary ceremony in mammoth Griffith Stadium in Washington, D.C. The ceremony included her new backup group, the Rosette Gospel Singers, Vivian Cooper, the Sunset Harmonizers, the Harmonizing Four, Katie Bell Nubin, and a backing band. Tharpe performed before, during, and after the ceremony, and more than 20,000 people paid to see the extravaganza.[31] Tharpe wore "a $1,000 white nylon lace gown with a sequin-trimmed three-foot train,"[32] a $350 white orchard hand corsage, a $350 veil, and followed a 200-foot white carpet from the dugout to a platform ending at second base.[33] The entire ceremony and all of the musical performances were later released as *Wedding Ceremony of Sister Rosetta Tharpe* (Decca DL 5382).

Among those who didn't perform, however, was Marie Knight, since Morrison, an executive of the Savoy Ballroom, wanted to re-establish Tharpe as a solo artist rather than as part of a duet. The slight ended their long friendship and partnership. Even without Knight, the wedding boosted Tharpe's career enough for one more barnstorming tour of the United States, performing with as many as twenty other gospel acts in a series of "anniversary" concerts. But the close proximity to more polished urban gospel artists such as Dorothy Love Coates and the Original Gospel Harmonettes only emphasized Tharpe's country roots. Gradually, the bookings slowed to a few strongholds in the South.[34]

Sister Rosetta Tharpe's twilight years were spent trying to reclaim the glory years. Her dalliances with jazz and nightclubs finally alienated her from virtually all of her former Holiness and Sanctified connections. The well-known French critic Hughes Panassie sponsored a successful year-long tour of Europe. Tharpe charmed the English. An unknown *Melody Maker* journalist dutifully reported a five-hour interview with Tharpe in 1958 that ended with an embrace and a kiss— and an admonition for the writer to quit smoking.[35] She played two well-received dates at the Apollo in 1960 with the Caravans and James Cleveland, and even tore up the 1967 Newport Jazz Festival, garbed in a stylish mink stole.[36] A stroke in 1970 was followed by the amputation of a leg and more health problems. When Anthony Heilbut recorded one of the few known in-depth interviews with

Sister Rosetta Tharpe performing at an outdoor music festival, late in her career (photo: Diana Davies, courtesy of the Center for Folklife and Cultural Heritage, Smithsonian Institution)

Tharpe in her final year, he found her as cheerfully irresistible as ever, planning yet another comeback, reminiscing on a life spent furthering the boundaries of gospel. "Someday I'm gonna write the story of my life—the people will cry and cry. I've been robbed, cheated, married three times," she told Heilbut, "but God is so good." Tharpe died on October 9, 1973, following another stroke, just as she was returning to the recording studio for her first album in several years.[37]

Among those who heard her in the early 1960s was a young Maria Muldaur ("Midnight at the Oasis"), who later paid tribute to Tharpe by performing on *Shout, Sister, Shout*: "I had heard black gospel music before, but it was nothing like this. She came out in this blue taffeta skirt, plugged in and turn it up to 10. Her performance was electrifying. She just had this crackling, ebullient joy. Energy, conviction and joy. It was irresistible."[38]

Clara Ward

Which was the greatest gospel group of all time? The pantheon of greats usually begins and ends with the Roberta Martin Singers, the Caravans, and the Clara Ward Singers. And, in the end, it would be difficult to name anyone but the Clara Ward Singers as Queens of Gospel.

Not that Gertrude Ward would have allowed it any other way.

George and Gertrude Ward moved from South Carolina to Philadelphia following World War I and it was there that their daughters Willarene (Willa) and Clara were born. Although Baptists, the Wards were active in the "programs," Sanctified-styled singing sessions. Gertrude reported receiving a message from God in 1931: "Go sing my Gospel and help save dying and lost men and women." As early as 1934, she was organizing gospel concerts in Philadelphia that included the likes of Sallie Martin and Thomas A. Dorsey. Gertrude, Willa, and Clara formed the Consecrated Gospel Singers, with Clara showing precocious skill on the piano. The group was soon performing in a wide radius around the tristate area.[39]

Gertrude, a fine singer herself, was the "textbook stage mother" and her "truest talents were . . . of an entrepreneurial nature."[40] But young Clara was most influenced by gospel singers Clara Hudson (the "Georgia Peach") and Queen C. Anderson, of Memphis. The Georgia Peach was a frequent visitor to the Wards' home in Philadelphia, as was Thomas Dorsey, Rosetta Tharpe, and Pearl Bailey.[41] Anderson was a protégée of Herbert Brewster at East Trigg Baptist and something of an enigma. She is reputed to have had an astounding voice, one of the best in all of gospel music. "She had the most beautiful voice you ever heard," Brewster once said. "She could make a high voice and with her low soprano she would louden it and widen it and deepen it. It was just amazing to anybody that heard it."[42] But despite some of Brewster's best songs, including the first version of "Move On Up a Little Higher," her recordings were erratic at best.[43]

However, Anderson's recordings with the Brewster Singers profoundly moved Clara Ward, and as the young group searched for songs to sing, they continued to return to Brewster's music.

The group's turning point was the 1943 National Baptist Convention in Chicago, where they were frequent visitors at Mahalia Jackson's house and beauty salon. After passing muster with the imposing Lucie Campbell, they sang four songs, including Dorsey's "If We Never Needed the Lord Before."[44] Their exhilarating performance created a "sensation" at the convention, and the Consecrated Gospel Singers moved from semi-pro to professional, performing as far away as Buffalo, New York, and their one-time hometown of Anderson, South Carolina. With the additions of Henrietta Waddy and Marion Williams, the group became the Famous Ward Singers.[45] In time, the group's reputation expanded to the point that they were touring as far as Japan, Canada, and Mexico, though their records with Savoy had not been best-sellers.

The group's second breakthrough came in 1949, following a tour of California. Prior to an engagement in Knoxville, Clara unveiled a new arrangement of Brewster's "Surely God Is Able" in the revolutionary (for gospel music) three-quarter or waltz time. When Savoy didn't move quickly enough, the Wards took the song to the small Gotham label and enjoyed gospel music's second million-selling record.[46] Among the first to call to congratulate the group was Herbert Brewster. This began a long and successful collaboration.[47]

Brewster, who had been at East Trigg since 1930, was at the peak of his songwriting powers. Anthony Heilbut calls him the "key architect" of the Golden Age of Gospel. His music is theatrical and melodic, his lyrics are an uncanny blend of African-American idiom and his own vast reservoir of classical education.[48] Clara Ward and Brewster in particular formed an unbeatable bond. He liked her intelligent, demanding arrangements; she liked that he often wrote songs especially for her alto voice and distinctive phrasings.[49] Eventually, the Wards recorded more than twenty Brewster songs, including "Surely God Is Able," "How I Got Over," "God's Amazing Love," and "The Old Landmark." Other artists also found career-defining songs from his seemingly inexhaustible creative well—including Brother Joe May's "Leaning and Depending on Him," "Lord, I've Tried," recorded at different times by both the Soul Stirrers and the Swan Silvertones, and gospel's *first* million-seller, "Move on Up a Little Higher" by Mahalia Jackson.[50]

There is no "typical" Brewster song. They range from a "house-wrecker" like Mahalia's version of "Just Over the Hill" to the apocalyptic "The Book of the Seven Seals":

> *When the lamb had opened seal number two*
> *A blood-red horse came galloping through*
> *It was to make the earth tremble beneath his tread*
> *With ten thousand battlefields strewn with the dead.*[51]

As the Soul Stirrers' lead vocalist R. H. Harris once told Heilbut, "With all the other writers, you need to work to bring out the message. With Old Man Brewster, the message's already there, a singer can really go to town."[52] "Old Man" Brewster continued to write and preach at East Trigg Baptist Church in Memphis for nearly fifty-four years. He was an active participant in the civil rights movement, honored by the Smithsonian with concerts and a symposium in 1982 and remained active in the church until his death in 1987.[53]

Fueled by Brewster's songs and their own compositions—as well as by Gertrude's unfettered ambition—the Wards estimated that they racked up more than a million miles of nonstop touring between 1943 and 1957, wearing out fifteen automobiles in the process.[54] But the touring—and talent—paid off. Soon the group was appearing on major radio and television programming, including shows hosted by Dinah Shore, Ed Sullivan, as well as *The Today Show, The Tonight Show,* and Philadelphia's *Mike Douglas.* One notable appearance at Carnegie Hall with Mahalia Jackson marked the first performance by a gospel group in one of the world's great musical venues. Among those who heard them sing "Each Day," "Come Ye Disconsolate," "Stretch Out," and "Surely God Is Able" that night was actress Grace Kelly, whose boyfriend John Hyde immediately tried to sign the group to the William Morris theatrical booking agency "to sing pop music with a guarantee of megabucks." Gertrude Ward responded by screaming, "John Hyde, you're trying to tear down all I've built up. You're the Devil's disciple. You hear me? You're the Devil's disciple!"[55] In 1953, Clara founded Ward's House of Music, a publishing company designed to print, promote, and sell her original compositions and those of William Herbert Brewster. The operation began offering sheet music exclusively, but eventually sold recordings, greeting cards, and gospel's first souvenir tour books.[56] It was also during this period that the Wards began performing with the Reverend C. L. Franklin. Willa's biography *How I Got Over* claims that Clara and Franklin also began a long-term relationship. Clara and Franklin's daughter Aretha became lifelong friends during this time.[57]

The Reverend Franklin was one of the many graduates of Brewster's "schools" in Memphis and perhaps the dominant African-American preacher of the era. Another Mississippi native, he became a preacher, sometimes preaching at four different rural services in a day, before eventually being called to New Bethel Baptist in Detroit after stops in Memphis and Buffalo. Buoyed by a popular radio broadcast, he quickly built the church into one of Detroit's largest with more than ten thousand members.[58] Following his wife, Barbara's, death from a heart attack in 1951, he recorded a series of extraordinary sermons for Chess, JVB, Battle, and Jewel Records, some of which are still in print more than fifty years later, including "The Eagle Stirreth Her Nest," "The Prodigal Son," "Dry Bones in the Valley," "Give Me This Mountain," and "Except I Shall See in His Hands the Print of the Nails and Thrust My Hand into His Side." Some of these sermons have also been transcribed and collected in Franklin's biography, *Give Me This Mountain*.[59]

While as a young boy Franklin is known to have listened to the recorded sermons of Rev. J. M. Gates,[60] nothing can prepare the listener for the ferocious vocal attack on these recordings. Franklin uses his rough and raspy voice, sandpapered from years of preaching several high-energy sermons in a day, as a musical instrument, attacking and retreating, spitting the words in a harsh staccato, then breaking into a crooning hymn.

A few early recordings also feature the startling voice of his daughter Aretha, who would become the dominant rhythm-and-blues and soul singer of her generation. Aretha has admitted emulating her idol, Clara Ward, and years later recorded an album of hymns "which were not only taken from Clara's repertoire, but were in every phrase and cadence the style of her mentor."[61]

The group was also in the process of changing the "look" of gospel music. According to Willa Ward's *Mommie Dearest*-styled biography *How I Got Over*, the Wards were initially forced to perform in nightclubs to pay the medical bills following an accident that injured a relative,[62] although other sources say that Clara had always been interested in taking their music out of the church. It was during this time that the Wards adopted a wardrobe that consisted of diaphanous gowns instead of choir robes and an array of towering, elegant wigs. Clara designed and sewed many of the distinctive gowns and wigs, which prompted one awestruck fan to exclaim, "The Ward Singers were a psychedelic light show, and the other groups looked like an old silent movie."[63]

The Ward Singers were also among the first to perform in Harlem's famed Apollo Theater as part of Thurman Ruth's Gospel Caravans. Gospel artists performed four grueling shows a day and were required to remain onstage to maintain a "church-like" atmosphere when others were singing.[64] Ruth recalled that patrons used to come expressly to see what the Ward Singers were wearing that day:

> They were great singers and they'd dress fabulously, and their hairpieces were so nice. A group might outsing them, but they couldn't outdress them. They were real showmen. . . . [T]hey went out to Vegas and places like that. They used to go back to the old landmark singing and shouting and stuff in the service of the Lord. But the dressing was what really put them over. Clara was kind of ahead of her time. They had a big Rolls-Royce, or some big car. She was pretty smart. She paid some news guy to do public relations. Clara kept something about her or the Ward Singers in the papers all the time.[65]

In 1956, the Wards joined Mahalia Jackson and the Drinkard Singers as the first gospel artists to perform at the prestigious Newport Jazz Festival. Since so few mainstream publications were writing about African Americans or gospel music in the mid-1950s, this detailed account of the event printed in the then-popular *Coronet* magazine is an all-too-rare glimpse of the Wards at their peak:

> Out onto the stage, shyly yet with dignity, walked a slight woman dressed in a long, flowing gown of white. She sat down at the piano. Following her came five other women, dressed in filmy gowns of pink, yellow, blue and orange.
>
> They seemed nervous as they arranged themselves around a microphone and the women at the piano, Clara Ward, played a few bars of introduction. They glanced at each other as though to muster strength. And then with a smiling placidity—they sang.
>
> Rhythmic, high, clear in perfect harmony they sang, the words in metered, driving cadence, underscored by the piano. They began to clap their hands; and within seconds hundreds in the audience were clapping with them. The singers threw back their heads and went into a second chorus, fervent and joyous. The voice of one, a young girl of ample girth, soared above the others, whose voices beat a counterpoint behind her.[66]

The author's inappropriate remark about Marion Williams's weight aside, this is a fine contemporary description of two of the Wards' distinctive qualities: the group's inherent "dignity" and their beautiful, elegant gowns.[67] Other publications were equally effusive in their praise. *Ebony* magazine called Clara the "Glamour Girl of Gospel Singers" and trumpeted her $50,000 wardrobe: "Clara

Ward, a petite singer with the rhythmic genius of a jazz star, the emotional power of a great preacher and the flair of a sophisticated entertainer, is the current rage of the multi-million dollar gospel field."[68]

At the peak of their popularity in the mid- to late-1950s, Franklin and Clara Ward toured Israel following a whirlwind visit to Europe. By now acclaimed "the Queen of Gospel Singers," she gave an exclusive account (with photographs) of her tour to *Color* magazine, "How a Visit to the Holy Land Changed My Life." In addition to claiming that the visit deepened her songwriting, Ward used the article to defend the group's increasing presence in secular venues:

> . . . I now feel that God intended for His message to be heard not solely by those who attend churches, but also by the outsiders who, in many cases, never attend a house of worship. For that reason, the Ward Singers have taken our gospel singing into the Apollo Theatre in New York City, which brought some criticism from church leaders and laymen throughout the country. I don't mind that so much—since my visit to the Holy Land, I know whatever and wherever we sing, it will be done with new meaning and new inspiration.[69]

Sister Willa notes that the trip was one of the few times Clara was able to slip away from her mother's hawk-like scrutiny and adds ruefully, "As it turned out, this was the only vacation my sister ever had."[70]

Clara and C. L. eventually parted ways. She told *Ebony* magazine in 1957 that she had nearly married "a prominent . . . western minister" two years earlier: "We were going steady for about six years, which I believe is what was wrong with our courtship. I think a long courtship is just no good. You get to learn too much about a person."[71] Still, the Wards continued on their hot streak, releasing numerous memorable albums for Savoy: *Lord, Touch Me* (1956), *That Old Landmark* (1958), and *Down by the Riverside: Live at the Town Hall, New York City* (1958). All featured an unbeatable combination of Brewster and Ward originals, Clara's stunning arrangements, and Marion Williams's powerful, effortless vocals.[72] Following one particularly scintillating rehearsal for *The Ed Sullivan Show*, Elvis Presley—who called Clara "Little Sister"—approached the Wards about recording an album together, only to see Colonel Tom Parker nix the idea, fearing that "some of Elvis' fans might not approve of the race mix."[73]

But all was not well with the Famous Ward Singers. Despite the group's success, Gertrude was by all accounts notoriously tightfisted with the receipts, funneling most of the money to her own accounts. When Williams finally quit over her low salary, she was soon followed by the other core members, Frances Steadman and Kitty Parham. Though Gertrude and Clara hired other first-rate singers in the years that followed (including Thelma Houston), the Wards never recovered.[74]

To combat half-empty churches, the newly reconfigured Wards began performing at Disneyland and in 1961 signed a lucrative (for the time) contract to perform forty weeks a year at the New Frontier in Las Vegas. They also relocated from Philadelphia to Los Angeles.[75] Eventually, even Willa was estranged from her mother and started her own groups, though the Wards reformed for President Lyndon Johnson's inaugural ceremonies and gala.[76]

Gertrude assembled several other groups bearing the "Ward" name, which toured extensively from Japan to Europe. Clara, fresh off a Broadway production of Langston Hughes's *Tambourines to Glory*, even headlined a USO tour of Vietnam in 1966.[77] But the following year, while performing at the Castaways in Miami, she suffered what appeared to be a severe aneurysm and stroke on the stage. Weeks later, she made what was widely reputed to be a "miraculous" recovery. Now billed as "God's Miracle Girl," Clara even made a film with Hank Williams, Jr., *A Time to Sing* (1968), as an angelic gospel singer who mysteriously counsels wayward country singer Grady Dodd (Williams).

Clara continued to perform into the 1970s with the Ward Singers at venues such as Caesar's Palace and the Monterey Jazz Festival, and with the Ward Singers continued to record for Verve, including *The Faith, the Heart, the Soul of Clara Ward*, which sold very well.[78] But the group never regained its former status. Clara died of a second stroke in January 1973 at forty-eight, exhausted from a lifetime of overwork and Gertrude's manic domineering control. Two subsequent memorial services, both organized by Gertrude, featured most of the best-known names in gospel music. Following an impassioned sermon by her father, Aretha Franklin sang Clara's "The Day Is Past and Gone" in Philadelphia, while Marion Williams sang "Surely God Is Able" in Los Angeles. Gertrude Ward would outlive her daughter by more than a decade.[79]

Most of Clara Ward's admirers prefer even now to remember the lovely young lady with the towering hair of the 1950s rather than the haggard self-parody playing Vegas in the late 1960s. "I watched her carry gospel into many, many places where it hadn't been before and where it hasn't been since," James Cleveland is quoted as saying. "Giants fall and little chips grow. Many young persons who were inspired by her, as I am, will pick up and carry on like Clara would have wanted them to."[80]

"It's all from the heart," Clara Ward once told *Newsweek*. "It gets you so much all over you, you just can't be still. You just can't imagine what it's like. But we don't just sing music that has no meaning. Our songs plead for sinners just like Billy Graham does in Madison Square Garden."[81]

Mahalia Jackson

Mahalia Jackson towers over the history of gospel music like Louis Armstrong towers over the history of jazz. Like Armstrong, Jackson was originally from New Orleans but initially made her mark in Chicago. And like Armstrong, her later years are marred by charges of sell-out and compromise. But nothing can diminish Mahalia's impact on gospel music, even today. Jackson is a larger-than-life figure, an icon, an Earth Mother with a once-in-a-lifetime presence and voice.

Ralph Ellison writes that Mahalia Jackson was not primarily a concert singer but a "high priestess (who) sings within the heart of the congregation as its own voice of faith."[82] To those lucky enough to have heard her in a church setting, it was indeed a transcendent, mystical experience.

Jackson is the best-chronicled of all gospel artists, the subject of several books, including a nondescript "autobiography" (*Movin' on Up*) and an alternately wonderful/infuriating biography with Laurraine Goreau, *Just Mahalia, Baby*. She was the subject of several documentaries and—unlike most of her contemporaries—regularly interviewed by some of the best-known newspapers and magazines in the United States. Because of her numerous television appearances, for many people, Mahalia Jackson will always be the "face" of gospel music. At a time when precious few African Americans were ever seen on TV, Mahalia was a *star*.

The circumstances of her impoverished childhood in New Orleans are well known, even to noninitiates, although the exact year of her birth is still uncertain (probably 1912). Mahala (which she later changed to the more euphonious Mahalia) rarely saw her father, Johnny Jackson, a Baptist preacher and longshoreman. When her mother died when Jackson was five, she was raised by an extended family that included a brother, six aunts, and a number of half siblings—also children of her father.

While she grew up attending the hymn-filled services of Mount Moriah Baptist Church, her adopted family's house was next door to a rockin' Holiness church, complete with instruments and the rhythms of New Orleans' hardscrabble Pinching Town.

One of Jackson's earliest memories was of Blind Frank, who played his guitar and sang in Holiness churches for "Sanctified people" throughout the Crescent City. "They sang the way I liked," she recalled years later, "with free expression. That's where I think jazz caught its beat. From the Holiness people. Long before Buddy Bolden and Bunk Johnson, they were clapping their hands and beating their tambourines and blowing their horns."[83]

And to get from home to church and back again, she had to pass the bars and clubs playing Buddy Bolden and Louis Armstrong and New Orleans' rich gumbo of blues, jazz, and Dixieland.[84]

Just where this voice comes from is even less clear. Years later, her longtime friend Studs Terkel once asked Jackson when she first began singing:

> You might as well ask when did I first begin to walk and talk. In New Orleans . . .
> I remember singing as I scrubbed the floors. It would make the work go easier.
> When the old people weren't home, I'd turn on a Bessie Smith record. And play
> it over and over. "Careless Love," that was the blues she sang. . . . That was before
> I was saved. The blues are fine, but I don't sing them. Just remember, all I'm

saying about my listening to Bessie and imitating her when I was a little girl: just remember this was before I was saved.

I'd play that record over and over again, and Bessie's voice would come out so full and round. And I'd make my mouth do the same thing. And before you know, all the people would stand outside the door and listen.

I didn't know what it was at the time. All I know is it would grip me. It would give me the same feeling as when I'd hear the men singing outside as they worked, laying the ties for the railroad. I liked the way Bessie made her tones.[85]

Today, it's Smith voice that listeners sometimes still hear on Jackson's classic recordings. "Bessie was my favorite," she said, "though I never let people know I listened to her. She dug right down and kept it in you. Her music haunted you even when she stopped singing."[86]

A talented singer as a young girl, Jackson devoted herself exclusively to the church following an emotional conversion experience at age fourteen. Even then, recalled a friend, "That voice *carry!* She [Mahalia] told the story of how she prayed and got converted . . . told her vision and the moment when the Lord spoke to her . . . how she *knew* she had religion; there was not a doubt. Then she came through with that long meter and she set that church on *fire.*"[87] Jackson's uninhibited performance, complete with a Holiness-inspired "spirit" dance, was already taking form.

Eager to work and strike out on her own, Jackson accepted an invitation from an aunt to relocate to Chicago on the Illinois Central in late November 1927. Shortly after her arrival, she attended the Greater Salem Baptist Church. "It was the most wonderful thing that ever happened to me," Jackson said later.[88] She soon found employment in a succession of low-paying jobs, frequently heard some of Chicago's finest musical talent on the South Side (including Louis Armstrong), and founded a singing group at Greater Salem with the three Johnson brothers, Robert, Prince, and Wilbur. Powered by Prince's piano playing and Mahalia's solos, the quartet was immediately popular in the church.[89] "Looking back," Jackson recalled, "I'd say that Prince really was the first gospel piano player in Chicago and we were really the first Negro gospel group in the city." Soon, the Johnson Singers were invited to perform at other churches in Bronzetown.[90]

But as Thomas Dorsey had already discovered, black Chicago's conservative Protestant churches were not ready for Mahalia. During their first performance, the pastor rose in anger and shouted for the group to get "that twisting and that jazz" out of his church. Jackson coolly responded, "This is the way we sing down South! I been singing this way all my life in church!"[91] Fortunately, there were numerous storefront churches along State Street on the South Side. And even closer than Greater Salem was the prosperous Pilgrim Baptist, where a young man named Dorsey was making a name for himself. "It was in this time that I heard Mahalia," he later told Laurraine Goreau. "She had a voice that nobody

More than thirty years after her death, Mahalia Jackson remains the most famous gospel singer in the world. (courtesy of Southern Folklife Collection, University of North Carolina, Chapel Hill)

ever had or anybody ever will have . . . the trills, tones, the spirit. They enjoyed her religion—that was the key, the core."[92]

Dorsey quickly asked Jackson to sing and promote his new sheet music business in 1929. "She was the only singer who would take my music," he recalled. "Mahalia would stand on a street corner and demonstrate it; then we'd sell a batch: 10 cents each. She was actually about the only gospel singer, besides Sallie Martin, when she came in."[93] While Martin handled the bulk of the out-of-state travel, Jackson continued to perform both with the Johnson Singers and as a solo, often singing from a battered copy of *Gospel Pearls*. In time, as word of her prodigious talent spread, her requests at first included churches and revivals in nearby states, then venues as far away as New York as well. "Gospel music in those days of the early 1930s was really taking wing," she said. "It was the kind of music colored people had left behind them down South and they liked it because it was just like a letter from home."[94]

Eventually, Jackson began accompanying Dorsey to larger and larger church meetings and conventions, still promoting his songs. Acceptance still ranged from slow to hostile among the large African-American churches. At one church, still another pastor denounced her singing in the pulpit. "I got right up, too," Jackson writes in her autobiography. "I told him I was born to sing gospel music. Nobody had to teach me. I was serving God. I told him I had been reading the Bible every day most of my life and there was a Psalm that said: 'Oh, clap your hands all ye people! Shout unto the Lord with the voice of a trumpet.' If it was undignified, it was what the Bible told me to do."[95]

"I want my hands . . . my feet . . . my whole body to say all that is in me. I say, 'Don't let the devil steal the beat from the Lord! The Lord doesn't like us to act dead. If you feel it, tap your feet a little—dance to the glory of the Lord!'"[96]

It was dawning on everybody who heard her that Mahalia Jackson, still just a teenager, was a special talent. Couple that voice with the new, looser Dorsey gospel songs and her slow, dramatic renditions of beloved Baptist hymns, and she became an irresistible force. "Jackson's appeal," writes Michael Harris, "rested on her adherence to the deeply emotive manner of singing that one finds referred to among enslaved African Americans as being heard in their secret meetings."[97] And in Chicago, the new southern immigrants found the closest substitute for their secret meetings in the Holiness storefront churches. "She [Jackson] and the Johnson Singers regularly performed at storefronts, the most common sites for the new settlers' urban bush harbor meetings," Harris adds. "There, where she was literally among her own, she helped them retain the old spirituality: 'Halie was a fresh wind from the down-home religion.'"[98] Besides the storefront churches, only the "progressive" Baptist churches like Pilgrim and Greater Salem allowed this kind of music. Through the sheer force of her will—and talent—Mahalia Jackson slowly broke down long-held barriers:

> In those days, the big colored churches didn't want me and they didn't let me in. I had to make it my business to pack the little basement-hall congregations and storefront churches and get their respect that way. When they began to see the crowds I drew, the big churches began to sit up and take notice because even inside the church there are people who are greedy for money.[99]

Jackson, like Dorsey, arrived at a particular point in time, a point where—in retrospect—it is always easy to identify the intersection of demand and talent. It's possible that Mahalia's gift was such that had she arrived earlier or later she still would have had an overpowering impact. In writing about Frank Sinatra, musicologist Henry Pleasants says that he was "neither pioneer nor radical." Instead, he claims Sinatra was "simply a musical genius who arrived at a moment predestined for that genius."[100] The parallel with Mahalia is unmistakable. Hindsight indicates that where the demand for this kind of music meets this kind of talent, something lasting always occurs:

> And with the changing music came a new style of performance, a style that emphasized movement and improvisation, a style that demanded emotional involve-

ment and personalized expression. Dorsey's model singers—those who initially presented the songs and then coached the young choruses—all came straight out of the sanctified church. Sallie Martin, Mahalia Jackson and Willie Mae Ford Smith all believed in letting the Holy Ghost have Its way; each of them made this belief performatively obvious in her singing. The new choruses, under these vocalists' careful tutelage, thus learned more than just new tunes. They also received training in the freedom and faith of singing in the Spirit.[101]

Especially in the African-American Holiness churches, "experience pervades all description of worship and performance." Each service, each song, is designed to invite the presence of the Holy Spirit, the third member of the Protestant church's "Holy Trinity." What Jackson was apparently able to do better than virtually all singers before or after her, according to numerous eyewitness accounts, was take listeners to a place where they could feel the "touch" of the Holy Spirit. This is an experience, writes Glenn Hinson, that is best "described in metaphors of fire and mystery":

> Transcending emotion, this spiritual "anointing" is upheld as the pinnacle of human experience. Its advent—said to be facilitated by the mind-focusing power of praise and prayer, song and sermon—serves as the experiential leitmotif of religious expression in the sanctified church.[102]

How Mahalia Jackson came to possess such a voice, one that so effortlessly brought about this "anointing," may ultimately be impossible to determine. Perhaps it was simply a gift, like the one bestowed on Mozart. Its origins—and its recipient's worthiness—may vex the likes of a Salieri in Milos Forman's *Amadeus*,[103] but it is readily apparent to all who hear it. In many African-American churches, the absence or presence of such a gift is signaled by a series of responses from the congregation. According to a study by Mellonee Burnim, respondents repeatedly and consistently reported that for the Holy Spirit to be present, the singer is required to possess a voice that "must transmit intensity, fullness, and the sense that tremendous energy is being expelled." If this happens, the congregation will spontaneously respond with phrases such as:

> "She's blowing!"
> "She's jamming; she can't help it!"
> "(The) girl is burning!"
> "Now that's getting it, boy."
> "She's tough."
> "Sing!"
> "She's getting down."
> "The girl needs to sit down and rest a while!"
> "I guess after that song that's all you need to do."[104]

This, of course, is exactly what happened in the numerous contemporary accounts of Mahalia Jackson's performances. During a particularly emotional church service during this period, Laurraine Goreau records one overwhelmed congregant as shouting, "That woman sing too *hard*; she going to have TB!"[105]

And thus, in the heart of the Depression, began the rise of one of America's greatest singers. Jackson soon began singing for local Democratic politicians, a precursor of her deep involvement in the civil rights movement. She signed with her first manager, Robert H. Miller, the owner of a South Side funeral home who not only got her $2 per funeral, but who upped her out-of-town fee to fifty cents per person. She also married her first husband, Isaac "Ike" Hockenhull.[106] In 1937, J. Mayo "Ink" Williams heard her sing at a funeral. Williams, a talent scout for industry giant Decca Records, made her Decca's first gospel artist. Jackson recorded four songs, including "God's Gonna Separate the Wheat from the Tares" and "You Sing On, My Singer." "God's Gonna Separate the Wheat from the Tares" was only a modest seller outside of Chicago, although it did well in the Deep South. It also prompted both Earl "Fatha" Hines and Louis Armstrong to invite her to join their groups. Mahalia declined both offers and did not record again until 1946.[107]

As her bookings increased, Jackson saved enough money in 1939 to open Mahalia's Beauty Salon near Pilgrim Baptist and soon had enough employees to cover the business while she traveled nearly every weekend from Detroit to St. Louis to sing.[108] The salon and Jackson's kitchen became the center of an informal group of singers who supported one another personally and professionally: Theodore Frye, Robert Anderson, Roberta Martin, Ruth Lee Jones (who would become Dinah Washington), and, when they were in town, Willa Mae Ford Smith, Sister Rosetta Tharpe, and the Ward Singers.[109]

By now, the Johnson Singers had quietly dissolved and Jackson was no longer able to tour in support of Dorsey's sheet music, in part because he never gave her a percentage of the sales. But one night in December 1940, when her regular pianists were elsewhere occupied, Dorsey agreed to accompany Mahalia on the piano for a standing-room-only program at the large Morning Star Baptist Church. Following performances by Roberta Martin and Frye, Jackson sang "The Day is Past and Gone." According to Goreau, it was on this night that Dorsey made official Jackson's status as the premiere gospel singer in Chicago:

> Ecstasy swept the church like a wave, people bobbing, rising, running on its crest, even Dorsey, the always contained Dorsey unable to keep his seat, to still his voice so that he rose from the piano and cried, "Mahalia Jackson's the Empress of gospel singers! She's the Empress! The Empress!"[110]

Members of the congregation would certainly catch the unmistakable allusion in Dorsey's ecstatic praise—revered blues singer Bessie Smith had long since earned the coveted sobriquet "the Empress of the Blues" by selling millions of records in the 1920s.[111]

Through the war years, Jackson's reputation continued to spread through church circles. She became friends with the Reverend C. L. Franklin, his wife, Barbara, and their daughter Aretha. In the days before he became famous, a young man named James Cleveland hung around the salon, looking for work, picking up tips on singing from some of gospel music's biggest stars. In the fall of 1946, top African-American promoter Johnny Meyers booked Jackson in New York City's Golden Gate Auditorium for the unheard of sum of $1,000.[112]

Meyers also arranged a meeting with Bess Berman, director of A&R for the new Apollo label. Jackson was just happy to have *anybody* interested in her music. Goreau's quirky biography says that Jackson sang an a cappella solo in the Apollo offices and that Berman said, "You could sing the blues." Mahalia's response, apparently recorded verbatim, is an informative glimpse into Jackson's motivations:

> Honey, what Negro couldn't sing the blues? That's the Devil working on you. Sing the blues, what you got? You down in a deep pit, crying for help. You end up—you ain't got it; you where you started. Despair. But gospel. Now gospel might start sad—you down; but honey, you already know there's hope; and time you finish, you have found the cure. And so have the people listening. That's singing for the Lord. Plenty people like it.[113]

Apparently satisfied with Jackson's response, Berman approved four sides: "I'm Going to Tell God All About It One of These Days," "I Want to Rest," "He Knows My Heart," and "Wait Till My Change Comes." But Mahalia's records initially fared poorly, save for in Chicago where young DJ Studs Terkel played them religiously. Berman was ready to drop Jackson from the label, but producer Art Freeman wanted to give her one more chance with a song he'd heard her warm up with, Herbert Brewster's "Move on Up a Little Higher."[114] With the then-unusual backing of both an organ and a piano to help retain the New Orleans beat of Mahalia's "head arrangement," the song was an immediate smash in early 1948. Stores couldn't keep up with the demand for "Move On Up a Little Higher Parts I and II" and it became gospel's first million-selling release, ultimately selling an astonishing two million copies. "Virtually overnight," says one source, "Jackson became a superstar."[115]

Paired with her greatest accompanist, pianist Mildred Falls, and soon aligned with the William Morris Agency, Mahalia enjoyed an unparalleled twenty years of commercial success. The Apollo albums in particular are classics, untouchable renditions of gospel songs by a voice in the prime of its power and command. Picking standout tracks from the Apollo years is a archivist's nightmare, but the *New Grove Gospel Blues and Jazz* cites the more bluesy tracks, such as "In the Upper Room," "Let the Power of the Holy Ghost Fall on Me," and "I'm Glad

Salvation Is Free" because of the "majesty of her singing and the remarkable melisma of the vocal line."[116] Other classic tracks include "Even Me," "Prayer Changes Things," "Dig a Little Deeper," and "In My Home Over There." Of the singing during these years, musicologist Wilfred Mellers expressively notes:

> The magnificent voice and the fervent faith are almost inseparable; a voice of such vibrancy, over so wide a range, creates a sound that is as all-embracing, as secure as the womb, from which singer and listener may be reborn.
> The breathtaking beauty of the voice and the superbly controlled transitions from speech to prayer to song heal and anneal.[117]

What Jackson may have been the most gifted at ties her closely to the most ancient of the African threads that knitted the spirituals: "surge" singing. When singing in this style, John Storm Roberts writes that Mahalia would slow down certain spirituals and the older "long meter" Baptist hymns, stretch out the syllables, and spontaneously add soaring, sometimes breathtaking trills, whoops, glissandos, and moans.[118] William H. Tallmadge also ties it to the ancient practice of "lining out" hymns and the "long meter" singing of the beloved "Dr. Watts" songs in the African-American church.[119] Again, it is Mellers who perhaps best describes a typical Mahalia Jackson "surge" treatment of a familiar gospel song:

> "In the Upper Room" begins very slowly, with tremolando chords on organ. From that womb of sound the vocal line tenebrously emerges, gradually taking wing in coloratura of immense range, while the chorus throbs in chromatic harmony that is a sophistication of the improvised homophony of plantation choirs. The performance is the experience, as the voice climbs from the sultry register of the "low room" to the ethereal heights of the "upper room." Transcendence is enhanced as the tempo quickens and jazz elements—blue notes, scoops, slides, elisions and syncopations—grow more obtrusive.[120]

Only Marion Williams and Aretha Franklin have been able to come close to matching Mahalia Jackson's brand of surge singing, and even then only on selected songs in selected venues.

With the commercial success came increasing recognition. Jackson brought gospel to Carnegie Hall in late 1950, the first of several triumphant concerts in that legendary venue. She was regularly featured first on Terkel's Chicago television series, then as one of the first African Americans on a host of national television programs, including Arthur Godfrey's number-one show, the *Dinah Shore Show* (Shore became a lifelong friend), and Dave Garroway's *Garroway at Large*. Her recording of "I Can Put My Trust in Jesus" won *Grand Prix du Disque* of 1950 from the Charles Cros Academie of France, followed the next year by a triumphant tour of Europe. In 1954, she even became the host of her own weekly radio series on CBS, which soon generated high ratings even with white listeners.[121] But Jackson was not receiving appropriate royalties for her work with

Apollo, and when she received an offer from Mitch Miller with industry leader Columbia Records, she called one of the few people she trusted in the music industry, John Hammond. Hammond's memory of his advice was: "Mahalia, if you want ads in *Life*, and to be known by the white audience, do it. But if you want to keep on singing for the black audience, forget signing with Columbia, because they don't know the black market at all."[122]

But Jackson, while doing better financially, had never moved far from her poverty-stricken roots. She took Columbia's offer, which—while financially lucrative—exacted hidden costs. To reach the white audience, the label insisted her songs be "cluttered" with the addition of "large choruses and orchestras with sweeping strings."[123] When the much slighter tune "Rusty Old Halo" was a surprise *Billboard* hit, producers such as Percy Faith soon saddled her with even less overtly religious songs, such as "Danny Boy," "Trees," "Summertime," "You'll Never Walk Alone," and even "Guardian Angel" with Harpo Marx (!) on harp. Virtually everything Hammond had predicted quickly came to pass:

> . . . [S]he lost the black market to a horrifying degree. I'd say that by her death she was playing to a 75 percent white audience, maybe as high as 90 percent. Columbia gave her the fancy accompaniments, and the choirs, but the wonderful drive and looseness from the Apollo recordings was missing. Did Mahalia miss the black audience? Mahalia was only interested in money, to be specific with you.[124]

If Hammond's comments sound harsh, they only reflect the critical comment that followed most of her recordings in the 1960s. As Anthony Heilbut sadly notes, "Mahalia, the musical daughter of Bessie Smith, was effectively modified into a black Kate Smith."[125] By the late 1950s, her fees put her out of reach of virtually every African-American church in America. Jackson, of course, was well aware of the criticism. In an interview with Nat Hentoff in 1958, she frankly admitted she was not happy with her relationship with Columbia:

> One thing I'll say about Columbia, is that they put me in a new field. They got me on TV and they paid me well. The only thing they haven't been too particular about is my songs. I like to sing the songs I feel. They got ideas of what's commercial. Some of the songs they pick for me I don't understand, and those I couldn't put myself into. At least at Apollo I picked what I wanted.[126]

Fortunately, nothing could forever dim the voice of an age. Old-friend Duke Ellington convinced her to sing in his jazz symphony *Black, Brown and Beige* that year, and her rendition of "Come Sunday" with Ellington playing aching simple piano accompaniment is unforgettable.[127] Several stunning performances at the Newport Jazz Festival in the late 1950s regained much of Jackson's cachet with critics (she was named one of the top four jazz vocalists in a *Downbeat* magazine poll—much to her dismay) and resulted in a memorable album by the same name.[128] In 1959, she even appeared in the film *Imitation of Life* with Lana Turner, singing the "23rd Psalm" during the movie's emotional funeral sequence.[129] Also of merit is *In the Upper Room* from 1965, featuring Mildred Falls and two gospel groups—one of the few times Mahalia "sings with an incendiary passion that rivals her classic '40s recordings."[130] Of the later work, Jackson told Hentoff that she was happy with the single "God Is So Good" and the album *Bless This House*:

> They [Columbia] didn't want to make that, I just begged them. The song was so much of my life, I thank God who brought me from down in Louisiana to the present day. I forgot I was in the studio making it when I sang. And as for the albums, there's more original Mahalia in *Bless This House* than the other albums made for Columbia.[131]

Where Jackson did make a difference was in the political arena. A staunch Democrat, Mahalia worked for both President Harry S Truman and Chicago Mayor Richard Daley, and her singing of "I Been 'Buked, I Been Scorned" was a highlight of the Prayer Pilgrimage for Freedom before 35,000 people at the Lincoln Memorial on May 17, 1957. "She had a strange effect on the secularists present," wrote Hentoff in the *Reporter*. "Most of them were amazed at the length of time after the concert during which the sound of her voice remained active in the mind."[132] Jackson also sang "The Star-Spangled Banner" at President John F. Kennedy's inauguration in 1961 and sat on the president's platform as a Distinguished Guest.[133]

Following a second triumphal tour of Europe where she was treated to an Elvis-like frenzy in every city—including Rome, where she had an audience with Pope John XXIII—Jackson toured the Holy Land.[134] Jackson aligned herself with longtime friend Dr. Martin Luther King, Jr., performing constantly at a host of fund-raising and consciousness-raising events for the civil rights movement, despite increasing health problems brought on by her ballooning weight, cardiac hypertension, and multisystem sarcoidosis.[135] She almost single-handedly raised more than $50,000 with a gala concert in Chicago to make bail for the two thousand sympathizers arrested in Birmingham in April 1963 for protesting segregation in that city.[136] In August, she was one of the headliners for the March on Washington for Jobs and Freedom, singing "Take My Hand, Precious Lord" and "I Been 'Buked" in front of a crowd of more than 200,000 just before King's legendary "I Have a Dream" speech.[137] A later biography cites activist Ben Hooks as saying it was Jackson's suggestion to King to deliver the "I Have a Dream" speech, which she had heard at a previous engagement together in Detroit. According to Hooks, King agreed and scrapped the previously approved address.[138]

And in the manic hours following President Kennedy's assassination, Jackson was everywhere in Chicago, appearing on television, during nonstop radio interviews, pleading for calm, praying for peace, singing "Nearer My God to Thee" and "Deep River," though it would be years before she was emotionally able to sing "Deep River" again.[139] Despite a still worsening physical condition and heart problems that left her bedridden for nearly a year and a second disastrous marriage and an even more disastrous divorce, she continued to work with King and plan both a church and a "temple" for the disadvantaged in Chicago. The murders of King and Robert Kennedy devastated Mahalia, who vowed to continue the fight:

> When I sang "Precious Lord, Take My Hand" at Martin Luther King's funeral, my grief seemed almost too much to bear. But when a reporter came to me after Dr. King and Senator Kennedy had been killed and said, "How do you carry on?" I said to him, "There can be no turning away. There's a right to feel doubtful and despondent about things, but that is the time when you can't let your spirit and determination weaken. We've got to remember these men lived for the good because it's needed so much now."[140]

Jackson's death from heart failure on January 27, 1972, prompted worldwide headlines, from a "visibly moved" Indian premiere Indira Gandhi to U.S. president Richard Nixon, who declared a statement of mourning for the nation. Lying in state at Greater Salem Baptist Church in Chicago, forty thousand mourners braved the icy winds to file past her coffin.[141] At the Chicago service in the Arie Crown Theatre, ten thousand bereaved listeners heard a variety of elegies, none more touching than that of Coretta King, "A woman with extraordinary gifts as a singer, singing songs, of her people. She was my friend and she was a friend of mankind." And after an emotional pause, King recalled how her husband had once said of Mahalia, "'A voice like this one comes not once in a century, but once in a millennium.'" Albertina Walker and Ella Fitzgerald both sang, followed by Aretha Franklin, who closed with "Take My Hand, Precious Lord." Back home in New Orleans, thousands lined the streets and another sixty thousand paid their respects in a New Orleans auditorium. A long procession delivered her body to Providence Memorial Park in nearby Metairie, just as the pre-Lenten carnival was about to begin and funeral dirges turned into high-stepping Dixieland jazz.[142]

Perhaps it is just an odd coincidence, but Mahalia's passing was followed in a year and a half by the deaths of both Clara Ward and Sister Rosetta Tharpe.

Three strong black women: gifted, indefatigable, undeniable.

Chapter Eleven

The Great Gospel Groups:
Six Unforgettable Voices

"The girls worked in the starching department used to sing spirituals to enable them to breathe standing ten hours and sticking their hands into almost boiling starch."
"Boiling?" I interrupted.
"Almost. It's so hot that they have to put camphor ice on their hands before they can put them into the starch. Cold starch is better but hot starch is cheaper—and you know the bosses," she winked. "As I said before, the starchers used to sing, 'Go Down, Moses,' 'Down by the Riverside,' and God, the feeling they put in their singing. As tired as we were, those spirituals lifted up our spirits and we joined in sometimes. That was too much pleasure to have while working for his money, said the boss, and the singing was out.
"But that was where the boss made his mistake. While singing we would forget our miserable lot, but after the singing was cut out, it gave us more time for thinking—thinking about our problems."

—Evelyn Macon[1]

I mean, it's a wonderful thing that Afro-American people gave to us. I mean, without that music, I mean, just imagine. We'd be living like those English folks, and those French folks, man. It'd be a horrible existence, you know what I mean? And because of those wonderful Afro-Americans, the whole world is now enjoying all that music.

—Wolfman Jack[2]

The post–World War II era, from 1945 to 1965, is often called gospel's "Golden Age." And while different writers identify different events that "end" this unofficial time frame, many of the genre's best-known artists recorded much of their greatest music during this period. To even mention all of them would turn this into little more than a laundry list of names. But what an experience it must have been to have the world's best gospel artists performing live every weekend in virtually every city in America!

The postwar era signaled a profound shift in the public's taste for popular music. When pricing ceilings were lifted after World War II, everything suddenly cost more, including gasoline, hotel rooms, and musician's salaries. One by one, the big bands folded—save those of Duke Ellington and Count Basie, which had always counted pennies. In their wake, hundreds of smaller groups emerged, including those playing rhythm and blues and gospel. As the final travel restrictions were lifted, those groups hit the roads.[3]

The postwar era saw important technological advances as well, including "high fidelity," which permitted a greater range of frequencies to be captured on vinyl records. By the early 1950s, the new 45-rpm disks had finally eclipsed the fragile ten-inch 78s. In 1952, not only had fifteen million 45s been produced for jukebox use, but many labels were re-releasing their older 78s in the new 45-rpm format.[4]

Equally important is the corresponding rise of small record labels to service the suddenly burgeoning interest in rhythm and blues, blues—and gospel. The small independent labels moved much quicker in response to public demand than the prewar giants Decca, Victor, and Capitol.[5] Between 1942 and 1952 a host of aggressive new labels sprang up:

Savoy Records—founded by Herman Lubinsky in Newark
Apollo Records—founded by Bess and Ike Berman in New York City
King Records—founded by Syd Nathan in Cincinnati
Modern Records—founded by Jules, Joe, and Sual Bihari in Los Angeles
Bronze Records—founded by Leon Hurte in Los Angeles
Specialty Records—founded by Art Rupe in Los Angeles
Atlantic Records—founded by Herb Abrahamson and Ahmet Ertegun in New York
Aristocrat/Chess Records—founded by Leonard and Phil Chess in Chicago
Peacock Records—founded by Don Robey in Houston
Imperial Records—founded by Lew Chudd in Los Angeles
Nashboro Records—founded by Ernie Young in Nashville.[6]

Much of the world's greatest gospel music was originally recorded on these labels, preserving the sound of gospel's greatest era. Today, the modern owners of many of these labels have begun actively reissuing their classic albums, including Fantasy, Inc., which is systemically rereleasing the famed Specialty line, and MCA, which is reissuing the gospel albums of the Peacock label.[7]

The owners were as eclectic as the labels themselves. Specialty's Art Rupe was a graduate student in business administration. He moved to Los Angeles during the defense-industry boom of World War II when half a million African Americans came to southern California in search of work. Though white, Rupe studied black music with a clinical eye, spending his small paychecks on 78s from record stores in Watts, trying to understand the appeal. "Some of this music moved me so much it brought tears to my eyes," he recalled later. "I looked for an area neglected by the majors and in essence took the crumbs left off the table of the recording industry."[8]

Specialty quickly scored with rhythm-and-blues hits by Roy Milton, Joe Liggins, Jimmy Liggins, and Percy Mayfield. Rupe then turned to gospel and built an impressive roster. "Gospel music was the real thing," he said, "and R&B its child, a derivative, an off-shoot." Like most indie operators, Rupe was tight with his money: the Soul Stirrers were signed for $600 per session, plus royalties of one cent per recorded side. "One thing about Art," recalled the Stirrers' S. R. Crain, "he might not have offered you too much, but whatever he offered you, he paid you!"[9]

Across the country in New York City, when Mahalia Jackson was signed to Apollo, she joined the Georgia Peach (actually Clara Hudman Gholson) and the Dixie Hummingbirds.[10] Just across the Hudson River, Savoy Records' founder Herman Lubinsky was a "tight-fisted, cigar-chomping record entrepreneur" from Newark, New Jersey, who founded his hometown city's first radio station (WNJ) in the 1920s. Early Savoy signees included Lester Young, Big Joe Turner, Billy Eckstine, Johnny Otis, Cannonball Adderly, Charlie Parker, and a host of top jazz and rhythm-and-blues artists. Savoy also featured terrific gospel artists, including the Ward Singers, the Davis Sisters, the Roberta Martin Singers, Dorothy Love Coates and the Original Gospel Harmonettes, the Reverend James Cleveland, and the Caravans.[11]

By keeping expenses low and aggressively signing promising talent, the new breed of labels—for a while—fought the major labels on even terms. According to Bob Krasnow, who started with King Records before joining Elektra in later years, "Hey, [we were] a small group of people who were like Green Berets. It was the opposite of England beating up on the Falklands, you know. It was like the Falklands beating up on England. It was reverse warfare."[12]

Once again, this presented significant rewards to the nimble entrepreneur present at the intersection of talent and opportunity. Labels needed radio stations to play their records. To meet the changing demands of the public, the first stations playing gospel music also emerged in the years following World War II, including:

KXLW in St. Louis
WERD in Atlanta
WLOU in Louisville
WDIA in Memphis
KRKD in Los Angeles

WYLD in New Orleans
WMBM in Miami
WLAC in Nashville[13]

If it was a golden age for gospel music, it was certainly a golden age for gospel radio. While few of the disk jockeys and fewer of the stations were owned by African Americans, most nurtured a proprietary interest between announcer and listener. Curiously, the two best-known stations regularly playing gospel music were both in Tennessee, WLAC in Nashville and WDIA in Memphis. WLAC's muscular 50,000 watts of power broadcast easy listening by day and rhythm and gospel at night, reaching thirty-eight states.[14]

Three white DJs, Bill "Hoss" Allen ("Hossman"), Gene Noble, and especially John "John R" Richbourg played fifteen minutes of gospel every hour when they weren't selling "baby chicks, hair pomade, recordings, garden seeds, choir robes and skin-lightening cream" for sponsors Randy's Record Shop of Gallatin, Tennessee, or Ernie's Record Mart of Nashville.[15] Among the groups popularized by WLAC was the Fairfield Four:

> We was on WLAC every morning at 6:45 for Sunway Vitamin out of Chicago. When we'd get through singing in the morning, we'd have to go out and get breakfast and come back to the station and be recording, maybe three or four hours sometime during the day, getting transcripts for all those other 19 stations that we had. We'd come on in Philadelphia at 5:05 in the morning, and went off in San Antonio, Texas, at 11:05 each night. So anywhere you went in the states just about, you could hear Fairfield. That went on for 12 years.[16]

Even more tied to the African-American public was WDIA, AM 1070, in Memphis. Jethroe "Jet" Bledsoe, manager of the Spirit of Memphis, said one of the group's turning points was when WDIA's signal was boosted dramatically in July 1954:

> It surprised me . . . how the group kicked off because I didn't think we'd ever get twenty miles out of town to be booked. . . . When WDIA went 50,000 watts, that's what blew the top! We were getting letters from all over, far as the station would reach.[17]

Kip Lornell's research on WDIA has made the station the best-chronicled of all African-American radio enterprises. *Happy in the Service of the Lord* includes programs from all-star revues (the station had its own charitable fund that sponsored or supported little leagues, schools, and medical clinics), which billed WDIA as the "FIRST—and the ONLY 50,000-watt station programmed exclusively for Negroes—truly one of America's GREAT radio stations." It also featured all African-American DJs.[18] WDIA regularly sponsored and promoted "programs" with the top gospel artists and usually provided the emcee, often

Theo "Bless My Bones" Wade.[19] The station was also the home of the Reverend W. Herbert Brewster's famed "Camp Meeting of the Air" that regularly featured Queen C. Anderson and the Brewsteraires.[20]

Perhaps the most famous gospel DJ was Joe Bostic of New York City, "the dean of Gospel Disk Jockeys." In addition to his popular show on WLIB in New York, he aggressively produced gospel concerts and programs, including the well-known "Negro Gospel and Religious Festivals" at Carnegie Hall that featured the likes of Mahalia Jackson and the Selah Jubilee Singers. Bostic also sponsored shows in Madison Square Garden, aiming primarily for an African-American audience that "wept, clapped, shouted and fainted to a music that was not rendered for form and fashion, but for 'soul salvation.'"[21]

The number of full-time black radio stations grew exponentially during this period. In 1943, only four stations were known to be programming exclusively for African Americans. By 1953, that number had jumped to 260 stations.[22]

Thus all of the elements were in place—the American road beckoned, there was music on the radio—and so a thousand quartets and trios and duos and soloists hit the so-called "gospel highway," a loose connection of churches, high school auditoriums, union and Veterans of Foreign Wars halls across the United States. Unfortunately, conditions for African Americans on the highway were not much improved from minstrel days. Prejudice and segregation, stated and de facto, were ever-present, save for a few cities such as New York and Philadelphia. Many gospel performers avoided trains, where their second-class citizenship meant third-class, overcrowded accommodations in the last car or two, usually with a filthy or unusable toilet. Additionally, few restaurants or hotels would accept blacks. As Mahalia Jackson once said, "The minute I left the concert hall, I felt as if I had stepped back into the jungle."[23]

Instead, until groups could afford their own buses, the automobile was the preferred mode of transportation. Performers could buy crackers, sardines, and bologna ("gospel chicken") to eat in the cars when restaurants would not serve them and, when no accommodations were available, they could sleep in their automobiles, if necessary. That is, of course, if a gasoline station could be found that would sell them gasoline. "It was a nightmare," Jackson recalled. "There was no place for us to eat or sleep along the major highways."[24]

Not that the smaller roads were much better. Perhaps the most horrific story from the gospel highway comes from Shirley Caesar. While traveling by automobile along highway 15 in the Carolinas, her small party stopped at a gas station. They were unexpectedly attacked by a group of white men and beaten with hammers and chased with pitchforks. Caesar fled and hid in a car lot, narrowly escaping serious injury. The local sheriff refused to press charges against the assailants.[25]

Of the many quartets on the gospel highway, none were greater road warriors than the Soul Stirrers, the "real creators of the modern gospel sound."[26] First begun by S. R. Crain in the small East Texas town of Trinity in 1926, Crain learned songs from mail-order copies of disks by the Norfolk Jubilees and the Birmingham Jubilees. At one of the teenage group's first performances, a member of the audience told Crain that his group's singing had "stirred his soul"— hence the name.[27]

Texas at the time was a particular hotbed of quartet singing. Both the Famous Blue Jays and the Kings of Harmony had moved to Texas. The Blues set up shop on radio station KTBC in Dallas, while the Kings of Harmony moved to Houston. "The Kings of Harmony took Texas by storms and jumps," remembered singer James Singleterry. "They used to come on the radio every Thursday morning at 2:15 A.M. You could walk up and down the street, I guarantee you could hear the Kings of Harmony. It's incredible. People would set their alarms to get up." Doug Seroff believes that these groups heavily influenced the nascent Texas quartets of the day. He calls the Blue Jays' emotional Silas Steele the first of the "new era" of gospel lead singers. Both the Blue Jays and the Kings of Harmony were among the first to travel extensively and sing as a "full-time undertaking."[28]

Crain's new group eventually splintered and he moved to Houston during the Depression. He joined an existing group on the condition that they, too, change their name to the Soul Stirrers. Despite regular performances on Houston-area radio stations, this began a long period of membership churn. One of the most significant additions was A. J. Johnson, already a veteran of the gospel highway. Two early members, the Reverend Walter LeBeau and Johnson, were natural lead singers. Rather than change either of them, Crain elected to have both sing the high leads. "The double leads," notes Daniel Wolff, "would revolutionize the quartet sound."[29] Seroff, however, also gives credit to the Blue Jays and Kings of Harmony for the creation of the "switch lead" format. Regardless of who was the "first" group to employ the technique, this innovation is a crucial moment in the onset of the "golden age of gospel quartet singing."[30]

This incarnation of the Soul Stirrers was recorded by Alan Lomax for the Library of Congress in 1936. Lomax called their sound "the most incredible polyrhythmic music you ever heard." LeBeau boasted a soaring falsetto, and "the arrangements show a strong rhythmic base and the beginnings of the more emotional style that represented a change from both the rhythmic spirituals and jubilee style of the Golden Gate Quartet and the even harmony singing of the university groups such as the Fisk Jubilee Singers or the Southernaires."[31] The most startling number in the Lomax recording is "How Did You Feel When You Come Out the Wilderness," with its "piercing falsetto runs by the high lead after long sustained notes." According to Ray Funk, "No other known recordings from that time are at all close in style."[32]

In short, the group merged the musical preferences of both the Baptist and Holiness churches into something new. And, because Johnson owned an automobile, they were one of the earliest professional quartets.[33]

In 1937, the Soul Stirrers moved to Chicago, then the domain of legendary quartet trainer Norman R. McQueen, who—like the Famous Blue Jays and the

Kings of Harmony—originally hailed from Bessemer, Alabama.[34] Once in Bronzeville, the Stirrers added a strong-voiced young man named Rebert H. Harris, a Texan who trained by imitating birdsong and the blues of Blind Lemon Jefferson. While in Chicago, the group quickly became immersed in the gospel blues of Thomas Dorsey. Harris, called "the most spiritual man on the road" by his peers, took the words he sang seriously:

> Most lead singers do not study the e-ssential word or phrase in the song. They don't read, don't define, don't insert themselves into the composer's condition and bring the thing to a picture. You must say it so clearly, so expressional . . . so forcefully that it demands a fellow to accept it.[35]

The combination of dominant lead singers and Harris's "high, crystalline voice remains the inspiration for virtually all great male quartet leads to follow."[36] Funk cites Harris's "distinctive clear voice filled with emotion" and writes that there was a "piercing, yet smooth quality to his voice which is utterly unmistakable." Notes Funk, "To this day, no one has ever been able to imitate him."[37] With Harris, the group ruled Chicago's quartet scene and continued to travel, until World War II slowed travel nationwide. The Soul Stirrers began a Sunday morning show on Chicago radio station WIND in 1940, which continued for ten years. If they were out of town, they recorded their selections ahead of time. Using their radio show as a promotional tool, the group also promoted gospel shows at the local African-American high schools, bringing such groups as the Golden Gate Quartet and the Fairfield Four to Chicago.[38]

Since travel was difficult, the quartets built their own circuit in Chicago of Baptist and COGIC churches, ending at 3838 South State Street, the headquarters of the new National Quartets Union. Patterned after Dorsey's gospel chorus convention, the building was the home of the "Battle of Quartets" every Thursday night. The Soul Stirrers so dominated, despite the presence of top-flight groups like the Famous Blue Jays, the Pilgrim Travelers, and the Kings of Harmony, that Harris was named the national president. Remembering those epic "battles," Lou Rawls, then with the Kings of Harmony, recalls, "You didn't win nothing. And you never knew who won, 'cause it wasn't even put on like a contest. The people would come 'cause there was *good* stuff."[39]

On one Thursday night near the end of the war, two hundred people had paid 75 cents each to witness the latest battle. On that night, "The Stirrers had Old Man Harris fluting out the lead like a bird, J. H. Medlock trading raw shouts, and S. R. Crain driving the group along as he beat time with a clenched fist in his palm." And in the audience, a willowy teenager with the voice of an angel sat mesmerized. His name was Sam Cook (he would add an "e" to Cook several years later).[40]

When the war ended, the Soul Stirrers, now with baritone Paul Foster, exploded, crisscrossing the country, and soon only the Dixie Hummingbirds could match their influence. In October 1946, the Stirrers recorded W. Herbert Brewster's "Lord, I've Tried," a "gospel-blues" considered by Horace Boyer to be one of the most significant tracks in gospel music history in the transition from jubilee to hard gospel. Other groups quickly recorded songs in a similar vein.[41] In 1950, after a number of additional hits for the Aladdin label, the Soul Stirrers were signed by the potent new Specialty label and cut more than two dozen tracks. Propelled by Harris's lead vocals and a strictly enforced professionalism, "By and By," "I'm Still Living on Mother's Prayer," "In That Awful Hour," and others were immediate hits, and widely imitated.[42]

But Harris was tiring of the constant travel and the "commercialization" of gospel music. Additionally, he'd been elected mayor of Bronzeville and was operating the Soul Stirrers' Cleaning and Pressing in a building that also served as the group's headquarters, booking office, and rehearsal hall.[43] When Harris decided to retire (although he would "un-retire" several times in the years to come to form new groups), the Soul Stirrers made a radical move. Instead of adding another well-known singer from one of their rivals, they asked twenty-year-old Sam Cook of the Highway QCs to replace the best-loved voice in gospel music. While many of their fans didn't know it, the Soul Stirrers' R. B. Robinson had actually been training Cook for the past four years.[44]

Samuel Cook, fourth child of the Reverend Samuel Cook and Annie May Cook, was born in Clarksdale, Mississippi on January 22, 1931, when Clarksdale was perhaps the most African-American enclave of New World and where the world's great blues singers, from Robert Johnson to Skip James, plied their trade.[45] The Reverend Cook pastored various Holiness churches where

> [T]he cymbals, drums and tambourines were let into the Holiness churches specifically to produce that rhythm that brought on ecstatic visions. So, at the same time a reverend like Charles Cook might denounce the devil's music, his own church was relying heavily on a hand-clapping, foot-stomping beat. To the outside observer, the height of a Spirit-raising service looked a lot like a juke joint on a particularly hot Saturday night. Of young Sam, his father later recalled, "Didn't nobody teach him no singing. He was born with that gift."[46]

During the Depression, Rev. Cook moved the family to Chicago, where he again pastored various churches in Bronzeville and Chicago Heights and worked as an unskilled laborer and stockyard employee. Through hard work and a special appeal to other new refugees from the Deep South, he transformed a small Holiness church into a thriving congregation.[47]

Around the start of World War II, Sam and his siblings formed the Singing Children and began singing around Chicago Heights in other African-American churches. Albertina Walker, who grew up in the same neighborhood, said, "They *all* could sing!"[48] Eventually, Rev. Cook became a traveling evangelist. With the Singing Children as one of his primary assets, he traveled from Washington,

D.C., to California. Back in Chicago between tours, young Sam heard numerous gospel programs headlined by the Soul Stirrers.[49]

In the years that followed, Sam formed various groups in high school that all wanted to sound like the Ink Spots. The most lasting was the Teenage Highway QCs—although in later years, no one remembered what the "QC" stood for.[50] The Teenage Highway QCs soon were regulars in Chicago churches and programs—and very popular, mostly because of good-looking young Sam Cook. Like many gospel groups of the era, they honed their skills with professional trainers, usually older, more experienced singers. For their vocal training, the Highway QCs naturally turned to the Soul Stirrers.[51]

The Soul Stirrers, like most quartets, continued to lose and add new members and, a few years earlier, had added T. L. Bruster and R. B. Robinson. It was Robinson the QCs asked to train them. Shortly thereafter, several members of the Soul Stirrers asked Sam to sing with them at a neighborhood church service.[52]

Robinson trained the young singers using Soul Stirrers recordings—and raved about the group to anyone who would listen. In time, they were referred to as the Soul Stirrers Juniors, performing many of the Soul Stirrers early hits, including "Canaan Land," "Remember Me," and "He Knows How Much I Can Bear." Harris also began training the promising sixteen-year-old Cook.[53] The quartet's big break occurred on September 26, 1948, when the Highway QCs appeared with the Soul Stirrers, the Fairfield Four, and the Flying Clouds of Detroit. Among those in the audience was Louis Tate, a friend of Harris's who had once managed and booked the Harmonizing Four of Bessemer, Alabama. "I just sat there and I was spellbound," Tate recalled. "'Cause I didn't know no kids could sing like that. This is something I always wanted to do."[54]

With Tate as manager, the group debuted February 20, 1949, in Detroit on a bill with the Harmony Kings of St. Louis and the Flying Clouds. Among those in attendance was the Reverend C. L. Franklin, who promptly invited them home. The QCs were soon asked to perform on WDIA in Memphis, by now already called the "Mother Station of Negroes." Dwight "Gatemouth" Moore, one of the first African-American DJs on the station, was also a showman, musician, and an excellent judge of talent.[55] So on the same station that inspired young Elvis Presley, Moore began featuring the QCs, mostly because he recognized Cook's talent, on the radio and booking the QCs for his regular "Spiritual Midnight Rambles" on Friday night. The whole group moved to Memphis and even joined Moore's church. They performed relentlessly in programs throughout the Midwest, but never quite made it to the next level—in part because Tate was never able to sign them to a record deal.[56]

Back in Chicago, after Harris had announced his retirement, Robinson insisted that the remaining members listen to Cook. He auditioned with another vocalist, singing Brewster's "How Far Am I from Canaan" and easily won. Tate graciously released Cook from his contract and replaced him in the Highway QCs with Johnnie Taylor.[57] Years later, Tate said he knew Cooke was destined

The Reverend W. R. Richardson of the Fairfield Four—named National Heritage Fellows by the National Endowment for the Arts in 1989 (courtesy of Southern Folklife Collection, University of North Carolina, Chapel Hill)

for stardom in music: "This was his life. He'd eat it, sleep it, walked it, talked it. Singing was his life."[58]

Cooke's first concert in Chicago a few days later was an unqualified success.[59] His first single with the group in 1951, "Jesus Gave Me Water" (which he wrote), was a smash hit, selling 17,000 copies within a few months, then doubling its sales again in the next quarter. By contrast, Harris's best-selling single never sold more than 10,000 copies for Specialty.[60]

Thus began a remarkable partnership, one that solidified the Soul Stirrers' hold on the gospel market. Harris was an innovator, one of the first to popularize improvised call and response measures and the rhythmic repetition of certain phrases behind other singers. But Cooke soon exceeded Harris's popularity "by injecting a youthful, sweet sexuality into his performances," writes Nelson George. "Instead of the hoarse shouting so typical of male gospel singing, Cooke used understatement to showcase his satiny midrange and natural vibrato." Certainly, Cooke could shout when he wanted to, but other singers, including J. W. Alexander of the Pilgrim Travelers, urged him to modulate between the two extremes. This gave Cooke "greater emotional range," adds George, "[a]nd greater sex appeal. According to every account from the period, his voice, along with his smooth, honey-brown skin and innocent yet masculine features, made Cooke gospel's first teen idol."[61]

What is less well known is that Cooke was a memorable gospel songwriter as well. His composition "Touch the Hem of His Garment" is still considered a classic, and Cooke wrote prolifically throughout his short career,[62] including "Be With Me, Jesus," "Nearer to Thee," "Wonderful," "Until Jesus Calls Me Home," "Jesus Wash Away My Troubles," and "Just Another Day." During Cooke's tenure with the group, he and Crain arranged most of the Soul Stirrers' songs.[63] Cooke stayed with the Soul Stirrers until 1956, and the group dominated the gospel marketplace like few others in the history of the genre. Thurman Ruth recalls that at the always sold-out Soul Stirrers' Apollo shows, whenever Cooke would sing "Touch the Hem of His Garment," women would jump on stage to touch Cooke: "The women used to just go crazy when he walked out there."[64]

Eventually, Cooke saw the opportunity for success beyond gospel. In 1957, his advisors Robert "Bumps" Blackwell and J. W. Alexander urged him to enter the popular music market. That year, Cooke wrote and released "You Send Me," which was an immediate Top 10 hit. "Specialty owner Art Rupe was outraged," notes Nelson George wryly, "not out of any real concern for the music but because a backlash by church-goers could endanger his company's gospel sales. The gospel catalogue was the backbone of his profit, and the last thing he wanted to do was anger a loyal audience (and proven source of income)."[65]

No one was more hurt by Cooke's decision than Harris. He once told *Rejoice!* magazine, "It broke my heart when Sam went to pop. He was so great and the church community loved him so much. He came to me and told me they were offering him too much money and that he just couldn't turn it down. . . . He was the greatest singer that I ever had or ever heard."[66]

While Cooke tried to straddle both worlds by producing and writing for the Soul Stirrers, he eventually chose work in the pop realm exclusively, though he would unexpectedly show up at programs periodically—always to a warm response. Stories later circulated that gospel audiences would boo and hiss when he took the stage, but longtime Stirrer Leroy Crume said, "That's a lie! Everybody wanted to hear him sing; I don't care what he was doing . . . I have never, ever in my life heard anybody boo—and I was there every time Sam stepped on a stage with the Soul Stirrers."[67] Cooke later co-founded SAR Records, the first full-fledged soul record company. Cooke also produced Johnnie Taylor, the Valentinos featuring Bobby Womack, Lou Rawls, and others, "all gospel singers Cooke met with the Soul Stirrers and then 'turned out,'" singers who "recorded rough, gritty love songs that reflected Cooke's deepest musical yearnings and his understanding of black America."[68] Before his still-suspicious shooting death in 1964, Cooke was responsible for a host of Top 40 hits, including "Wonderful World," "Chain Gang," "Twistin' the Night Away," "Another Saturday Night," the prophetic "A Change Is Gonna Come," and many others.[69]

The Soul Stirrers replaced Cooke with Johnnie Taylor, another Highway QCs alumnus, who himself left after a few years to perform rhythm and blues, including "Who's Making Love," "Cheaper to Keep Her," and "Disco Lady." J. J. Farley recalled that Taylor helped "break" the group in New York City. But Cooke's death had a "devastating" effect on the band. Promoters drastically cut the price they charged for the Soul Stirrers and eventually Specialty dropped the group from its roster. Other fine singers followed, including Arthur Crume, Jimmy Outler, Willie Rogers, and the group recorded several fine sides for Cooke's SAR label.[70] Two different touring versions of the Soul Stirrers—one led by Farley, the other by Crume—continued to perform and occasionally record into the 1990s, though the group never again regained the stature it once enjoyed first with R. H. Harris and later with Sam Cooke.[71]

"Cooke was an adventurous, experimental, and contradictory figure," concludes George, "who molded his talent to entice whites, while pioneering new directions for black artists as a producer, songwriter, and businessman."[72] Harris continued to record and occasionally tour, but channeled most of his efforts into the National Quartet Convention, which endured deep into the 1970s with more than thirty thousand members. He continued to give concerts in his hometown of Trinity, Texas,[73] before he died in Chicago at the age of eighty-four on September 3, 2000. At the time of Harris's death, Heilbut told the Associated Press: "If Sam Cooke was the architect of soul, R. H. Harris was tickling his ear. Considering the time he sang, he had an interesting synthesis of elements: bluesy moans, cowboy yodels, and the epicene purity of an Irish tenor."[74]

Harris was, Heilbut added, "the most influential figure in soul music."[75] The Soul Stirrers' legacy endures into the twenty-first century as well. The group was inducted into the Rock and Roll Hall of Fame in 1989.[76] *Sam Cooke with the Soul Stirrers: The Complete Specialty Records Recordings* was nominated for two Grammy awards in 2003, in both the Historical Album and Album Notes categories.[77]

At the height of the Stirrers' success, their record label, Specialty, was also riding high with a potent roster of high-profile gospel artists. Specialty's main competition came from, of all places, Houston, Texas. Peacock Records had an advantage over virtually all of the new indie labels that sprang up in the late forties and early fifties—owner Don Robey was an African American who inspired both trust and sometimes fear among his stable of singers. Robey worked initially as a music promoter (Duke Ellington, Cab Calloway, Count Basie, among others) who opened his first nightclub, the Bronze Peacock Dinner Club, in the heart of Houston's rough-and-tumble Fifth Ward in 1945. It seemed a natural transition to eventually found his own record label as well. Robey chose the name "Peacock Records," perhaps in tribute to the first two black-owned (and short-lived) record labels of the 1920s, Harry Pace's Black Swan label and J. Mayo Williams's Black Patti. Peacock's first significant artist was Clarence "Gatemouth" Brown.[78]

Working primarily with both traditional blues and rhythm-and-blues artists, Robey and his brilliant associate Evelyn J. Johnson slowly assembled a strong lineup of artists, including Memphis Slim, the Tempo Toppers (with future superstar Little Richard), and Big Mama Thornton. When he bought the Memphis-based Duke label, he inherited Bobby "Blue" Bland, the Gospel Travelers, and the talented, but troubled, Johnny Ace.[79] Additionally, Robey and Johnson created two booking agencies, Buffalo Booking and Spiritual Artists, to handle concerts for all of Robey's own artists, as well as for B. B. King.[80]

But Robey's most significant contribution to popular music may have been his gospel roster. Beginning in 1950, he signed artist after artist until by the early 1960s, when labels such as Apollo and Gotham had already gone bankrupt, Peacock boasted more than 100 gospel acts.[81] Robey, a hard-nosed businessman by all accounts, might not have committed to gospel so completely if his first group, the Five Blind Boys of Mississippi, had not soon provided Peacock with a monster hit, "My Father."[82]

Few quartets had a more varied past than the Five Blind Boys of Mississippi, a past that begins in an African-American school for the blind outside Jackson, Mississippi, with an extraordinary singer, Archie Brownlee. Originally called the Cotton Blossom Singers, in 1937 they recorded four songs for the ubiquitous Alan Lomax during a Library of Congress field trip, though their game songs and humorous ditties bear little resemblance to their later sound. As the Jackson Harmoneers, the group was based first in Jackson, then New Orleans. In New Orleans, they were joined by their only sighted member, the Reverend Percell Perkins. Perkins had performed with the Fairfield Four, the Chosen Five, and the Swan Silvertones and was a talented writer and arranger.[83] Additionally, Per-

Led by the glorious falsetto of Claude Jeter, the Swan Silvertones have been thrilling audiences since 1938. (courtesy of Southern Folklife Collection, University of North Carolina, Chapel Hill)

kins's voice had a "piercing urgency in his tone and the ability to move back and forth from singing to a piercing shout that made churchgoers fall out wherever it was heard." It was Perkins who claimed to have moved the quartet from the jubilee style to hard gospel.[84]

They recorded under several names with various smaller labels with spotty success until Robey signed them to an exclusive contract. Their third cut for Peacock, Perkins's arrangement of "Our Father," was released in the holiday season of 1950 and has become a staple in the field. The song is actually a mostly spoken word recitation of "The Lord's Prayer," with the Five Blind Boys chanting "Our Father" in the background and supported by a slowly building, somewhat martial, drumbeat. "Like many other great gospel renditions," writes Ray Funk, "the group's intensity gathered momentum as the song progressed from start to finish." The song was No. 10 on *Billboard*'s most-played list in December 1950.[85]

In later years, Robey cited the song as one of his crowning achievements:

"Our Father" [by the Five Blind Boys] and "Peace in the Valley" by Red Foley on Decca were the first two gospel records to ever hit the jukebox. I must add that I'm the one who put the beat into religious records. I was highly criticized when I started it, but I put the first beat—which was not a drum—and then after the public started to buy the beat, why, then I put a drum into it. Then a guitar, then a trombone. I found that the public wanted something new in religious music, and I tried it with different instruments to see which one they would take to. They did not take to the trombone, but they did take to the guitar and drum-beat, and it got to a point where, if you didn't have a beat in a religious record, you had no sales.[86]

While Robey overstates his impact—other artists were also adding instru-ments about this same time—the new sound signaled the final death knell of the older jubilee groups, such as the Golden Gate Quartet. Still, the Five Blind Boys' greatest instrument was not a guitar but Brownlee's "wondrous" voice. Accord-ing to one writer, Brownlee's "riveting, chilling screams and yells were among gospel's most amazing." The Blind Boys recorded five classic albums and twenty-seven singles for Peacock, then moved on to record a number of equally brilliant releases for Chess and Vee-Jay before Brownlee's sudden death of pneumonia (some say a perforated ulcer) in 1960. He was only thirty-five.[87]

Writers are often forced to resort to exotic images to describe Brownlee's singing. Heilbut describes how Brownlee influenced first Ray Charles, then all subsequent soul singers, and how he could "demolish huge auditoriums" with his singing: "Brownlee would interrupt his songs with an unresolved falsetto shriek that conjured up images of witchcraft or bedlam."[88]

Even the Blind Boys' entrance—the five were always led onto the stage a linked human chain, each man with a hand on the shoulder of the man in front of him—was electrifying. In the throes of a particularly strong manifestation of the Holy Spirit, the completely blind Brownlee would miraculously rush about the stage and sometimes down the aisles. One awestruck observer once reported, "I seen him at Booker T. Auditorium jump *all the way* off that balcony, down on the floor—*blind!* I don't see how in the world he could do that. People would just fall out all over the house!"[89]

In time, Perkins left the Blind Boys to enter the ministry—he spent forty years as pastor of a Baptist church in Helena, Arkansas—but did record four solo albums before his death in January 2003. And he lived long enough to see the group's induction in the Gospel Hall of Fame in 2000.[90] The remaining mem-bers added several fine singers in the years that followed, most notably Willmer Broadnax, once of the Spirit of Memphis. Different variations of the quartet continued into the 1990s, still singing Blind Boys hits such as "My Robe Will Fit Me," "Jesus Loves Me," "No Need to Cry," "Let's Have Church," "Love Lifted Me," "Speak for Jesus," and "Jesus Satisfied." But no one could ever match Brownlee, whose vocals, one writer claims, "have been known to slay souls and reduce grown men to tears."[91]

After he left gospel, Sam Cooke once told a friend that he would always tear up when he would listen to Brownlee: "He's the only one who could do that—to move me like that."[92]

By 1952, Peacock was the home of yet another transcendent male vocalist, the Dixie Hummingbirds' Ira Tucker. The quartet had had several successful recordings for a number of labels, including Regis, Apollo, and Gotham, before a long stint with Columbia/OKeh. But seeing the across-the-boards acceptance of the Five Blind Boys of Mississippi, and feeling marginalized with OKeh, they signed with Robey during a tour of Texas.[93] About the same time, just as the electric guitar was becoming accepted in gospel music, the Birds were joined by Howard Carroll, an accomplished guitarist with a distinctively percussive style that incorporated both "jazzy chords and the feel of swing blues." The group gave him free rein to play whatever felt right.[94]

In June 1953, the Dixie Hummingbirds recorded what would become their signature tune, "Let's Go Out to the Programs." Only a singer as gifted as Tucker would attempt something quite so audacious. "Programs" features Tucker perfectly mimicking the Soul Stirrers' "Jesus Gave Me Water," the Blind Boys' "Our Father," the Pilgrim Travelers' "Mother Bowed," and the Bells of Joy's "Let's Talk About Jesus." More impressively, Tucker was not only able to sound like Sam Cooke and Archie Brownlee live, he was also able to replicate their motions and performance quirks. The song was an immediate smash and remained the most-requested song in the Birds' repertoire.[95]

Even the gospel music reviewer for *Billboard* magazine was impressed and gave the song a whopping eighty-five rating: "This group accomplishes quite a feat here in inviting everyone to a program of religious music and then successfully staging the same by imitating the styles of other famous spiritual groups, somewhat after the Modernaires' 'Juke Box Saturday Night.' It's a great idea and ought to create a big stir in the market."[96]

R&B great Jerry Butler, then just a thirteen-year-old boy, still vividly remembers "Let's Go Out to the Programs":

> Now, Archie Brownlee was one of the great singers of the time—and nobody sounded like Archie Brownlee. And there was Sam Cooke. And then here comes Ira Tucker saying, 'I'm good enough to sing like that guy!' They say imitation is the greatest form of flattery, so, here they were imitating the giants![97]

Of course, mimicry, no matter how perfect, is not enough to sustain a group through a multidecade career. The Dixie Hummingbirds were among the first to wear white tuxedoes in performance and, according to Tucker, "got to be known as the dressing-est group on the road." There was even a Sons of the Birds, a quartet comprised of the children of the active members who, by the mid-1950s, were opening for their fathers.[98] Of course, the Birds also thrived because they always seemed to be loaded with talent, especially bass singer William Bobo. But few vocalists could compare with Tucker. Heilbut says he was a "virtuoso" among gospel singers:

He looks to seduce his audience vocally. So within a few bars of his opening note, he will scoop down between beats in a dizzying combine of wit and breath. It takes a split second before the audience responds, and then orgiastic "Oohs" and "Help yourself, son" inform Tucker he's home safe.[99]

In addition to "Programs," the Dixie Hummingbirds scored a wide array of hit singles in the gospel market in the years that followed, including "Lord, Come See About Me," "Trouble in My Way," "Christian's Testimonial," "Devil Can't Harm a Praying Man," "Christian's Automobile," and "Search Me, Lord." In the early 1950s, they toured extensively with the Angelic Gospel Singers, an all-female, piano-accompanied group, also from Philadelphia. That union spawned numerous hit singles, including "Jesus Will Answer Prayer" and "Dear Lord, Look Down Upon Me."[100]

In 1959, the Dixie Hummingbirds released their sequel, "Let's Go Out to the Programs No. 2," which featured Tucker's uncanny recreations of top female artists, including the Angelic Gospel Singers, the Davis Sisters, the Caravans, and even the Ward Singers. Throughout their long career, the Birds would adapt the song to reflect whichever artists were currently atop the gospel charts.[101] Also in 1959, Peacock released its first long-play $33^{1}/_{3}$ rpm gospel album, *The Dixie Hummingbirds and a Christian Testimonial* (PLP-1000), two years after other major independents had released gospel LPs. The jacket featured the Birds resplendent in their white tuxedoes against a starry sky.[102]

The Birds continued through the 1960s, influencing first countless doo-wop groups, then early rock and rollers at every stop. R&B legend Hank Ballard claimed that the Dixie Hummingbirds were his "heroes" and that when they came to town, "it was like the Rolling Stones." Soul pioneer Solomon Burke credited the Birds with starting his career.[103] The group remained steady sellers for Peacock, even as gospel sales overall declined in the late 1960s and early 1970s. One of their best-loved numbers from this era, "In the Morning," featured both a boogie-woogie guitar and thumping drum line. It was such a hit that Jackie Wilson, another big Birds fan, re-worked it into "I Just Can't Help It," freely acknowledging that he "borrowed" the song from Tucker.[104]

In 1972, Paul Simon, another long-time follower of gospel music, heard the quartet perform at the Newport Jazz Festival, which by then had relocated to New York City. Simon asked the Birds to record behind him on "Loves Me Like a Rock" for *There Goes Rhymin' Simon* (Columbia LP KC 32280). The song was a smash hit, peaking at number two on the Top 100 and garnering the group their first Grammy. It also generated a firestorm of criticism in the gospel world.[105] Two years later, the Birds' James B. Davis told the African-American-oriented magazine *SEPIA* that the group was still feeling the impact:

> It would be a blessing if SEPIA could help make it clear to our people that the Dixie Hummingbirds are religious men, living God-fearing lives who function as ambassadors for Jesus.

We feel in a night club something like we do in a church and we prove it to the people.[106]

William Bobo died in 1976 after recording the ironically titled *Wonderful to be Alive*, ending a splendid thirty-year career. He once told *SEPIA* that he had originally been a baritone but nearly froze to death in a freak accident. When he recovered, his voice had changed into one of the most resonate basses in all of gospel music.[107] Two years later, *Ebony* dubbed the Birds "the World's Greatest Gospel Group," and Tucker soldiered on, in the process becoming one of the most in-demand producers in gospel music. Other awards included induction into both the Gospel Music Hall of Fame and the Vocal Group Hall of Fame, followed in the fall of 2000 by their selection by the National Endowment for the Arts as National Heritage Fellows. The designation as "national treasures" was accompanied by a $10,000 gift.[108]

In 1986, the Dixie Hummingbirds made yet another triumphant tour of Europe, enjoyed sold-out crowds and shamelessly gushing reviews. Following a two-hour show in Switzerland, Tucker told an English music magazine that the Birds were not finished yet:

We don't care about the money, just go ahead and work, try to keep goin' on. Because if you stop, you're finished. You tighten up and forget about what's happenin'. I know we gotta stop some day, but so what? Until that time, we try to stay three or four concerts a week. That's enough to keep us going.[109]

Almost unbelievably, Robey's Peacock label boasted still another lead singer with a hard-driving gospel quartet who was nearly the equal of Harris, Cooke, Brownlee, and Tucker: Julius "June" Cheeks of the Sensational Nightingales. The group originally came out of the Philadelphia-based Lamplighters but after various personnel changes switched to gospel as the Nightingales in 1949. Shortly after World War II, Barney Parks, a former Dixie Hummingbird, came on board as their manager and assembled a mostly new group around guitarists Howard Carroll and Jo Jo Wallace. Parks retired from singing and devoted himself to managing the 'Gales—as they were called—drilling them relentlessly. Years later, Parks admitted he enforced a military-styled discipline into the group: "I had them just like they were in the army."[110]

After a few fine sides for Coleman and King Records, Parks relocated the group to Spartanburg, South Carolina, where they added the unknown Cheeks. Cheeks left school after the second grade and remained illiterate all his life. He had had a desperately hard life, one of thirteen children of a widowed mother, working in the cotton fields and singing at night with a local group, the Baronets. With the hard-singing Cheeks, Parks found the final piece to his puzzle. The group signed with Peacock in 1952.[111]

The Sensational Nightingales' *Songs to Edify* **was nominated for a Grammy in 2003 for Best Traditional Soul Gospel Album. (photo courtesy of Malaco Records)**

The group's first recordings for Robey, "A Soldier Not in Uniform" and "Will He Welcome Me There," were immediate hits. In fact, they were called a "sensation" so often that the Nightingales quickly added the word "Sensational" to their name. And much of it had to do with Cheeks's "overpowering" singing. Boyer writes that Cheeks approached singing with his "thick, baritone voice" as he approached preaching—with a dazzling array of "falsetto, growls and screams."[112] Cheeks would sing so hard, even in the studio, that he would "overdrive" the microphones, distorting the sound. Soon, his style was heavily "bor-rowed" by the likes of Wilson Pickett, Bobby "Blue" Bland, and others.[113]

Parks recalled that Cheeks made the group unforgettable in concert: "When I got June Cheeks in there, they were unstoppable. Any group, I don't care how famous, they knew just to get up and sing, 'cause June Cheeks and those guys, going to turn out on you. Spirit-killers! If they didn't get you one way, they'd get you another. They were just that hard."[114]

Soon, the 'Gales' popularity was such that they were included with the Pilgrim Travelers, the Five Blind Boys of Mississippi, the Caravans, the Harmonizing Four, and the Dixie Hummingbirds on the first "Gospel Caravan" in December 1955 at the Apollo Theater in New York City.[115] It was during this period that Wallace wrote a nonsense dance song after a gospel show with the Davis Sisters. Wallace eventually gave the song to Hank Ballard, saying, "We can't record this, we're a spiritual group—see what you can do with it." Ballard recorded the little ditty, called "The Twist," only to see Chubby Checker record an even bigger version.[116]

Cheeks left the Sensational Nightingales on a couple of occasions, always to return. He briefly joined the Soul Stirrers in 1954. According to S. R. Crain, Cheeks's short tenure with the Stirrers was invaluable in that it prompted the shy Sam Cooke to be more animated on the stage: "He did a noble service for me. He inspired Sam. Old June was a yeller; he'd get Sister Flute or die! He'd tear the house down on you and he didn't care who you are or where you came from. He'd do everything!"[117]

"Sister Flute" was the Golden Gate Quartet's affectionate nickname for the staunch, elderly African-American women who populated most of their church services and concerts. For a show to be successful, any group had to "win over" Sister Flute. The Birds, the Soul Stirrers, and other groups adopted the term.[118] Cooke had always performed flat-footed and nearly motionless onstage. But during one show, in an effort to reach Sister Flute, Cheeks shoved Cooke, who fell off the platform. "People thought he was happy," Cheeks recalled. "I said, 'Move, man,' and the two of us fell into the audience."[119] The two became best friends, with Cheeks "egging" Cooke on to become more animated at every concert. "That scoundrel do anything!" Crain once said of Cheeks. "He and Sam jumped off a stage ten-feet-high in Washington D.C."[120] Apparently, they finally reached Sister Flute on that occasion, at least.

Many credit Cheeks as the "father" of such audience-grabbing antics—derisively called "clowning" by some in gospel music. But Cheeks was a deeply religious man and, like Archie Brownlee, always believed that reaching his audience was paramount. "I was the first to run up aisles and shake folks' hands," Cheeks said. "Man, I cut the fool so bad, old Archie started saying, 'Don't no-body ever give me trouble but June Cheeks.'" But Brownlee had the final say. Just months before his death, Brownlee left the hospital in New Orleans to sing at a double bill with the Five Blind Boys and the 'Gales. "Man, I woke up in the dressing room," Cheeks recalled, exhausted from trying to match Brownlee's vocal power. "That's the first and only time I ever fell out. Man, that Archie Brownlee was *tough*."[121]

The Sensational Nightingales flourished during Cheeks's stay. The group added pianos to the guitar/drum and developed new tempos behind Cheeks's voice and produced hit after hit: "See How They Done My Lord," "Somewhere to Lay My Head," "To the End," "Burying Ground," "Standing in Judgment," and many of his ad-libs were adopted by other quartets. But the constant one-nighters and Sister Flute's demands eventually shredded Cheeks's once magnificent baritone and left him with little more than a hoarse whisper. Cheeks went into semiretirement, occasionally resurfacing with his own group, the Sensational Knights, the Mighty Clouds of Joy, and occasionally even the Nightingales before his death in 1981.[122] The modern artist who most resembles Cheeks, soul legend Wilson Pickett, continues to pay tribute to Cheeks, sometimes performing his trademark numbers, often with the Clouds. "Pickett," writes Heilbut, "duplicates his every vocal and physical trait. Even his dance steps are parodies of Cheeks' shouts, with muscular arms flapping in the air. One guesses if Pickett could have his way, he'd be another June Cheeks."[123]

The Sensational Nightingales have continued into the twenty-first century with original members Wallace and Bill Woodruff and new lead singer Charles Johnson releasing a series of dynamic CDs with Malaco Records and still enjoying standing-room-only houses, particularly in the South. But there will only be one Julius "June" Cheeks, "[t]he hardest-singing lead in gospel."[124]

The last of the Golden Age's most transcendent male quartet vocalists is Claude Jeter, who is, like Tucker, still performing into the twenty-first century. Although his group, the Swan Silvertones, were not on Peacock, they recorded for virtually every other major label, including Specialty, during their long career.

Born outside Montgomery, Alabama, Jeter moved with his family to West Virginia at a young age when his father died. "I didn't really learn to sing," Jeter said in an interview from 1988, "I was born with that. I've never taken any music or anything. My mother was a beautiful singer who sang in the church and the choir and had a group, and I think that's where it began, by me loving it."[125]

A few years later, Jeter was among the four West Virginia coal miners who founded the Four Harmony Kings in 1938. After countless hours of rehearsals and weekend performances in tiny mountain churches, they auditioned and won a regular radio spot on a powerful Knoxville, Tennessee, radio station during the early years of World War II. So as to avoid confusion with the popular jubilee-styled Kings of Harmony, they changed their names to the Silvertone Singers. And when the Swan Bakery became the primary sponsor for their daily fifteen-minute show at 12:15 P.M., they switched their name again to the Swan Silvertones.[126]

Though an admirer of the Dixie Hummingbirds, the tall, thin Jeter purposefully set out to make the Swans distinctive by emphasizing a "sweet-singing" sound. The greatest difference was Jeter's soaring falsetto and his preference for "crooning" the older Baptist hymns. At his prime, Jeter would "seduce" audiences rather than bludgeon them.[127] After the war, the quartet moved to Cincinnati to record for King Records and was joined by the powerful bass Henry Brossard, late of the Famous Blue Jays. Brossard's booming, percussive bass would become the prototype for many early rhythm-and-blues and rock-and-roll acts in the 1950s and early 1960s.[128]

When it became obvious that the older jubilee sound was fading, the Swans recruited the powerful lead singer Solomon Womack. The group rehearsed incessantly and scored a few hits with King, mostly built around Womack's full-throated roar: "Use Me Lord" and "I've Got a Witness in Heaven." But it was not to last. "Poor Womack," Jeter said later. "He was the best lead I ever had. But he sang himself to death. He'd come out of the singing, raining sweat and then go bareheaded in zero-degree weather. . . . [T]he next thing we knew, Womack was dead."[129]

Success initially eluded the Swan Silvertones even after a move to Specialty in 1951. However, shortly thereafter they added another "shrill, gravelly" shouter in the Reverend Robert Crenshaw and former Dixie Hummingbird Paul Owens. Owens was a fine singer but a better arranger. Suddenly, everybody wanted the Swans' records, complete with gorgeous, note-perfect harmonies, Jeter's silky falsetto hymns, and the hard-driving shouts of Owens and Crenshaw. A host of hits followed, including "An Old Lady Called Mother," "My Rock," and "How I Got Over."[130]

In 1955, the Swans moved yet again, this time to Chicago's Vee-Jay label, where they added another raspy-voiced lead singer, Louis Johnson, and guitarist extraordinaire Linwood Hargrove. Hargrove's guitar expertise made the group one of gospel's most adventuresome in the recording studios. But Johnson's soulful tenor sparked the final change in Jeter's already famed falsetto. "Louis made me add this growl," Jeter told Heilbut. "I'd be switch-leading with him, and I didn't dare get smooth behind his part. I tried to make a little growl and then smooth it over."[131] Among the many fans of the Swans' new sound—besides countless R&B groups—was a young Paul Simon, who later said Jeter's rendition of "Mary Don't You Weep" provided the inspiration for "Bridge Over Troubled Water."[132]

This configuration, for many, constituted the definitive Swan Silvertones. Hit after hit—"Savior Pass Me Not," "Love Lifted Me," "I'll Be Satisfied," "End of My Journey," "Jesus Is Alright With Me"—followed in rapid succession. Thurmon Ruth, himself a wonderful singer with the famed Selah Jubilee Singers, was responsible for booking gospel artists for the Apollo Theater. Although he saw all of gospel's greatest (save Mahalia Jackson, who refused to perform at the Apollo) at the theater's Gospel Caravan, he told Ted Fox that the Swans with Jeter of the late 1950s and early 1960s had few peers:

I saw the Swan Silvertone Singers [sic] do something at the Apollo that I've never seen any other group do. The Caravans and Albertina Walker were closing the show. . . . They had so many folks shouting and getting happy that the Caravans and Albertina Walker couldn't even go on. It was just curtain time. Just cut the last act off. They couldn't go on, the Caravans—they were out there with the Swan Silvertones and were shouting and happy themselves.[133]

While Owens and Johnson were superb singers, it is Jeter's falsetto that remains the Swans' greatest legacy. Many writers, including Horace Boyer, consider him gospel's greatest practitioner, even better than the Soul Stirrers' R. H. Harris:

More striking than the beauty of his falsetto is Jeter's judicious use of the device. Not content to discard the natural voice altogether, like Eddie Kendricks and the Bee Gees, Jeter essays his beautiful and firm lyric tenor voice in most of his singing. But for special climaxes and emotion he turns to falsetto, one of the purest and strongest among singers to date.[134]

In fact, only the Reverend Al Green and Russell Thompkins, Jr., of the Stylistics have ever approached Jeter's "elastic, dazzling" command of the falsetto. When Vee-Jay closed in 1965, the Swans moved to Hob and recorded one more sterling release before Jeter left the group to enter the ministry in Harlem.[135] Jeter has since devoted himself to the ministry, recording sporadically, and occasionally showing up for the rare Swan Silvertone reunion shows. Johnson kept the group going, relying on the pristine harmonies first forged in the "billion-dollar" mountains of West Virginia, before the Swans' run finally ended in the late 1970s.[136]

But from his vantage point in Harlem, near the Hotel Cecil, home for most gospel groups when they performed in New York City, Jeter told Heilbut that it was his strong faith, not his glorious falsetto, that has sustained him along the gospel highway:

This is a thing where you can only survive by being real. Out of all the people we can fool, we can't fool God. He knows our intentions. So I'd rather fool nobody in the gospel field. If I don't feel the spirit, I won't move. I believe in the soft approach. The Bible tells us, "If you pray in secret, I'll reward you openly." I tried to practice that during my career.[137]

The end came quickly for most of the indies. Vee-Jay Records, one of the few independent labels besides Peacock owned by African Americans, was auctioned off bankruptcy in early 1967.[138] Changing tastes in music and the aggressive signing of their top artists by the major labels were among the factors that eventually doomed most of the independents. Lew Chudd finally sold Imperial to Liberty Records in the mid-1960s after larger labels signed away his biggest acts, Fats

Domino and Ricky Nelson.[139] The great Savoy label continued, but Chess Records was sold to GRT in January 1969, and co-founder Leonard Chess died that same year.[140] Art Rupe phased himself out of the music business in 1963 but returned after a few years, occasionally re-releasing Specialty's enormous catalog of hits until finally selling to Fantasy in 1991.[141]

As for Don Robey, his strong gospel roster enabled him to last a full decade past previous competitors such as Apollo and Gotham. But even he finally buckled in May 1973, selling his 2,700 song copyrights, 2,000 unreleased masters, and 100 contracted artists to ABC Records. The feisty, forthright Robey, who once punched out Little Richard over a contract, was dead within a year. He was seventy-one.[142]

Chapter Twelve

Gospel on the Freedom Highway

Aretha was continuing what Ray Charles had begun, the seculariza-
tion of gospel, turning church rhythms, church patterns and especially church feelings into personalized love songs. Like Ray, Aretha
was a hands-on performer, a two-fisted pianist plugged into the main
circuit of Holy Ghost power.

—Jerry Wexler[1]

We are a little fed up with this voter registration business . . . we want
our colored people to live like they've been living for the last hundred
years—peaceful and happy.

—Sheriff Z. T. Mathews, when he broke up a
civil rights meeting in Terrell County, Georgia.[2]

The freedom songs are playing a vital role in our struggle. These songs
give the people new courage and a sense of unity. I think they keep
alive a faith, a radiant hope in the future, particularly in our most
trying hours.

—the Rev. Martin Luther King, Jr.[3]

When this thing first started, this business of the diocese and Reverend Bacon, Fiske used to play Reverend Bacon's mother's records in
his apartment at night and sing along, at the top of his lungs, with
ecstatic abandon—"The mil-len-ni-al rei-eiggn!"—a song made famous by Shirley Caesar . . . oh, he knew his gospel singers . . .

—*The Bonfire of the Vanities,* Tom Wolfe[4]

The evolution of gospel music is not a straight, linear progression. It has
changed and adapted from the very beginning. In attempting to chart the
path from work songs/spirituals to jubilee to gospel, it has not been with
the intention of implying that this was the *only* road.

The spirituals, in something close to what we understand to be their classic form, have continued to be sung throughout this musical evolution. In 1905, Booker T. Washington writes that the spirituals survive in "the smaller towns and country districts" and that "new ones appear from time to time."[5] In 1942, researchers Lee and Marianne Seal visited a remarkably unchanged religious service near Clayton, Louisiana. Once there, they heard African-American musical performances that appeared to unchanged for a century. When researcher Harry Oster accompanied the Seals back to the same "Easter Rock" celebration in 1958, the spirituals were still being sung.[6] Marshall Stearns, a music historian and early supporter of Mahalia Jackson, writes of hearing spirituals being performed in the "old" style in the village of Bluffton, South Carolina, about thirty miles north of Savannah, in 1951,[7] while Richard Raichelson notes that they were still being sung, but with modern accompaniment, in a Sanctified church in Philadelphia in 1974.[8]

Nor did jubilee singing entirely vanish. The Golden Gate Quartet, which had been touring regularly in Europe and the Middle East since 1955, did not move permanently to France until 1959, although the United States Department of State continued to book them as goodwill ambassadors throughout Africa and Asia into the 1960s. But their original move to Europe had been prompted, in part, by declining attendance at concerts and dwindling record sales.[9]

A cappella gospel was fading as well. Virtually all of the major quartets continued to sing some songs without instrumental accompaniment, but the number of groups without at least a guitarist diminished each year. One of the last holdouts, the stirring Spirit of Memphis—in part because the quartet always boasted topflight soloists such as Silas Steele, Willie "Little Ax" Broadnax, Jet Bledsoe, and Joe Hinton—continued for several years without a band. A testament to their power is a rare live recording of "Lord Jesus Part I and Lord Jesus Part II," available on *Acapella Gospel Singing*.[10] The thundering attack eventually spills out into the audience and is marked by spine-tingling moans and orgiastic shouts. A few groups, like the Jubilee Four (who appear as themselves with Elvis Presley in 1964's *Viva Las Vegas*) continued performing a cappella into the 1960s. A collection of songs and artists captured midstream in the transition from a cappella to "hard gospel" is found on *The Golden Age of Gospel Singing*.[11]

With the addition of musical instruments, especially electric bass, the importance of the bass singer waned as well since the bass guitar generally replaced the bass singer's parts. This change made the "beat" harder and more pronounced and further emphasized the role of a solo lead vocalist.[12]

There were other changes afoot. Despite the restrictive economic opportunities and unequal protection under the law, a significant African-American middle class was finally emerging in the 1950s.[13] This, too, impacted what black music sold well. In the world of entertainment, the interest in straight ahead rhythm and blues and the electric blues that originally built the Vee-Jay, Peacock, and Chess labels gradually morphed into the "soul music" craze of the 1960s. Many of the greatest soul artists, Aretha Franklin, James Brown, Lou Rawls, Wilson Pickett, and literally dozens more, began in professional or amateur gospel groups before moving into the secular realm.[14] According to Cornel West, "Soul music is the populist application of be-bop's aim: racial self-consciousness among black people in light of their rich musical heritage."[15] One observer, however, makes a credible argument that soul music is, in fact, "the popular and secular offspring" of Thomas Dorsey's innovative "gospel blues."[16]

The result was that by the mid-1960s, a few influential individuals and groups were able to move (relatively) easily between the two worlds, most significantly Aretha Franklin and the Staple Singers.

The daughter of the Reverend C. L. Franklin, "The Man with the Million Dollar Voice," Aretha Franklin's bloodline is unmatched. It's the voice behind "Respect," "You Make Me Feel Like a Natural Woman," "Chain of Fools," and "I Never Loved a Man (the Way I Love You)." "Most of what I learned vocally came from him," she told reporter Phyl Garland while talking about her father. "He gave me a sense of timing in music and timing is important in everything."[17]

But it's also a bloodline heavily influenced by a lifelong friendship with Clara Ward. Years later, Aretha recalled a moment at an aunt's funeral when Ward sang Thomas Dorsey's "Peace in the Valley" and, caught up in the moment, threw her expensive hat on the ground. "That," Franklin said, "is when I wanted to become a singer."[18]

As a young girl, Franklin sang in her father's churches and the one recording from those days that survives, *The Rev. C. L. Franklin, Aretha Franklin and the New Bethel Baptist Church Choir,* combines C. L.'s hoarse exhortations with a teenage Aretha wailing on the old hymns. The era's other greatest "soul" singer, Ray Charles, marvels at recordings like these, saying that Aretha's prodigious talent "was just born with her." As he told *SEPIA* magazine, "She didn't have to be *made* into a great singer."[19] It was during this period that a young James Cleveland, like the Highway QCs before him, moved into the expansive Franklin household. Cleveland taught Aretha "some real nice chords" on the piano: "I liked his deep sound. There's a whole lot of earthiness in the way he sings and what he was feelin', I was feelin'. But I just didn't know how to put it across. The more I watched him, the more I got out of it."[20]

Aretha, mostly self-taught on the piano, memorized Clara Ward's records: "I learned how to play 'em because I thought one day she might decide she didn't want to play anymore and I'd be ready."[21]

Like Mahalia Jackson, Franklin was signed to Columbia by John Hammond. But after a series of uneven albums, she joined Atlantic, where she enjoyed her greatest success as a singer. And like Mahalia, her personal life has been as heart-wrenching as her public life has been successful.[22] She suffered through two unhappy marriages and her beloved father was shot by intruders in his Detroit home in 1979. The Reverend Franklin never recovered, lingering in a coma until his death in 1984.[23] Through it all, Aretha has remained in close contact with the church: "I feel a real kinship with God and that's what has helped me pull out of my problems. I have my career and my family and plenty of friends everywhere. The reason why is that through the years, no matter how much success I achieved, I never lost my faith in God."[24]

To date, she has recorded two extraordinary gospel albums, *Amazing Grace*, a two-record set with the Reverend James Cleveland (1972), and a second two-record set, *One Lord One Faith One Baptism*, with the Reverend Jesse Jackson and Mavis Staples (1987). Reviews of *Amazing Grace* were especially rapturous. Musicologist Wilfrid Mellers's description of Franklin's version of the title track is a good example:

> Gradually, her roulades become more extended until she's soaring on top of the homophony, now screeching or squawking in a wilder version of Arizona Dranes' bleat, now sobbing and sighing with a warm liquidity recalling Mahalia Jackson. Chorus and congregation rise to a frenzy that, in winging lyricism, hints at "mystical" incandescence.[25]

A tireless worker in the civil rights movement, Franklin appeared regularly, first with Dr. Martin Luther King, Jr., and the Southern Christian Leadership Conference, then with the Reverend Jesse Jackson—often singing "Precious Lord, Take My Hand" at their request.[26]

Now in her fifth decade of singing professionally, Aretha has few worlds left to conquer and is universally revered by younger female singers. But, according to Guralnick, at least, Franklin is truly happy only when she is singing gospel. "If you want to know the truth," he quotes her late father as once saying, "Aretha has never left the church. If you have the ability to feel, and you have the ability to hear, you know that Aretha is still a gospel singer."[27]

With the whole of gospel music's greatest singers to choose from to accompany her on *One Lord One Faith One Baptism* in 1987, Franklin chose Mavis Staples of the Staple Singers. Like Aretha, the Staples moved freely between the two camps. Founder Roebuck "Pops" Staples grew up on the plantations near Winona, Mississippi, listening each weekend to the world's greatest blues singers, including Robert Johnson, Charley Patton, and Howlin' Wolf:

> Charley Patton was a good man, far as I know—I was young, and didn't know about his life or anything. But Wolf, I thought he was the greatest thing. . . . He was just a few years older than me, but he was so powerful I wouldn't even dare speak to him. They were already calling him Wolf then. . . . As far as I was concerned, he was the blues.[28]

Staples and his wife, Oceola, joined the Great Migration to Chicago in the 1940s, working in a meatpacking plant. In Chicago, Staples at first performed solo in three-room "joints" that had only a kitchen, gambling room, and a dancing room:

Even then, I'd do the gospel on Sunday. Pick up $3 at the joint, $5 from the offering plate at church, and make $8 for the weekend and live high on the hog when my peers were happy just to get the $3. But I wanted to be playing only gospel even then. It just never quite worked out.[29]

After his wife died, Staples formed a gospel group with his children Pervis, Cleotha, and the youngest, Mavis. The group performed regularly throughout the city before signing with Vee-Jay Records. Propelled by Mavis's deep contralto and "Pops"'s bluesy, vibrato-laced guitar, distinctive for its heavy use of the "tremolo" bar, they recorded a host of stellar sides for the label, including "Uncloudy Day," "Will the Circle Be Unbroken," "Don't Drive Me Away," and "Pray On."[30]

The group (now christened the Staple Singers after Pops dropped the "s" from their name) moved to Riverside Records in 1960, adding sister Yvonne along the way. The Staple Singers broadened their output on their Riverside releases, recording carefully chosen covers and message-oriented folk songs. Bob Dylan frequently cited Mavis as his favorite "soul vocalist." (More than forty years later, Mavis would be a part of *Gotta Serve Somebody—The Gospel Songs of Bob Dylan* for Sony in 2003, and their duet on "Gonna Change My Way of Thinking" would receive a Grammy nomination in the "Best Pop Collaboration with Vocals" category.) Hits during this period included a cover of Buffalo Springfield's "For What Its Worth" and a wonderful Christmas album, *The 25th Day of December.*[31]

During this time, the Staple Singers became indelibly linked to the civil rights movement. Mahalia Jackson and Aretha Franklin may have been better known and more visible, but neither recorded many overtly political songs. (Although Mark Anthony Neal argues that Aretha's readings of "Respect" and "Young, Gifted and Black" were tacitly understood by African-American audiences to be about civil rights).[32]

For a brief moment, "gospel music was involved in cross-fertilizations that embraced the music of the core-culture church, the entertainment arena, and the fight for social and political equality, thereby beginning to insinuate itself into the larger society."[33] It was here that the gospel and freedom highways merged in the quest for civil rights:

I would think that a movement without music would crumble. Music picks up people's spirits. Anytime you can get something that lifts your spirits and also speaks to the reality of your life, even the reality of oppression, and at the same time is talking about how you can really overcome; that's terribly important stuff.—the Reverend C. T. Vivian[34]

The freedom riders, the freedom singers (with Bernice Johnson Reagon) sit-ins, voter registration drives, and marches were invariably accompanied by reworked spirituals, gospel songs, and soul songs like the Impressions' "People Get

The Staple Singers, featuring Mavis Staples, bridged the gap between gospel and soul music. (courtesy of Southern Folklife Collection, University of North Carolina, Chapel Hill)

Ready" and the Chi-Lites' "(For God's Sake Give More) Power to the People." Even the gospel DJs got into the act. During the spring 1963 demonstrations in Birmingham, announcer Erskine Fausch used coded words and the Highway QCs' "All Men Are Made by God" as cues to help protestors avoid the notorious Sheriff Bull Connor's violent tactics.[35] According to Pops, Dr. King's 1965 violence-marred march from Selma to Montgomery, Alabama, was the impetus for the Staples' *Freedom Highway,* while the song "Marching Up Jesus' Highway" was about the unrest in Selma, Alabama. *Freedom Highway* was recorded in a church and was dedicated to the freedom marchers.[36]

However, the song most associated with the civil rights movement was "We Shall Overcome," which combined the old Baptist hymn "I'll Be Alright" with the text of C. A. Tindley's "I'll Overcome Someday." Marchers reworked the lyric into a more corporate expression:

From:	To:
I'll overcome someday	*We shall overcome*
I'll overcome someday	*We shall overcome*
I'll overcome someday	*We shall overcome someday*
If in my heart I do not yield	*If in our hearts we do believe*
I'll overcome someday	*We shall overcome someday.*[37]

For the participants, this particular gospel song took on a sacred significance:

One cannot describe the vitality and emotion this one song evokes across the Southland. I have heard it sung in great mass meetings with a thousand voices singing as one; I've heard a half-dozen sing it softly behind the bars of the Hinds County prison in Mississippi; I've heard old women singing it on the way to work in Albany, Georgia; I've heard the students singing it as they were being dragged away to jail. It generates power that is indescribable.—Wyatt Tee Walker[38]

When the Staples moved to Stax Records, they recorded some of their greatest songs, several albums' worth of funky, memorable tunes that deftly merged genres and provided a showcase for Mavis's raspy purr: "Respect Yourself," "Heavy Makes You Happy," "I'll Take You There," and others. The group was featured in two movies, *Soul to Soul* with Santana and Wilson Pickett in 1971 and *Wattstax* with Richard Pryor and Isaac Hayes in 1973. Other hits followed for a variety of labels, though none could rival their gospel-flavored releases for Stax.[39]

Mavis Staples continues to tour and record with everybody from Bob Dylan to Prince. Recent projects include both a CD and tour behind *Spirituals & Gospel: A Tribute to Mahalia Jackson* (Polygram, 1996). As she told reporter Misha Berson after a scintillating live performance of "Soon I Will Be Done with the Troubles of the World" in Seattle, "I tell you, when that spirit hits you, you don't know which way you're goin'."[40] Mavis's tribute becomes all the more poignant with the memory of Mavis coming onstage to finish "Precious Lord" for a feeble Mahalia during one of Jackson's last concerts in Harlem. Staples calls the moment the "highpoint" of her long career.[41]

But it was her scorching duet on *Gotta Serve Somebody* with Bob Dylan—who has recorded precious few duets in his career—that reintroduced Staples to the public. After a few bars of "Gonna Change My Way of Thinking," Dylan stops the song in midverse and carries on a funny, if slightly surreal, conversation with

Staples: "Why look, someone's coming up the road, boys. It's Mavis Staples!" Invigorated, Dylan and Staples deliver a furious, guitar-driven rendition of the song.[42]

Ultimately, Staples has said that the best music, be it mainstream or religious, is about healing. And that's what she's always tried to sing:

> If somebody's burdened down and having a hard time, if they're depressed, gospel music will help them. We were singing about freedom. We were singing about when will we be paid for the work we've done. We were talking about doing right by us. We were down with Martin Luther King. Pops said, "This is a righteous man. If he can preach this, we can sing it."[43]

As for Pops, he released two widely praised solo albums for Virgin Records, *Peace to the Neighborhood* in 1992 and *Father Father* in 1994. He would live to see the Staple Singers receive a National Heritage Fellowship from the National Endowment for the Arts in 1998 and be inducted into the Rock and Roll Hall of Fame in 1999 before his death in the final days of 2000.[44] On *Father Father*, he recorded a very personal version of "Why (Am I Treated So Bad)?"—which the Staples first recorded in response to civil unrest in Little Rock, Arkansas. Just before Dr. King's assassination in Memphis in April 1968, King told Pops that this was his "favorite" song. "To this day, I still sing it every night in honor of him," Pops said in an interview a few years before his death. "I still miss him."[45]

But the most ferocious warrior for civil rights among gospel's elite died virtually unnoticed in April 2002 in her home in Birmingham, Alabama, near the site of some of the movement's bloodiest moments. Dorothy Love Coates, tall, impassioned, elegant, unpredictable, considered being incarcerated for the cause an honor and a privilege. She wrote eloquently and angrily about man's inhumanity to man—and about a heavenly home that awaited those who persevered.

Born in poverty in Birmingham, Dorothy McGriff was a childhood friend of Alex Bradford (see Chapter 13). After dropping out of high school, Dorothy worked as a domestic by day and sang gospel by night. As a singer, she achieved acclaim throughout northern Alabama and at age sixteen married Willie Love of the Fairfield Four.[46] She became seriously ill during her first pregnancy and, when her daughter Cassandra was born with cerebral palsy, was prostrate with grief for months. R. H. Harris and the Soul Stirrers drove to the Love's house and at her bedside sang Brewster's "I Never Reached Perfection . . . Lord, I Tried." "That girl got up," Harris recalled, "and been up ever since."[47]

Birmingham's best-known female gospel group of the day was the Harmoneers, who often toured behind evangelist Bishop Williams, along with Arizona Dranes. Renamed the Gospel Harmonettes, the group enjoyed some success and even appeared on Arthur Godfrey's popular *Talent Scouts* radio program. But several early sides for RCA Victor garnered little attention. In 1947, the Harmonettes recruited the striking Dorothy Love who, after only a short time, was forced to leave the group to care for Cassandra. After her divorce, Dorothy rejoined the group in 1951, just in time to appear on their first recordings for Specialty Records.[48]

In the years that followed, the Gospel Harmonettes released a series of thrilling, emotional songs, often supported by the gifted organist Herbert "Pee Wee" Pickard: "I'm Sealed," "Get Away, Jordan," "(You Can't Hurry God) He's Right On Time," "Strange Man," "I Wouldn't Mind Dying," "Come On in the House," "Jesus Knows It All," "These Are They," "Everyday Will be Sunday," "There's a God Somewhere," "Just to Behold His Face," and "Am I a Soldier," many of which Dorothy wrote.[49] She left the group again in 1959 and married Carl Coates of the Sensational Nightingales the following year, only to return to a reorganized Harmonettes in 1961.

Dorothy Love Coates's contralto was rough and raspy, more like Sallie Martin's than Mahalia Jackson's, but in her best work there is a fierce intensity rare even in gospel music. In "You've Been Good to Me" (for Vee-Jay Records) and "I Won't Let Go of My Faith" (Nashboro Records), her "intense vocalizations" drew listeners to their feet. She was also an electrifying performer, physical, animated, and unpredictable.[50] Coates's "vocal gymnastics" often caused Art Rupe, president of Specialty, to fear she would suffer a heart attack in the recording studio.[51]

But it is for her uncompromising support of the civil rights movement that Coates is best remembered today. At a time when few popular artists, save for Nina Simone, were at the forefront of the movement, Coates and Julius Cheeks of the Nightingales were powerful voices demanding an end to segregation. In 1958, Coates's blistering attack on lynchings and violence, "That's Enough," was one of the first songs to tackle sensitive subjects head-on. That righteous anger appears in other songs, including "How Much More of Life's Burdens Must We Bear?"[52]

Through the heady days of the movement, Coates marched the streets of Birmingham with Dr. Martin Luther King, Jr., spent nights in jail, and worked in voter registration drives. In 1967, she narrowly missed death in the nightmarish Newark riots. But her unflinching calls for equality, as well as her uncompromising spiritual stance, earned her the sobriquet of "prophet." Marveled her old friend R. H. Harris, "Dot's the only one still out on the road keeping this thing alive."[53]

Coates's most riveting performance, however, may have been "The Hymn," written in the uncertain days following the murder of President John F. Kennedy, and featuring one of her most impassioned spoken word intros, delivered in the clipped cadence of an old-time brush arbor preacher:

> When the president was assassinated, the nation said, "Where is God?" When the little children lost their lives in the church bombing, the nation cried, "Where is God?" I got the answer for you today: God is still on the throne.[54]

She disbanded the Gospel Harmonettes in 1970 but continued to sing, some-times with the Dorothy Love Coates Singers (which included her sister Lillian McGriff), sometimes solo. She also continued to write and her songs were re-corded by the likes of Johnny Cash, Ray Charles, Etta James, the Blackwood Brothers, the Statesmen Quartet, and Andrae Crouch, as well as by many others who "appropriated" them for their own. "I feel like I'm feeding the entire gospel field," she told her longtime friend Anthony Heilbut. "They all take my songs or my sayings." She reserved even harsher words for promoters and pastors who routinely bilked gospel artists.[55]

Heilbut once speculated that had Coates lived in Chicago or even Philadel-phia, she could have rivaled gospel's greatest. But she rarely left Birmingham, then called "Bombingham" by African Americans, despite the horrors she had once seen on its streets, and only then to ride the gospel highway once more. "Why not?" she told Heilbut. "I've stayed in the North. It's the same every-where—if you look like me."[56]

The world found Coates anyway. She appeared several times at the Newport Jazz Festival, and her regal, commanding presence earned her appearances in two films, *The Long Walk Home* (1990) and *Beloved* (1998). In *Beloved,* she leads a chorus of former slaves in an old spiritual. Her song "No Hiding Place" can even be heard in the movie *Ghost* (1990).[57] In late 2000, PBS aired a documentary titled *Still Holding On: The Music of Dorothy Love Coates and the Original Gospel Harmonettes,* produced by Dwight Cammeron and the University of Alabama Center for Public Television and Radio.[58] Of the production, *New York Times* columnist Margo Jefferson wrote, "We use the word 'wonderful' too often, so let me say, she [Coates] is a wondrous performer. She delights, but she aston-ishes, too."[59]

Craig Werner's book on music and race in America ranks her with Mahalia Jackson, Claude Jeter, and Marion Williams as one of the four "greatest gospel singers of all time." To Werner, Coates's music presents the "best" of gospel music:

> . . . [A] model of call and response rooted in an unflinching engagement with history; an understanding of the world that sends pulses of energy back and forth between gospel and the blues; an unwavering commitment to the beloved community; a refusal to be seduced into the mainstream where the value of life is measured in money; and music so powerful it can change your life.[60]

The posthumous tributes, in publications as diverse as the *Times* (London) and the folk journal *Dirty Linen,* were equally effusive in their praise, but the best paean to Dorothy Love Coates, singer, songwriter, freedom fighter, may be found in the words of her stomping gospel rave up, "I Won't Let Go of My Faith":

> *Old Satan is busy stirring up wrath*
> *Gathering stones to block my path*

Enemies inflicting all the hurt they can
Throwing their rocks and hiding their hands
If you dig one ditch, you better dig two
The trap you set might be for you
He put it in my heart, you can't change me
My soul's on fire, and the world can't harm me[61]

Musically, Coates's songs bore a strong resemblance to those of her idol, W. Herbert Brewster, and she was among the first female gospel artists to insert the "vamp" at the end—a repetitive rhythmic sequence that allowed her to "preach" short sermons. Most of Coates's innovations came in the form of her lyrics. She melded Brewster's more literary allusions with her own folksy idioms and immediately grabbed her listeners' heartstrings. Coupled with her blistering rhetoric and spirit-filled (some would say "spirit-possessed") performances, Coates was a true original.[62]

Another group changing gospel music during this period was the Caravans. Half a century later, gospel superstars like Yolanda Adams still pay tribute to the "cutting edge" innovations pioneered by the "Vans," as they were affectionately called.[63] While most quartets featured one exceptional vocalist, the Caravans were a collection of stars, each a famed soloist in her own right. As soon as one topflight singer left, another replaced her. Like the great college football and basketball teams of the twenty-first century, the Caravans never rebuilt—they simply reloaded.

The Caravans were founded and built around Albertina Walker who, although a memorable soloist herself, preferred to stay in the background after the troupe's early years. Walker—or "Tina" as she has universally been called for more than fifty years—began singing as a child in Chicago, and while still a teenager she was invited to join Robert Anderson's prestigious ensemble. "I had seen Roberta Martin and Mahalia Jackson," she once told a reporter. "I wanted to stand up before audiences and deliver the message, win souls for Christ. I wanted to touch dying men and slipping women."[64]

In 1952, a record label asked Walker to record for them. "I said I didn't want to sing by myself," Tina recalled. "I asked if the girls could record with me and the record company said it was OK."[65] Consequently, Tina and several other members of the Anderson group split off to form the Caravans, initially most notable for Walker's "husky contralto with a characteristic crack of three or four descending tones as she moves through a melodic line"—a feature most recently heard in soul singer Gladys Knight.[66] The Vans' unofficial headquarters was Mahalia Jackson's house at 37th and Prairie streets: "I used to go to [Mahalia's] house all the time. She used to cook soul food, and we'd sing and have a good time. James Cleveland was there. I had grown up with James and asked him if he wanted to play for my group. He did."[67]

A year later, Walker added New Orleans native Bessie Griffin (born Arlette B. Broil), whose "contralto is huge and lustrous," and who was raised, like another

Crescent City native, Mahalia Jackson, on a steady diet of "Amazing Grace," twelve-bar blues, and the singing/preaching of Blind Frank. As a member of the Southern Harps, Griffin ruled New Orleans. On two different occasions, once while the Southern Harps were singing "Just Over the Hill" and once during "I Want to Rest," overwrought listeners actually died during the performances.[68]

But the Southern Harps never broke through, despite Griffin's house-wrecking abilities. It wasn't until a 1951 gospel concert in Chicago, when she stole the show from host Mahalia, the Dixie Hummingbirds, and Rosetta Tharpe, that Griffin attracted national attention—and that of Albertina Walker. Griffin joined the Caravans in 1953.[69] Tina wisely stepped back from the limelight and allowed Griffin to soar. Horace Boyer marvels at Griffin's vocal "pyrotechnics," which included the ability to both sustain tones for uncommonly long periods of time and still moan and whoop uncontrollably in the choruses. Her short tenure with the Caravans resulted in some legendary performances. Griffin's trademark was a twenty-minute version of Alex Bradford's "Too Close to Heaven," sung in such a way that each verse gathered momentum with additional "embellishments and volume."[70]

As blues singer Linda Hopkins once told Heilbut, "Bessie Griffin . . . that woman *sang* . . . Lord, letmetellyou. She'd get up, start moaning, raise her hands up in the air, *mmmm!* Never heard nothing like it."[71] Griffin enjoyed only mild successes in the years that followed, performing in both sacred and mainstream venues, but never found the acclaim that her memorable contralto deserved before her death of breast cancer in 1989.

Inexplicably, the Vans did not make much of a living in the early days, performing primarily in high school auditoriums and churches. "It was a lot of hard work and no money," Walker said. "The Lord blessed me with all those singers who were interested in singing."[72] With the departure of Griffin after only a year, Walker recruited an astounding series of soloists, each seemingly more compelling than the last. Walker's keyboardist/arranger for the mid-1950s, James Cleveland, persuaded Birmingham native Inez Andrews to join the Caravans in 1957. Andrews was a powerful preacher with a crystalline contralto, and she specialized in the slower, more dramatic songs. Her best-known Vans songs are the spiritual "Mary, Don't You Weep," with its thundering arrangement by Claude Jeter (and covered by no less than Aretha Franklin on *Amazing Grace)* and James Cleveland's bluesy "Soldiers in the Army." Andrews left in the early 1960s to perform both as a solo artist and with her own group, the Andrewettes, enjoying hit after hit into the twenty-first century.[73]

Andrews' biggest song thus far is "Lord, Don't Move the Mountain," which crossed over into the R&B charts and remained on the gospel charts for more than a year in the late 1970s. " 'Mountain' has been with me for years," she said. "I never even bothered to record it. I'd just sing it when I needed to."[74] At the time, Andrews started noticing more and more rock-and-roll singers in her audiences—and all were paying close attention to what they were hearing:

They come purposely to see what they can learn—or what they can steal. They'll come backstage and say, "Hey girl, I've got to know what you did on those last eight bars." Rock 'n' roll singers steal even worse than gospel singers. Because we had something to steal from the very beginning, while they had nothing.[75]

Dorothy Norwood was another one of Walker's early recruits. The Atlanta native arrived in Chicago with the gift of storytelling, a gift that has sustained her through five decades of singing and preaching. Like Andrews, she learned much of the craft of gospel singing from Cleveland: "James Cleveland was my mentor. I grew up under James, and in later years I worked with him, singing in his group. He was such a great influence, a person after my own heart. His music was not compromised."[76]

Norwood's career soared after leaving the Caravans in the late 1950s. She joined James Cleveland's Gospel Chimes, then formed her own group. As a storyteller, she has no peer, racking up impressive sales with mostly spoken-word songs, such as "The Boy and the Kite," "The Old Lady's House," and the runaway hit, "The Denied Mother." Most of her best songs were recorded live, which allowed Norwood's voice to build in volume and intensity. Midway through the narration, the instrumentation begins to build as well until the story bursts into song, invariably accompanied by the roar of the crowd.[77]

The Stones tapped Norwood and her group to open their mammoth 1972 tour, performing nightly before crowds often in excess of 60,000 people. Mick Jagger in particular would stand in the wings and watch Norwood perform. "You could see them crying when I did 'Johnny and Jesus,'" she said later. "And they loved 'When the Saints Go Marching In.'"[78] At this writing, Norwood has recorded nearly fifty albums, been nominated for a host of Grammy and Dove awards, attends Caravan reunion concerts, and still preaches as a traveling evangelist. "I can't go at the pace I've been going for many years," she said in 1997. "But I want to continue to do the work of the Lord. God has preserved me to do a work for Him. Why shouldn't I?"[79] In 2003, Norwood's release *Live at Home* for Malaco Records was nominated for a Grammy award in the "Best Traditional Soul Gospel" category. Why not, indeed?

Some of Walker's recruits had enjoyed successful careers before joining the Caravans. Cassietta George was a member of both the a cappella Songbirds of the South and the Brewster Ensemble before joining the Vans in 1954. The tiny George's biggest number with the Caravans was "Somebody Bigger Than You and I," which nearly crossed over into the pop charts as well. George was an accomplished songwriter and while her post-Caravan career never matched her heights with the Caravans, she wrote several hits, including "To Whom Shall I Turn?" and "I Believe in Thee." She died in Los Angeles in 1995.[80]

But the best-known Caravans alumnus is the incomparable Shirley Caesar. Caesar today is known by many names: "The Queen of Gospel Music," "pastor" (she leads a flourishing church in Raleigh, North Carolina), "councilperson"

After becoming a star with the Caravans, Dorothy Norwood once opened for the Rolling Stones. (photo courtesy of Malaco Records)

(she served four years on the Durham City Council), "doctor" (she received an honorary doctorate from Shaw University, where she also earned a Bachelor of Arts in business—graduating magna cum laude), and "director" (she heads up Shirley Caesar Outreach Ministry, which works with the poor and elderly in Durham). In the meantime, she has also managed to record more than forty albums, receive a fistful of gold records, and accepted a dozen Grammy awards.

One of thirteen children reared by a widowed, invalid mother, Caesar was a gospel music child prodigy, traveling by age twelve as "Baby Shirley Caesar." She nursed her ailing mother from ages seventeen to nineteen, when she heard Dorothy Love Coates and the Gospel Harmonettes perform with the Caravans in Winston-Salem. On the second night, Caesar wrote a note that read, *Please ask Shirley Caesar to sing* and slipped it to Albertina Walker during the performance. "I felt that if she would only hear me, she would want me," Caesar recalled. Walker did and Caesar happily joined the group four days later:

> I rehearsed with them for a day and we sang Friday, and I stayed with them for six years. I never missed one concert in that time. One night all of them but me had the flu, so I went on the road with the Soul Stirrers. They backed me, I performed, came home, paid off everybody. This went on for two weeks while they were sick.[81]

"I thought she was still a little girl in school because she had socks on," Walker once told the *Chicago Sun-Times*. "She told me she was grown and she could go on tour because she was out of school. I told her I had to talk to her mother."[82] Caesar joined a lineup that included Walker, Andrews, and Dolores Washington, which by 1956 had moved into gospel music's highest echelons. Famed for their "telepathic" teamwork, "the combination of the young soprano phenom Caesar and the shrieking contralto Andrews was a powerhouse one-two punch and as the decade drew to a close, the Caravans were the queens of the gospel circuit."[83]

With the Caravans, young Caesar was "schooled" by Walker and Andrews, and this particular incarnation of the Vans resulted in some extraordinary sides for Savoy, including "Sweeping Through the City, "No Coward Soldier," "Running for Jesus," and "The Lord Keep Me By That Day." Caesar became known as "the Clean Up Lady," or "the House Wrecker," or "the Little Trouper" (Walker's pet nickname) in those days, hurling herself from stages, dancing in the Holy Spirit, and suddenly erupting into a fervent sermon. "I was full of energy in those days," she said later. "Backstage at the Apollo, I could run all of the way up all of those stairs and in thirty seconds be on the top floor." And when she was not onstage, Caesar could often be found backstage, Bible in hand, witnessing to a stagehand.[84]

For eight years, the Caravans traveled in a single Cadillac, performing in everything from small churches to Madison Square Garden, handling their own bookings and arrangements, and when racial prejudice was just as likely to keep them out of decent hotels as the frequently inadequate freewill offering at many churches.[85]

According to one gospel historian, "The Caravans cut new territory in terms of their dynamics, their arrangements, and their performance style." In the midst of it all would be the diminutive Caesar, who would perform "these little jerks with her feet and shoulders and the hall would just go up in flames."[86]

Eventually, however, Caesar's desire to preach became a "call." For a time, she and Walker tried to coordinate Caesar's preaching engagements and revivals around Caravans dates, but it quickly became obvious that the arrangement was untenable. When the small Hob label offered Caesar a recording contract, she left the Vans in August 1966.[87] "Finally, the Lord told me to preach or perish," Caesar recalls. "I didn't want to die, so I gave the Caravans two weeks' notice that I had had the call to the ministry."[88]

Caesar's early years were difficult. Billed as "the Singing Evangelist," even church congregations wanted her to sing and the gospel highway is particularly perilous for single females. Gradually, she formed the Shirley Caesar Singers (which included her sister Anne), found reliable keyboardists, and overcame the usual trials of stingy congregations and thieving promoters. Fortunately, artists like Clarence Fountain of the Blind Boys of Alabama and J. J. Farley of the Soul Stirrers "adopted" the spunky young woman, counseling and encouraging her along the way.[89] Eventually, the quartets began opening for her instead of the other way around.

Caesar is blessed with a remarkably supple voice, one that is able to "sell" a country-tinged hit ("No Charge" or "King Heroin") just as believably as a traditional gospel shout ("Bread of Heaven"). Her ability to preach has also enabled her to release a long line of successful story songs, including the ten-minute hit, "Don't Drive Your Mama Away." "I describe myself as a 'traditional gospel singer with a contemporary flavor,'" Caesar said. "Or, another way, as a 'down to earth singer serving an up-to-date God.' That's just the way it happened."[90]

After Hob Records, Caesar joined first Roadshow Records (where she scored another major hit with "Faded Rose"), then industry leader Word Records, where she was the contemporary Christian music giant's first true gospel artist. "I chose Word over some of the better-known black gospel labels because I knew they were all gospel," Caesar said. "I wouldn't have to worry about them trying to get me to sing about Jesus in the second person—you know, 'He' songs or 'You' songs. They knew I was a 'Jesus' woman and I knew I'd have no problem with Word."[91]

The combination of Word and Caesar has resulted in nearly twenty releases (several of them gold), twelve Grammy awards (at press time she was nominated both for her own *Shirley Caesar and Friends* for Word and as part of the *Gotta Serve Somebody—The Gospel Songs of Bob Dylan* project), and literally dozens of Stellar and Dove awards. Her songs have been featured on *The Preacher's Wife*, *The Prince of Egypt*, *Rosewood*, and *Why Do Fools Fall in Love* soundtracks. Caesar's church, Mount Calvary Word of Faith Church in Raleigh, has 1,500 members and she married Bishop Harold I. Williams in 1983. But in interviews, she's just as likely to talk about the families touched by Shirley Caesar Outreach Ministries. "I can't take a bag of sugar and sweeten the Atlantic Ocean," she said, referring to the ministry, "but I can dip a pitcher out of the ocean and sweeten that."[92]

Since joining Word (and later as part of the Word imprint Rejoice), Caesar has recorded an unbroken streak of memorable songs—enough to fill a couple "best of" collections. While the music has ranged from traditional gospel blues to more contemporary, her "old school" testifying and unashamedly Christian lyrics have not changed. During the recording of *Live in Chicago* (which remained number one on the gospel charts for fifty weeks in 1989), an improvised riff in E-flat catapulted the story-song "Hold My Mule" into becoming one of the best-selling gospel songs of all time. [93] In gospel's beloved and time-honored "song and sermonette" format, Boyer writes that Caesar has no equal.[94] A song and video in honor of her late mother Hallie Martin Caesar was one of the first gospel videos to receive "gold" certification the following year.[95]

Along the way, the Evangelist Shirley Caesar has sung for presidents Carter, Bush Sr., and Clinton, as well as for Nelson Mandela. She is continuing her quest for a master's degree in theology from Duke University. And she will drive all night from a concert to be back in time for Sunday morning services at Mount Calvary. "Music can heal," she once said. "I've seen what it can do. Spirits are lifted, yokes are broken. As far as I'm concerned, music and preaching go together like ham and eggs."[96]

Caesar has also managed to resist the lure of popular music and "safe" songs—commercial tunes with "inspirational" rather than overtly Christian lyrics. And because she has remained committed to her faith in the process, Boyer notes that she has achieved unusual stature within the close-knit gospel community: "She stands above the rest of us. When Shirley Caesar does something new, the rest of us feel it is okay to do that. There are those of us in the church who believe we sing because we want to and some of us sing because we have to. Shirley is a preacher who sings."[97]

As for the Caravans, Caesar's departure in 1966 effectively ended the Vans' long run. The other remaining members left in the months that followed. Albertina Walker recruited new singers, including future disco diva Loleatta Holloway, but shortly thereafter officially disbanded the group. Walker continued to record sporadically as a solo and occasionally hosted Caravan reunion concerts, which almost always attracted all surviving members—a tribute to her genial, compassionate leadership. Her generosity in sharing the spotlight was the Vans' secret weapon. In later years, however, Tina has unsuccessfully tried to downplay her role: "What made the Caravans so unique was the fact that everyone was a soloist. We came together and worked as a group. That's why, when everyone went their separate ways, they were successful."[98]

Chapter Thirteen

Gospel's Evolution: From Alex Bradford to James Cleveland to Andrae Crouch

Just as it became second nature for the singers that they listened to—
Mahalia Jackson, the Staple Singers, Shirley Caesar—to play around
with a note, so too did they become comfortable about straying into
uncharted territory on their quilting style, producing compositions
quite unlike the norms of American quilt-makers. Off of the radio,
into their heads and hands, a new quilt is formed.

—Gee's Bend: The Women and Their Quilts[1]

A garrulous man in a mohair suit, with the ample girth and well-
manicured demeanor of a successful corporation man, James Cleveland is probably America's most successful and most influential gospel performer. Pastor of the Cornerstone Institutional Baptist
Church, Los Angeles; best-selling recording artist and producer;
Founder and President of the Gospel Music Workshop; soul food res-
taurant proprietor and—in a world where the apparent contradic-
tions between liturgy and high theatre, spirituality and material
success are effortlessly reconciled—superstar.

—Mick Brown, 1981[2]

Alex Bradford

The evolution of gospel music accelerated in the late 1960s, spurred by the
creative genius of a handful of singer/songwriter/performers who continued to look both forward and backward for inspiration. Building on the
advances found in the music of the best of the male quartets and the Caravans,
Alex Bradford emerged as one of gospel's greatest innovators—and greatest char-

acters. In his too-short career, there appeared to be no world Bradford could not conquer. Charismatic, complex, and extravagantly talented, Alex Bradford was destined to be a star.

Born in the heart of the Great Depression in Bessemer, Alabama, Bradford's parents somehow managed to pay for piano and dance lessons for their child. By age four, he was appearing on local stages. By age thirteen, he had his own gospel group and a year later had his own radio show. He studied briefly in New York, then returned to Alabama to attend the prestigious Snow Hill Institute, founded by William James Edwards—the great-grandfather of filmmaker Spike Lee. At one point, he even taught school briefly, thus earning him the lifelong title "Professor."[3]

Gospel-mad Bessemer and nearby Birmingham were regular stops on the gospel highway, and Bradford heard many of the genre's immortals. One frequent visitor to local Holiness churches was the ubiquitous Arizona Dranes, who "regaled" young Alex with stories whenever she was in town.[4] On a tour of Alabama, the Roberta Martin Singers visited the small church where Bradford was directing the choir. According to longtime Martin associate Leona Price, the legendary songwriter was impressed with young Alex's style and fervor: "Miss Martin took him under her wing and encouraged him to such heights that he became world renowned."[5]

Bradford migrated to Chicago after World War II and worked with Martin, Robert Anderson, and was briefly employed by Mahalia Jackson before joining Martin alumnus Willie Webb and his group. Webb allowed Bradford to sing his startlingly original arrangement of the old Protestant hymn "Every Day and Every Hour" on his next record. While only a mild commercial success, the arrangement and Bradford's multioctave voice caught the ears of industry veterans, including Specialty's Art Rupe. When the Professor formed the Bradford Specials in 1953, Rupe offered him a contract. The result was *Too Close to Heaven,* a tour de force that sounds remarkably fresh today. In the midst of the title track, Bradford's husky baritone suddenly shoots to a true high C in falsetto—and back again. "Too Close to Heaven" was a career-making single and only the first of many hits.[6] The song sold a million copies, and Bradford's record label modestly dubbed him "The Singing Rage of the Gospel Age."[7]

The Specials were an all-male gospel group, *not* a quartet, built around two tenor voices, soprano and alto, more like the Roberta Martin Singers than the Dixie Hummingbirds. It was a daring combination, but Bradford's songwriting and arranging skills meant that hit after hit followed, including "Let God Abide," "He'll Wash Whiter Than Snow" (with Sallie Martin), "He's a Wonder," "Lord, Lord, Lord," and "God Is Good to Me." Throughout his career, Bradford worked with countertenor Charles Campbell and their recordings were immediately popular with African-American choirs across the country.[8]

But unlike many artists, the more popular the group got, the more daring Bradford became. His songs were supported by instruments new to gospel, in-

Alex Bradford is one of gospel's greatest innovators—and this is his most famous gospel song. (author's collection)

I'M TOO CLOSE TO HEAVEN — 3 — 2

cluding the celeste and bongos, he instituted outrageously elaborate choreography, and he dressed the Specials in flamboyant robes of his own design. All of this was underpinned by Bradford's sometimes overpowering vocals and instinctive piano accompaniment. Within a few months, he became the highest paid male artist in gospel.[9]

During this period, Bradford was chosen as one of the featured artists at the Apollo Theater's first gospel program. "Bradford was always a winner," recalled promoter Thurman Ruth. "He was always a showman. A great singer, maybe not the best singer in the world, but he was a great singer. He went over very big at our first show."[10] But Bradford's emotional performances often ran longer than the group's allotted slot. After several performances, Bradford was confronted by production manager Leonard Reed, who cautioned the gospel singer to stay within his scheduled sixteen minutes. "Listen, Mr. Reed," Bradford said, "what do we do if the Holy Spirit arrives?" Reed stared evenly at Bradford and replied, "Make sure He leaves by the end of the record, that's all."[11] According to Etta James, Bradford was *also* a regular at the parties that invariably followed shows at the Apollo and other New York venues, whether they were gospel shows or not.[12]

As the 1960s deepened, so did Bradford's interest in other forms of expression. "I want to record all kinds of music," he told Anthony Heilbut, "and I mean all kinds."[13] He left Specialty in 1959 and moved restlessly to various other labels, including Gospel, Choice, Vee-Jay, Checker, Nashboro, Savoy, and Atlantic. With each release, both the instrumental and vocal arrangements became "increasingly intricate and polished."[14] Bradford's first two releases for Vee-Jay are particularly noteworthy. As in the past, he takes the bulk of the vocals, including the curious "Angel on Vacation"—which lyrically can be interpreted either as a secular love song or a standard gospel number. However, on the Vee-Jay albums, he allows various members of the Specials to step forward. The most memorable cuts are by the only female member of the group, Madeline Bell, who will gain fame later singing with the Stones and Joe Cocker. Here, however, her "stunning" contralto shines on "What About You," "Daniel Is a Prayin' Man," and "Just Know I Made It In."[15]

Bradford also wrote, produced, and performed for other artists during this period, including early rock-and-roll star LaVern Baker, creating what is arguably her best work.[16] Ray Charles transformed one of Bradford's songs into his groundbreaking "I Got a Woman." "Never had a secular song had this kind of spiritual passion," wrote one writer, "this kind of down-home fervor, this kind of 'home cookin'.'" The remake did not sit well with some listeners, who called it "blasphemous."[17]

Bradford continued to surprise his audience. He resettled in Newark, New Jersey, to become minister of music for the famed Abyssinian Baptist Church in the heart of the Newark ghetto. Soon, his thrilling arrangements and the choir's thundering performances (often featuring Madeline Bell as soloist) were the talk of the industry. Veteran talent scout John Hammond convinced Columbia to agree to the risky venture of recording a live album with a hundred-voice choir. However, as Hammond later wrote, Bradford himself was signed to Savoy at the time, so he could direct the choir and write their songs, but he could not sing on the record itself:

> The congregation was present and we recorded its responses. The Columbia engineer and I were the only white people there. I even hired a black photographer to take pictures of the choir in action. Later I found out that one other white was present: Herman Lubinsky, president of Savoy, showed up to make sure his star, Alex Bradford, did not open his mouth during the session![18]

The album, *Shakin' the Rafters*, credited to "the Abyssinian Baptist Choir, Under the Director of Professor Alex Bradford," was a moderate success. Recorded in stereo, it remains a steady-seller in Columbia's otherwise skimpy gospel catalog and is a pivotal, if somewhat underrated, release in the history of gospel music.

But Bradford continued to search for new avenues of artistic expression. In 1961, he joined old friend Marion Williams in bringing poet/essayist Langston Hughes's gospel-flavored retelling of the Christmas story, *Black Nativity*, to Broadway. Producer Gary Kramer got the idea from a delightful Christmas album Williams had released some years earlier, and her fresh arrangements of hoary Christmas carols and overfamiliar seasonal hymns captivated audiences.[19] Early reviews did not have much to say about the sets, choreography, or book, but loved the singing: "The voices plunge into sudden dark growls like muted trombones and soar in ecstatic squeals and frantic clarinets."[20] Later, Williams admitted that the daily grind of rehearsals and performances made everyone work harder than they had worked in years. "Alex and I wasn't doing much in church," she said. "We knew this was our big chance, and we'd better sing."[21] The play was a mild success in New York but was a smash hit overseas, where it ran for several years. Madeline Bell stayed in London to become one of the most in-demand backup session singers in England.[22] *Black Nativity* was also the direct source of later rock-gospel shows, such as *Jesus Christ Superstar* and *Godspell*.[23]

Black Nativity also boosted Williams's career. Despite being "gospel's leading lyric soprano and one of its greatest growlers," the irrepressible Williams had been little more than an afterthought with the Clara Ward Singers. She finally left in 1958 after numerous financial disputes with the legendary penny-pincher Gertrude Ward and formed Marion Williams and the Stars of Faith with some of the Wards' best singers, including Kitty Parham and Henrietta Waddy. Their most popular number was a fiery remake of the Wards' "Packing Up," which outshines the original. While singing the song, Williams would march through the auditorium or church collecting purses, then unerringly return them to their rightful owners at the song's conclusion.[24]

In the years that followed, Bradford's concerts were populated by the stars of rock and R&B, from the Beatles to Little Richard. Bradford continued to tour Europe and Australia, and his costumes and stage persona grew increasingly ostentatious. Ray Charles told Bradford that he was his "ideal" as a gospel singer, and invited the Professor to send him songs any time.[25]

Bradford's next foray into theater came in 1969, as the arranger for Vinnette Carroll's groundbreaking African-American adaptation of *Alice in Wonderland*, called *But Never Jam Today*. The production wowed critics, who praised it as "original and entertaining," but the show never found a steady audience.[26] Bradford toured in the mid-1970s for two years with Carroll's *Don't Bother Me, I Can't Cope*. The original production in 1972 made Carroll the first African-American woman to direct on Broadway. "I want to be an all-around singer," Bradford said at the time. "I'd love to do musical comedy. I'm too late for opera. I want to sing 'I've Got to Be Me' and also be the embodiment of 'earth.'"[27]

Bradford returned to Broadway again in 1976 when he wrote the songs for Carroll's *Your Arms Too Short to Box With God*—a gospel-styled reworking of the New Testament book of St. Matthew. The original production made a star of Delores Hall and introduced Bradford's music to a new audience. Critics lauded the music's "durability and soulfulness."[28] *Your Arms Too Short* featured several innovations, including a black Jesus who communicated only through dance. At a time when African-American-oriented productions such as *The Wiz*, *Bubbling Brown Sugar*, *For Colored Girls Who Have Considered Suicide/When the Rainbow Is Enuf*, and a revival of *Porgy and Bess* were rife on Broadway, *Newsweek*'s Jack Kroll liked it best of all, calling it "irresistible."[29] Theater critic Warren B. Burdine hailed it as well, calling it an important bridge for African Americans, combining "a profound faith in Christianity" with an "uncompromising black pride." A revival in 1982 with Patty LaBelle and the Reverend Al Green fared nearly as well.[30]

But in 1978, Bradford, just fifty-one, suffered a stroke while working on still another musical, *Don't Cry, Mary*, and died a few weeks later. A few years earlier, he had been one of the speakers at Clara Ward's funeral. After first looking around the church where most of gospel's elite had gathered to pay their respects, he offered this eerily prophetic tribute: "The choir's getting smaller down here. Used to be twenty or thirty, looked around the other day and found only two or three. Clara, I want you to know I'm too close to heaven to turn around."[31]

Little footage of any kind remains of the electrifying Bradford in performance. The Center for Black Music Research in Chicago has a nearly complete collection of Sid Ordower's *Jubilee Showcase*, a weekly gospel music program that aired in Chicago from 1963 until 1984. Much of the footage is priceless, including some of the only known shots of Thomas Dorsey playing his distinctive boogie-woogie piano from an episode that aired December 1, 1964. But perhaps the most haunting show is from November 1, 1964. In it, Alex Bradford, resplendent in a tailored robe, is joined by Prince Stewart and a young Marion Williams and the Stars of Faith performing selections from *Black Nativity*. Bradford is beaming, caught up in the music, but always cognizant of the camera's blinking red light.[32]

The author of "more standards than any other gospel composer of his generation," Professor Alex Bradford's music was "reverently traditional and restlessly innovative, true to its spiritual roots, but never out of step with the advances of contemporary pop and jazz."[33]

James Cleveland

The definitive biography of Bradford's main rival and successor—James Cleveland—has yet to be written. But when it is completed, it will reveal the sheer scope of the man's influence. And like Bradford—whom he soon eclipsed—Cleveland's impact was felt far beyond gospel. At one point in Cornel West and Henry Louis Gates, Jr.'s prophetic *The Future of the Race*[34], the two great African-American historians present a short list of the "most profound black cultural products" African Americans have given the modern world. This list includes John Coltrane's sax solos, James Baldwin's essays, and "James Cleveland's gut gospels."[35]

Born in Chicago, Cleveland heard gospel music on every corner. "I was exposed to some of the greatest names in gospel," he recalled, "and got a chance to work with them at an early age—Mahalia Jackson, Beatrice Lux, Robert Anderson and the Barrett Sisters."[36] He took piano lessons at age five, was Mahalia's paperboy, daily pressing his ear to the door of her beauty shop to hear her sing, and made his first public appearance at age eight as a boy soprano in Thomas Dorsey's Junior Gospel Choir at the famed Pilgrim Baptist Church.[37] According to Cleveland, his first solo for Dorsey came about in a somewhat roundabout fashion: "My grandmother was in his choir and I had to go to rehearsal with her all the time. I just got bored and started singing. Then he wrote a song for me and that's how I got started."[38]

Like Bradford, Cleveland consciously learned Roberta Martin's piano style (he studied with "Little" Lucy Smith) and incorporated it into his first group, the Thorne Crusaders. Cleveland was also composing and, at age sixteen, the Roberta Martin Singers recorded his "Grace Sufficient," which quickly became a gospel standard. Eventually, the demands of hitting the high notes in the days before public address systems ravaged his vocal cords, and by age twenty-three Cleveland already possessed a gravelly voice that only became more raspy with age.[39]

Cleveland always claimed that his early involvement in gospel music was as much due to persistence as to any talent on his part. For instance, he said he made it his business to attend every gospel concert or recording session in Chicago:

I'd stand around by the door and hope somebody's musician didn't show up. Then I'd offer to play for them. They'd ask me, "Boy, can you play such-and-such?" And I'd always say I could even if I never heard of it before in my life. Then they'd say, "All right. I need an E-flat," and I'd go right out there and start playing.[40]

Cleveland experienced a tumultuous tenure as pianist and musical director with the Caravans, leaving and joining several times, writing some of their best-known songs, perfecting his "half-crooning, half-preaching" performance style—always supported by his fluid, funky piano accompaniment. He relished the call and response format of the spirituals and often wrote repetitive "vamps" into his songs, which both allowed him room to preach and his best soloists room to wail.[41]

Through the course of working first with the Caravans, then the Gospel Chimes, the Gospel All Stars, and eventually his own James Cleveland Singers in the 1950s and 1960s, Cleveland entered one of the most prolific and creative individual periods in gospel music history, writing such standards as "I Get a Blessing Every Day," "Walk Around Heaven All Day," "Lord, Do It for Me," "I've Been in the Storm Too Long," and "Where Is Your Faith in God"—perhaps 500 songs in his lifetime. Other artists quickly took notice. Chess Records' legendary Leonard Caston often played Cleveland's LPs in the Chess studios, and Mitty Collier's two biggest hits for the label were unapologetic rewrites of Cleveland songs: "I Had a Talk with My Man" ("I Had a Talk With God Last Night") and "No Faith, No Love" ("No Cross, No Crown").[42]

By the early 1960s, Cleveland was at the top of his profession. And yet, like Bradford, Cleveland later told an interviewer that he was still dissatisfied: "I'd felt I'd been with all the gospel greats . . . I had my group, the All Stars, and on and on, but it didn't seem fulfilling enough. So I moved to California with the idea of getting a job, finding a church to work with, and just leaving gospel alone for a while."[43]

Cleveland joined the westward migration of gospel artists—which in time included Bessie Griffin, Clara Ward and the Ward Singers, Cassietta George, Raymond Rasberry and the Mighty Clouds of Joy—that had begun in earnest following World War II. Once there, they were assimilated into a flourishing gospel community, built around Thurston Frazier, Gwendolyn Cooper Lightner, Albert Goodson, J. Earle Hines, Doris Akers, and others. Cleveland's arrival in January 1962 sparked a giant concert honoring "James Cleveland Day" and featuring most of California's gospel elite.[44] It was a good move for most artists. It was only in California that Griffin was finally able to escape Mahalia Jackson's long shadow, appearing on a host of television shows, including *Shindig*, and performing in the gospel musical, *Portraits in Bronze*.[45]

Once in southern California, Cleveland opted not to enter the world of popular music or work to make gospel more contemporary-sounding. Instead, he looked back to a childhood spent singing in the choirs of Thomas Dorsey. Cleveland had recently signed a long-term contract with Savoy Records and was eager to try a different choral approach. He began recording with the First Baptist Church Choir of Nutley, New Jersey, using the massed voices of the choir as a single instrument. In 1963, Cleveland and the choir released *Peace Be Still*, a landmark live recording that would eventually sell more than a million copies. The "complex voicings and odd time signatures" of the title track—actually a re-working of a sixteenth-century English madrigal—and the subsequent release with the Voices of Tabernacle of the hit single "The Love of God" suddenly made massed choirs fashionable among young people.[46]

Invigorated by the discipline he heard in California's choirs, the result of a long tradition of exacting musicianship,[47] Cleveland began working systematically with a variety of choirs, including the Voices of Tabernacle, the Prayer Tabernacle Choir in Detroit ("God Has Smiled on Me"), the Salem Inspirational Choir ("No Ways Tired"), the Angelic Choir ("Stood on the Banks of the Jordan"), and finally with his own Southern California Community Choir, sometimes called "James Cleveland personified."[48]

The image of a choir in white robes surging in unison around a hot rhythm section has grown to iconic status in American popular culture, joining both scenes of a well-dressed male quartet and a diva-like female singer moaning in front of a piano as the three most readily identifiable "faces" of gospel music to the public. Cleveland, writes Mick Brown, almost single-handedly gave the world that picture of a modern black gospel choir:

> Choir music is gospel at its most musically developed. It is music springing on its heels, propelled by piano, organ, electric bass and a hard and relentless drum beat, with the lead singer taking the refrain, the choir echoing the response, building through a series of immaculate, often complex vocal arrangements to a climactic emotional release. In it one recognizes one of the cornerstones of rock 'n' roll, yet the music here bursts with a contagious sense of joy and celebration that much contemporary rock seems to have lost altogether.[49]

Not that Cleveland somehow "invented" the mass choir. The famed Wings Over Jordan Choir had been on the airwaves since the late 1930s, and in Los Angeles, J. Earle Hines's St. Paul's Church Choir had both a radio show and a hit record in the late 1940s.[50] But spurred by the success of Bradford's Abyssinian Choir and Cleveland's various aggregations, other big gospel choirs emerged in the 1960s, most notably Mattie Moss Clark's Southwest Michigan State Choir and, later, the Church of God in Christ Convocation Choir. The "close harmonies and crisp rhythms" of these choirs provided the perfect showcase for a number of soloists as well, including Moss's daughters (who would achieve stardom as the Clark Sisters) and Douglas Miller.[51] Cleveland's success was such that, for many years, Savoy was known as the "choir" company, which differentiated it from the more quartet-oriented Peacock and Specialty labels. Cleveland served as a de facto artist and repertoire man for Savoy, wielding significant power over who the label signed or didn't sign.[52]

Fred Mendelsohn, who succeeded Herman Lubinsky as head of Savoy, said that—during his prime—Cleveland was the most powerful figure in gospel music:

> There's nobody bigger. . . . [Cleveland] also presents new artists. On the album, he sings one of the songs, and the [new] artist takes it from there. The fact that he is on the album sells it and introduces a new artist. The follow-up is an album by the new artist alone. There's no promotion. You send the new releases to the jockeys and wait. At times, a record will not take off until six months after it's released, but then it will go on selling for sixty years.[53]

By all accounts, Cleveland had a gift for working with choirs. "He could make you see the song," explained the Reverend Marvin Winans, a noted choir director himself.[54] Cleveland's gruff demeanor—explained partly by his urgent, hoarse voice—rarely masked his genuine love for the singers and the music: "Within everybody, there's a certain well of creativity. There are so many sitting there in the choir that don't even know their own potential. I draw them out, and I get a whole lot of stuff out of them that they're not aware they have."[55]

Cleveland soon recognized something significant happening with the nationwide rise of the choirs and was the first to capitalize on it. In late 1968, he founded the Gospel Music Workshop of America (GMWA). The organization spread rapidly until there are currently more than 200 chapters, with a membership in the tens of thousands. The GMWA's annual convention has become one of gospel music's preeminent events. Cleveland used the convention to teach participants his new songs and arrangements and then record with an all-star "mass" choir. The resulting albums would invariably sell well.[56] More than thirty GMWA mass choir albums have been released and the careers of artists such as Kirk Franklin and John P. Kee have been launched through these popular projects.[57] Neither of the two older gospel organizations, Dorsey's National Convention of Choirs and Choruses nor the National Quartets Union, have managed to maintain the GMWA's pace.

In November 1970, Cleveland, now firmly established as "the Crown Prince of Gospel," fulfilled a lifelong dream and founded the Cornerstone Institutional Baptist Church in Los Angeles. As senior pastor, Cleveland's sermons were—like his music—"part Baptist, part Sanctified."[58] One early visitor to the church was Mick Jagger. While the Stones were in Los Angeles finishing their *Exile on Main Street* album in January 1972, Cleveland protégée Billy Preston took Jagger to Cornerstone to hear Cleveland.[59] It was shortly thereafter that the Stones invited Dorothy Love Coates to open their 1972 world tour for them.

But Cleveland's best-known and best-loved project may have been Aretha Franklin's *Amazing Grace*, recorded in two days at the New Temple Missionary

Baptist Church in Los Angeles in 1972. Cleveland arranged and directed the music and the album, which "offers a stunning tribute to the scope and influence of the black Christian tradition on black public life and the black popular music tradition."[60] Together, Franklin and Cleveland provide a rich overview of all significant trends in gospel music. And from a sociological viewpoint, commentator Mark Anthony Neal believes that *Amazing Grace* "documents the end of perhaps [the black church's] most influential period, a period defined by its willing partnership with the black protest movement."[61]

Cleveland's later years were filled with the kind of financial security and public acclaim few gospel artists achieve in a lifetime. He was asked to work on Elton John's *Blue Moves* album in 1976,[62] undertook a mostly unsuccessful tour of Europe with Liza Minnelli,[63] worked with Quincy Jones on *Roots,* recorded the opera *Porgy and Bess* with Ray Charles and Cleo Laine, lobbied hard with the GMWA to increase the number of gospel categories for the Grammy Awards in 1975,[64] and in 1981 became the first gospel artist with a star on the "Hollywood Walk of Fame."[65]

In the end, Cleveland recorded more than 100 albums, including sixteen that went gold. He was awarded a fistful of Grammy awards and virtually every other award a gospel artist could win. His performances were always sold out, and when he entered the annual GMWA convention, his adoring public always stood and applauded feverishly. Cleveland "invigorated the traditional choir," wrote one journalist, "reintroducing it into contemporary gospel after years of dominance by quartets and soloists."[66]

According to Anthony Heilbut and others, Cleveland's death, at the young age of fifty-nine, on February 9, 1991, was the result of complications from the AIDS virus.[67] Fortunately, for the most part, the gospel community he had led for so long rallied around his memory and his memorial service was moved to the Shrine Auditorium to handle the overflow crowd of more than four thousand mourners. The tributes were loving and emotional, including one from Shirley Caesar: "A lot of people didn't know they could sing before James Cleveland came along. Don't let anybody tell you, 'Don't cry.' I say, 'Cry.'"[68]

Also in attendance was Aretha Franklin who, as a child, sang in Cleveland's choir in her father's church. "Anyone who heard him," she said, "you were touched by him. He was a motivator, an innovator. A great soul has passed on. I'm thankful that he touched my life. He leaves the greatest legacy."[69] Perhaps the Reverend Al Green said it best: "He brought excitement to gospel music."[70]

Edwin Hawkins

One of the many musicians who considered himself a "legacy" of James Cleveland was Edwin Hawkins, who was also at the Shrine Auditorium that day. Of Cleveland, Hawkins told a reporter, "We have all been influenced by him. I grew up with his music. We all bought his records as children—that's how we learned to sing gospel music."[71] But Hawkins would take Cleveland's lessons one step further—he would take the mass choir out of the church and put it on the nation's Top 40 radio stations.

Hawkins's song was an anomaly that has yet to be repeated, a jolt of energy that cut through the static and the airwaves in the spring of 1969. Amid the riots and chaos that wracked America that year, it provided the soundtrack for when humanity first reached the moon:

> *Oh happy day*
> *Oh happy day*
> *When Jesus washed*
> *When Jesus washed*
> *When Jesus washed*
> *He washed my sins away!*[72]

The composer of "Oh Happy Day," Edwin Hawkins was something of a child prodigy. When his family formed a gospel group and recorded an album in 1957, they turned to seven-year-old Edwin to play the piano. "Music ran in my family," he recalled later. "My mother and most of her brothers were musical. She was one of eleven children and one of her brothers was even a jazz musician."[73] Hawkins was also the first accompanist for an early gospel choir in the Bay Area in the 1950s, the Original Joy Spreaders of Oakland. Years later, one of the founders, Joyce Beasley, recalled that their high school pianist had a flair, even in the beginning:

> When Ed was playing, it was a very unique situation because he could only play in one key and that was F-sharp. So we all sang in F-sharp. When you begin to see a man become famous and he's playing in all keys now, I have to tease him from time to time. Later we changed from him to Roger Payne. But Ed had that sound that was much different.[74]

In 1967, Hawkins was a student at Berkeley, a member of the Ephesian Church of God in Christ (COGIC) in Oakland, and apparently somewhat more proficient on the piano. In that year, along with friend Betty Wright, he co-founded the Northern California State Youth Choir, drawn from Pentecostal churches in Berkeley, San Francisco, Oakland, San Jose, and Richmond, to perform at the Pentecostal Youth Congress in Washington, D.C.[75]

In two years, the popular choir had a full rhythm section, nearly fifty voices, and a flair for performing the bright new songs Hawkins was composing. The choir voted to attend the next youth congress in Cleveland but needed to raise enough money to finance their trip. They went to a San Francisco church that had an old two-track stereo machine where, in just a few hours, they recorded an album's worth of songs, *Let Us Go into the House of the Lord*.[76] Notes one writer, "The record was a happy blend of amateurism, the room sound was both cheap and spacious, and ambition; the music was loaded with foreign influences from bossa nova to soul jazz."[77]

In one of those great, unfathomable coincidences, a copy of one of the tracks, a surging, joyous remake of a Philip Doddridge hymn, found its way into the hands of a DJ at underground FM radio station KSAN in San Francisco two years after it had originally been released. Prior to that point, Tramaine Hawkins, who was one of the "Singers," recalled that *Let Us Go into the House of the Lord* had been ignored by gospel radio:

> You know, sometimes it takes that. It takes someone from the outside to really show you . . . what you have here. . . . [Y]ou're sitting on a gold mine and don't even know it.
>
> And then when the secular industry got a hold to it and . . . went crazy with it, then our own people in the church . . . turned on us, and started criticizing that particular recording because it was played in clubs.[78]

Buddha Records, sensing something special, renamed the group the Edwin Hawkins Singers, released it as Pavilion 2001, and watched—like everyone else—as in nine weeks it peaked at number four in May 1969. Almost exactly one year later, the Edwin Hawkins Singers backed Melanie on "Lay Down (Candles in the Rain)," another unlikely gospel-tinged song that hit number fourteen.[79]

But the song raised the hackles of some church leaders. Petitions were organized to have the song removed from the playlists of secular stations, and "Oh Happy Day" was denounced from dozens of pulpits. Shaken, Hawkins began daily devotional times to handle the attacks:

> It made me really begin to search the Word of God again. Because from when I was a child, I was taught that the gospel should be spread to the "highways and the hedges," that we should "go into all the world." Well, isn't the radio—secular radio—part of the world?[80]

Hawkins never broke through into the Top 40 charts again, and his lead singer, Dorothy Combs Morrison, never replicated her success on "Oh Happy Day," despite going solo the following year. After an appearance at the famed Big Sur Folk Festival in 1969 (later made into a documentary with Crosby, Stills, Nash & Young, among others), the Edwin Hawkins Singers were one of the top-billed acts in the concert documentary *It's Your Thing*, filmed in Yankee Stadium in 1970 and featuring Tina Turner and the Isley Brothers.[81] In 1979, the songwriters of "He's So Fine" successfully sued former Beatle George Harrison, alleging that the music in his hit "My Sweet Lord" was an exact copy of their original. Harrison ruefully replied that his music had *actually* been inspired by "Oh Happy Day." Hawkins graciously refused to sue.[82] *Let Us Go into the House of the Lord* ultimately sold nearly seven million copies.

However, songs this bold—no ambiguous "he" lyrics here!—are too confrontational to appear regularly on pop radio. Without other hits, the cost of keeping a choir of this size together eventually reduced the Edwin Hawkins Singers to seven family members. But Hawkins has continued to be a significant presence in the gospel world, regularly releasing sharp, imaginative choir albums for a variety of labels.[83] He's received nearly a dozen Grammy nominations, winning in 1983 for "If You Love Me." He also founded the Edwin Hawkins Music and Arts Seminar, a showcase for young gospel artists that attracts thousands of musicians to Florida each year.[84]

"I never saw the success of 'Oh Happy Day' as a fluke," Hawkins said. "I've always deemed it a miracle. We were just kids with no idea in the world what we were doing. But our motives were pure—to give glory to God. We did—and He did the rest."[85]

However, Edwin's brother Walter Hawkins would become an even more significant presence in the gospel world. As pastor of the Love Center COGIC in Berkeley, which he founded in 1973, Walter took his "Love Alive" choir into the studio two years later. The first *Love Alive* album featured his wife, Tramaine, on vocals and Edwin on piano and was an out-of-the-box smash hit, selling 300,000 units and staying on the gospel charts for three years. In 1978, *Love Alive II* also sold 300,000 copies and received multiple award nominations. *Love Alive III,* released in 1985, sold a million copies, while 1989's *Love Alive IV* sat on top of the gospel charts for nearly a year. The series is still gospel's best-selling set of mass choir albums.[86] During the period, Walter worked with some of the genre's biggest stars, as well as top secular artists, including Van Morrison. Tramaine and Walter later divorced, but she, too, would emerge as a major gospel star in the 1980s.[87]

Andrae Crouch

The second, and most significant, artist to come out of California's fertile gospel ranks was Andrae Edward Crouch, born with his twin sister Sandra Elaine, to Benjamin and Catherine Dorothea Crouch in 1942. The Crouch family ran a cleaning store in the Compton district in Los Angeles, but Benjamin Crouch's passion was street-corner preaching. The Crouch family worshiped at Emmanuel COGIC (which had once hosted Arizona Dranes), where Andrae's great-uncle Bishop Samuel M. Crouch was the pastor. The Crouches were a musical family in a musical church.[88]

Andrae's musical background was eclectic, listening not just to gospel (especially the Davis Sisters and the Caravans) but to jazz, rock and roll, rhythm and blues, and classical—the music of southern California was as varied as the immigrants who arrived daily.[89] He was also a natural musician, although he remembers stuttering "uncontrollably" until he underwent an intense religious experience at age twelve, when he was cured.[90] As Andrae grew older, he formed

Pastor Andrae Crouch now splits his time between music and his southern California congregation. (photo courtesy of New Christ Memorial COGIC)

the first of several groups with his siblings while his father went into full-time "church planting" for the COGIC bishop, first in Val Verde, then in San Fernando. Eventually, the San Fernando church was organized as Christ Memorial and settled on its current location in Pacoima, where it continues as one of the dominant Pentecostal churches in southern California. While still a teenager, Andrae formed a group of seven young African Americans, called the COGICS. The COGICS included Billy Preston, Edna Wright (the Honeycombs), Gloria Jones (later a Motown songwriter), and sister Sandra (who, too, would become a successful gospel artist).[91] Later, Crouch formed the first Disciples, which included Billy Thedford and Sherman Andrus, both of whom would also become topflight gospel artists.[92]

Crouch began composing at an early age and at fourteen wrote his first song, "The Blood Will Never Lose Its Power." James Cleveland and California gospel music legend Thurston Frazier thought so much of "The Blood"—as it is now commonly called—that they published it through their new music publishing firm, Frazier-Cleveland and Company.[93] "The Blood" has become a gospel standard. Since its first recording by the Caravans, it continues to be heard in choirs, both black and white:

> When I hear it, it's almost like I didn't write it because it seems like its been around all my life. When I wrote it, I didn't know that I was a good songwriter. I had written some of the words on a piece of paper that I threw away. Then my sister picked it up and said, "This is a good song." She was on the piano with me and when we started to sing, there were people at the house at the time who came around and started crying. Then it became a song that everybody was singing and it's still that way.[94]

By the mid-1960s, Crouch and the Disciples were appearing regularly throughout the West Coast, a gospel-rock group that performed unapologetically Christian songs, usually written by Crouch. A chance meeting with producer Ralph Carmichael of the new Light label led to the group's first album, *Take the Message Everywhere*. A world tour with evangelist John Haggai followed.[95] Eventually, Crouch—who obviously has an uncanny eye for talent—assembled the best-known lineup of the Disciples, one that included his sister Sandra, percussionist Bill Maxwell (later a gospel songwriter and producer), Danniebelle Hall (another gospel solo artist), and horn player Fletch Wiley (still another popular gospel writer/producer).[96]

Crouch and the Disciples emerged at a unique time in American religious history. Southern California was the epicenter of the new "Jesus movement," a widespread phenomenon among young people that emphasized the "accessibility" of Jesus Christ. The accompanying "Jesus music" melded traditional religious lyrics with contemporary rock music. Crouch and the Disciples were multiracial and their music was a catchy mixture of gospel and rock. And like their northern California counterparts, Sly and the Family Stone, the group was an immediate hit with white audiences.[97]

In the years that followed, some observers claimed that Crouch's constant performing for primarily white audiences caused him to "eventually give up some of the hard-edged improvisations in his performances."[98] But no less an authority that the Reverend James Cleveland once had a different take, celebrating the connections that the Disciples created:

> Andrae has bridged the gap between black and white audiences . . . The white artists are very interested in the more soulful type of gospel music. . . . [M]any

black musicians are now embracing the contemporary sound. There is a great upsurge of white choirs that sing like blacks, and the blacks have always tried to excel and perfect performances relating to sound, arrangement and instrumentation. Orchestrations and the like bring us closer to what the white man has been doing all the time. . . . So they're coming our way and we're going their way. Somewhere in the middle of the road, we're bound to run into one another.[99]

It does not take a trained ear to hear the differences in the recordings released during this period by Cleveland and the recordings released by Crouch. This dichotomy exemplifies the next stage in the evolution of gospel music. To Horace Boyer, Cleveland typifies the "traditional" sound of gospel music:

If the sound, devices, and accompaniment of the gospel music prove to be an extension of the established tradition—that is, the tradition as established by Thomas A. Dorsey, Mahalia Jackson, Roberta Martin, the Pilgrim Travelers, and Brother Joe May, it is called *traditional* gospel music. If the sound, devices and accompaniment of the music are distinctly, recognizably "borrowed" from another already established tradition—that is, jazz, soul or blues, and it is difficult to translate the music into the traditional gospel sound, it is called contemporary gospel music.[100]

Crouch and the Disciples, by contrast, were the first popular proponents of what Boyer calls "contemporary" gospel. The rise of contemporary gospel, however, did not come without a cost:

Generally speaking, contemporary gospel is rejected by the mainstream Black church, though Andrae Crouch has successfully developed a Black church following—only, however after first building an audience of white people, high school- and college-age Black students, and jazz lovers.[101]

The main protest against leveled against Andrae Crouch and the Disciples was that the group was taking gospel music out of the church—although these complaints bear more than a passing similarity to those launched against first Thomas A. Dorsey, then Sister Rosetta Tharpe.[102] Still, through the entire 1970s, Crouch and the Disciples were the best-known, best-selling group in what would be known as contemporary Christian music (CCM). Their albums—*Keep On Singing, Soulfully, This Is Another Day, Take Me Back*, and others—set numerous sales records. *Live in London,* with its futuristic cover of an UFO-like piano soaring above the United Kingdom, in particular has been cited by numerous artists as the most influential album in their musical development. *Live in London* is an ambitious double album—then a rarity in either gospel music or CCM—a powerful mixture of straight-ahead gospel, rock, and what would later be called "praise and worship" music.

It was also during the 1970s that Crouch wrote and introduced a number of original songs that would become standards themselves: "My Tribute," "Soon and Very Soon," "Through It All," "Start All Over Again," "Satisfied," "Bless His Holy Name," "Everything Changed," and others. Artists ranging from Elvis Presley to Pat Boone recorded his songs, and Paul Simon performed "Jesus Is the Answer" in his live show for years.[103] At the same time, some of Crouch's songs were also being included in new hymnals such as a revised *Songs of Zion* and *The National Baptist Hymnal*.[104]

While Crouch experimented incessantly with his music in the 1970s, his foundational music still remained gospel. Like African-American musicians almost from their arrival in the New World, Crouch's performance of a popular song varies from concert to concert. He retains other gospel characteristics as well. He has recorded radically different versions of the same song on different albums. He always allowed his musicians "room" to solo during certain numbers. He has shown a liking for recasting old hymns in new ways. And finally, like the very best gospel artists, "he brought 'church' into his performance."[105]

At the same time, Crouch has always attracted a large white audience, even though songs such as "Through It All" and "Soon and Very Soon" are "traditional" gospel. Boyer wryly says the multitalented Crouch is a 'split-compositional' personality."[106]

Crouch is pivotal for yet another reason. He was among the first gospel artists to leave behind the lyrics of the spirituals and Dorsey and devote entire songs to praising and worshiping God. The emphasis has shifted from detailing humanity's problems and ultimate salvation to focusing instead exclusively on the person of Jesus Christ or "glorifying" an almighty God.[107]

Crouch's innovations have generated controversy, primarily in the gospel music world. More than one artist and critic has wondered if, in fact, the music of Hawkins and Crouch should truly be termed "gospel" at all.[108] One of the most interesting approaches to resolving the dispute is to be found in George Ricks's *Some Aspects of the Religious Music of the United States Negro: An Ethnomusicological Study with Special Emphasis on the Gospel Tradition*. One of the questions Ricks sought to answer was that, by 1977, contemporary gospel music had

> shifted away from basic values of the folk tradition in United States Negro religious music, by means of a combination of methods (ethno-historical and ethnomusicological), a direct relationship in terms of structural characteristics, a relative dating in time, and a continuity of musical values and practices have been established for the spiritual, jubilee, and gospel styles.[109]

But Ricks observed that the decades-long evolution of gospel into what ultimately culminated in contemporary gospel instead "smoothly integrated" the skilled use of mostly European instrumental accompaniment and full harmony, while still "maintaining basic patterns and values of the African musical tradition."[110] In short, while gospel has been changing from the beginning, contemporary gospel is only the latest permutation—and it is *still* gospel.

Music historian Samuel A. Floyd, Jr., writes that during this period the "down-home gut-bucket fervor" was largely replaced by "the slick veneer of Motown-like productions." But Floyd agrees that the "the more refined contemporary black gospel music retains the character of its predecessors, and its performance still depended on a performer-audience call and response rapport unlike that of any other music experience."[111]

Crouch eventually sought to broaden his musical horizons and disbanded the Disciples in 1981. On his solo albums, such as *Don't Give Up,* he worked with some of the top musicians in the country, including Stevie Wonder and Joe Sample. But the releases never caught on with the public in either mainstream or religious music. Eventually, he worked with Michael Jackson ("Man in the Mirror"), Madonna ("Like a Prayer"), and Quincy Jones (on the soundtrack of *The Color Purple,* which earned Crouch on Oscar). He was also involved with the Broadway musical *The Lion King* and performed "Precious Lord, Take My Hand" with his choir in the movie *A Time to Kill.*[112]

One measure of an artist is his or her influence on other artists. Few young artists have even tried to emulate Andrae Crouch's distinctive, original blend of musical styles presented in a gospel format. A few African Americans have gone into CCM since Crouch—Leon Patillo, Morris Chapman, and Larnelle Harris— but all have tended more toward the rock or pop side of the musical spectrum rather than gospel.[113]

Crouch went ten years between releasing albums, from 1984's *No Time to Lose* to *Mercy* in 1994. One writer called *Mercy* a "complete triumph" and predicted that the song "The Lord Is My Light" was "destined to be one of the greatest of all choir songs."[114]

Mercy, which earned two Grammy awards, also marked a return to the church. In 1995, Crouch succeeded his late father, Benjamin, as pastor of the 900-member Christ Memorial COGIC in Pacoima, with an installation ceremony in the posh Century Plaza Hotel, followed by a concert. Crouch had been ordained in 1990. "I didn't know how it was going to happen, but I knew that someday I would be pastor of this church," he told *Jet* magazine.[115] "It's pretty much his nature to be a shepherd," added his sister Sandra, "because he's always had a shepherd's heart."[116]

Since becoming a pastor, Crouch has slowed his once frantic pace. Like James Cleveland before him, he now serves as somewhat of an elder statesman in the gospel community—his "sin" of making gospel "contemporary" long since forgiven. In an article on Crouch in *Ebony,* Walter Burrell noted, "Andrae Crouch insists he isn't an entertainer. If you ask him, he'll tell you he's 'a minister spreading God's word through song.'"[117] A decade after his induction, Crouch is still senior pastor at the renamed New Christ Memorial COGIC, located at 13333 Vaughn Street in Pacoima, with his sister Sandra serving as associate pastor. The church is now located in a predominantly Hispanic neighborhood, so many church services are conducted in Spanish. And, continuing Crouch's lifelong commitment to the disadvantaged, New Christ Memorial has aggressive programs targeting the homeless, the hungry, the incarcerated, the dispossessed, as well as at-risk youth.[118]

Crouch continues to juggle the roles of pastor and musician, however. He recently founded his own record label, Slave Records—its provocative title drawn from Romans 6. He continues to both write and record and is still in demand as a producer. "As I walk through real life, every day a song will come up," Crouch has said. "I'm always in the studio."[119]

Crouch closes his autobiography with these words, which would seem to be the words of an artist at peace with himself and his God: "God just happens to use me. I'm not His first choice, not His second, maybe not even His hundredth; but so be it, He chose me. He gave me some songs and you just happen to hear those songs. I trust that through it all, something I write or sing will be a blessing to you."[120]

The advent of Cleveland, Hawkins, and Crouch marks a significant phase in the evolution of gospel music. For the first time, a significant number of artists are performing in theaters, convention centers, concert halls, and even in open-air stadiums, often to both black and white audiences. At the same time, mass choirs are emerging, forming in hitherto unlikely places, such as college campuses.[121] But for Crouch, the form and the venue are lesser considerations in gospel music. Only the lyrics matter:

> For a person to just hear my story is OK for history, but along with that there needs to be something else in there if it's going to change a life. Music has to have a concept of the Word in it, because the Word changes a situation. So I ask, Who is the song about? What is the song talking about? Why are you talking about it? When did it happen and what went on? And why? What is God trying to tell you through this? That's what I have always tried to pattern myself after— who, what, when, where, how and why. The similarity of the music comes from the art-form, but the story-telling is where the strength is.[122]

Chapter Fourteen

The Last Great Male Quartets

She cried, looking at the men who now stepped up to the microphone; the Mighty Clouds of Joy. So much expansiveness, so much lightness, expressed in the name they gave themselves, she thought. . . . So at home, also, with the spirit they sang to and for. They were real, earthy, generous-hearted, scarred and puffy-eyed, singing for Jesus. And she loved them because they remained who they were through it all.

—Alice Walker, *The Way Forward Is With a Broken Heart*[1]

When this young fellow sang those [gospel] songs, his voice seemed to have gained a new melody. It was something about it that was most spiritual; it had something about it that was heart-warming and had a meaningfulness. He personalized it and made it his own testimony, and that of itself is one of the highest points, I think, in his impact on gospel songs, on gospel singing.

—W. Herbert Brewster on Elvis Presley[2]

The Mighty Clouds of Joy

The dual rise of the mass choirs and Andrae Crouch in the 1970s appeared to sound the death knell of the old "gospel blues" style first codified by Thomas A. Dorsey. But Crouch kept reinventing himself and returned to the form from time to time, especially in the twelve-bar blues format of songs like "Take a Little Time (Thank You, Lord)."[3] James Cleveland also returned to the gospel blues format in 1980 with the song "I Get a Blessing Every Day," a tribute to gospel's roots, performed by the Mighty Clouds of Joy.[4]

Cleveland's choice of the Mighty Clouds of Joy to record the song was deliberate. The Clouds may be the last great quartet—they are certainly among the

The Mighty Clouds of Joy have been one of gospel's most electrifying live shows for more than thirty years. (photo courtesy of Zach Glickman)

most progressive in gospel history. In their nearly five decades, the Clouds have flourished because of their ability to embrace musical change, while still keeping their core distinction—Joe Ligon's hard-driving gospel voice—in the forefront.

The group—originally called the Sensational Wonders, then the Mighty Mighty Clouds of Joy—began in southern California's musical scene in the late 1950s. The Clouds were built around Ligon, lately arrived from Alabama with his family, and bass singer Richard Wallace, himself originally from rural Georgia. Ligon grew up in a religious home, spending most waking hours in churches where his grandfather preached and his grandmother moaned the hymns rather than singing them, so as to better "confuse the Devil." In the Los Angeles area, he heard the great quartets and learned from them, especially June Cheeks and the Sensational Nightingales.[5] After gigging around small churches in the Los

Angeles area, the group signed to Don Robey's Peacock label in 1960, beginning a fifteen-year career that was much more lucrative for Robey than for the Clouds.[6] Critics still rave over some of their Peacock releases, including *Family Circle* from 1963 ("Pyrotechnic performances by this sensational group"), *The Mighty Clouds of Joy Live at the Music Hall* from 1966 ("More church wrecking"), and others.[7]

The Clouds were soon the biggest quartet in gospel music, and their performances were invariably filled with the elite from R&B and soul music. Their famed "Gospel Explosion" tours with the Gospelaires and Violinaires was one of the most successful "packages" of the era. By 1972, *Ebony* magazine proclaimed them "the nation's hottest quartet."[8] But when some of their peers began to leave gospel for secular music, Ligon said he flatly refused:

> Sam Cooke took me to his house once and he said, "Joe, I could write you some R&B songs and you could become rich and famous—look at me." He had this big mansion near Hollywood. He said, "You could have all of this, man, with all that talent! Let me write for you; I'll even put you on my own label and take good care of you." But I . . . never wanted to do that, I just wanted to do the music I love.[9]

At the peak of their popularity, Ligon said the Mighty Clouds of Joy sensed the changes coming in both the gospel and mainstream music industries: "When we first started, we did traditional gospel because that was popular then. In the mid-'70s, we saw the new sounds coming. We were always ahead of ourselves. It was a new day when we tried. My own father didn't even like it."[10]

On tour, the Clouds saw the need for standard small combo (bass, guitar, drums, and keyboards) accompaniment, Ligon said, even though it stretched the small paychecks even further: "You have to be able to change. You can't just say, 'We'll sing just one style and that's all we can do.' A lot of my friends started out in this business, and when the music changed and they couldn't change, the audience left them. And these were big groups, groups that inspired me."[11]

The Clouds broke with tradition in other ways. Ligon said they added razor-sharp choreography, stylish pompadours, and suits so colorful that they outshone even Alex Bradford's colorful robes: "I didn't really want to wear a black suit or a brown suit or a white suit—the basic in churches then. We came out in peach, green, blue, lavender, and we had the same tailor as the Temptations."[12]

Now dubbed "the Temptations of Gospel," the Clouds undertook a series of breakthrough tours and recording sessions, working with the likes of the Stones, Marvin Gaye, James Brown, and Paul Simon, whom they once backed for a months of dates in Madison Square Garden. They released a series of memorable singles, including "What a Friend" and the sermonette "Pray for Me"—which was a hit twice, once as a morality story about a young boy going off to fight in Vietnam and, a few years later, as a cautionary tale about a young boy going off to join a rock-and-roll band.[13] After leaving the Sensational Nightingales, June Cheeks—Ligon's idol and father figure—sometimes toured with the Clouds, who returned the favor by recording an entire album of the Nightingales' most memorable songs.[14]

In the mid-1970s, they recorded "Ride the Mighty High," which remains their biggest hit. The song, with its propulsive beat, was a mild hit on the rock charts, a bigger hit on the disco charts, and suddenly took them before still another new audience. Ligon remembered initially being somewhat unsure about "Ride the Mighty High"'s lyrics:

> It was the most difficult song of all for me to understand. At that time, the people they called "flower children" used to talk about getting high on pot. So I finally asked the song's writer what he meant by "ride the mighty high." He explained that it was a positive message praising the mightiest high of all, the Lord, and that won me over.[15]

The Clouds' performance of "Ride the Mighty High" on *Soul Train*—certainly the first gospel group to ever appear on the popular syndicated dance show—left even some of their most ardent fans in shock. "We caught a lot of flak," Ligon admitted years later. "When we went on *Soul Train,* my dad got so mad. It was unheard of. People thought we'd lost our minds."[16]

But it gained them new fans as well. President Jimmy Carter chose the Mighty Clouds of Joy to be one of the first groups to appear on the White House lawn, performing their hits for families sitting on blankets outside the Rose Garden.[17] A few years later, Roger Troutman, formerly of Zapp, asked the group to record Wilson Pickett's "In the Midnight Hour" on his *The Saga Continues* album.[18] And when Paul Simon assembled the music for his stint as host of the *Cinemax Sessions* in 1987, he included the Clouds, along with Andrae Crouch and the Edwin Hawkins Singers. But never, Ligon has declared, at the expense of their mission: "The Clouds have never sung a song about babes, about breakin' up, makin' up, makin' love. We've had plenty of chances. But even though we might play in night clubs, we're still singing to lift the name of the Lord."[19]

The years have been both kind and unkind to the Clouds. Like many gospel artists, they've recorded for a variety of record labels: Peacock, ABC, MCA, Hob, Word, Intersound, and Light Records. The typical Mighty Clouds of Joy album or concert includes a wide variety of styles, from gospel blues to contemporary gospel to a cappella spirituals. "You have to mix your songs," Ligon said in an interview from 1997. "Go traditional, then go contemporary. Traditional music will never die because the church will never die."[20] As if to underscore the importance of the gospel blues, Aretha Franklin asked Ligon to sing with her "I've Been in the Storm Too Long" in 1988. The scorching duet is one of the highlights of Franklin's *One Lord, One Faith, One Baptism.*[21]

The group has undergone almost consistent personal changes, save for the two surviving original members, Wallace and Ligon. But they are one of the few quartets still on the road. Along the way, they have appeared on a host of television shows and received three Grammy awards. Through it all, the main constants have been an ability to adapt and Ligon's ferocious voice. It's so distinctive, Ligon even has a pet name for it—"the Growl": "When I sing hard with the Growl, I'm giving it all I have. I'm digging deep, way down. I get caught up in what I do. It's a blessing from God that I have. I'm not bragging, but I'm proud of my voice and that it's stayed so strong for 40 years."[22]

The Mighty Clouds of Joy were inducted into the Gospel Music Hall of Fame in 1998, and hip surgery in 2003 only slowed Ligon briefly. In early 2004, at age sixty-six, Ligon was back on the road again with the Clouds, "the Growl" intact, with new worlds yet to conquer.

The Five Blind Boys of Alabama

A second old-time quartet, once considered an anachronism, found new life in the 1980s with one of the most audacious plays in Broadway history—and then became one of America's most improbable music stars in the twenty-first century. The story of the Blind Boys of Alabama begins at the Talladega School for the Negro Deaf and Blind in Alabama, with five young men who studied the classics but listened to the Golden Gate Quartet on the radio from Birmingham at night. "They must have been the only gospel group making records back then," recalled quartet member Jimmy Carter, "because that's the only recorded gospel we heard."[23]

A small glee club became the Happy Land Jubilee Singers, which included Clarence Fountain, George Scott, and Carter in 1939. They supported themselves performing in churches in rural Alabama before turning professional in 1944. In 1948, a promoter in Newark, New Jersey, who was booking both groups, suggested to the Happy Land Jubilees that they change their name to the Five Blind Boys of Alabama to draw attention to their upcoming double bill with the already successful Five Blind Boys of Mississippi.[24] Fountain said the group agreed, then proceeded to get blown off the stage by Archie Brownlee: "They whipped us so good, I got embarrassed. But you got to get a good whippin' before you can learn somethin'."[25]

Although Fountain was never able to outshout Brownlee, the two groups became friends and the Blind Boys gradually evolved from a jubilee quartet into the raw, impassioned "hard gospel" style. Since then, Fountain said he has systematically worked to keep the group growing musically. Like the Clouds, they have incorporated each of gospel's new stylistic changes with grace and style. "We can do it all," Fountain told *Billboard*, "four-part harmony, five-part harmony, jubilee, contemporary, and we sing traditional. We're trying to market to the masses of people, not just to black audiences or the saved."[26]

During gospel's Golden Age, the Blind Boys of Alabama "were among the most dynamic, energetic gospel quartets" in the business, consistently topping the charts and filling the pews wherever they went. They eventually recorded for every major gospel label—Specialty, Vee-Jay, Elektra, Savoy, Peacock, Hob, MCA, Jewel, Philly International, Keen, Wajji, Atlanta International—and enjoyed numerous hits. The group's best-known numbers, however, almost all had "mother" themes, including "I Can See Everybody's Mother But Mine," "My Mother Used to Pray for Me," "Let Me Hear My Mother Pray Again," "Mother's on the Train," and others.[27]

Like most of the great gospel acts, Fountain said the Blind Boys were regularly tempted to defect to the mainstream music world, be it R&B, soul, or rock and roll:

> I was in the studio with Sam Cooke when he signed his contract. The man offered me one just like he did him. But I turned it down because that ain't what I told the Lord I wanted to do. I wanted to sing gospel, that's what I wanted to do and that's what He allowed me to do, so I'm satisfied. . . . I [once] told the Lord, "If you do this and you do that, then I'll stay out in the gospel field and work for You alone, as a Christian." It's what I promised him. When you promise God something, you don't go back on that.[28]

Still, like most gospel quartets, even the Blind Boys of Alabama fell on hard times in the mid-1970s. Fountain even left the group for a few years to record as a solo artist. When he returned, there were—briefly—two competing Blind Boys of Alabama groups.[29] Despite several fine albums, bookings dried up and venues became smaller and smaller. The group survived by repeatedly touring Europe and because of Fountain's business management acumen. "We know exactly where to go when things get hard," he said. "We got certain spots to go, just like a following of a football team."[30]

Like Alex Bradford, the Blind Boys' renaissance began in an unexpected locale: off-Broadway. Composer Bob Telson and director/adapter Lee Breuer had created a visionary retelling of Sophocles' *Oedipus at Colonus* (the second play in the *Oedipus Rex* trilogy), but a trial run in the early 1980s in Europe with a doo-wop group failed miserably. The producers then turned to the Blind Boys. "We came in and put our stamp on it," Fountain said, "a little rock and roll beat to get it up. A rock band would've been too much. You need a gospel group to give it just the right beat and put it in perspective."[31] Telson and Breuer had collaborated on an earlier musical, *Sister Suzie Cinema,* with only nominal success. But Telson, who had once toured with the Blind Boys on keyboards, reconfigured the storyline and music to set it in a Sanctified church. The resulting pairing of the blind Oedipus and the Blind Boys of Alabama made *Gospel at Colonus* an immediate hit in 1983.[32]

Gospel at Colonus, with Morgan Freeman as the Messenger, enjoyed a lengthy run at the Brooklyn Academy of Music and won an Obie award for Best Off-

Broadway Musical. While the Broadway production only lasted sixty-one performances in 1988, the production's national tours were commercially successful and were followed by a cast album and presentation on the Public Broadcasting System's *Great Performances* series. *Gospel at Colonus* has also enjoyed multiple revivals.[33]

Although the *Gospel at Colonus* is not overtly Christian, Fountain noted the similarities between gospel call and response and the "Greek chorus" format. Likewise, he had no problem reconciling his faith with its message:

> Oedipus was all screwed up. He killed his papa and went with his mama, had children by her. Oh man, things were all messed up. He wanted to find some peace before he died. You gotta get things right with God. If you don't get it right, there's devastation. But if God is in you and you in Him, all things are possible. That's the message of the play. I'll hang with that philosophy. You have to believe that to sing gospel.[34]

In his book *The Power of Black Music,* Samuel A. Floyd, Jr., lavishly praises *Gospel at Colonus* and suggests that it somehow captured the symbolism of both Greek myth *and* African-American ritual: "This remarkable integration of acting, speaking and singing in Call-Response delivery is a stunning reinterpretation that summarizes the gospel tradition while revealing and expressing the universality of human experience."[35]

Gospel at Colonus raised the Blind Boys' profile significantly and they worked steadily again—still playing some churches, but now adding jazz and blues festivals, enjoying a Sunday brunch residency at the House of Blues in Los Angeles, opening for Tom Petty and the Heartbreakers, and continuing to tour Europe.[36] The group recorded several more memorable albums, including *Deep River* (Nonesuch, 1992) and *I Brought Him With Me* (House of Blues Records, 1995), but the dramatic turnaround came with the release of *Spirit of the Century* on Peter Gabriel's Real World Records in 2001. *Spirit of the Century* is both a radical departure and a systematic return to the gospel roots of the Blind Boys of Alabama. Booking agent Chris Goldsmith and producer John Chelew conceived of the project, which wedded a simple, funky accompaniment (by guitarist John Hammond, Jr., harmonica-player Charlie Musselwhite, David Lindley on strings, and others) with dramatic renditions of songs by Tom Waits, Ben Harper, and the Stones, along with some traditional gospel. Chelew's vision was to produce music that would pair the Blind Boys "with Delta blues and the real scary gospel background—that ghostly aura that original gospel has. My mission was to bring the sound of the Blind Boys up to the current moment by going back into their past."[37]

The pair shopped the completed project, and Gabriel, whose label specializes in world music, loved it. "For us, it was a no-brainer," he told *Billboard*. "As soon as we heard the music, we were hooked."[38] The album received the Best

Traditional Soul Gospel Grammy and sold extremely well. Even publications not noted for their gospel sensibilities concurred—*Rolling Stone* called *Spirit of the Century* "transfixing."[39]

The following year, the group again mixed traditional gospel with a variety of well-chosen, if offbeat, covers and released *Higher Ground*. Among the more intriguing numbers are a passionate reading of "The Cross" by Prince, Curtis Mayfield's "People Get Ready," and the words of Psalm 23 sung over Funkadelic's "You and Your Folks." Singer/songwriter Ben Harper eagerly offered his services and, along with sacred steel artist Robert Randolph and the Family Band, provided the musical accompaniment. *Higher Ground* sold even better than *Spirit of the Century* and earned the group its second Grammy. "If you hang in there—in God's own time—He'll bless you," Fountain said of the acceptance of both albums. "Not in your time, 'cause you ain't got no time, but in God's time, He will give you your just reward. And we're receiving it now."[40] As before, *Rolling Stone* concurred and raved that *Higher Ground* "is another stunning set of songs from Alabama's finest." The magazine awarded the release four stars.[41]

In late 2003, the Blind Boys released their first Christmas project, *Go Tell It on the Mountain,* which featured an even more remarkable array of pop superstars, including Mavis Staples, Aaron Neville, and George Clinton. It, too, received a Grammy for Best Traditional Soul Gospel Album. Though their recent releases have featured eclectic musical choices, Fountain said that the Blind Boys carefully discuss the lyrics of each song brought to them by their producers before they agree to record it—including "The Cross." "Prince wrote it but he don't have to be gospel to write a good gospel song," Fountain noted. "And it *is* a good gospel song."[42]

Sixty years after their debut performances in small white churches in rural Alabama, the Blind Boys have found themselves performing on *The Tonight Show with Jay Leno, David Letterman, 60 Minutes II,* and in the movie *The Fighting Temptations* with Cuba Gooding, Jr. In 2003, they were inducted into the Gospel Music Association's Hall of Fame. According to Fountain, the Blind Boys of Alabama are now, as they always have been, a ministry first. "My theory has always been just to do what we can while we can," Fountain said. "And, in return, the Lord will make a way."[43]

Gospel Labels

None of the record labels releasing recent Blind Boys of Alabama projects—Nonesuch, House of Blues, Real World—are "typical" gospel labels. This continues a trend that began in the 1970s and 1980s, which saw further changes in the distribution of gospel product. As gospel labels like Specialty, Aladdin, and Peacock closed or were sold, the major labels—Warner, Capitol, Columbia/CBS, MCA—showed little interest in recording and releasing gospel music, particularly traditional gospel. Four labels in particular emerged to fill the void: Nashboro, Tyscot, Atlanta International (AIR Gospel), and Malaco.

Nashboro was founded in 1951 by Ernie Lafayette Young, of Ernie's Record Mart in Nashville fame. Nashboro's R&B offshoot, Excello, also flourished for years because of Young's "ear for robust, rollicking R&B in all its diverse strains" and irresistible 45s by Slim Harpo.[44] For years, the Nashville-based Nashboro dominated the American South with a steady stream of gospel reissues and new product from the likes of Brother Joe May, the Consolers, the Angelic Gospel Singers, and others.[45] But in 1994, Young sold Nashboro/Excello to Harry Anger/AVI Entertainment Group. Anger, a former Motown executive, rereleased several classic Nashboro LPs on CD, including the Fairfield Four's *Standing on the Rock*, and the gospel compilations *The Best of Nashboro Gospel* and *It's Jesus, Y'all.*[46] But Anger eventually sold the catalog to MCA/Universal. Like AVI, MCA/Universal announced an ambitious reissue schedule in late 1998 of Nashboro's best gospel product, along with classics from the Peacock, Chess, ABC, and Decca labels.[47] But a sluggish economy eventually slowed to a crawl the release of many long out-of-print Nashboro albums.

Tyscot Records was founded in 1976 by Dr. Leonard Scott (a practicing dentist) and his nephew L. Craig Tyson, though Scott assumed full control a few years later. In 2004, it is one of the largest African-American-owned record companies in the country, with a roster that includes the Rance Allen Group and the Inner City Mass Choir, featuring John P. Kee and Morris Chapman.[48]

Scott was once a member of the biracial 1960s rock group the Soul Messengers, which opened for a number of well-known acts. But when the Soul Messengers failed to secure a recording contract, he returned to Indianapolis and joined the Christ Church Apostolic Choir. When a self-pressed recording of the choir did well, Tyscot Records was formed. Scott quickly attracted a number of talented gospel artists, including the Reverend Bill Sawyer, Derrick Brinkley, the group Witness, and Kee. Scott was called to the ministry in 1986 and, while he remains active with the label, his son Bryant now serves as president.[49]

Alan Freeman, who at the time owned a wholesale one-stop that handled a number of gospel labels, established Atlanta International Record Company, Inc., in 1980. Like Tyscot, many of the greats of gospel were without record deals at the time, and artists like the Dixie Hummingbirds, the Five Blind Boys of Alabama, Dorothy Norwood, the O'Neal Twins, the Reverend Cleophus Robinson, Sr., and others recorded one or more albums for what came to be called AIR Gospel.[50]

AIR Gospel is based in Atlanta, the third largest retail market for black gospel in the United States in 2002—trailing only New York and Los Angeles.[51] Freeman slowly built a traditional gospel dynasty around the Barnes family, the Reverend F. C. Barnes and the prolific Luther Barnes. Luther Barnes, as a solo artist, with the Redd Budd Gospel Choir or the Sunset Jubilaires, is a potent force in the traditional gospel music marketplace. Other AIR Gospel artists include Dottie

The Rev. F. C. Barnes who, with the Rev. Janice Brown, created one of gospel's greatest songs: "The Rough Side of the Mountain." (photo courtesy of AIR Gospel)

Peoples, the Consolers, the Christianaires, the Reverend Timothy Wright, Tommy Ellison, and the Fantastic Violinaires. AIR is also notable as one of the last labels to release feature-length sermons by the likes of the Reverend Jasper Williams, the Reverend Leo Daniels, and the Reverend Timothy Fleming.[52]

Fifty years after Mahalia Jackson, gospel artists continue to endure bad paydays, infrequent airplay, and sometimes hostile churches, but continue to sing out of a sense of mission. That's why Freeman says he "absolutely loves the

Luther Barnes has had hits with the Red Budd Gospel Choir, the Sunset Jubilaires, and as a solo artist. (photo courtesy of AIR Gospel)

hearts of gospel artists" and continues to support older groups like the Consolers or the Fantastic Violinaires:

> They are very clear about what they're doing and why. There is no conflict in the choices they've made, whether they're barely making bills or they're very successful. It's the only form of music where the artist is truly committed to the music and the message.[53]

But the great survivor, and one of the great stories of gospel music, is the continued success of the feisty Malaco label in Jackson, Mississippi. The label was begun on a shoestring by white fraternity brothers Tommy Couch and Gerald (Wolf) Stephenson in 1969 to record the earthy rhythm and blues artists they craved but had difficulty finding. When Stax Records, which had dominated the southern soul market, closed a few years later, Malaco was able to fill the void. The label was bolstered by steady sales from artists like Z. Z. Hill, Denise LaSalle, Bobby "Blue" Bland, Dorothy Moore—and the work of legendary promotions director Dave Clark.[54]

Malaco's entry into gospel was equally nonchalant. The label's first signing— hometown gospel heroes the Jackson Southernaires, led by Frank Williams— came about because the group approached Malaco. "I'd like to say that I was a visionary," Couch said, "but the truth is that the opportunity just presented itself. Frank and the other group members had been traveling some distance to record, and wanted to stay closer to home."[55] Attracted by Couch and Clark, other gospel artists soon followed.

The label's second pivotal decision came in 1985 when it purchased what was perhaps the greatest gospel label, Savoy. Since its founding in 1942, the New-York-based Savoy had been the premiere gospel label. But despite the presence of artists such as James Cleveland, it, too, was struggling in the 1980s. Couch left Savoy independent under executive director Milton Biggham but combined all promotional and advertising budgets.[56]

Soon, the combined Malaco/Savoy roster was outselling the label's blues and R&B artists. Even as the industry's fortunes fluctuated, Malaco survived by keeping its overhead low, doing most of its production in-house, and handling its own distribution. And, because gospel fans are so loyal, Malaco executives are proud of never having "cut out" any releases from its enormous back catalog.[57]

But gospel music aficionados can surprise the savviest record exec from time to time. In 1988, Frank Williams, by then Malaco's executive vice president, advertised for a new mass choir in the Jackson area and paired the singers with the Jackson Southernaires' hot rhythm section on a variety of hymns and traditional gospel songs.[58] Dubbed the Mississippi Mass Choir, the group's eponymous debut album for Malaco—with music that would be instantly familiar to devotees of the genre's Golden Age—sold 400,000 copies, remained at number one on the gospel charts for most of 1989 and 1990. A follow-up with Detroit-based Rev. James Moore did nearly as well.[59]

Williams managed the Mississippi Mass until his death in March 1993. Jerry Mannery, who had been Williams's assistant director, then took over the reins. "The Mississippi Mass Choir was Frank's dream," Mannery said. "He wanted to bring gospel music back to the church."[60]

Two other major players in the gospel music field during this era, Word and Benson, had originally specialized in more traditional religious music and white southern gospel. But Word, led by the dynamic young Jarrell McCracken, was

The Rev. James Moore's work with the Mississippi Mass Choir and as a solo artist is in the innovative tradition of the Rev. James Cleveland. (photo courtesy of Malaco Records)

one of the first to enter the contemporary Christian music field. McCracken brought a number of first-rate executives into the company, including Kurt Kaiser, Billy Ray Hearn, and Ralph Carmichael. In the 1980s, Word (with its boutique labels Myrrh and Rejoice!) concentrated on the more contemporary side of gospel, signing Shirley Caesar, the Mighty Clouds of Joy, and the Reverend Al Green (what Anthony Heilbut derisively calls "gos-pop"). Soon, Hearn and Carmichael started their own labels and eventually left Word.[61]

Carmichael's Light Records tended toward contemporary gospel and, in addition to Andrae Crouch, included Walter Hawkins, Tramaine Hawkins, Sandra Crouch, the Winans, and others.[62] Sparrow's contemporary artists at the time included pop star Deniece Williams and BeBe & CeCe Winans, both of whom benefited from cross-licensing with major secular labels.[63] Word finally entered the traditional market with Reverend Milton Brunson and Albertina Walker in the late 1980s, but then signed a distribution agreement with the more contemporary-oriented Command Records.[64]

The Mississippi Mass Choir revitalized gospel choirs across America and dominated the charts in 1989 and 1990. (photo courtesy of Malaco Records)

Although both Caesar and the Clouds did well for Word, it was Green's gospel releases that generated the most publicity—and controversy.

Al Green

In the tumultuous days of the 1970s and 1980s, the Reverend Al Green made a significant impact on gospel music. One of ten children born to a sharecropper outside Jacknash, Arkansas, Al Greene (he would later drop the "e") sang with his family's gospel group, the Greene Brothers.[65] Later, he moved to Grand Rapids, Michigan, to form Al Greene and the Soul Mates (which had a midsized R&B hit with "Back Up Train") before connecting with legendary producer/songwriter Willie Mitchell in a Midland, Texas, honky-tonk.[66] Back in Memphis with Hi Records, the duo would record some of America's most transcendent soul music.

Green holds an important position in the evolution of soul music into the silky Philadelphia-styled soul of the 1980s and what Nelson George eventually calls *The Death of Rhythm and Blues* in his book by the same name. The socioeconomic forces that eventually doomed soul music also forever altered gospel.[67] Green instinctively knew a sea change was coming in popular music: "The era of the 'soul-shouter' seemed to be sputtering out and it would bring along something altogether more smooth and sophisticated. Maybe it was just my long-standing love of jazz that put the notion in my head, but I was convinced that soul music was about to take on a whole new mood."[68]

Mitchell and Green quickly sold millions of copies of songs like "Sha-La-La (Make Me Happy)," "Look What You've Done for Me," "Love and Happiness," and "How Can You Mend a Broken Heart." But Green experienced a religious conversion in a hotel room outside of Disneyland in 1973 and his music—and personal life—changed dramatically.[69]

According to Craig Werner, Green's songs "Tired of Being Alone," "Let's Stay Together," "I'm Still in Love with You," and others mingle "blues confession and gospel testimony." Unable to reconcile his conflicting feelings, Green increasingly "turned to the gospel tradition in his search for an answer." The result is a remarkable series of songs that somehow blend the sacred and the profane: "Call Me (Come Back Home)," "Here I Am (Come and Take Me)," "Take Me to the River," and the entire *Belle Album* chronicle that journey.[70]

Green finally abandoned popular music and moved exclusively to gospel, recording a fine series of pop gospel albums for Word in the 1980s and early 1990s. They sold reasonably well, earned Green a few long-overdue Grammy awards, and culminated with one of the era's greatest hits, the soaring, incandescent "Sailing (On the Sea of Your Love)," a duet with Shirley Caesar. Green's music was still gospel-based, but lighter, smoother, and less emotionally charged. The beat was still there, but gone was the throaty rasp of a June Cheeks or James Cleveland. Green's success helped pave the way for the groups Commissioned and Anointed, as well as BeBe and CeCe Winans, and others.[71]

"Yet when Al Green returned to the church," notes Werner, "it marked the end of a concerted effort to let white America in on the secret, the burden and the joy." No matter how transcendent gospel music is at its best, "enough evidence had accumulated to convince a whole lot of black folks that whites simply didn't want to know."[72]

Green founded the Full Gospel Tabernacle in 1976, and although he would eventually return to recording popular music, in early 2004, he was still pastor of this thriving church in the quiet Memphis neighborhood of Whitehaven.[73] Green still records religious-based songs periodically and what makes them special is what has always made his mainstream love songs special: that *voice*. In his candid, introspective autobiography, Green recalls his answer when Willie Mitchell once asked him where he learned to sing like that:

> I thought back to the birds outside the farmhouse window, the radio tuned to Jackie Wilson way out across the Arkansas night, a moaning and a groaning such as no human tongue can utter as the Holy Spirit swept in under Mother Bates' revival tent. I never did learn it, I wanted to tell him. It just comes through me, like a breeze through the trees.[74]

The death of Memphis's best-known musical export—Elvis Presley—in 1977 brought about another intriguing juxtaposition of old and new. Growing up in

Memphis, Presley listened faithfully to WDIA, "The Mother Station of the Ne-groes," especially to the Spirit of Memphis Quartette, and to WHBQ, where Rev. W. Herbert Brewster's sermons were broadcast live on Sunday nights from the East Trigg Baptist Church, only a mile from Presley's original Memphis home. Even when Elvis moved into Graceland, it was located just up Bellevue/Highway 51 from East Trigg.[75]

Presley's long love affair with gospel—both southern gospel and black gospel—was apparent from his recordings and concerts. One classmate remem-bers Elvis rushing home after school in Tupelo to listen to Sister Rosetta Tharpe on station WELO.[76] And when he died, among the first to arrive at Graceland after his death was soul singer James Brown, who shared Presley's gospel roots.

"When this young fellow Elvis passed, it was a saddening thing," said Brew-ster shortly after Presley's death. "It was like the clouds themselves wept.[77]

The Winans Family

Ultimately, it wasn't the Mighty Clouds of Joy or the Blind Boys of Alabama or even Al Green who had the most impact on gospel music in the 1980s, it was a family—albeit a *big* family—from Detroit. Delores and David Winans and their ten children are not just gospel music's greatest dynasty, they may be the greatest family dynasty in American musical history. An ever-increasing number of dif-ferent Winans family units—including Mom and Pops Winans, the Winans (brothers Marvin, Carvin, Ronald and Michael), BeBe and CeCe Winans, Angie and Debbie, and solo artists Daniel Winans and David Winans II, among oth-ers—have had recording contracts, sold hundreds of thousands of units, and/or won Grammy awards. To make matters more confusing, both BeBe and CeCe and Ronald Winans have had successful solo careers as well. In 2002, the family's Together We Stand Tour was joined by Winans Phase 2, four sons of the original Winans quartet. The tour marked the first time in a decade the far-flung mem-bers of gospel's First Family were able to unite for a joint venture.[78]

The Winans siblings grew up in a home dominated by gospel music—both David and Delores once sang with the Lemon Gospel Chorus. They faithfully attended the Pentecostal Mack Avenue Church of God in Christ, founded by their great-grandfather, but listened on every street corner to artists like Gladys Knight and the Pips, the Jackson Five, and Marvin Gaye.[79] The children would sing at the church's Christmas and Mother's Day gospel pageants, then return home and secretly award each other imaginary "Grammy" awards for their per-formances, just as they had seen on television.[80]

After oldest brother David Winans II left for a musical career in California, the next four brothers formed a group originally called the Testamonial Singers, then eventually renamed themselves the Winans. But instead of emulating the quartets that performed regularly at their church, the Winans were attracted to a more contemporary sound. When the brothers started writing their own songs—long before they signed their first record deal—Carvin Winans recalled that what they wrote was always in a contemporary vein:

> Some of the saints around the church didn't really agree with our type of music because it wasn't the "tradition," so we ended up singing at other churches where they had a lot of young people living a more open lifestyle of music. The music our parents made us sing, we never liked those songs. We wanted to write music that would be pleasing to our ears and maybe to other young people, too.[81]

Fortunately, their parents were sympathetic and supported the fledgling group. The Winans' breakthrough came in the early 1980s when they were championed by Andrae Crouch and with the release by Light Records of *Introducing the Winans* in 1981. In the years that followed, the brothers would enjoy hit after hit, though none so controversial as the heavily rhythmic "It's Time" in 1992. Produced by Teddy Riley (Bobby Brown, Keith Sweat), the song crossed over into the pop and rap charts. Carvin Winans said the group expected a backlash with the release: "We looked at Teddy as someone who knew what he was doing in his style of music. It's a plus when we get our music played on secular stations, because we're reaching those who we feel need to be reached."[82]

The Winans began cutting back their touring in the late 1990s, though they continued to record and produce other artists, in part because of brother Ronald's near-fatal heart attack in 1997.[83] Like many of his gospel contemporaries, Marvin Winans also became a pastor of a church, while Ronald started a solo career.[84]

The second set of Winans to draw national attention were the brother-and-sister duo of CeCe (Priscilla) and BeBe (Benjamin), who first formed the Winans Part II with the remaining siblings and three family friends while still teenagers. This group was also influenced by the Hawkins and Crouch families and often sang with choirs led by Mrs. Mattie Moss Clark, then president and director of the music department for the entire COGIC denomination.[85] In 1981, BeBe and CeCe were invited by music director Howard McCrary to audition for spots on *The PTL Show*, the flagship program of Jim and Tammy Faye Bakker's PTL network based at the religious theme park, Heritage USA. The show had a national audience, although neither BeBe nor CeCe had heard of it at the time. They auditioned and won spots as part of the PTL Singers.[86]

The outgoing BeBe and the angelic-voiced CeCe soon became the stars of the program, and they performed regularly with the top gospel artists in the country, black and white, who often appeared on *PTL*. After a few years, Tammy Faye Bakker rewrote with religious lyrics the hit song "Lift Us Up Where We Belong" from the movie *An Officer and a Gentleman* and insisted the duo perform it. They did and the song immediately became their "signature" number as "Lord, Lift Us Up Where We Belong."[87] The success of "Lord, Lift Us Up" led to an album by the same name for the small PTL label, which, too, was a success—in part due to the constant airplay and promotion on the PTL network.[88]

Although the PTL empire eventually collapsed in scandal, BeBe and CeCe became the first African-American artists to sign with contemporary Christian music powerhouse Sparrow Records in 1985 and released the first in a long series of contemporary gospel albums, *Introducing BeBe & CeCe*. The album sold more than 300,000 copies and earned the first of several Grammy awards for the duo.[89] Their second Sparrow release, *Different Lifestyles*, which was distributed in the mainstream marketplace by Capitol Records, did even better. It was certified "gold" and spawned two number one R&B hits, "Addictive Love" and a remake of "I'll Take You There" with Mavis Staples.[90] Both as a duo and as solo artists, BeBe and CeCe Winans have continued as hit-makers into the twenty-first century. As for the dual careers, BeBe told *Billboard* that no record buyers should misunderstand their roots:

> And we're committed to gospel, and we will always be committed to that. If our gospel goes over in the mainstream and we become successful in the commercial market, it is only because we were committed to the Gospel itself. It can be done and I think it will—but we won't ever change.[91]

In time, Mom and Pops Winans, the Sisters (Angie and Debbie), Daniel Winans, and Winans Phase 2 (Marvin Winans, Jr.; Carvin Winans III; Juan Winans; and Michael Winans, Jr.) would all be nominated for Grammy awards for their various releases.[92]

For all of the uncertainties during the late 1970s and through the 1980s, gospel music eventually split between contemporary and traditional gospel. Although some artists passed easily between the two worlds, most found their niche in one or the other. It is not by accident that two of the best-selling albums by the end of the 1980s define the two emerging streams of gospel.

The first is Rev. F. C. Barnes and Rev. Janice Brown's *Rough Side of the Mountain* for AIR Gospel. The fiercely traditional album sold 400,000 units and is often credited as being a critical element in the national revival of traditional gospel, according to AIR's Juandolyn Stokes: "That record dropped at exactly the right time, when Reagan had just come into office and times were getting hard. Since then, contemporary gospel can be up and down, but traditional is solid as a rock."[93]

The second, Tramaine Hawkins's "Fall Down"—or, "Spirit Fall Down on Me" in the gospel charts—became the first gospel song to climb to number one in *Billboard*'s dance-floor hits chart in 1985. With its throbbing beat, "Fall Down" was a lightning rod for criticism within the gospel community. But Hawkins, who had sung with the Edwin Hawkins Singers on "Oh Happy Day," said she was prepared for the backlash this time:

> When "Fall Down" was a hit, [other people] all over the country lifted me up in prayer. No matter how I was being attacked, they never let me get discouraged.

My drive and determination come from the Scripture that says, "In all these things we are more than conquerors through Him that loved us." Why settle for less?

No matter what I sing or what the accomplishment is, I always sing about the Lord—and about what I believe, [and] about what I live for.[94]

Sometimes gospel artists are forced to find creative solutions to the sticky problems arising from the traditional/contemporary dichotomy. With the massive Winans' family tour of 1992, one of the featured numbers was the older brothers' "It's Time," which, on record, featured a rap by Teddy Riley. But in concert, knowing that they would be performing primarily for gospel music fans, Marvin Winans wisely recast the rap into an old gospel song that was instead sung each evening by his mother, Delores, to avoid alienating his audience.[95]

Proving, once again, that there doesn't have to be a dichotomy between contemporary and traditional styles. Sometimes there are creative solutions that combine the best of *both* worlds.

Chapter Fifteen

Contemporary Gospel: Six Defining Voices

The singing from the church vibrated through [Bigger Thomas], suffusing him with a mood of sensitive sorrow. He tried not to listen, but it seeped into his feelings, whispering of another way of life and death. . . . The singing filled his ears; it mocked his fear and loneliness, his deep yearning for a sense of wholeness. Its fullness contrasted so sharply with his hunger, its richness with his emptiness, that he recoiled from it while answering it.

—Richard Wright, *Native Son*[1]

[T]he blues won't die because spirituals won't die. Blues—a steal from spirituals. And rock is a steal from the blues . . . blues singers starts out singin' in the church.

—Big Bill Broonzy[2]

Gospel artists in the latter days of the twentieth century and the early days of the twenty-first still faced the traditional/contemporary divide. They created as many ways to reconcile that split as there are musicians. For a happy few—the Consolers, Luther Barnes, the Gospel Keynotes—the decision was an easy one. They remained firmly in the traditional camp. But for most, how much contemporary to incorporate into their music was a question to be answered not just on a CD-by-CD basis but on a song-by-song basis.

In the end, short of creating an encyclopedic listing, there is no way to survey an entire industry. Instead, here are six reasonably representative artists and how they have both bridged the musical gap and sought to follow what they believe is their highest calling.

Tramaine Hawkins

Few artists have experienced success at so many levels as Hawkins, "an astonishingly beautiful woman," according to the frankly admiring historian Anthony Heilbut.[3] She sang on the legendary "Oh Happy Day" sessions, was a featured soloist on her ex-husband Walter Hawkins's Love Alive Choir albums, and had a number one dance-floor hit with "Fall Down." After a series of mostly traditional albums, she signed with Sparrow, whose distribution agreement with mainstream giant Capitol had paid big dividends for BeBe and CeCe. Regardless of the label, for Hawkins, the desire to take her message beyond the church has always been paramount:

> . . . [I]t seemed like from talking to other artists that their desire was just to reach the Christian marketplace. It seemed as though we'd built ourselves into a narrow vise. Both the other artists and the record labels just assumed that the secular audience didn't want what we were offering or that it wouldn't appeal to them.[4]

Following her Sparrow releases, Hawkins tried a variety of styles for a variety of labels in the years that followed, sometimes with a mass choir, sometimes with an orchestra—sometimes sounding like Clara Ward, sometimes like Whitney Houston. Artists such as M. C. Hammer, El DeBarge, and the actor Danny Glover showed during the taping of a live album in 1990.[5] She later returned the favor by singing on a revamped version of "Saviour, Do Not Pass Me By" on Hammer's *2 Legit 2 Quit* CD. For her first Columbia release in 1994, *To a Higher Place,* Hawkins combined all of her favorite musical styles: traditional, contemporary, even orchestral. The album's most arresting track is a "duet" with Mahalia Jackson on "I Found the Answer" that sounds eerily like the real thing, thanks to digital technology. "The Bible says to praise Him on the high-sounding cymbals," Hawkins said. "The orchestration complements my voice, and I think it takes gospel to a higher place, and that's good."[6]

Finally, after a long hiatus, Hawkins resurfaced on the decidedly contemporary Gospo Centric label, home of Kirk Franklin. In 2001, she released *Still Tramaine.* Hawkins's way of dealing with the different forces that pulled at her was to record an album of beat-heavy music and shimmering ballads but with straight-ahead religious lyrics. After two Grammy awards, hundreds of thousands of units sold, she eventually decided that there was a significant difference between "secular" and "commercial" in music. She now calls her music "inspirational":

> I don't think we need to be so concerned about whether someone or their music is traditional or whatever. What really concerns me is not so much the music but the lyric content of what young people are hearing. It puts down women; it talks about violence; it is very negative. I feel that somebody has got to combat that.

So, as long as it inspires and uplifts and makes alive and people receive joy and happiness and get a good feeling from it, I don't think anything else is important.[7]

John P. Kee

They call John P. Kee the "Crown Prince of Gospel." They used to call him "drug addict" and "pusher." Today, his parishioners call him "Pastor." Kee is one of gospel music's most remarkable talents—and stories.

The fifteenth of sixteen children, Kee was born on the outskirts of Durham, North Carolina, a child prodigy who taught himself to play on the family's old upright piano. His father, John Henry Kee, had been with the Southland Gospel Singers and ran a strictly religious household: "There was Sunday morning prayer, eight o'clock prayer, Scripture reading during the week and then the family sang. We had a little gospel thing going around the house 24 hours a day."[8]

Kee graduated from the North Carolina School of the Arts in Winston-Salem at age fourteen, toured the country with the opera *The Toymaker,* and was accepted by the prestigious Yuba College Conservatory of Music in northern California at age fifteen. Soon he was playing piano for artists as varied as Donald Byrd and the funk group Cameo. He also began taking drugs. When he moved back to Charlotte, using and selling drugs eventually outstripped his interest in music, and he was forced to use a grocery store as his cover. It took the death of a close friend to halt Kee's downward spiral: "He died for a little bit of money and it could have been me. So I started saying around this time—it was '81 or '82—that I didn't want to die on the streets. . . . I gave my life to the Lord the night I saw the brother get killed. It was a major turning point."[9]

Shaken, Kee returned to the church and started a small inner-city group, the Combination Choir, which included a number of former drug addicts. Looking back, Kee said he sees the hand of God on his life:

Everything that happened in my life was a lesson that needed to be learned. The hard knocks kind of made me, and they made me appreciate what I went through, what I took advantage of and the things I took for granted. It certainly caused this little country boy to grow. I paid those old debts and walked away from that lifestyle.[10]

The choir became the New Life Community Choir, and Kee's songwriting blossomed during this period as well. Eventually, his songs were recorded by Daryl Coley, the Hawkins Family Singers, and Rev. James Cleveland. In 1985, he wrote and sang two songs on the annual Gospel Music Workshop of America Mass Choir, led by Rev. Cleveland. This was the first time Cleveland had ever allowed more than one song by the same writer on an album. "I made gospel

John P. Kee has won dozens of awards and received several gold records for his various choir and solo projects. (photo courtesy of Verity/New Life Records)

history with that," Kee recalled, "and doors began to open. Things started to happen very, very fast."[11]

Kee financed a demo, which led to his first release for Tyscot Records in 1987, *Wait on Him.* "We had a small budget, kept it simple, and kept the tunes traditional," he said. "Well, the shocker is that overnight it has become a hit."[12] The album did so well that secular giant Jive/Zomba signed a seven-year deal with Tyscot, giving Jive worldwide rights to Kee's recordings, and inked a separate production deal with Kee. The arrangement marked Jive/Zomba's entry into gospel, which eventually led to the founding of the Verity label,[13] now the largest in the industry.

Wait on Him marked the first in a steady series of releases from the prolific Kee, ranging from traditional to contemporary to songs with a little of both. In addition to his New Life Community Choir CDs, Kee also recorded three solo albums and several more releases with the Victory in Praise Seminar Mass Choir.[14] Powered by a strong promotional push from the newly named Verity label, Kee's 1995 release, *Show Up!*—his eleventh album in just eight years— debuted at number seven on *Billboard*'s influential "Heatseekers Album Chart" on February 11, 1995. This was the highest debut by a gospel album in the history of the chart. Verity took the unusual approach of buying time on mostly secular media outlets, including the BET television network, and ads in a variety of African-American-oriented magazines. Faced with criticism from the gospel industry, Jive/Verity's James "Jazzy" Jordan, senior director of marketing, defended the label's approach: "The biggest thing gospel needs is exposure. If we can provide that, then we're giving the world a balance in music. Gospel is filling in some void from less-than-great R&B artists."[15]

But eventually Kee tired of the pace and, in 1996, talked of retirement. He began building a church in Durham, the New Life Christian Center, just blocks from the grocery store where he once sold drugs. When the church was completed, he became its first pastor.[16] Not surprisingly, the church soon developed an extensive street ministry and began working with addicts and former addicts in Charlotte. Other ministries soon included tutors for schoolchildren, food pantries, and homeless shelters: "My dream is that one day the entire gospel community will reach out as one to show the love of Christ to those who need it the most. That means more to me than awards, and deals, and business. That's the business of the Lord and that's what I'm here to accomplish."[17]

Although Kee's absence was felt throughout the industry—his New Life production offices reported receiving as many as 300 requests per week for appearances—his records continued to sell. Kee threw himself into full-time ministry for more than a year. The demands of being a pastor helped him "grow up," he told *Billboard,* and enabled him to rediscover his passion for music:

> Pastoring a church made me really recognize what real ministry was. There were some folks who were really hurting in church who looked good . . . looked saved. I had to really seek the Scriptures and get in God's word. I had decided I didn't want to [make music] anymore, so I didn't write, I didn't sit at the piano. I had really stopped, and it was then that the songs began to come.
>
> The songs are all encouraging, and what I found is that I have a prophetic message for today's youth, on- and off-stage. In the inner city, we're doing some real work, and that's where I see my destiny.[18]

Renewed by the time away from touring, Kee released *Strength* in 1997, his biggest-selling CD to that point. He also further expanded his production duties, working the boards for a number of artists, both old and new. His Back to the 'Hood Tour that year was sponsored by Pepsi, Denny's, and Bojangles and drew record crowds in a variety of venues.[19] Kee also radically slowed his release schedule. In November 2000, *Billboard* gave *Strength*'s follow-up, *Not Guilty*, a highly laudatory review and called Kee "one of gospel's most sparkling gemstones, shining brighter than ever." As with Kee's previous projects, *Not Guilty* featured overtly religious lyrics set to everything from pop ballads to hip-hop to salsa-flavored dance tunes.[20] In 2003, another New Life Choir project, *Blessed by Association*, did equally well and earned another Grammy nomination.

John P. Kee has earned a host of awards, sold hundreds of thousands of units, and appeared before an untold number of people in concert. He is happily married, and his church is thriving. The Victory in Praise Music & Arts Convention, which Kee founded in 1990, continues to thrive as well, attracting thousands of young choir members to Charlotte each year to work with some of the industry's top stars.[21]

But for Kee, musician/songwriter/producer/pastor, the details of how to get the message out are always less important than the message itself: "Every album I've recorded has been done with the conscious intention of capturing the heart and mind of everyone from the baby to the grandma. I want to tear the categorizations apart and then put them back together in a way that creates a new musical common denominator—music that brings people into oneness of worship."[22]

Vickie Winans

Like so many gospel artists, Vickie Winans's life has been filled with heartache and pain. And like the best of them, she has transformed that hurt into a powerful musical testimony. Born Vickie Bowman in Detroit, the seventh of twelve children, she began her singing career at the age of six: "There was a wonderful spiritual environment at home, with lots of prayer, lots of spiritual talk, and we sang, sang, sang all the time. That was the order of the day."[23]

She sang her first church solo at eight and often harmonized with family members while neighbors would gather outside their open windows to listen. Vickie's earliest influences included Andrae Crouch and Tramaine Hawkins, and she decided on a career in music at sixteen. It was through her church choir that she met her future husband, Marvin Winans. Following the birth of their two boys, she resumed her singing career, usually singing with Winans Phase 2, which included three Winans siblings, Daniel, BeBe, and CeCe. When BeBe and CeCe left, Marvin recorded a demo with Vickie and pitched it to Light Records. The resulting album, *Be Encouraged*, included her signature song, the powerful "We Shall Behold Him," and earned Winans her first Grammy nomination.[24]

Gifted as both a singer and a designer, Vickie Winans is also a talented comedian. (photo courtesy of Verity)

Winans said all the musicians involved knew that the recording session for "We Shall Behold Him" was special from the opening moments in the studio:

The anointing of the Lord came into the studio while we were recording "We Shall Behold Him." We did it in one take and we all knew it was anointed. The children were crying, my husband Marvin was in tears, we were all throwing up our hands in joy. It was all caught up in the Spirit. We could have all just gone on up right then and there.[25]

A subsequent release in 1988, *Total Victory,* hit number one in the gospel charts.

Following her divorce in 1995, Winans battled depression and a variety of physical problems, but found the recovery and peace she was searching for at a revival led by the Bishop T. D. Jakes, who himself has now recorded a series of best-selling sermons and mass choir albums. Like Bradford and the Blind Boys of Alabama, Winans's comeback was fueled by a number of outstanding performances on Broadway and in national touring companies, including *Don't Get God Started, The First Lady, Perilous Times,* and *The Christmas Celebration.*[26] *First Lady* was directed and choreographed by Waymon Thompson, the genius behind the Broadway hit *Dreamgirls.* Winans played a recently widowed pastor's wife trying to lead her late husband's congregation, and she co-starred with Louis Price, previously of the Temptations.[27]

From there a series of stunning releases followed, all capitalizing on Winans's multioctave voice and old-time gospel energy onstage. In 1991, MCA Records signed her directly to the label and released the first single, "Don't Throw Your Life Away," directly to urban radio outlets, with several hot new mixes. While the single was not a major hit, Winans was happy with the response, noting "there are more people who just would not have listened to gospel music at our concerts than ever before."[28]

The sparkle that caught MCA's eye also caught the attention of Wrigley Gum and Johnson Hair Products, both of whom hired her as a national spokesperson. She also served as the host of the nationally syndicated television show *Singsation* for many years.[29]

Winans still handles much of her management and booking through her own company, Viviane, Inc. Consequently, she has been called "the hardest working woman in gospel music," frequently performing 200 to 250 dates per year. "I like to be hands-on, down-to-earth and loving," she said. "Most representation is horrible, and if you can't represent me like I can represent me, then there is no point to me having you."[30]

In 2003, her release *Bringing It All Together* debuted at number one on the gospel charts, stayed there nine weeks, and featured her sons Mario (Yellowman) and Marvin (Coconut) Winans producing.[31] The album, for Verity, was also nominated for a Best Contemporary Soul Gospel Album Grammy. Winans closed 2003 out in style by marrying Detroit businessman Joe McLemore in late November in Las Vegas. During the Nineteenth Stellar Awards, held in Houston on January 19, 2004, *Bringing It All Together* also won four awards, including Artist of the Year for Winans—who also cohosted the event with Kirk Franklin, Donnie McClurkin, and Yolanda Adams. Shortly thereafter, Winans left to star in the stage play *Torn Between Two Lovers,* which she also produced.[32]

Torn Between Two Lovers, like most of her projects, soon generated contro-versy in some segments of the gospel community. But Vickie Winans, as she has done most of her life, shrugged it off:

> I want to be whatever I am now. We're all talking about one man and one spirit, right? I don't understand why people call the music things like "Hispanic gospel." However my first album came out, people labeled it "traditional black gospel." I didn't call it anything. I sing everything. I can sing jazz, contemporary gospel, whatever. All I'm concerned about is if it is being anointed. The anointing is what breaks the yoke of oppression.[33]

Donnie McClurkin

Donnie McClurkin grew up in Copiague, New York, one of ten children and the son of a weekend alcoholic. McClurkin's young life was marred by abuse and violence, with predictable results.[34] At age eight, he was raped by a relative. A few years later, he was raped by still another relative. But at age eleven, he was introduced to Andrae Crouch by his aunt Bea Carr. Carr had once sung backup for Crouch, and Andrae, with his long history of working with troubled young people, began mentoring the boy. McClurkin is a gifted pianist and performer and soon had his own gospel group, which rented public address systems and performed on street corners in tough urban neighborhoods. In time, he founded the New York Restoration Choir. When Marvin Winans, by then pastor of Per-fecting Church in Detroit, heard the group in 1983, he remembered McClurkin's name. In 1989, Winans appointed him associate pastor of his church.[35]

McClurkin survived a leukemia scare and a near nervous breakdown to pen the song "Stand" in twenty-five minutes, which he included on his first album—also called *Stand*—in 1996. The album went gold and earned him his first Grammy nomination. " 'Stand' was my own personal story," McClurkin said later. "I didn't think everybody would gravitate to it."[36]

The album was a smart, catchy mix of traditional songs by Thomas Dorsey ("Search Me, Lord") and contemporary songs by Andrae Crouch ("We Expect You"). In addition to McClurkin's own compositions, he covered the Pointer Sisters' funky "Yes, We Can Can"—but with a decidedly gospel twist. The al-bum's sales were helped by Oprah Winfrey, who held up the CD on her televi-sion show and urged her listeners to buy it, in part because of the powerful title track. "And within two weeks, it went gold," McClurkin said. "Right now, she won't let me sing anything else on her show."[37]

McClurkin's second release in 1999 did even better, receiving platinum certi-fication in less than two years. *Live in London & More* did so well—the title was an obvious tribute to Crouch—that one writer said the "year 2001 belonged to Donnie McClurkin." McClurkin almost alone of all major artists in any genre saw an increase in sales in the devastating week following "Black Tuesday," Sep-

Donnie McClurkin has been the most dominant gospel artist of the first years of the twenty-first century. (photo courtesy of Verity)

tember 11, 2001. In fact, McClurkin actually witnessed the first explosion while flying out of New York's LaGuardia Airport en route to Chicago.[38]

McClurkin's other signature song, "We Fall Down" by Kyle Matthews, was also recorded following a time of intense personal crisis. The inspirational "We Fall Down" remained at number one on the gospel charts for more than forty weeks and even reached the Top 20 on R&B charts. For McClurkin, the lyrics offered hope at a particularly crucial moment in his life:

I almost got to the point of giving up, not giving up my relationship with God, but my ministry. I had jacked up so badly, [and] then the song came. I realized that I am no better than anyone, but then, I am no worse, either. . . . [W]hen we mess up, we punish ourselves because we don't realize that everybody in this world messes up—sometimes royally.[39]

Today he is easily one of gospel's two or three biggest stars, "gospel music's hidden treasure," according to *Jet* magazine, although it is hard to imagine how a multi-platinum artist could exactly be "hidden." In 2002, McClurkin founded the Perfecting Faith Church on Long Island, New York, not far from his boyhood home in Copiague. The decision to become a minister at the peak of his career has required serious adjustments in his busy schedule, even to the point of flying back to Long Island on Saturday nights from wherever he is on tour. "Preaching is my passion," McClurkin said, "and music is a by-product of that. My church duties are first and foremost."[40]

Whether he is preaching or performing, audiences want to hear the message of hope contained in songs like "Stand," "Speak to My Heart," and "Fall Down." "It's got nothing to do with me," McClurkin said. "I'm just standing back amazed at what God's doing."[41]

> *We fall down*
> *But we get up*
> *We fall down*
> *But we get up*
> *For a saint is just a sinner who fell down*
> *And got up.*[42]

"We Fall Down"
Written by Kyle Matthews
© 1998 BMG Songs, Inc. (ASCAP)
All rights on behalf of BMG Songs, Inc.
(ASCAP) administered by BMG Music
Publishing
All rights reserved. Used by permission.

Yolanda Adams

In a culture that requires beauty more than talent in its popular artists, Yolanda Adams is that rare hybrid with both. More than six feet tall, she towers over most of her male co-stars. Dr. Bobby Jones, whose *Bobby Jones Gospel* and *Video Gospel* are the two most popular gospel-related shows in the United States in the first years of the twenty-first century, calls her "my tall, wonderful, gorgeous friend." But like all of the artists profiled in this chapter, her life was not without hardship.

Adams grew up in a Christian home in a mostly middle-class neighborhood of Houston, listening and—when she was old enough—playing gospel music. Both of her parents were teachers, and her mother also played piano:

> A lot of people don't think I should say this, but my influences in the music industry are people like Stevie Wonder and Nancy Wilson.[43]
>
> But gospel music was the heart of me. I was singing in the kids' choir at church when I was four. And, later, I was inspired by gospel artists like the Clark Sisters and O'Landa Draper.[44]

At age thirteen, Adams's idyllic life was shattered by the premature death of her father, then only thirty-five. As the oldest child of six, she assumed responsibility for the household but still managed to finish high school and college on time. With a degree in education, she taught elementary school but sang with the Southeast Inspirational Choir during the summers. Eventually, she became the lead singer with the twenty-five-voice ensemble.[45] The choir's music, Adams said, was more grounded in Walter Hawkins than James Cleveland:

> It was like the difference between Brandy and Aretha today. We were trying to make sure young people enjoyed gospel music, so we had really fresh beats and songs kids could sing along with when they heard them the first time. We were teen-agers; you wouldn't expect us to sing in 1980 like Mahalia Jackson sang in 1940.[46]

It was while she was with the Southeast Inspirational Choir that Adams met influential composer/producer Thomas Whitfield. "I did a song called 'Wash Me,' Adams recalled, "and he was in the front row crying. He said, 'I got to record you.'"[47] Whitfield produced Adams's debut release, *Just as I Am*, in 1987, which stayed on the gospel charts for two years.[48] She moved to the small Tribute label in 1990 and released three number-one singles, combining traditional gospel with jazz, soul, hip-hop, and funk accompaniments in her albums *Through the Storm* and *Save the World*: "Every type of music can be used as a ministry. Ministry is influencing someone else to believe what you believe. We just tend to think that ministry is only for the church."[49]

Adams appeared on *The Tonight Show with Jay Leno, The Arsenio Hall Show*, and received invitations to perform at both the Republican National Convention and a Democratic fund-raiser for then-presidential candidate Bill Clinton.[50] At the Tenth Stellar Awards in 1994, *Save the World* was named Contemporary Album of the Year, while the single "The Battle Is the Lord's" was selected Song of the Year.[51]

By 1999, Adams sat atop the gospel industry, at a pinnacle that included only Donnie McClurkin and Kirk Franklin. There were virtually no worlds left for her to conquer. It was at this time that she moved from Verity Records to mainstream powerhouse Elektra Records at the personal urging of Elektra CEO Sylvia

Rhone. Rhone attended a show in New York and promised Adams that the label would not change her music or lyrics—only her audience. Her first Elektra release, *Mountain High . . . Valley Deep,* debuted at number one on *Billboard*'s gospel charts. Featuring production by some of the top producers in both secular and Christian music—Keith Thomas, Jimmy Jam and Terry Lewis, Fred Hammond, Richard Smallwood, and Warren "Smiley" Campbell—*Mountain High* eventually went platinum, charted high on both the Top 200 and R&B charts, and prompted a sold-out tour with Hammond and McClurkin.[52] "We wanted her to do things she hadn't done, but still keep the Word in it," Lewis said. "We wanted to give it some R&B flavor so it would get played on some mainstream radio stations."[53]

Jam and Lewis were as good as their word. Their contemporary soul ballad "Open My Heart" was an immediate R&B hit, dominating the airwaves in late 2000, fitting nicely between hit radio songs with raunchy raps and throbbing beats. Adams said the success of the single was providential:

> You need my music between a Lil' Kim and a Mystikal. You have to have someone say, "You don't have to do it the way they're telling you to do it to be a success." Hopefully, some young person trying to make a decision in [his or her life] will say, "You know what? I do need to talk to God before I make this drastic decision or shake it fast."
> I just believe God chooses people to do this—and I'm one of them.[54]

Mountain High . . . Valley Deep earned Adams her first Grammy (after four previous nominations) for Best Contemporary Soul Gospel and spent a full year at either number one or number two in the gospel charts. Still, Adams told the *Houston Chronicle* that, despite repeated offers from mainstream labels, she is happy to remain a gospel artist:

> The beauty of gospel music is that you are not a one-hit wonder because of the truth you sing about. It's the love of God you sing about and that is a constant that you can sing about on and on and on.[55]
> The rhythm and blues and pop singers have to psych themselves up to sing what they sing. You don't have to get psyched up, you don't have to do drugs, you don't have to drink to do what we do. [Gospel music] is just about the joy of the Lord.[56]

In March 2001, Elektra released a double live album, *The Experience,* recorded in Washington, D.C.'s DAR Constitution Hall, which once would not allow Marian Anderson to sing (see Chapter 9). While the release does feature Adams's startling soprano on a few traditional choir numbers, it is marked, once again, by sizzling beats and bass-heavy contemporary accompaniment. Adams believes that consumers have a right to expect gospel music to be as good—or better—than its secular counterpart:

Since leaving Commissioned, Fred Hammond has become gospel music's most influential producer. (photo by Vic Toliva, courtesy of Verity)

If you're not finding innovative ways to get your music out there, you're pretty much preaching to the choir. Of course you want to encourage those folks, too. But you also want to broaden your audience and get your message to the people who really need hope, really need encouragement, need to have a sense that somebody loves them.[57]

Yolanda Adams's career has shown no signs of peaking. Her follow-up to *The Experience*, titled *Believe*, was another out-of-the-box smash. During the 2003–2004 race for the presidential nomination for the Democratic party, candidate Al Sharpton named *Believe* as his favorite album.[58] At the massive pregame Super Bowl concert in Reliant Stadium in Houston, Adams was one of the headliners, along with old friends John P. Kee and Donnie McClurkin.[59] From time to time, there is still criticism of her music, and while Adams has long since made peace with her career and ministry, she still feels compelled to respond, citing a gospel music legend:

I've always believed that in spreading God's Word, you should appeal to everybody—the oldsters, people who love pop music or jazz—everybody.
      And look at Thomas Dorsey. Everybody was saying, "Get him outta here" because he was playing blues. We just have to understand that change comes. The only thing that doesn't change is God.[60]

Kirk Franklin

Billboard magazine once referred to the enormously successful Yolanda Adams as "the female Kirk Franklin." As popular as she has been, Adams still is not on the same sales and influence level as Franklin. Few artists in any genre are. Gospel fans would have to go back to Andrae Crouch or, more accurately, Mahalia Jackson to find someone of similar stature in the music as the diminutive artist from Fort Worth. As for Adams, she does not even consider herself a serious rival:

I knew Kirk when he was a little kid because we were both gospel singers in Texas and we often crossed paths. He was a cool little kid, really sweet. I remember when he was about 13 and I was about 23. We got to talking and he said, "I want to do this for the rest of my life." I told him, "Then you have to be dedicated, because there are times when it's busy, there are also times when it's slow. But you can do it if you put your mind to it because you have the ability."[61]

Franklin did just that, but it was never a sure thing. As with Donnie McClurkin and John P. Kee, Franklin's childhood and young-adult years were rarely more than a heartbeat away from disaster. When his fifteen-year-old mother could not raise him in Fort Worth's tough Riverside neighborhood, his late grandmother's sister, Gertrude Franklin, sixty-four, offered to adopt the baby.

Gertrude's lone child had been stillborn more than forty years earlier. Gertrude and her husband, Jack, a fine piano player himself, raised young Kirk in a Christian home. Kirk began to pick out the tunes he heard on the piano at age four.[62] By age eleven, he was leading the choir at Mount Rose Baptist Church where he stayed until he was eighteen.[63] Poor and frequently abused because of his small size, Franklin soon found himself caught up in a wild lifestyle, even as he played in Fort Worth churches on weekends.[64]

In the summer between Franklin's ninth and tenth grade years, a close friend was killed: "One day he was there; the next day he was dead, and his death had a life-changing impact on me. He was the first person I knew around my own age who got killed, and it was a very emotional experience."[65]

Franklin transferred to another high school with an award-winning choir and found a new group of friends, and he had his first personal religious experience at age fourteen.[66] In the eleventh grade, he was admitted to the new Professional Youth Conservatory on the campus of Texas Wesleyan University in Fort Worth. An unknown benefactor paid his tuition, but when the school failed, Franklin dropped out of high school to become the minister of music at several nearby Baptist churches before ending up at Greater Stranger's Rest Baptist Church on the west side of Fort Worth.[67] Through his work at Stranger's Rest, Franklin was brought to the attention of the Dallas/Fort Worth Mass Choir, where he met legendary gospel producer Milton Biggham. With Biggham's encouragement, he was soon directing choir workshops throughout the Dallas/Fort Worth area.[68]

Franklin's big breakthrough came when Biggham invited Franklin to direct a choir in singing his original composition "Every Day With Jesus" at the Gospel Music Workshop of America convention in Washington, D.C., in 1990. Franklin, twenty, also became Biggham's regular pianist, and the two performed throughout the country.[69]

In the next few years, his songs were recorded by several top choirs, and in 1992 Franklin assembled his own group from longtime friends and musicians, which he dubbed "the Family."[70] Daryl Coley passed a copy of the group's first demo tape to a new label in Los Angeles, Gospo Centric. Label president Vicki Lataillade, a former Sparrow Records PR rep, had founded the label with a borrowed $6,000 just two years earlier. Ultimately, Franklin chose to record for Gospo Centric over offers from several larger gospel labels.[71]

Kirk Franklin & the Family's first release for Gospo Centric in June 1993 was a remixed and remastered version of the original demo, *Why We Sing*. It became a phenomenon. The album and title track both went to number one in a matter of months, won numerous Stellar, Dove, and GMWA awards, and "Why We Sing" even charted on the *Billboard* Top 200 charts and went Top 10 on the R&B charts, despite relatively little initial promotion.[72] *Why We Sing* ultimately sold more than two million units and invited comparisons with "Oh Happy Day," in part because Franklin's lyrics were more overtly Christian than those of other "crossover" gospel artists. Writer Mark Anthony Neal claims that Franklin is the first black artist since Edwin Hawkins to understand the specific purpose of using music as an evangelical tool in the African-American community: "[M]usic is a vehicle to attract and keep black youths in the church, but in order to pique their attention, the church has to be willing to inhabit the aural spaces that black youth culture constructs."[73]

Not growing up in a classic gospel-singing family, Franklin was the first gospel superstar of his generation not to have heard Andrae Crouch, and his music reflects instead the secular music of his youth—a heady mix of the latest beats, spiced with international influences. It was, in short, difficult to categorize. "It sounded like R&B and Franklin had the sex appeal of Teddy Pendergrass and Al Green," wrote one critic, "but the lyrics were focused on spiritual messages and very orthodox biblical ones at that."[74] One veteran gospel writer called Franklin's mix of modern music with transparently religious lyrics, "new traditional."[75]

Billboard magazine chronicled the album's crossover success with a front page story and noted that artists as diverse as Ice Cube and R. Kelly counted themselves among Franklin's "fans." Lataillade said the label never intended to position Franklin as an R&B artist, but that changed with a February 1994 appearance on *The Arsenio Hall Show,* which also featured Louis Farrakhan: "When he went on *Arsenio* is when it started. It did a whole lot for sales. Gospo Centric is a youth-oriented label and we want to provide alternative music for black youths. Our focus was to get a broad audience, but I had no idea [we'd be so successful]."[76]

In a matter of months, Franklin went from struggling financially to headlining, serving as a spokesman for Quaker Oats and generating Beatles-like enthusiasm in concert. Even Lataillade, who had worked with some of gospel's biggest stars, was taken aback: "I've never seen a gospel artist get his clothes ripped off him at a show. It's his magnetism. People just seem to be very excited about this young man talking about the Lord."[77]

Why We Sing logged 100 weeks at number one on the gospel charts and pushed the release of the even more contemporary-sounding *Whatcha Lookin' 4* back nearly six months into 1995. The edgy music, predictably, generated more criticism within his former church circles, with some claiming that Franklin had turned his back on traditional gospel music. Franklin addressed the accusation in his painfully honest biography, *Church Boy*:

> The music we play today wasn't *designed*. We weren't trying to make any kind of statement; it just evolved naturally. It was a natural development and direction that we felt the music should take.
>
> But I like to think that the growth and musical development are there because we were willing to let the music within us express itself. We weren't trying to imitate anybody's style or to make some kind of statement. We never pushed it. We just let the music take us wherever the Spirit led us and wherever the music wanted to go.[78]

Whatcha Lookin' 4 sparked a similar response to *Why We Sing,* including more than two dozen network television appearances, many national newspapers and magazines, ranging from the *New York Times* to *Guideposts* (where he appeared on the cover). The album took Franklin and the Family on an international tour and debuted at number twenty-three on *Billboard*'s top 200—the highest debut ever by a gospel artist.[79] *Whatcha Lookin' 4* also hit number five on the R&B chart and number one on the contemporary Christian chart—again, the first gospel release to do so on a chart that routinely featured Amy Grant and the Newsboys.[80]

But in November 1996, Franklin was nearly killed in a fall from a stage in Memphis. He suffered massive head injuries and was on life support for several hours. For a time, doctors feared he would never regain full control of his speech or thought processes, but he made a remarkable recovery and was soon touring again.[81] "What the accident did for me was take me from age 26 to age 40 in one day," Franklin said later.[82]

He returned in 1997 with the awkwardly titled *God's Property From Kirk Franklin's Nu Nation* and a thundering hit called "Stomp," featuring a rap by "Salt" (Cheryl James) of the rap duo Salt 'n' Pepa.[83] God's Property, a Houston-based choir that included a number of former gang members as well as arts-magnet-school students, was the ideal aggregation to sing over a bass line sampled from Funkadelic's "One Nation Under a Groove." The lyrics mixed "a liberal use of urban slang" and Christian doctrine, which, according to one writer, "mirrors the many rhetorical strategies used by black ministers in order to reach nontraditional audiences."[84] Musically, "Stomp" combines "funk, hip-hop and contemporary gospel into a street-friendly medley that asks for nothing short of a 'holy ghost party.'"[85]

God's Property would go on to sell three million units but, more important, it was the first phase of Franklin's youth outreach project, Nu Nation, which would eventually include summer camps and music conventions for young people. According to Franklin, the project was simply an extension of what he had been attempting from the beginning of his career: "All I am trying to do is reach people where they are. What you hear [on 'Stomp'] is what attracted me to [God's Property]. Their vocal ability . . . musically, they maneuver so smoothly."[86]

Led by Franklin's various projects, gospel music experienced an extraordinary surge in sales. Gospel music sales leaped more than thirty percent between 1995 and 1996, from $381 million to $538 million, then experienced another thirty percent increase in 1997. In 1997, Franklin had two of the best-selling albums in gospel, *God's Property From Kirk Franklin's Nu Nation* and *Whatcha Lookin' 4. God's Property* debuted at number three on the *Billboard* Top 200—once again, the highest debut ever by a gospel album—and ultimately sold more than three million copies. According to *Ebony,* Franklin's Tour of Life with Yolanda Adams and Fred Hammond (late of Commissioned) was "the most commercially successful tour in gospel music history," selling out venues in sixty-seven markets.[87]

The grumblings about Franklin's "suitability" and choices as a gospel artist only increased with the release of *The Nu Nation Project* the following year. His ballad preaching compassion for the homeless and dying, "Lean on Me," featured several guest vocalists, including U2's Bono, Mary J. Blige, and R. Kelly. "I wanted a 'We are the World' vibe," he said. "That was the song God gave me."[88]

Franklin told one reporter that he listened to everybody from Thomas Dorsey to Lauryn Hill and would not apologize for recording with mainstream artists:

> The first thing is not to try to justify it. I work with people because I'm compelled to work with them. There are things about my secular friends that I don't agree with. But at the same time, how am I ever going to reach them if I don't fellowship with them?
>
> When I deal with secular artists, it's not for financial gain. I'm trying to reach out to lost people. Imagine if a Garth Brooks or Celine Dion started talking about Christ. Can you imagine what kind of impact that would make? That's why I affiliate myself with secular artists. As long as I believe that the person I get to know behind closed doors has the same heart I have, then I'll work with anyone.[89]

Kirk Franklin's influence has extended unabated and undiminished into the twenty-first century. In 2000, *Kirk Franklin Presents 1NC (One Nation Crew)* featured ten culturally diverse vocalists and introduced a number of world music sounds, from South Africa to Latin America, in addition to the beats and raps. The live CD *The Rebirth of Kirk Franklin* was more of the same, a winning mixture of old-school gospel and highly danceable R&B songs with religious lyrics. Although there was nothing on either album to match the wildfire success of "Stomp," both *1NC* and *The Rebirth* were quickly certified gold.[90]

By 2003, Franklin had become such a cultural phenomenon that he was able to release a special remix project that was sold only in K Mart stores during the holiday season. Now happily married and an ordained minister, Franklin in recent years has slowed his frenzied schedule and lifestyle. Throughout 2003, he was on the road with "The Hopeville Tour," a unique combination of gospel tent revival and Broadway play. Also featuring Yolanda Adams and Donnie McClurkin, Hopeville's *West Side Story*-styled narrative is told with music, elaborate sets (a live band plays on a tenement balcony), costumes, video, dance, and, of course, song.[91] Despite the adulation of the sold-out tour and another hit record, Franklin is more adamant than ever in stating that he has a clearer picture of what's really important: "At no time do I want to come across as the new messiah. This isn't about me. I try to represent Jesus. The power is not in the messenger, it's in the Message. For anybody who wants to do this Christian thing for real, it's a hard job, whether or not you're in the public eye."[92]

Conclusion

The dispute between traditional and contemporary, church and secular applications of gospel music is, as several artists suggested, as old as gospel itself. It *is* a "hard job," as Franklin says. Most popular entertainers need only be concerned with entertaining. Gospel artists must both entertain *and* edify. An offstage scandal can actually help a pop artist's career. Even the hint of a scandal can bring a promising career in gospel screeching to a halt.

The dramatic increase in gospel sales in the 1990s heightened the divide between the contemporary and traditional camps. The level of affluence generated by CD sales in the millions would have been only a dream to gospel artists just a generation ago. And while relatively few artists—Franklin, Yolanda Adams, Donnie McClurkin—ever actually achieve those numbers, their success has not gone unnoticed by the great mass of gospel singers. For every John P. Kee or Fred Hammond, there are many more who still sing for love offerings on the weekends.

One of the most powerful—and poignant—essays in Susan Orlean's acclaimed book *The Bullfighter Checks Her Makeup* first appeared in the *New Yorker*. In 1995, Orlean traveled with the venerable Jackson Southernaires to Demopolis, Alabama, and McCormick, South Carolina, on their battered bus. She ate in truck stops, haggled for motel rooms, and sometimes saw the group sing their hearts out to half-empty halls—all for concert promoters who sometimes "misplaced" their money. By the end of the trip, Orlean is obviously crazy about the band.[93]

The dichotomy extends to the record labels themselves. On any given gospel chart, Verity Records, founded in 1994, will have nearly a quarter of the listings. Distributed by Zomba/Jive, a mainstream industry giant, the roster is dotted with superstars. By contrast, Doug Williams cofounded the fiercely traditional Blackberry label in 1991 with the aim of signing classic gospel artists like the Reverend Clay Evans: "Today, there are a lot of artists who tend to sound alike, but with the older artists there's an identity. When you hear the voice, you know who it is, because no one else sounds like that. That's legacy."[94]

There is another distinctive facet of gospel. Traditional or contemporary, gospel artists are aware, as are the practitioners of the blues, folk, and bluegrass, of the unbroken line of musicians and singers who precede them. They are keenly aware, as well, of the songs and sources that precede them. Artists as diverse as Kirk Franklin, Fred Hammond, and Richard Smallwood have based a number of their songs on the Psalms from the Old Testament. Kurt Carr and Donnie McClurkin have repeatedly shown a fondness for the old Dr. Watts-styled hymns.[95] John P. Kee sums it up nicely: "Gospel music is a part of who I am as a person. It's the hand-clapping, foot-patting, throw-your-hands-up-in-the-air kind of music my granddaddy taught me as a child, and that can't be easily replicated."[96]

The Jackson Southernaires are still on the road, wrecking churches. (photo courtesy of Malaco Records)

Each generation of gospel artists has passed on this feeling, this music, to the next generation with the fervor of an apostolic succession. In 1992, Horace Boyer declared that "Tindley influenced Dorsey, Dorsey influenced Martin, Martin influenced Cleveland, and the genealogy goes on and on."[97] But had Boyer written those words ten years later, he would have added, "and Cleveland influenced John P. Kee." In her testimony, Albertina Walker talks about being influenced by Mahalia Jackson and then, as a member of the Caravans, mentoring a young Shirley Caesar.[98]

Of course, that succession has led to a few odd quirks along the way. Flamboyant rock-and-roll artist Little Richard has bounced back and forth between pop and gospel numerous times during the course of recording several gospel albums. He has publicly acknowledged his singing debt to Brother Joe May and the Ward Sisters, but his greatest influence may stem from an encounter with Sister Rosetta Tharpe. During a concert at Macon City Auditorium, Tharpe invited Richard Penniman—who had been selling sodas—onstage to sing with her. The ensuing applause, Little Richard once said, "was the best thing that had ever happened to me."[99]

Perhaps the sacred connections of gospel are best exemplified by Marion Williams, who electrified audiences first with the Clara Ward Singers, then with her own group, the Stars of Faith. Williams also influenced Little Richard—who claimed he learned his thrilling octave-leaping vocal "swoops" from her. But in the late 1980s, she was living virtually in poverty, hampered by ill health and undergoing regular dialysis.[100] In 1991, Bill Moyers taped her singing "Amazing Grace" in his PBS special on the song and suddenly the world could not do enough for her.[101] She appeared in the hit movie *Fried Green Tomatoes* the following year singing "A Charge I Have to Keep"; the producers even dedicated the movie to her.[102] That same year, she was a guest soloist for the premiere of Wynton Marsalis's gospel-flavor jazz suite, *In This House/On This Morning*.[103]

In 1993, Williams became the first gospel artist to receive a grant from the MacArthur Foundation, which strives to recognize and reward bona fide genius in the creative arts. She learned of the $374,000 grant while working her church's soup kitchen in downtown Philadelphia. At the tribute for the awardees at the Kennedy Center, Aretha Franklin sang several of the Ward Singers' best-known numbers, including "Surely God Is Able." Williams died a year later on July 2, 1994. She was sixty-six.[104] Anthony Heilbut is unapologetically direct in his assessment: "Marion is simply the most lyrical and imaginative singer gospel has produced."[105]

But if gospel music is *only* about the voice, then Williams would have been just another gifted gospel singer in a long line of gifted singers. Instead, Marion Williams is the bridge that returns us to Vera Hall, the nearly blind singer of spirituals first discovered by Alan Lomax. It is Hall's haunting voice that graces most of Moby's most powerful songs on his album, *Play* (see Chapter 1). Musicologist/historian Wilfred Mellers cites Hall's tortured field holler "Trouble So Hard" as a direct line descendant of gospel's pre-Christian African heritage. But Mellers doesn't stop there. He then states that those same roots, that same power, is also present in the voice of Marion Williams—and it is a power that cannot be constrained by either modern gospel songs or older hymns. This wild, heartfelt moan bursts through on a number of Williams's songs, but most notably in the a cappella hymn, "They Led My Lord Away" from *Brighten the Corner Where You Are*:

[S]he here creates a pentatonic incantation no less primitively disturbing than Vera Hall's field holler. Infusing body with spirit, she appeals to Christ for release from the suffering that is vicariously yours; and release becomes audibly incarnate in the wild upward slides on the word "away," and in the frantic sweep on "Calvary's hill." Similarly the refrain—"He never said a mumblin' word, not a word, mmm-mmm, not a word, no, no did he say"—effaces time in inducing hypnosis, while the intermittently spoke "nuff saids" and the visceral tone on "They pierced Him in the side" center us in the painful present. Again, God and Devil, Word and Flesh, are integrated.[106]

From African rhythms through the spirituals through gospel through today—this is what the great ones do. They synthesize, then they create something new, something wonderful, something *transcendent.*

In the end, the divide that caused preachers to throw Thomas Dorsey out of their churches still exists in gospel music. Is it a music designed primarily for the edification of the saints? Or is it primarily an evangelical tool for the church?

"Gospel music was never made for the church [alone]," says Donnie McClurkin. "Gospel was always supposed to be preached to the secular. That's how conversion happens."[107]

"It's not the music that really makes it gospel," says Shirley Caesar. "We have to always listen to the lyrics. And it's the lyrics that's going to bring deliverance."[108]

And somewhere in the middle is a legend like Albertina Walker: "That old music will never die. Contemporary music is great, but it's the message, the feeling of traditional gospel, that moves you. Traditional music is the Word. In place of preaching it, we sing it."[109]

In the beginning was THE WORD . . .
And when THE WORD got the funky beat, it became GOSPEL.

Discography

This is a strictly subjective listing of representative music by the artists mentioned in *People Get Ready*. In addition to taking into account personal preference, the list is further limited to releases readily available to the general public. Alas, an appalling number of gospel's greatest releases are currently out of print. In addition to the record labels themselves, as well as the usual Internet vendors such as Amazon.com and CDnow.com, information for this listing was gleaned from the following sources:

AIR Gospel (Atlanta International)—*www.airgospel.com*
Blackberry Records—www.*blackberryrecords.com*
Columbia Records—*www.legacyrecords.com*
Document Records—*www.document-records.com*
Gospo Centric Records—*www.gospocentric.com*
Library of Congress—*www.loc.gov/folklife/rounder.html*
Malaco/Savoy Records—*www.shopmalaco.com*
Collectables Records—*www.Oldies.com/genre*
Rhino Records—*www.rhino.com*
Roots 'n' Rhythm—*www.Rootsandrhythm.com*
Rounder Records—*www.rounder.com*
Specialty Records—*www.fantasyjazz.com*
Tyscot Records—*www.tyscot.com*
Verity Records—*www.verityrecords.com*

Chapter 6

Afro-American Spirituals, Work Songs, and Ballads
Various artists
Library of Congress
Archive of Folk Culture
Rounder Records, Rounder CD 1510

The Ballad Hunter, Volumes VII and VIII
"Spiritual: Religion Through Songs of Southern Negroes"
Various artists

Folk Music in America
Library of Congress AFS 52

The Ballad Hunter, Volumes IX and X
"Jordan and Jubilee: Songs from Livingston, Alabama"
Various artists
Folk Music in America
Library of Congress AFS 53

The Birmingham Jubilee Singers, Complete Recorded Works, Volume II, 1927–1930
The Birmingham Jubilee Singers
Document Records DOCD 5346

Black Secular Vocal Groups, Volume I, 1923–1929
Various artists
Document Records DOCD 5546

Black Secular Vocal Groups, Volume II, 1931–1939
Various artists
Document Records DOCD 5550

Fisk Jubilee Singers, Volume I, 1909–1911
Fisk Jubilee Singers
Document Records DOCD 5533

Fisk Jubilee Singers, Volume II, 1915–1920
Fisk Jubilee Singers
Document Records DOCD 5534

Henry Thomas, Complete Recorded Works in Chronological Order, 1927–1929
Henry Thomas
Document Records DOCD 5665

I Believe in the Angels Singing: Songs from the Underground Railroad Era
Various artists
Highlander Center
1959 Highlander Way
New Market, TN 37820

Jim Jackson, Complete Recorded Works in Chronological Order, Volume I, 1927–1928
Jim Jackson
Document Records DOCD 5114

Louisiana Blues
Various artists
Wolf Records, WSE 109

Negro Religious Field Recordings, 1934–1942
Various artists
Document Records DOCD 5312

Negro Religious Songs and Services
Various artists
Library of Congress
Archive of Folk Culture
Rounder Records, Rounder CD 1514

Religious Music: Congregational and Ceremonial
Various artists
Folk Music in America
Library of Congress, LCB 1

The Rev. E. D. Campbell, the Rev. Isaiah Shelton, and the Rev. R. F. Thornton, 1927
Rev. E. D. Campbell, the Rev. Isaiah Shelton, and the Rev. R. F. Thornton
Document Records DOCD 5389

The Rev. J. C. Burnett, Volume I, 1926–1927
Rev. J. C. Burnett
Document Records DOCD 5557

The Rev. J. C. Burnett, Volume II, 1927–1945
Rev. J. C. Burnett
Document Records DOCD 5558

Sacred Harp Singing
Various artists
Library of Congress
Archive of Folk Culture
Rounder Records, Rounder CD 1503

Sanctified Jug Bands, 1928–1930
Various artists
Document Records DOCD 5300

Southern Journey, Volume 12: Biblical Songs and Spirituals
Georgia Sea Island Singers
Rounder Records 1712

Too Late Too Late, Volume II, 1897–1935
Various artists
Document Records DOCD 5216

Tuskegee Institute Singers/Quartet, 1914–1927
Tuskegee Institute Singers/Quartet
Document Records DOCD 5549

Chapter 7

Acapella Gospel Singing
Various artists
Folklyric/Arhoolie Records 9045

Afro-American Spirituals, Work Songs, and Ballads
Various artists
Library of Congress Archive of Folk Culture
Rounder Select ROUNCD 1510, 1998

Arizona Dranes, 1926–29
Arizona Dranes
Document DOCD 5186, 1994

Atlanta, GA Gospel, 1923–1931
Various artists
Document Records DOCD 5485

Bessemer Sunset Four, 1928–1930
Bessemer Sunset Four
Document Records, DOCD 5379

Black Vocal Groups, Volume 3, 1925–1943
Various artists
Document DOCD 5551

Black Vocal Groups, Volume 7, 1927–1941
Various artists
Document DOCD 5555

Black Vocal Groups, Volume 9, 1929–1942
Various artists
Document Records DOCD 5606

The Complete Blind Willie Johnson
Blind Willie Johnson
Columbia/Legacy C2K 52835, 1993

Cotton Belt Quartet, 1925–1927
Cotton Belt Quartet
Document Records, DOCD 5439

The Earliest Negro Vocal Quartets, Volume I, 1894–1928
Various artists
Document Records DOCD 5061

The Earliest Negro Vocal Quartets, Volume II, 1893–1922
Various artists
Document Records DOCD 5288

Fisk Jubilee Singers Volume III, 1924–1940
Fisk Jubilee Singers
Document DOCD-5535,

I Am Born to Preach the Gospel
Washington Phillips
Yazoo Records 2003, 2009

Negro Songs and Services
Various artists
Library of Congress Archive of Folk Culture
Rounder Select ROUNCD 1510, 1999

Norfolk Jazz and Jubilee Quartets, Volume I, 1921–1923
Various artists
Document Records DOCD 5381

Norfolk Jazz and Jubilee Quartets, Volume II, 1923–1925
Various artists
Document Records DOCD 5382

Norfolk Jazz and Jubilee Quartets, Volume III, 1925–1927
Various artists
Document Records DOCD 5383

Norfolk Jazz and Jubilee Quartets, Volume IV, 1927–1929
Various artists
Document Records DOCD 5384

Pace Jubilee Singers, Volume I, 1926–1927
Pace Jubilee Singers
Document DOCD 5617, 2000

Pace Jubilee Singers, Volume II, 1928–1929
Pace Jubilee Singers
Document DOCD 5618, 2000

Preachers & Congregations, Volume I, 1927–1938
Various artists
Document Records DOCD 5529

Preachers & Congregations, Volume II, 1926–1941
Various artists
Document Records DOCD 5530

Rev. F. W. McGee, Volume I, 1927–1929
The Reverend F. W. McGee
Document Records BDCD 6031, 1992

Rev. J. M. Gates, Volume I, 1926
The Reverend J. M. Gates
Document Records DOCD 5414

Rev. J. M. Gates, Volume II, 1926
The Reverend J. M. Gates
Document Records DOCD 5433

Rev. J. M. Gates, Volume IIII, 1926
The Reverend J. M. Gates
Document Records DOCD 5442

Silver Leaf Quartette of Norfolk, 1928–1931
Silver Leaf Quartette
Document Records DOCD 5362

Songsters and Saints, Volume I
Various artists
Matchbox Records MSEX 2002/2002

Songsters and Saints, Volume II
Various artists
Matchbox Records, MSEX 2003/2004

Storefront and Street Corner Gospel, 1927–1929
Various artists
Document DOCD 5054, 1993

Chapter 8

Complete Recorded Works in Chronological Order, Vol. 1, 1928–1930
Georgia Tom Dorsey
Document Records, DOCD, 1996

Complete Recorded Works in Chronological Order, Vol. II, 1930–1934
Georgia Tom Dorsey
Document Records, DOCD 1996

Georgia Blues and Gospel, 1927–1931
Various artists
Document Records DOCD 5160

Georgia Tom Dorsey—The Essential
Georgia Tom Dorsey
Document Records, CBL-200034

The Hokum Boys, Volume 1, 1929
The Hokum Boys
Document Records DOCD 5236

Precious Lord: The Great Gospel Songs of Thomas A. Dorsey
Various artists
Sony/Legacy CK 57164, 1994

Throw Out the Lifeline
Sallie Martin Singers/Cora Martin
Specialty Records SPCD 7043-2

Chapter 9

Best of the Dixie Hummingbirds
Dixie Hummingbirds
MCA Special Products MCAD 22043

Diamond Jubilation: 75ᵗʰ Anniversary
Dixie Hummingbirds
Rounder Records ROUN2181

Dixie Hummingbirds Completed Recorded Works 1939–1947 in Chronological Order
Dixie Hummingbirds
Document Records DOCD 5491

Jesus Has Traveled This Road Before
Dixie Hummingbirds
Gospel Friend 1503

Thank You for One More Day
Dixie Hummingbirds
MCA Records MCA 11882

Precious Lord: The Great Gospel Songs of Thomas A. Dorsey
Various artists
Sony Records CK 057164

Freedom: The Golden Gate Quartet and Josh White in Concert
Great Performances from the Library of Congress, Vol. 14

The Golden Gate Quartet and Josh White
Bridge Records 9114
1940

Golden Gate Jubilee Quartet: Complete Recorded Works in Chronological Order, Volume 1—1937–1938
Golden Gate Jubilee Quartet
Document Records DOCD 5472

Golden Gate Jubilee Quartet: Complete Recorded Works in Chronological Order, Volume 2—1938–1939
Golden Gate Jubilee Quartet
Document Records DOCD 5473

Golden Gate Quartet: Complete Recorded Works in Chronological Order, Volume 5—1945–1949
Golden Gate Quartet
Document Records DOCD 5638

The Best of the Roberta Martin Singers
The Roberta Martin Singers
Savoy Records SGL 7018

Working the Road: The Golden Age of Chicago Gospel Featuring Robert Anderson
Various artists
Delmark Records DE-702

All God's Sons and Daughters: Chicago's Gospel Legends
Various artists
Shanachie Gospel

The Great Gospel Men
Various artists
Shanachie Gospel

The Great Gospel Women
Various artists
Shanachie Gospel

Kings of the Gospel Highway
Various artists
Shanachie Gospel

Say Amen, Somebody Soundtrack
Various artists
DRG Records

Chapter 10

Legendary Sermons
The Reverend C. L. Franklin
MCA Special Projects

My Favorite Sermons
The Reverend C. L. Franklin
MCA Special Projects

Sermons and Hymns
The Reverend C. L. Franklin
MCA Special Projects

The Best of Mahalia Jackson
Mahalia Jackson
Columbia/Legacy 66911

Bless This House
Mahalia Jackson
Columbia Records, CL 899

The Essential Mahalia Jackson
Mahalia Jackson
Metro Records METRCD034

Gospels, Spirituals & Hymns, Volume I
Mahalia Jackson
Columbia/Legacy 65594

Gospels, Spirituals & Hymns, Volume II
Mahalia Jackson
Columbia/Legacy 65597

How I Got Over: Apollo Sessions, 1946–1954
Mahalia Jackson
Westside Records 303

In Concert, Easter Sunday 1967
Mahalia Jackson
Columbia/Legacy 85298

The Power and the Glory
Mahalia Jackson
Columbia/Legacy 65201

Recorded Live in Europe During Her Latest Concert Tour
Mahalia Jackson
Columbia/Legacy 85282

16 Most Requested Songs
Mahalia Jackson
Columbia/Legacy 64991

Sunday Morning Prayer Meeting With Mahalia Jackson
Mahalia Jackson
Columbia/Legacy 63592

The Essence of Mahalia Jackson
Mahalia Jackson
Columbia/Legacy 57705

Sister Rosetta Tharpe: The Gospel of Blues
Sister Rosetta Tharpe
MCA Records MCA 005330

Shout, Sister, Shout: A Tribute to Sister Rosetta Tharpe
Various artists
M.C. Records

Sister Rosetta Tharpe: The Original Soul Sister
Sister Rosetta Tharpe
Proper Records Properbox 51

Jumpin' at the Savoy
Sister Rosetta Tharpe with the Lucky Millinder Orchestra
EPM Musique CD

Up Above My Head
Sister Rosetta Tharpe
Indigo Records IGO CD 2108Z

I Feel the Holy Spirit
Clara Ward and the Ward Singers
Gospel Friend 1502

Somebody Bigger Than You or I
Clara Ward and the Clara Ward Singers
Peacock Gospel Classics

Take My Hand, Precious Lord
Clara Ward Singers
MCA Special Products

The Very Greatest
Clara Ward and the Famous Clara Ward Singers
Nashboro 4010

Chapter 11

The Best of the Blind Boys of Mississippi
The Blind Boys of Mississippi
MCA Special Products

The Great Lost Blind Boys of Mississippi Album
The Blind Boys of Mississippi
Collectables Records COL 7236

I Never Heard a Man
The Blind Boys of Mississippi
Jewell Records Gospel Series

I'll Make It Alright
The Blind Boys of Mississippi
Jewell Records Gospel Series

The Rev. Julius Cheeks and the Four Knights
The Reverend Julius Cheeks and the Four Knights
Savoy Records

Somebody Left on the Morning Train
The Reverend Julius Cheeks
Savoy Records

We'll Lay Down Our Lives
The Reverend Julius Cheeks and the Young Adult Choir
Savoy Records

The Very Best of the Dixie Hummingbirds and the Angelics: Up in Heaven
The Dixie Hummingbirds and the Angelics
Collectables Records VCL 6103

Best of the Sensational Nightingales
Sensational Nightingales
MCA Special Products MCAD 22044

God Is Not Pleased
Sensational Nightingales
Malaco Records

Live So God Can Use You
Sensational Nightingales
Malaco Records

Seek Ye First the Kingdom of God
Sensational Nightingales
Malaco Records

Sensational Nightingales Greatest Hits
Sensational Nightgales
Malaco Records

Songs to Edify
Sensational Nightingales
Malaco Records

Stay on the Boat
Sensational Nightingales
Malaco Records

Heaven Is My Home
The Soul Stirrers, featuring Paul Foster and Johnnie Taylor
Specialty SPCD 7040-2

Jesus Gave Me Water
The Soul Stirrers, featuring Sam Cooke, Paul Foster, and Julius Cheeks
Specialty SPCD-7031-2

Shine on Me
The Soul Stirrers, featuring R. H. Harris
Specialty SPCD 7013-2

Happy With Jesus Alone
Swan Silvertones
Liquid 8/Roadshow 82004-12021-2

Heavenly Light
Swan Silvertones
Specialty SPCD 7044-2

Love Lifted Me/My Rock
Swan Silvertones
Specialty SPCD 7202-2

Pray for Me/Let's Go to Church Together
Swan Silvertones
Collectables Records COL 7234

Savior Pass Me Not
Swan Silvertones
Collectables Records COL 7227

Singin' in My Soul/Blessed Assurance
Swan Silvertones
Collectables Records COL 7226

The Very Best of the Swan Silvertones: Do You Believe?
Swan Silvertones
Collectables Records VCL 6111

The Best of King Gospel
Various artists
Ace Records CDCHD 873

Gotham Gospel Volume I
Various artists
Collectables Records VCL 5312

Gotham Gospel Volume II
Various artists
Collectables Records VCL 5325

New Orleans Gospel Quartets
Various artists
504 Records 81

O Gospel, Where Art Thou?
Various artists
Morada Records 102

The Specialty Story Box Set
Various artists
Specialty SPCD 4412

Chapter 12

Lord Lift Us Up
Inez Andrews
Savoy Records

My Testimony: Live
Inez Andrews
Savoy Records

Sinner's Prayer: Live
Inez Andrews
Savoy Records

The Best of Shirley Caesar
Shirley Caesar
Savoy Records 14202

The First Lady of Gospel
Shirley Caesar
Liquid 8/Roadshow Records 82004-12013-2

Hymns
Shirley Caesar
Word Records 080688615420

Shirley Caesar's Greatest Hits
Shirley Caesar
Rhino Records Rhino 73898

The Very Best of Shirley Caesar: To Be Like Him
Shirley Caesar
Collectables VCL 6100

The Best of the Caravans
The Caravans
Savoy

The Caravans Sing . . .
The Caravans
Savoy Records

Seek Ye the Lord/The Soul of the Caravans
The Caravans
Collectables COL 7237

The Very Best of the Caravans
The Caravans
Collectables VCL 6101

Walk Around Heaven All Day/In Concert
The Caravans
Collectables COL 7212

Camp Meeting/God Is Here
The Original Gospel Harmonettes
Collectables 7231

A City Built Four-Square
Dorothy Love Coates & Singers
Savoy Records

Get on Board
Dorothy Love Coates and the Gospel Harmonettes
Specialty SPCD 7017-2

The Soul of the Original Gospel Harmonettes/Peace in the Valley
The Original Gospel Harmonettes
Collectables 7229

Gotta Serve Somebody: The Gospel Songs of Bob Dylan
Various artists
Columbia CK 89015

Amazing Grace: The Complete Recordings Live
Aretha Franklin, the Rev. James Cleveland and others
Rhino Records
Rhino 75627

One Lord, One Faith, One Baptism
Aretha Franklin, the Reverend Jesse Jackson, the Rev. Jasper Williams, Mavis
    Staples, Joe Ligon and others
Arista Records
AL 8497

The Rev. C. L. Franklin, Aretha Franklin, and the New Bethel Baptist Church Choir
The Reverend C. L. Franklin, Aretha Franklin, and the New Bethel Baptist
    Church Choir
Jewel Records Gospel Series

Cassietta George
Cassietta George
Savoy Records

Answer Me, Dear Jesus
Dorothy Norwood
Savoy Records

Better Days Ahead
Dorothy Norwood
Malaco Records

Denied Mother
Dorothy Norwood
Savoy Records

Golden Classics
Dorothy Norwood
Collectables COL 5218

Hattie B's Daughter
Dorothy Norwood
Malaco Records

Live
Dorothy Norwood
Malaco Records

Live at Home
Dorothy Norwood
Malaco Records

Look What They've Done to My Child
Dorothy Norwood
Savoy Records

The Lord Is a Wonder
Dorothy Norwood
Malaco Records

Ol' Rickety Bridge
Dorothy Norwood
Malaco Records

Shake the Devil Off
Dorothy Norwood
Malaco Records

Up Where We Belong
Dorothy Norwood
Savoy Records

Freedom Highway
The Staple Singers
Columbia 47334

Swing Low, Sweet Chariot
Staple Singers
Collectables COL 7132

The 25th Day of December
The Staple Singers
Specialty 7051

Uncloudy Day
Staple Singers
Koch Jazz/Rhino KOC CD-51408

The Very Best of the Staple Singers: Live, Volume I
The Staple Singers
Collectables VCL 6109

The Very Best of the Staple Singers: On the Way to Heaven, Volume II
The Staple Singers
Collectables VCL 6110

God Is Able to Carry You Through
Albertina Walker and the Metro Mass Choir
Savoy Records

Sweet, Sweet Spirit
Albertina Walker and the Lighthouse Baptist Church Choir
Savoy Records

Work on It
Albertina Walker and the Charlotte I.M. Choir
Savoy Records

Give Your Hands to Struggle
Bernice Reagon
Paredon Records P-1028.
(P.O. Box 889, Brooklyn, NY 11202)

Chapter 13

A Lifetime of Believing/Black Man's Lament
Professor Alex Bradford
Collectables COL 6812

One Step/Angel on Vacation
Professor Alex Bradford and the Bradford Singers
Collectables COL 7235

Pop Gospel From London/The Soul of Alex Bradford
Professor Alex Bradford
Collectables COL 7211

Rainbow in the Sky
Professor Alex Bradford
Specialty SPCD 7015-2

Shakin' the Rafters
The Abyssinian Baptist Choir, Under the Direction of Professor Alex Bradford
Columbia 47335

Too Close
Professor Alex Bradford
Specialty SPCD 7042-2

Breathe on Me
The Reverend James Cleveland and Albertina Walker
Savoy Records

The Rev. James Cleveland: A Tribute to the King, Volume 2
Various choirs accompanying the Reverend James Cleveland
Malaco Records

The Rev. James Cleveland and the Angelic Choir III: Peace Still
The Reverend James Cleveland and the Angelic Choir
Savoy Records

The Rev. James Cleveland and the Charles Fold Singers
The Reverend James Cleveland and the Charles Fold Singers
Savoy Records

The Rev. James Cleveland and the Los Angeles Gospel Messengers
The Reverend James Cleveland and the Los Angeles Gospel Messengers
Savoy Records

The Rev. James Cleveland and the Salem Inspirational Choir
The Reverend James Cleveland and the Salem Inspirational Choir
Savoy Records

The Rev. James Cleveland and the Southern California Community Choir
The Reverend James Cleveland and the Southern California Community Choir
Savoy Records

I Don't Feel Noways Tired
The Reverend James Cleveland
Malaco/601 Music

I'm Giving Up My Life to You
The Reverend James Cleveland
Savoy Records

I Stood on the Banks of the Jordan
The Reverend James Cleveland
Savoy Records

The King of Gospel
The Reverend James Cleveland
Malaco/601 Music

Live with the New Jersey Mass Choir
The Reverend James Cleveland
Savoy Records

Please Be Patient With Me
The Reverend James Cleveland and Albertina Walker
Savoy Records

Soon I Will Be Done with the Troubles of the World
The Reverend James Cleveland
Savoy Records

The Very Best of the Rev. James Cleveland: Great Day
The Reverend James Cleveland
Collectables VCL 6102

The Best of Andrae
Andrae Crouch and the Disciples
Light Records LS 5678

The Classics, Volume 1
Andrae Crouch and the Disciples
Platinum Entertainment

Live at Carnegie Hall
Andrae Crouch and the Disciples
Light Records LS 5602

Live in London
Andrae Crouch and the Disciples
Light Records LS 5717

Mercy
Andrae Crouch
Qwest/Warner Brothers 9-45432

More of the Best
Andrae Crouch and the Disciples
Platinum Entertainment

Pray
Andrae Crouch
Warner Brothers Records

This Is Another Day
Andrae Crouch and the Disciples
Light Records LC 5683

The Best of the Edwin Hawkins Singers
The Edwin Hawkins Singers
Savoy Records 7707

Oh Happy Day
The Edwin Hawkins Singers
BMG Special Products

The Original Edwin Hawkins Singers Reunion: Oh Happy Day
The Edwin Hawkins Singers
Intersound CRD 7005

Chapter 14

Go Tell It on the Mountain
Blind Boys of Alabama
Real World Records

Gospel at Colonus: 1985 Philadelphia Cast Recording
Blind Boys of Alabama and others
Nonesuch Records

Higher Ground
Blind Boys of Alabama
Real World Records 7243 8 50918 2 7

1948–1951
Five Blind Boys of Alabama
Flyright Records

Oh Lord, Stand by Me
The Blind Boys of Alabama
Specialty Records SP 2123

Spirit of the Century
Blind Boys of Alabama
Real World Records 7243 8 12793 2 8

The Very Best of the Blind Boys of Alabama: Have Faith
The Blind Boys of Alabama
Collectables VCL 6104

Precious Lord
The Reverend Al Green
Myrrh Records MSB 6702

A Bright New Side
The Mighty Clouds of Joy
MCA Special Products

The Best of the Mighty Clouds of Joy, Volume 1
The Mighty Clouds of Joy
MCA Special Products MCAD 2045

Changing Times
The Mighty Clouds of Joy
Song Records 66898

Family Circle
The Mighty Clouds of Joy
MCA 28008

Live
The Mighty Clouds of Joy
MCA Special Products MCAD 22022

Live in Charleston
The Mighty Clouds of Joy
Intersound Records

Memory Lane: The Best of the Mighty Clouds of Joy
The Mighty Clouds of Joy
Sony Records

The Mighty Clouds Live at the Music Hall
The Mighty Clouds of Joy
MCA 28017

Pray for Me
The Mighty Clouds of Joy
Word Records 701920608

God Gets the Glory
The Mississippi Mass Choir
Malaco Records MCD-6008

It Remains to be Seen
The Mississippi Mass Choir
Malaco Records MCD-6013

The Mississippi Mass Choir
The Mississippi Mass Choir
Malaco Records MCD-6003

BeBe Winans
BeBe Winans
Atlantic

Love and Freedom
BeBe Winans
Polygram Records

BeBe and CeCe Winans
BeBe and CeCe Winans
Capitol Records

Different Lifestyles
BeBe & CeCe Winans
Capitol Records

Heaven
BeBe & CeCe Winans
Capitol Records

Relationships
BeBe & CeCe Winans
Capitol Records

Alabaster Box
CeCe Winans
Sparrow/EMD

Alone in His Presence
CeCe Winans
Sparrow/EMB Records

Everlasting Love
CeCe Winans
Atlantic Records

Throne Room
CeCe Winans
Sony Records

For the Rest of My Life
Mom and Pops Winans
Capitol

Mom and Pops Winans
Mom and Pops Winans
Capitol

All Out
The Winans
Warner Brothers Records

Decisions
The Winans
Warner Brothers Records

Introducing the Winans
The Winans
Platinum Entertainment

Let My People Go
The Winans
Warner Brothers Records

Long Time Comin'
The Winans
Platinum Entertainment

Return
The Winans
Warner Brothers Records

The Very Best of the Winans
The Winans
Rhino Records

Chapter 15

Believe
Yolana Adams
Elektra Asylum

Best of Yolanda Adams
Yolanda Adams
Verity Records

The Experience
Yolanda Adams
Elektra/Asylum

Live in Washington
Yolanda Adams
Verity Records

More Than a Melody
Yolanda Adams
Verity Records

Mountain High . . . Valley Deep
Yolanda Adams
Elektra Asylum

Songs from the Heart
Yolanda Adams
Verity Records

God's Property
Kirk Franklin Presents God's Property
Gospo Centric

Kirk Franklin and the Family
Kirk Franklin and the Family
Gospo Centric 72119-2

Kirk Franklin and the Nu Nation Project
Kirk Franklin and the Nu National Project
Gospo Centric

Kirk Franklin Presents 1NC (One Nation Crew)
Kirk Franklin Presents 1NC
Gospo Centric

The Rebirth of . . .
Kirk Franklin
Gospo Centric 75751-70037-2

Whatcha Lookin' 4
Kirk Franklin and the Family
Gospo Centric

All My Best for You, Volume I
Tramaine Hawkins
Sparrow/EMD Records

All My Best for You, Volume II
Tramaine Hawkins
Chordant

Determined
Tramaine Hawkins
Platinum Entertainment

Live
Tramaine Hawkins
Sparrow Records

Still
Tramaine Hawkins
Gospo Centric

Tramaine
Tramaine Hawkins
Light Records

To a Higher Place
Tramaine Hawkins
Sony Records

Treasury
Tramaine Hawkins
Platinum Entertainment

Any Day
John P. Kee and the V.I.P. Music and the Arts Mass Choir
Verity Records

Blessed by Association
John P. Kee and the New Life Community Choir
Verity Records

Color Blind
John P. Kee
Jive Records

Just Me This Time
John P. Kee
Jive Records

Lily in the Valley
John P. Kee and the V.I.P. Music and the Arts Mass Choir
Jive Records

Mighty in the Spirit
John P. Kee and the V.I.P. Music and the Arts Mass Choir
Verity Records

Not Guilty . . . The Experience
John P. Kee and the New Life Community Choir
Verity Records

Show Up!
John P. Kee and the New Life Community Choir
Jive Records

Stand
John P. Kee and the V.I.P. Music and the Arts Mass Choir
Jive Records

Strength
John P. Kee and the New Life Community Choir
Verity Records

There is Hope
John P. Kee
Jive Records

Wait on Him
John P. Kee and the New Life Community Choir
Jive Records

Wash Me
John P. Kee and the New Life Community Choir
Jive Records

The Collection
Donnie McClurkin
Savoy Records

Donnie McClurkin
Donnie McClurkin
Warner Alliance 9 46297-2

Donnie McClurkin . . . Again
Donnie McClurkin
Verity Records

Live in London . . . and More
Donnie McClurkin
Verity Records

Can't Keep It to Myself
Marion Williams
Shanachie Records

God and Me/Let the Words of My Mouth
Marion Williams
Collectables Records COL 7230

Gospel Soul of Marion Williams
Marion Williams
Shanachie Records

The New Message/Standing Here Wondering
Marion Williams
Collectables Records COL 7484

O Holy Night
Marion Williams
Savoy Records

This Too Shall Pass
Marion Williams
Nashboro Records

Through Many Dangers
Marion Williams
Shanachie Records

Be Encouraged
Vickie Winans
Light Records

Bringing It All Together
Vickie Winans
Verity Records 01241-43214-2

Live in Detroit
Vickie Winans
Light Records

Live in Detroit II
Vickie Winans
Light Records

Vickie Winans
Vickie Winans
Light Records

Notes

Chapter 1

1. Cone, James H., *The Spirituals and the Blues: An Interpretation* (New York: Seabury Press, 1971), 5.

2. Johnson, James Weldon, ed., and Johnson, J. Rosamund, musical arranger. *The Book of African Negro Spirituals* (New York: Viking Press, 1925), 12–13.

3. Lovell, John, Jr. *Black Song: The Forge and the Flame. The Story of How the Afro-American Spiritual Was Hammered Out* (New York: Paragon House Publishers, 1972), 126.

4. Parrish, Lydia. *Slave Songs of the Georgia Sea Islands.* (New York: Creative Age Press, 1942), 20.

5. Dobie, J. Frank, ed. *Follow de Drinkin' Gou'd* (Austin: Texas Folk-Lore Society, 1928), 184.

6. Ibid., 81.

7. Ibid.

8. Ibid., 82.

9. Ibid.

10. Ibid.

11. Ibid., 83.

12. Ibid., 84.

13. Ibid.

14. Lovell, John, Jr. "The Social Implications of the Negro Spiritual," *Journal of Negro Education,* Oct. 1939, 635 + .

15. Wallis, Jim. "America's Original Sin: The Legacy of White Racism," *Sojourners,* Nov. 1987, 4 + .

16. Truesdale, Albert L., Jr. "A Tillichian Analysis of White Racism in the South" (Ph.D. diss., Emory University, 1976), 7.

17. Ibid.

18. Wink, Walter. *Unmasking the Powers: The Invisible Forces That Determine Human Existence* (Philadelphia: Fortress Press, 1986), 41–51.

19. Higginson, Thomas. *Army Life in a Black Regiment* (Boston: Osgood & Co., 1870), 17–18.

20. Kirk-Duggan, Cheryl A. *Exorcising Evil* (Maryknoll, NY: Orbis Books, 1997), 36.

21. Garland, Phyl. *The Sound of Soul* (Chicago: Henry Regency Company, 1969), 86.

22. Robertson, Edwin H., ed. *No Rusty Swords: Letters, Lectures, and Notes, 1928–1936. From the Collected Works of Dietrich Bonhoeffer* (New York: Harper & Row, 1947), 113.

23. Dvořák, Antonin. "Real Value of Negro Melodies: Dr. Dvorak Finds in Them the Basis for an American School of Music," *New York Herald,* 21 May 1893, 28.

24. Du Bois, W. E. B. *The Souls of Black Folk* (New York: Bantam Books, 1989), 178.

25. Welding, Pete. "John Lee Hooker: Blues Is My Business," *Down Beat,* 7 May 1964, 24 +.

26. Marsh, J. B. T. *The Story of the Jubilee Singers: With Their Songs* (New York: AMS Press, 1971), 173.

27. Lomax, John A., collector. *Afro-American Spirituals, Work Songs, and Ballads.* Rounder CD 1510.

28. Lomax, John, and Lomax, Alan. *Our Singing Country* (New York: The MacMillan Company, 1941), 34.

29. Oliver, Paul. *Conversation with the Blues* (New York: Cambridge, 1965), 30.

30. Broonzy, Big Bill. *Black, Brown and White.* Smithsonian Folkways, 400131.

31. Moby. *Play.* V2 Records, 63881–27049–2, 1999.

32. Dixon, Christa K. *Negro Spirituals: From Bible to Folk Song* (Philadelphia: Fortress Press, 1976), 82.

33. Thurman, Howard. *Deep River* (New York: Harper & Brothers, 1955), 22.

34. Garland, Phyl. *The Sound of Soul* (Chicago: Henry Regency Company, 1969), 179.

35. Kernan, Michael. "Around the Mall and Beyond," *Smithsonian Magazine,* Apr. 1996, 24 +.

36. Wooten, James T. "Mississippi 'Loyalist' Democrats Nominate Evers for Governor," *New York Times,* 19 April 1971, 1 +.

37. McNulty, Jennifer. "UCSC Responds to September 11," *UCSC Santa Cruz,* Winter 2002, 15.

38. No author listed. "50 Selections for Registry," *New York Times,* 20 Jan. 2003, sec. E, 7.

39. Cone, 84–85.

Chapter 2

1. Curtin, Philip D., ed. *Africa Remembered: Narratives by West Africans from the Era of the Slave Trade* (Madison: University of Milwaukee Press, 1968), 72.

2. Scarborough, Dorothy. *On the Trail of Negro Folk Songs* (Cambridge: Harvard University Press, 1925), 25–26.

3. Davidson, Basil and F. K. Buah. *A History of West Africa to the Nineteenth Century* (Garden City, NY: Anchor Books, 1966), 105–287.

4. Davidson, Basil. *Black Mother: The Years of the African Slave Trade* (Boston: Little, Brown and Company, 1961), 111.

5. Ibid., 221.

6. Ibid., 242.

7. U.S. Department of Health, Education, and Welfare Office of Education Bureau of Research, *Project in African Music: In Search of a Common Musical Language in Africa* (Washington, D.C.: 1970), 93.

8. Merriam, Alan P. *African Music in Perspective* (New York: Garland Publishing, Inc., 1982), 68.

9. Herskovits, Melville J. *The Myth of the Negro Past* (New York: Harper & Brothers Publishers, 1941), 54–85.

10. Jones, A. M. *Studies in African Music, vol. 1* (London: Oxford University Press, 1959), 199.

11. Ibid., 199–201.

12. Ibid., 215–216.

13. Ibid.

14. Lomax, Alan. "Africanisms in the New World Negro Music," *The Haitian Potential: Research and Resources of Haiti,* eds. Rubin, Vera and Richard P. Schaedel (New York: Teachers College, Columbia University 1975), 39.

15. Ibid., 44.

16. Ibid., 188.

17. Ibid., 197–198.

18. Nketia, J. H. *The Music of Africa* (New York: W.W. Norton & Company, 1974), 4.

19. Lomax, 197–198.

20. Roberts, John Storm. *Black Music of Two Worlds* (New York: Praeger Publishers, 1972), 3.

21. Heine, Bernd and Derek Nurse, eds. *African Languages: An Introduction* (Cambridge, U.K.: Cambridge University Press, 2000), 1–10.

22. Jobson, Richard. *The Golden Trade or A Discovery of the River Gambra, and of the golden trade of the Aethiopians* (Reprint, London: Penguin Press, 1932), 152–153.

23. Park, Mungo. *Travel in the Interior Districts of Africa* (London: Eland Books, 1983), 151–152.

24. Ibid.

25. Burton, Richard F. *The Lake Regions of Central Africa* (Reprint, New York: Harper & Brothers, Publishers, 1860), 248–249.

26. Ibid., 468–469.

27. Ibid., 487–488.

28. Lovell, John, Jr. *Black Song: The Forge and the Flame: The Story of How the Afro-American Spiritual Was Hammered Out* (Reprint, New York: Macmillan, 1972), 14.

29. Roberts, 5.

30. Maultsby, Portia Katrenia. "Afro-American Religious Music, 1619–1861" (Ph.D. diss., University of Madison, 1974), 13.

31. Ibid., 14.

32. Herskovits, 207.

33. Ibid., 215.

34. Roberts, 6.

35. Ibid.

36. Ibid., 7–8.

37. Ibid., 9.

38. Gorlin, Dan. *Songs of West Africa* (Forest Knolls, CA: Alokli Press, 2000), 3.

39. Ibid.

40. Nketia, J. H. "The Musical Languages of Subsaharan Africa." African Music Meeting in Yaounde, Cameroon, 23–27 February 1970. Organized by UNESCO La Revue Musicale Paris 1972, 37.

41. Gorlin, 51.

42. Ibid., 105.

43. Ibid.

44. Waterman, Richard A. and William R. Bascom. "African and New World Negro Folklore," *Dictionary of Folklore, Mythology and Legend*, ed. Maria Leach (New York: Funk & Wagnalls, 1949), 21.

45. Chief Fela Sowande. "The Role of Music in Traditional African Society." African Music Meeting in Yaounde, Cameroon, 23–27 February 1970. Organized by UNESCO La Revue Musicale Paris 1972, 64.

46. Ibid.

47. Clark, Kenneth S. "Penetrates Jungle for Primitive Folk Tunes," *Musical America*, 6 Mar. 1915, 3.

48. Floyd, Samuel A., Jr. *The Power of Black Music* (New York: Oxford University Press, 1995), 32.

49. Belinga, Samuel Eno. "The Traditional Music of West Africa." African Meeting, UNESCO, 71–75.

50. Curtin, Philip D. *The Atlantic Slave Trade: A Census* (Madison: University of Wisconsin Press, 1969), 157.

51. von Hornbostel, Erich M. and Curt Sachs. "Systematik der Musikinstrumente," *Zeitschrift fur Ethnologie*, XLVI (1914), 553–590.

52. Merriam, Alan. "African Music," *Continuity and Change in African Cultures*, eds. William R. Bascom and Melville J. Herskovits (Chicago: University of Chicago Press, 1959), 57.

53. U.S. Department of Health, Education, and Welfare Office of Education Bureau of Research, 93.

54. Ibid.

55. Ibid., 94.

56. Ibid., 95.

57. Merriam, *African Music in Perspective*, 98–99.

58. Ibid., 99.

59. Ibid., 98.

60. Waterman, Richard A. "Hot Rhythm in Negro Music," *Journal of the American Musicological Society*, vol. 1, 1948, 25.

61. Rublowsky, John. *Black Music in America* (New York: Basic Books, Inc., 1971), 50.

62. Miley, Bubber, cited in Burns, Ken. *Jazz: The Story of America's Music. A Film by Ken Burns*, PBS Jazz951. 2000.

63. Waterman, "Hot Rhythm in Negro Music," 29.

64. Merriam, *Continuity*, 53–4. A. M. Jones, "African Music in Northern Rhodesia and Some Other Places," (Rhodes-Livingstone Museum, Occasional Papers, No. 4, [Livingstone, 1949]), 11–12. Cited in: *Continuity and Change in African Cultures*. Edited by William R. Bascom and Melville J. Herskovits (Chicago: University of Chicago Press, 1959).

65. Waterman, "Hot Rhythm in Negro Music," 30.

66. Jones, A. M. "African Rhythm." *Africa* XXIV, January 1954 26–27.

67. Talbot, Amaury P. *The Peoples of Southern Nigeria* (Reprint, London: Frank Cass & Co. Ltd., 1926), 802.

68. Ibid., 802–803.

69. Ibid.

70. Jones, *Studies in African Music*, 96–97.

71. Talbot, 803.

72. Ibid.

73. Stanley, Henry M. *In Darkest Africa* (New York: Charles Scribner's Sons, 1891), 437.

74. Talbot, 802–803.

75. Stuckey, Sterling. *Slave Culture: Nationalist Theory and the Foundations of Black America* (New York: Oxford University Press, 1987), 25.

76. Raboteau, Albert J. *Slave Religion* (New York: Oxford University Press, 1978), 7.

77. Park, 29.

78. Curtin, *Africa Remembered*, 78.

79. Burton, 502.

80. Mbiti, John S. *African Religions & Philosophy*, 2nd revised and enlarged ed. (Portsmouth, NH: Heinemann International, 1969), 29.

81. Ibid.

82. Ibid., 49.

83. Ibid., 48.

84. Ibid., 52.

85. Nketia, J. H. *African Music in Ghana* (Evanston, IL: Northwestern University Press, 1963), 13.

86. Lovell, 30.

87. Herskovits, 232.

87. Ibid., 233–234.

88. Fage, J. D. *A History of Africa* (New York: Alfred A. Knopf, 1986), 237.

89. Davidson, *Black Mother: The Years of the African Slave Trade,* 38–39.

90. Fage, 237.

91. Davidson, *Black Mother*, 204–205.

92. Ibid.

93. Ibid.

94. Curtin, *The Atlantic Slave Trade: A Census*, 49.

95. Ibid., 46.

96. Ibid., 71.

97. Ibid., 118.

98. Ibid., 157.

99. Ibid., 158–161.

100. Ibid., 258.

101. Ibid., 15.

102. Schneider, Dorothy and Carl J. Schneider. *Slavery in America, from Colonial Times to the Civil War* (New York: Checkmark Books, 2000), 53.

103. Curtin, *The Atlantic Slave Trade: A Census*, 118–119.

104. Ibid., 268.

105. Fage, 253.

106. Curtin, *The Atlantic Slave Trade: A Census*, 269.

107. Fage, 255.

108. Curtin, *The Atlantic Slave Trade: A Census*, 113.

109. Ibid., 279.

110. Ibid., 285.

111. Ibid., 286.

112. Curtin, *Africa Remembered,* 129–130.

113. Ibid., 78.

114. Ibid., 274–276.

115. Ibid., 275–280.

116. Botkin, B. A., ed. *Lay My Burden Down: A Folk History of Slavery.* Slave Narrative Collection, Federal Writers' Project (Chicago: University of Chicago Press, 1937), 57–58.

117. Du Bois, W. E. B. *The Autobiography of W. E. B. Du Bois: A Soliloquy on Viewing My Life from the Last Decade of Its First Century* (United States of America: International Publishers, Co., 1968), 62.

118. Fage, 327.

119. Park, 81.

120. Ibid., 81–82.

121. Fage, 269.

122. Ibid.

123. Small, Christopher. *Music of the Common Tongue* (New York: Riverrun Press, 1987), 31.

124. Psalms 137: 1–4, King James Version.

125. Lovell, 63.

126. Haydon, Geoffrey and Marks, Dennis, eds. *Repercussions: A Celebration of African-American Music* (London: Century Publishing, 1985), 9.

Chapter 3

1. Thurman, Howard. "The Meaning of Spirituals," ed. Lindsay Patterson. *The Negro in Music and Art.* The International Library of Negro Life and History (New York: Publishers Company, Inc., 1967), 5.

2. Wright, Richard. *12 Million Black Voices* (Reprint, New York: Thunder's Mouth Press, 1988), 15.

3. Payne, Bishop Daniel Alexander. "Bishop Daniel Alexander Payne's Protestation of American Slavery, June 1839," *Journal of Negro History* LII (1967): 63.

4. Gates, Henry Louis, Jr. *The Signifying Monkey: A Theory of Afro-American Criticism* (New York: Oxford University Press, 1988), xxiv.

5. Bennett, Lerone, Jr. *Before the* Mayflower: *A History of the Negro in America,* 3rd ed. (Chicago: Johnson Publishing Co., 1966), 30.

(Note: Bennett adds that while there were apparently African-American slaves aboard the *Niña, Pinta,* and *Santa Maria,* the first African-American settlement was probably in 1525 when Spain established a colony in part of present-day South Carolina. The slaves soon revolted and fled into the primordial American forest to join the native Americans [373].)

6. Schneider, Dorothy and Carl J. Scheider. *Slavery in America, An Eyewitness History* (New York: Checkmark Books, 2000), 52.

7. Litwack, Leon F. *North of Slavery: The Negro in the Free States, 1790–1860* (Chicago: University of Chicago Press, 1961), 4.

8. Ibid., 3–4.

9. Bennett, 30.

10. Litwack, 10–11.

11. Ibid., 14.

12. Du Bois, W. E. B. *The Autobiography of W. E. B. Du Bois* (New York: International Publishers, 1968).

13. Duncan, John M. *Travels Through Part of the United States and Canada in 1818 and 1819*, vol. 1 (New York: W. B. Gilley, 1823), 60.

14. Galatians 3:28, King James Version.

15. Haynes, Leonard L. *The Negro Community Within American Protestantism 1619–1844* (Boston: Christopher Publishing House, 1953), 76.

16. Litwack, 197.

17. Ibid., 227.

18. Jordan, Winthrop D. *White Over Black: American Attitudes Toward the Negro, 1550–1812* (Kingsport: University of North Carolina Press, 1968), 183.

19. Schneider, 106–107.

20. Jordan, 183.

21. Ibid.

22. Ibid., 212.

23. Whitefield, George. *George Whitefield's Journal* (Reprint, London: Guildford and London, 1960), 422.

24. Wesley, Charles H. *Richard Allen, Apostle of Freedom*. (Washington, D.C.: Associated Publishers, Inc., 1935), 51–52.

25. Allen, Richard. *Life, Experience, and Gospel Labors of the Rt. Rev. Richard Allen* (Philadelphia: Martin & Boden, Printers, 1833), 14–21.

26. Wesley, 69–79.

27. Ibid., 71.

28. Ibid., 72–73.

29. Ibid., 78–79.

30. Litwack, 194.

31. Ibid.

32. Wesley, 140–142.

33. Litwack, 195.

34. Blackwell, Lois S. *The Wings of the Dove: The Story of Gospel Music in America* (Norfolk, VA: Donning Company/Publishers, Inc., 1978), 21.

35. Chase, Gilbert. *America's Music, From the Pilgrims to the Present* (New York: McGraw Hill Book Co., 1966), 31–32.

36. Tallmadge, William H. "Dr. Watts and Mahalia Jackson—The Development, Decline, and Survival of a Folk Style in America," *Ethnomusicology*, vol. 2 (1961), 96.

37. Chase, 41–46.

38. Benson, Louis F. *The English Hymn: Its Development and Use in Worship* (Reprint, Richmond: John Knox Press, 1962), 252–253.

39. Maultsby, Portia Katrenia. "Afro-American Religious Music, 1619–1861" (Ph.D. diss., University of Madison, 1974), 69–70.

40. Southern, Eileen. *The Music of Black Americans*, 2nd ed. (New York: W.W. Norton & Company, 1983), 75–79.

41. Maultsby, 72.

42. Nketia, J.H. Kwabena. *African Music in Ghana* (Great Britain: Northwestern University Press, 1963), 28–32, 108.

43. Southern, 76.

44. Wesley, 110.

45. Yarmolinsky, Avrahm. *Picturesque United States of America, 1811, 1812, 1813: A Memoir of Paul Svinin and his Sojourn in the United States.* (New York: William Edwin Rudge, 1930), 20.

46. Ibid., 21.

47. Watson, John F. "A Wesleyan Methodist," *Methodist Error; Friendly, Christian Advice, To those Methodists, Who indulge in extravagant emotions and bodily exercises* (Trenton, NJ: D. & E. Fenton, 1819), 29.

48. Ibid.

49. Ibid., 30–31.

50. Southern, 90.

51. Southern, Eileen J. "Musical Practices in Black Churches of Philadelphia and New York, ca. 1800–1844," *Journal of the American Musicological Society* XXX, (1977), 309.

52. Wesley, 10.

53. Ibid., 13.

54. Genovese, Eugene D. *Roll, Jordan, Roll: The World the Slaves Made* (New York: Pantheon Books, 1974), 185.

55. Ibid.

56. Steward, John, ed. *Bessie Jones: For the Ancestors* (Urbana, IL: University of Illinois Press, 1983), ix.

57. Schneider, 218.

58. Kemble, Frances Anne. *Journal of a Residence on a Georgia Plantation in 1838–1839.* ed., John A. Scott (New York: Alfred A. Knopf, 1961), 39.

59. Work, John W. *American Negro Songs and Spirituals* (New York: Bonanza Books, 1940), 2.

60. Cone, James H. *The Spirituals and the Blues: An Interpretation* (New York: The Seabury Press, 1972), 24.

61. Raboteau, Albert J. *Slave Religion, The "Invisible Institution" in the Antebellum South* (New York: Oxford University Press, 1978), 4.

62. Southern, 182.

63. Epstein, Dena J. *Sinful Tunes and Spirituals: Black Folk Music to the Civil War* (Urbana, IL: University of Illinois Press, 1977), 289.

64. Southern, *The Music of Black Americans*, 156.

65. Lomax, Alan. *Georgia Sea Islands*, New York: New World Records 80278. Liner notes, CD. Various artists.

66. Kebede, Ashenafi. *Roots of Black Music: The Vocal, Instrumental and Dance Heritage of Africa and Black America.* (Englewood Cliffs, NJ: Prentice-Hall, Inc., 1982), 130.

67. Ibid., 129.

68. Law, Frederick Omsted. *A Journey in the Seaboard Slave States in the Years 1853–1854, with Remarks on Their Economy*, vol. 2 (Reprint, New York: Dix & Edwards, 1856), 19.

69. Spencer, Jon Michael. *Sacred Symphony: The Chanted Sermon of the Black Preacher* (New York: Greenwood Press, 1987), ix.

70. Parrish, Lydia. *Slave Songs of the Georgia Sea Islands* (New York: Creative Age Press, Inc., 1942), 250–251.

71. Coleridge-Taylor, Samuel. *Twenty-Four Negro Melodies Transcribed by S. Coleridge-Taylor, Op. 59* (Boston: Oliver Ditson Co., 1905), viii.

72. Turner, Lorenzo Dow. *Africanisms in the Gullah Dialect* (Reprint, New York: Arno Press and the *New York Times,* 1969), 202.

73. Courlander, Harold. *Negro Folk Music, U.S.A.* (New York: Columbia University Press, 1963), 194–195.

74. Creel, Margaret Washington. *A Peculiar People: Slave Religion and Community Culture Among the Gullahs* (New York: New York University Press, 1988), 297–298.

75. Allen, William Francis, Charles Pickard Ware, and Lucy McKim Garrison, eds. *Slave Songs of the United States* (New York: A. Simpson & Co., 1867), xii–xv.

76. Parrish, 54.

77. Creel, 299.

78. Parrish, 55.

79. Ibid.

80. Epstein, 230.

81. Southern, 69.

82. Raboteau, 92.

83. Spencer, John Michael. *Protest & Praise: Sacred Music of Black Religion* (Minneapolis: Fortress Press, 1990), 136.

84. Parrish, 20.

85. Schneider, 43.

86. Schwerke, Irving. *Views and Interviews* (Paris: Les Orphelins-Apprentis D'Auteuil, 1936), 3.

87. Epstein, 115.

88. Windley, Lathan, complier, *Runaway Slave Advertisements, A Documentary History from the 1730s to 1790: Volume 1, Virginia and North Carolina* (Westport, CT: Greenwood Press, 1983), 248.

89. Ibid., 270.

90. Cimbala, Paul. "Fortunate Bondsmen: Black 'Musicianers' and Their Role as an Antebellum Southern Plantation Slave Elite," *Southern Studies* 18, 1979, 291–292.

91. Ibid., 293.

92. Ibid.

93. Ibid., 297.

94. Ibid., 301.

95. Ibid., 302.

96. Stampp, Kenneth M. *The Peculiar Institution: Slavery in the Ante-Bellum South* (Reprint, New York: Vintage Books, 1984), 30.

97. Curtin, 108.

98. Ibid.

99. Lomax, 1.

100. McWhiney, Grady. *Cracker Culture: Celtic Ways in the Old South* (Tuscaloosa: University of Alabama Press, 1988), 185–186.

101. Ibid., 185.

102. Ibid., 196.

103. Ibid., 188–189.

104. Ibid., 189.

105. Genovese, 185.

106. Ibid., 191–192.

107. Jones, Charles Colcock. *The Religious Instruction of Negroes in the United States* (Reprint, New York: Negro University Press, 1969), 175–176.

108. Raboteau, 209.

109. Epstein, 11.

110. Schneider, 107.

111. Farrison, William Edward. *William Wells Brown, Author & Reformer* (Chicago: University of Chicago Press, 1969), 25–26.

112. Ibid., 26.

113. Lovell, 152.

114. Small, Christopher. *Music of the Common Tongue* (New York: Riverrun Press, 1987), 85.

115. Holt, Grace Sims. "Stylin' Outta the Black Pulpit," *Rappin' and Stylin' Out: Communication in Urban America*, Thomas Kochman, ed. (Urbana: University of Illinois Press, 1972), 189–210.

116. Lovell, John, Jr. *Black Song: The Forge and Flame: The Story of How the Afro-American Spiritual Was Hammered Out* (Reprint, New York: Paragon House Publishers, 1986), 30.

117. Walker, Wyatt Tee. *Somebody's Calling My Name: Black Sacred Music and Social Change* (Valley Forge, PA: Judson Press, 1979), 19–20.

118. Gates, 4.

119. Kennedy, R. Emmet. *Mellows: A Chronicle of Unknown Singers* (New York: Albert and Charles Boni, 1925), 123–125.

120. Ibid.

121. Raboteau, 209.

122. Stuckey, Sterling. *Slave Culture: Nationalist Theory and the Foundations of Black America* (New York: Oxford University Press, 1987), 35.

123. Ibid., 38.

124. Du Bois, W. E. B. *The Souls of Black Folk* (Reprint, Greenwich, CN: A Fawcett Premier Book 1961), 144.

125. Ibid., 145.

126. Herskovits, M. J. *Man and His Works* (New York: Alfred A. Knopf, 1948), 552.

127. Tallmadge, William H. "The Black in Jackson's White Spirituals," *The Black Perspective in Music* 9:2, 1981, 159.

128. Fisher, Miles Mark. *Negro Slave Songs in the United States* (Reprint, New York: Russell & Russell, 1968), *passim*.

129. Ibid., 32–33.

130. Balmer, Randall and Lauren F. Winner. *Protestantism in America* (New York: Columbia University Press, 2002), 15.

131. Ibid., 44.

132. Ibid.

133. Ibid., 42.

134. Ibid., 46.

135. Williams, Peter W. *America's Religions, From Their Origins to the Twenty-first Century* (Urbana, IL: University of Illinois Press, 2002), 147.

136. Ibid., 182.

137. Ibid., 185.

138. Wilson, Olly. "The Association of Movement and Music as a Manifestation of a Black Conceptual Approach to Music-Making" ed. Jackson, Irene V. *More Than Dancing: Essays on Afro-American Music and Musicians* (Westport, CN: Greenwood Press, 1985), 13.

139. Ibid.

140. Trollope, Frances. *Domestic Manners of the Americans* (Reprint, New York: Alfred A. Knopf, 1949), 170–171.

141. Southern, 83.

142. Benson, 292.

143. Ibid., 293.

144. Bruce, Dickson D. *And They All Sang Hallelujah: Plain Folk Camp-Meeting Religion, 1800–1845* (Knoxville: University of Tennessee Press, 1974), 90–91.

145. Ibid.

146. Tallmadge, 140.

147. Ibid., 146–227.

148. Ibid., 263.

149. Lomax, John A. and Alan Lomax. *The 111 Best American Ballads: Folk Song U.S.A.* (New York: Duell, Sloan and Pearce, 1947), 329.

150. Tallmadge ,158.

151. Roberts, 168.

152. Oliver, Paul, Max Harrison, and William Bolcom. *New Grove Gospel, Blues, and Jazz, with Spirituals and Ragtime* (New York: W.W. Norton & Company, 1986), 9.

153. Waterman, Richard A. "African Patterns in Trinidad Negro Music" (Ph.D. diss., Northwestern University, 1943), 14.

154. Dett, R. Nathaniel. *The Dett Collection of Negro Spirituals, Third Group* (Chicago: Hall & McCreary Company, 1936), 3.

155. Ibid.

156. Ibid.

157. Krehbiel, Henry. *Afro-American Folk Songs* (New York: G. Schirmer, Inc., 1914), 70.

158. Spaeth, Sigmund. "Dixie, Harlem and Tin Pan Alley: Who Writes Negro Music—And How?" *Scribner's Magazine*, XCIX, Jan. 1936, 24.

159. Chase, 89.

160. Garst, John F. "Mutual Reinforcement and the Origins of Spirituals," *American Music 4*, Winter 1986, 404.

161. Shapiro, Anne Dhu. "Black Sacred Song and the Tune-Family Concept," ed. Josephine Wright, with Samuel A. Floyd. *New Perspectives on Music: Essays in Honor of Eileen Southern* (Warren, MI: Harmonie Park Press, 1992), 115.

162. Stampp, 160.

163. Pipes, William H. *Say Amen, Brother!* (Westport, CN: Negro University Press, 1970), 59.

164. Spencer, Jon Michael. *Sacred Symphony: The Chanted Sermon of the Black Preacher* (New York: Greenwood Press, 1987), 2.

165. Ibid.

166. Du Bois, W. E. B. *The Negro Church* (Atlanta: Atlanta University Press, 1903), 5.

167. King, Edward. *The Great South*, eds. W. Magruder and Robert R. Jones. (Reprint, Baton Rouge: Louisiana State University Press, 1972), 584–585.

168. Spencer, 3.

169. Pipes, 152–153.

170. Harrison, Paul Carter. *The Drama of Nommo* (New York: Grove Press, 1972), 44–45.

171. Pipes, 66.

172. Spencer, 6.

173. Davis, Gerald L. *I Got the Word in Me and I Can Sing It, You Know: A Study of the Performed African-American Sermon* (Philadelphia: University of Pennsylvania, 1985), 99.

174. Spencer, ix.

175. Ibid., x.

176. Spencer, Jon Michael. *Re-Searching Black Music* (Knoxville: University of Tennessee Press, 1996), 47.

177. Spencer, *Sacred Symphony: The Chanted Sermon of the Black Preacher*, xiii.

178. Ibid.

179. Ibid., xv.

180. Allen, iv–v.

181. Barrett, Harris. "Negro Folk Songs," *Southern Workman* 41, 1912, 241.

182. Spencer, 234–235.

183. Holt, 189–190.

184. Ibid., 191.

185. Cone, 30.

186. Stuckey, 24.

187. Levine, Lawrence. "'Some Go Up and Some Go Down': The Meaning of the Slave Trickster," *Articles on American Slavery, vol. 8: The Culture and Community of Slavery* (Reprint, New York: Garland Publishing, Inc., 1989), 246.

188. Epstein, 199.

189. Ibid., 200.

190. Ibid., 202.

191. Ibid., 203.

192. Ibid.

193. Ibid.

194. Work, 17–20.

195. Higginson, Col. Thomas W. *Army Life in a Black Regiment*, 2nd ed., ed. Eliene Southern (New York: W.W. Norton & Company, 1983), 183.

196. Lovell, 111.

197. Parrish, 5.

198. Ibid., 6.

199. Fisher, 183.

200. Lomax, John A. and Alan Lomax, eds. *The 111 Best American Ballads: Folk Song U.S.A.* (New York: Duell, Sloan and Pearce, 1947), 334.

201. Dett, 3–4.

Chapter 4

1. Coleridge-Taylor, Samuel. *Twenty-Four Negro Melodies Transcribed by S. Coleridge-Taylor, Op. 59* (Boston: Oliver Ditson Co., 1905), ix.

2. Southern, Eileen, ed. *Readings in Black American Music* (New York: W.W. Norton & Co., 1983), 203.

3. Lomax, John A. and Alan Lomax. *The 111 Best American Ballads: Folk Song U.S.A.* (New York: Duell, Sloan and Pearce, 1947), 329.

4. Colossians 3:16, King James Version.

5. Parrish, Lydia. *Slave Songs of the Georgia Sea Islands* (New York: Creative Age Press, Inc., 1942), 5.

6. Marcel (W. F. Allen). "The Negro Dialect," *Nation,* 14 Dec. 1865, 744–745.

7. Parrish, ii.

8. Southern, Eileen. *The Music of Black Americans* (Reprint, New York: W.W. Norton & Co., 1997), 180.

9. Jackson, Bruce, ed. *The Negro and His Folklore in Nineteenth-Century Periodicals* (Austin: University of Texas Press, 1967).

10. Tyler, Mary Ann L. "The Music of Charles Henry Pace and Its Relationship to the Afro-American Church Experience" (Ph.D. diss., University of Pittsburgh, 1980), 15.

11. Lovell, John, Jr. *Black Song: The Forge and the Flame: The Story of How the Afro-American Spiritual Was Hammered Out* (Reprint, New York: Macmillan, 1972), 215.

12. Southern, *The Music of Black Americans,* 188–189.

13. Spencer, Jon Michael. *Sacred Symphony: The Chanted Sermon of the Black Preacher* (New York: Greenwood Press, 1987), 6.

14. Southern, *The Music of Black Americans,* 188.

15. Ibid., 198.

16. Ibid.

17. Ibid, 176.

18. Allen, William Francis, Charles Pickard Ware, and Lucy McKim Garrison, eds. *Slave Songs of the United States* (Reprint, Mineola, NY: Dover Publications, Inc., 1995), iv.

19. Epstein, Dena J. *Sinful Tunes and Spirituals: Black Folk Music in the Civil War* (Urbana: University of Illinois Press, 1977), 225.

20. Tucker, George. *Letters from Virginia, Translated from the French* (Baltimore: F. Lucas, Jr., 1816), 29–34.

21. Southern, *Readings in Black American Music,* 205.

22. Spencer, 2–3.

23. Allen et al., vi.

24. Work, John W. *American Negro Songs and Spirituals* (New York: Bonanza Books, 1940), 26.

25. Southern, *The Music of Black Americans,* 191.

26. Ibid.

27. Southern, *Readings in Black American Music,* 214.

28. Krehbiel, Henry. *Afro-American Folk Songs* (New York: G. Schirmer, Inc., 1914), 42–43.

29. Southern, *The Music of Black Americans,* 197.

30. Ibid., 194.

31. Walker, Wyatt Tee. *Somebody's Calling My Name: Black Sacred Music and Social Change* (Valley Forge, PA: Judson Press, 1979), 52–58.

32. Raboteau, Albert J. *Slave Religion, The "Invisible Institution" in the Antebellum South* (New York: Oxford University Press, 1978), 74.

33. Leonard, Daisy Anderson, ed. *From Slavery to Affluence: Memoir of Robert Anderson, Ex-Slave* (Reprint, Steamboat Springs: Steamboat Press, 1967), 25–26.

34. Southern, *The Music of Black Americans*, 169–170.

35. Ibid., 170.

36. Work, 18–19.

37. Ibid., 27.

38. Raboteau, 247.

39. Ibid., 246.

40. Courlander, Harold. *Negro Folk Music, U.S.A.* (New York: Columbia University Press, 1963), 25.

41. Thurman, Howard. "The Meaning of Spirituals," *The Negro in Music and Art.* ed., Lindsay Patterson. (New York: Publishers Company, Inc., 1967), 3.

42. Peters, Erskine. "Spirituals, African American," *American Folklore: An Encyclopedia.* ed. Jan Harold Brunvard. (New York: Garland Publishing, Inc., 1996), 682–683.

43. Ibid., 683.

44. Murphy, Jeannette Robinson. "The Survival of African Music in America," *Popular Science Monthly* 55 (1899), 660–672.

45. Roberts, John Storm. *Black Music of Two Worlds* (New York: Praeger Publishers, 1972), 170.

46. Lovell, 257.

47. Ibid., 137.

48. Holt, Grace Sims. "Stylin' Outta the Black Pulpit," *Rappin' and Stylin' Out: Communication in Urban America*, Thomas Kochman, ed. (Urbana: University of Illinois Press, 1972), 189–190.

49. Ibid.

50. Steward, John, ed. *Bessie Jones: For the Ancestors* (Urbana: University of Illinois Press, 1983), x.

51. Ames, Russell. *The Story of American Folk Song* (New York: Grosset & Dunlap, 1955), 140–141.

52. Ibid.

53. Lovell, 172.

54. Gates, Henry Louis, Jr. *The Signifying Monkey: A Theory of Afro-America Literary Criticism* (New York: Oxford University Press, 1988), 46–50.

55. Ibid., 51.

56. Ibid., 52.

57. Kirk-Duggan, Cheryl A. *Exorcizing Evil* (Maryknoll, NY: Orbis Books, 1997), 80.

58. Ibid., 79–80.

59. Work, 25.

60. Dixon, Christa K. *Negro Spirituals: From Bible to Folk Song* (Philadelphia: Fortress Press, 1976), 45–46.

61. Dett, R. Nathaniel, ed. *Religious Folk-Songs of the Negro as Sung at Hampton Institute* (Reprint, New York: AMS Press, 1972), 78.

62. Ibid., 79.

63. Fisher, Miles Mark. *Negro Slave Songs in the United States* (New York: Russell & Russell, 1968), 29.

64. Conrad, Earl. "General Tubman, Composer of Spirituals," *Etude Magazine* IX, 1942, 305, f.

65. Scarborough, Dorothy. *On the Trail of Negro Folk Songs* (Cambridge, U.K.: Cambridge University Press, 1925), 22–23.

66. Ames, 151.

67. Ibid., 151–153.

68. Ibid.

69. Ibid.

70. Ibid., 157–158.

71. Southern, 144.

72. Ibid.

73. Parrish, xvii–xviii.

74. Ibid.

75. Lovell, 249.

76. Lawrence-McIntyre, Charshee Charlotte. "The Double Meaning of the Spirituals," *Journal of Black Studies* 12:4, 1987, 388.

77. Ibid., 388–389.

78. Ibid., 389.

79. Lovell, "Social Implications," 643–644.

80. Levine, Lawrence. *Black Culture and Black Consciousness* (New York: Oxford University Press, 1977), 50–51.

81. Ibid., 51.

82. Parrish, 134.

83. Levine, 51.

84. Ames, 142–143.

85. Ibid., 143.

86. Dixon, 23.

87. Southern, *Readings in Black American Music,* 87.

88. Cone, James. H. *The Spirituals and the Blues; An Interpretation* (New York: Seabury Press, 1972), 34–35.

89. Levine, 37.

90. Lovell, 640.

91. Levine, 37.

92. McGee, Daniel Bennett. "Religious Beliefs and Ethical Motifs of the Negro Spirituals," M. Theology, Southern Baptist Theological Seminary, 1960, 47–48.

93. Ames, 133.

94. Lovell, 189.

95. Work, 100.

96. Ibid., 103.

97. Ibid., 105.

98. Dixon, 70.

99. Ibid., 2–3.

100. Levine, 31.

101. Ames, 135–136.
102. Levine, 31.
103. Ibid., 31.
104. Ibid., 33.
105. Lovell, 276.
106. Lovell, *Social Implications*, 641–642.
107. Ibid., 642–643.

Chapter 5

1. Unsigned article. "Songs of the Blacks," *Dwight's Journal of Music* IX:7, 15 Nov. 1856, 51–52.

2. Garland, Phyl. *The Sound of Soul.* (Chicago: Henry Regency Company, 1969), 86. *Reprint of radio interview with blues legend W. C. Handy, transcription that appeared in the March 14, 1931, issue of the* Pittsburgh Courier.

3. Rublowsky, John. *Black Music in America* (New York: Basic Books, Inc., 1971), 92.

4. Lovell, John, Jr.. *Black Song: The Forge and the Flame: The Story of How the Afro-American Spiritual Was Hammered Out* (Reprint, New York: Macmillan, 1972), 137–139.

5. Conrad, Earl. "'General' Tubman, Composer of Spirituals," *Etude Magazine* LX. 5 (1942), 344.

6. Brown, William Wells, M. D. *The Rising Son or the Antecedents and Advancement of the Colored Race* (Reprint, Miami, FL: Mnemostyne Publishing Co, 1969), 537.

7. Conrad, 344.

8. Ibid.

9. Ibid., 352.

10. Still, William. *The Underground Railroad* (Reprint, New York: Ayer, 1992), 538.

11. Ibid.

12. Conrad, 352.

13. Still, 638–639.

14. Conrad, Earl. *Harriet Tubman* (New York: Paul S. Eriksson, Inc., 1943), 224.

15. Keck, George R. and Sherrill V. Martin. *Feel the Spirit: Studies in Nineteenth-century Afro-American Music* (New York: Greenwood Press, 1988), 2–3.

16. Epstein, Dena J. "Black Sprituals: Their Emergence into Public Knowledge," *Black Music Research Newsletter* 9.2, Spring 1986, 5.

17. Ibid.

18. Butler, Benjamin F. *Autobiography and Personal Reminiscences of Major-General Benj. F. Butler: Butler's Book* (Boston: A.M. Thayer & Co., 1892), 256–264.

19. Schneider, Dorothy and Carl J. Schneider. *Slavery in America: From Colonial Times to the Civil War* (New York: Checkmark Books, 2001), 293–294.

20. Ibid., 393.

21. Southern, Eileen, ed. *Readings in Black American Music*, 2nd ed. (New York: W.W. Norton & Company, 1983), 181–182. (Higginson, Thomas W. "Army Life in a Black Regiment," *Atlantic Monthly* 19, June 1867).

22. Ibid., 191–192.

23. Ibid., 194.

24. Ibid., 198.

25. Ibid., 199–200.

26. Ibid., 202.

27. Epstein, Dena J. "Lucy McKim Garrison, American Musician," *Bulletin of the New York Public Library* LXVII, 1963, 528–546.

28. Ibid., 540.

29. Southern, 149.

30. Ibid.

31. Allen, William Francis, Charles Pickard Ware, and Lucy McKim Garrison, eds. *Slave Songs of the United States* (Reprint, Mineola, NY: Dover Publications, Inc., 1995), preface by Harold Courlander.

32. Ibid., x–xi.

33. Ibid., xi.

34. Ibid., i–iii.

35. Ibid., vi–viii.

36. Ibid., 19.

37. Ibid., 41.

38. Ibid., 84.

39. Epstein, Dena J. "Black Spirituals: Their Emergence into Public Knowledge," *Black Music Research Newsletter* 8.2, Spring 1986, 59.

40. Allen et al., xi.

41. Holland, Rupert Sargent, ed. *Letters and Diary of Laura M. Towne: Written from the Sea Islands of South Carolina, 1862–1884* (Reprint, New York: Negro Universities Press, 1969), introduction.

42. Ibid., 34.

43. Ibid., 35.

44. Spaulding, Henry George. "Under the Palmetto," *Continental Monthly*, Aug. 1863, 196–200.

45. Forten, Charlotte. "Life on the Sea Islands," *Atlantic Monthly*, May and June 1864, iv–v.

46. Ibid., 69–71.

47. Ibid., 76–77.

48. Bernard, Kenneth A. *Lincoln and the Music of the Civil War* (Caldwell, ID: Caxton Printers, 1966), 91.

49. Ibid., 92.

50. Ibid., 94–95.

51. Emilio, Luis F. *A Brave Black Regiment: History of the Fifty-fourth Regiment of Massachusetts Volunteer Infantry, 1863–1865* (Reprint, New York: Arno Press and the *New York Times*, 1969), 415–416.

52. Ibid., 430.

53. Keck., 10.

54. Ibid.

55. Stern, Philip Van Doren. *An End to Valor: The Last Days of the Civil War* (New York: Bonanza Books, 1958), 198–199.

56. Williams, George W., LL.D. *A History of the Negro Troops in the War of Rebellion, 1861–1865* (Reprint, New York: Negro Universities Press, 1969), 168.

57. Ibid., 300–301.

58. Ibid., 303.

59. Ibid.

60. Washington, Booker T. *Up From Slavery: An Autobiography* (Garden City, NY: Doubleday & Co., Inc., 1948), 19–20.

61. Keck, 11.

62. Holland, 159.

63. Ibid., 162.

Chapter 6

1. King, Edward. *The Great South*. Reprint, eds. W. Magruder and Robert R. Jones (Baton Rouge: Louisiana State University Press, 1972), 608–609.

2. Murphy, Jeanette Robinson. "The Survival of African Music in America," *Popular Science Monthly* 55, 1899, 660.

3. Handy, W. C. *Father of the Blues: An Autobiography of W. C. Handy*, ed. Arna Bontemps (London: Sidgwick and Jackson, 1957), 62.

4. Ward, Andrew. *Dark Midnight When I Rise: The Story of the Jubilee Singers Who Introduced the World to the Music of Black America* (New York: Farrar, Straus and Giroux, 2000), 407.

5. Creel, Margaret Washington. *A Peculiar People: Slave Religion and Community Culture Among the Gullahs* (New York: New York University Press, 1988), 272.

6. Ibid., 271.

7. Ibid.

8. Fisher, Miles Mark. *Negro Slave Songs in the United States* (New York: Russell & Russell, 1968), 172–173.

9. Allen, William, Charles Pickard Ware, and Lucy McKim Garrison, eds. *Slave Songs of the United States*, (Reprint, New York: Peter Smith, 1927), 10–11.

10. Botume, Elizabeth Hyde. *First Days Amongst the Contrabands* (Reprint, New York: Arno Press, 1968), 222–223.

11. Bennett, Lerone, Jr. *Before the* Mayflower: *A History of the Negro in America*, 3rd ed. (Chicago: Johnson Publishing Co., 1966), 187.

12. Ibid., 188–189.

13. Ibid.

14. Walker, Wyatt Tee. *Somebody's Calling My Name: Black Sacred Music and Social Change* (Valley Forge, PA: Judson Press, 1979), 85.

15. Raichelson, Richard M. "Black Religious Folksong: A Study in Generic and Social Change" (Ph.D. diss., University of Pennsylvania, 1975), 187–188.

16. Walker, 20.

17. Litwack, Leon F. *North of Slavery; The Negro in the Free States, 1790–1860* (Chicago: University of Chicago Press, 1961), 187.

18. Brown, John Mason. "Songs of the Slave," *Lippincott's Magazine* 11, Dec. 1868, 618.

19. King, 609–610.

20. Macrae, David. *The Americans at Home* (Reprint, New York: E. P. Dutton & Co., Inc. 1952), 359–365.

21. Ibid., 365.

22. Ibid.

23. Payne, Bishop Daniel Alexander. *Recollections of Seventy Years* (Reprint, New York: Arno Press and the *New York Times*, 1968), 253–255.

24. Ibid., 253–254.

25. Ibid.

26. Ibid., 254–255.

27. Marsh, J. B. T. *The Story of the Jubilee Singers: With Their Songs* (Reprint, New York: AMS Press, Inc., 1971), 6–13.

28. Ward, 73–81.

29. Marsh, 13–14.

30. Graham, Sandra J. "The Fisk Jubilee Singers and the Concert Spiritual: The Beginnings of an American Tradition" (Ph.D. diss., New York University, 2001), 2.

31. Marsh, 26.

32. Ward, 139.

33. Marsh, 29.

34. Ibid., 30.

35. Ibid., 30–31.

36. Ibid., 32.

37. Epstein, Dena J. "Black Spirituals: Their Emergence into Public Knowledge," *Black Music Research Newsletter* 8.2, Spring 1986, 5–8.

38. Ibid., 6.

39. Pike, G. D. *The Jubilee Singers and their campaign for twenty thousand dollars* (Boston: Lee and Shepard, 1873), 91–92.

40. Epstein, 6–7.

41. Seward, Theodore P. *Jubilee Songs: As Sung by the Jubilee Singers* (New York: Bigelow & Main, 1872), 3.

42. Marsh, 36.

43. Ibid., 39.

44. Fulton, Joe, Assistant Professor of English at Baylor University, Personal interview, June 25, 2003.

45. Pike Rev. Gustavus D. *The Singing Campaign for Ten Thousand Pounds or The Jubilee Singers in Great Britain* (Reprint, New York: American Missionary Association, 1875), 14–15.

46. Ward, 211–215.

47. Seroff, Doug. "The Fisk Jubilee Singers in Britain," *Under the Imperial Carpet: Essays in Black History, 1780–1950*, eds. Ranier Lotz and Ian Pegg (Crawley, U.K.: Rabbit Press, 1986), 44–45.

48. Epstein, 7.

49. Graham, Sandra. "From Sacred to Sacrilege? Spirituals in Postbellum Blackface Minstrelsy," *2003 meeting of the Society of American Music* (unpublished paper, University of California, Davis), 9.

50. Ibid., 11.

51. Du Bois, W. E. B. *The Autobiography of W. E. B. Du Bois: A Soliloquy on Viewing My Life from the Last Decade of Its First Century* (United States of America: International Publishers, Co., 1968), 106.

52. Ibid., 120.

53. Trotter, James M. *Music and Some Highly Musical People: Remarkable Musicians of the Colored Race, With Portraits* (Reprint, New York: Johnson Reprint Corporation, 1968), 259.

54. Silveri, Louis D. "The Singing Tours of the Fisk Jubilee Singers: 1871–74," *Feel the Spirit: Studies in Nineteenth-century Afro-American Music*, eds. George R. Keck and Sherrill V. Martin (New York: Greenwood Press, 1988), 110.

55. Raichelson, Richard M. "Black Religious Folksong: A Study in Generic and Social Change" (Ph.D. diss., University of Pennsylvania, 1975), 234.

56. Seroff, Doug. *Gospel Arts Day Nashville: A Special Commemoration: Fisk Memorial Chapel*, 18 June 1989, P3. Fisk Jubilee Vertical file, Library of Congress.

57. Raichelson, 235.

58. Ibid, 241.

59. Hurston, Zora Neale. *The Sanctified Church* (New York: Marlow & Company, 1981), 5.

60. Ibid., 66–67.

61. Lott, Eric. *Love and Theft: Blackface Minstrelsy and the American Working Class* (New York: Oxford University Press, 1993), 3–12.

62. Mahar, William J. " 'Backside Albany' and Early Blackface Minstrelsy: A Contextual Study of America's First Blackface Song," *American Music* 6, (Spring 1988), 1–27.

63. Cockrell, Dale. *Demons of Disorder: Early Blackface Minstrels and Their World* (Cambridge, U.K.: Cambridge University Press, 1997), xi.

64. Ibid.

65. Ibid., xii.

66. Grey, Tobias. "White Men With Black Masks," *Financial Times of London*, 15 Sept. 2001, 4.

67. Lott, 236.

68. Southern, Eileen. *The Music of Black America*, 2nd ed. (New York: W.W. Norton & Company, 1983), 89–90.

69. Dett, R. Nathaniel. "The Emancipation of Negro Music," *Southern Workman* XLIV, Apr. 1918), 172.

70. Southern, 90–91.

71. Ibid., 228–229.

72. Troll, Robert C. *Blacking Up: The Minstrel Show in Nineteenth Century America* (New York: Oxford University Press, 1974), 271.

73. Ibid., 272–273.

74. Ibid., 237.

75. Ibid.

76. Ibid., 238.

77. Ibid.

78. Ibid., 239.

79. Ibid., 243.

80. Ibid.

81. Rublowsky, John. *Black Music in America* (New York: Basic Books, Inc., 1971), 101.

82. Ibid.

83. Tosches, Nick. *Where Dead Voices Gather* (Boston: Little, Brown & Co., 2001).

84. Handy, W. C. *Father of the Blues: An Autobiography of W.C. Handy*, ed. Arna Bontemps (London: Sidgwick and Jackson, 1957), 62.

85. Trotter, *passim*.

86. Ibid., 271.

87. Ibid., 272.

88. Ibid., 275.

89. Ibid., 275–277.

90. Ibid., 278–281.

91. Graham, 2.

92. Trotter, 281.

93. Cockrell, *Demons of Disorder*, 169.

94. Locke, Alain. *The Negro and His Music* (Reprint, New York: Arno Press, 1969), 59.

95. Graham, 4.

96. Troll, 273.

97. Lhamon, W. T., Jr. *Raising Cain: Blackface Performance from Jim Crow to Hip Hop* (Cambridge, MA: Harvard University Press, 1998), 104.

98. Kilham, Elizabeth. "Sketches in Color IV," *Putnam's Monthly* IV, Mar. 1870, 304–311.

99. Taylor, Marshall W. and W. C. Echols. *Plantation Melodies, Book of Negro Folk Songs* (Cincinnati: Marshall W. Taylor and W. C. Echols Publishers, 1882).

100. Wood, Henry Cleveland. "Negro Camp-Meeting Melodies," *New England Magazine*, Mar. 1892, 62.

101. Ibid., 61–64.

102. Barton, William E. *Old Plantation Hymns* (Boston: Lamson, Wolffe and Company, 1899).

103. Haskell, Marion Alexander. "Negro 'Spirituals'," *Century Magazine* XXXVI, Aug. 1899, 577.

104. Ibid.

105. Ibid., 579–581.

106. Levine, Lawrence W. *Black Culture and Black Consciousness* (New York: Oxford University Press, 1977), 158–159.

107. Lomax, Alan and Joan Halifax. "Folk Song Texts as Cultural Indicators," *Folk Song Style and Culture* (Washington, D.C.: American Association for the Advancement of Science), 274–275.

108. Levine, 160.

109. Ibid., 160.

110. Levine, 159–160.

111. Barton, 33–34.

112. Ibid., 35.

113. Edwards, Charles L. *Bahama Songs and Stories* (Reprint, Boston: Houghton, Mifflin & Co., 1895), 16.

114. Ibid., 17.

115. Ibid., 19.

116. Ibid., 26.

117. Ibid., 30.

118. Abbott, Lynn and Doug Seroff. *Out of Sight: The Rise of African American Popular Music, 1889–1895* (Jackson, MS: University Press of Mississippi, 2002), 461.

119. Ibid.

120. Dvořák, Antonín. "Music in America," *The Negro and His Folklore in Nineteenth Century Periodicals*, ed. Bruce Jackson (Austin: University of Texas Press, 1967), 269.

121. Ibid., 270.

122. Abbott and Seroff, 461.

Chapter 7

1. Litwack, Leon F. *Trouble in Mind: Black Southerners in the Age of Jim Crow* (New York: Alfred A. Knopf, 1999), 453.

2. Wright, Richard. *12 Million Black Voices* (Reprint, New York: Thunder's Mouth Press, 1988), 92.

3. Locke, Alain, ed. *The New Negro* (New York: Albert and Charles Boni, 1925), 6.

4. Wright, 128.

5. Hurston, Zora Neale. *The Sanctified Church* (New York: Marlow & Company, 1981), 104.

6. Harrison, Alferdteen, ed. *Black Exodus: The Great Migration from the American South* (Jackson, MS: University Press of Mississippi, 1991), vii.

7. Davis, Dernoral. "Toward a Socio-Historical and Demographic Portrait of Twentieth-Century African Americans," *Black Exodus: The Great Migration from the American South*, ed. Alferdteen Harrison. (Jackson, MS: University Press of Mississippi, 1991), 7.

8. Davis, George A. and O. Fred Donaldson. *Blacks in the United States: A Geographic Perspective* (Boston: Houghton Mifflin Company, 1975), 54–89.

9. Aptheker, Herbert, ed. *A Documentary History of the Negro People in the United States* (New York: Citadel Press. 1951), 861.

10. Wright, 64.

11. Litwack, 284.

12. Evers, Charles. *Evers* (New York: World Publishing Company, 1971), 23.

13. Davis, "Toward a Socio-Historical and Demographic Portrait of Twentieth-Century African Americans," 10.

14. Ibid.

15. Ibid., xv.

16. Davis and Donaldson, *Blacks in the United States*, 3.

17. Ibid., 44–47.

18. Marks, Carole. "The Social and Economic Life of Southern Blacks During the Migration," *Black Exodus: The Great Migration from the American South*, ed. Alferdteen Harrison (Jackson, MS: University Press of Mississippi, 1991), 48–49.

19. Davis and Donaldson, *Blacks in the United States*, 54–89.

20. Grossman James R. "Black Labor Is the Best Labor: Southern White Reactions to the Great Migration," *Black Exodus: The Great Migration from the American South*, ed. Alferdteen Harrison (Jackson, MS: University Press of Mississippi, 1991), 57–60.

21. Ibid.

22. Handy, W. C. *Father of the Blues: An Autobiography of W.C. Handy*, ed. Arna Bontemps (London: Sidgwick and Jackson, 1957), 79.

23. Grossman, 57–60.

24. Davis and Donaldson, *Blacks in the United States*, 89.

25. Barker, Danny. *A Life in Jazz* (London: MacMillan Press, 1986), 71–72.

26. Davis and Donaldson, *Blacks in the United States*, 198.

27. Langille, Douglas. "The Spatial Dynamics and Diffusion of a Culture-Specific Artform: The Geography of Blues" (B.A. thesis, University of Guelph, 1975), 127.

28. Ibid., 102.

29. Oliver, Paul. *Songsters and Saints: Vocal Traditions on Race Records* (Cambridge, U.K.: Cambridge University Press, 1984), 176.

30. Murphy, Jeannette Robinson. "The Survival of African Music in America," *Appleton's Popular Science Monthly* 55, 1899, 664.

31. Walker, Wyatt Tee. *Somebody's Calling My Name: Black Sacred Music and Social Change* (Valley Forge, PA: Judson Press 1979), 62.

32. Haralambos, Michael. *Right On: From Blues to Soul in Black America* (New York: Drake Publishers Inc., 1975), 30–32.

33. Warner, Jay. *The Billboard Book of American Singing Groups: A History 1940–1990* (New York: Billboard Books, 1992), 2.

34. Southern, Eileen. *The Music of Black Americans*, 2nd ed. (New York: W.W. Norton & Company, 1983), 257–258.

35. Johnson, James Weldon and J. Rosamund Johnson. *The Book of American Negro Spirituals* (New York: Viking Press, 1969), 35.

36. Johnson, James Weldon. *Along This Way: The Autobiography of James Weldon Johnson* (New York: Viking Press, 1933), 8–30.

37. Johnson, *The Book of American Negro Spirituals*, 35–36.

38. Ibid.

39. Lornell, Kip. *Happy in the Service of the Lord: Afro-American Gospel Quartets in Memphis* (Urbana, IL: University of Illinois Press, 1988), 18.

40. Simond, Ike. *Old Slack's Reminiscences and Pocket History of the Colored Profession from 1865–1891* (Chicago: Self-published, 1891), 26.

41. Rubman, Kerill Leslie. "From 'Jubilee' to 'Gospel' in Black Male Quartet Singing" (M.A. thesis, University of North Carolina, Chapel Hill, 1980), 45–46.

42. Warner, 2

43. Abbott, Lynn. "'Play That Barber Shop Chord': A Case for the African American Origin of Barbershop Harmony," *American Music* 10, Fall 1992, 289–319.

44. Ibid., 319.

45. Oliver, 176.

46. Garland, Phyl. *The Sound of Soul* (Chicago: Henry Regency Company, 1969), 25.

47. Melton, J. Gordon, ed. *Encyclopedia of American Religions*, 7th ed. (Detroit: Thomson Gale Publishers, 2003), 79.

48. Ibid., 80.

49. Ibid., 80–81.

50. Ibid., 85.

51. Ibid.

52. Ibid., 87.

53. Synan, Vinson. *The Holiness-Pentecostal Tradition: Charismatic Movements in the Twentieth Century*, 2nd ed. (Grand Rapids, MI: William B. Eerdmans Publishing Company, 1997), 178.

54. Ibid., 179.

55. Ibid., 178.

56. Psalms 150:3–6, King James Version.

57. Floyd, Samuel A., Jr. *The Power of Black Music: Interpreting Its History from Africa to the United States* (New York: Oxford University Press, 1995), 63.

58. Ibid., 65.

59. Hinson, Glenn D. "When the Words Roll and the Fire Flows: Spirit, Style and Experience in African American Gospel Performance" (Ph.D. diss., University of Pennsylvania, 1989), 96–97.

60. Litwack, 395–396.

61. Kalil, Timothy M. "Thomas A. Dorsey and the Development and Diffusion of Traditional Black Gospel Piano," *Perspectives on American Music, 1900–1950*, ed. Michael Saffle (New York: Garland Publishing, Inc., 2000), 174.

62. Charlesworth, Vernon J. *The Life of Rowland Hill: Life, Anecdotes and Pulpit Sayings* (London: Hodder & Stoughton, 1877), 156.

63. Work, John W. "Changing Patterns in Negro Folk Songs," *Journal of American Folklore* 2, 1949, 140–141.

64. Hinson, 98.

65. Levine, Lawrence W. *Black Culture and Black Consciousness: Afro-American Thought from Slavery to Freedom* (New York: Oxford University Press, 1977), 180.

66. Floyd, 63.

67. Lipsitz, George. *Rainbow Over Midnight: Labor and Culture in the 1940s* (Urbana: University of Illinois Press, 1994), 305.

68. Southern, 331.

69. Raichelson, Richard M. "Black Religious Folksong: A Study in Generic and Social Change" (Ph.D. diss, University of Pennsylvania, 1975), 400–404.

70. Oliver, 200.

71. Handy, 87.

72. Ibid., 88.

73. Murphy, 662.

74. Oliver, 1–2.

75. Ibid., 199–228.

76. Perkins, A. E. "Negro Spirituals from the Far South," *Journal of American Folk-Lore,* 35, 1922, 223.

77. Oliver, 140.

78. Ibid., 140–141.

79. Spencer, Jon Michael. *Sacred Symphony: The Chanted Sermon of the Black Preacher* (New York: Greenwood Press, 1987), 3.

80. Oliver, 141.

81. Broughton, Viv. *Too Close to Heaven: The Illustrated History of Gospel Music* (London: Midnight Books, 1996), 48–49.

82. Erlewine, Michael, Vladimir Bogdanov, Chris Woodstra, and Cub Koba, eds. *AMG All Music Guide to the Blues* (San Francisco: Miller Freeman Books, 2nd ed., 1999), 307.

83. Oliver, Paul, Max Harrison, and William Bolcom. *The New Grove Gospel, Blues, and Jazz with Spirituals and Ragtime* (New York: W.W. Norton & Company, 1986), 198–199.

84. Corcoran, Michael. "Praising Arizona: She influenced generations of musicians but died in obscurity. Texas gospel pioneer Arizona Juanita Dranes' barrelhouse piano set

the beat for a new kind of church music," *Austin-American Statesman*, 19 June 2003, sec. E1.

85. Boyer, Horace Clarence. *How Sweet the Sound: The Golden Age of Gospel* (Washington, D.C.: Elliott & Clark Publishing, 1995), 36–37.

86. Jackson, Jerma A. "Testifying at the Cross: Thomas Andrew Dorsey, Sister Rosetta Tharpe, and the Politics of African-American Sacred and Secular Music" (Ph.D. diss., State University of New Jersey, 1995), 159.

87. Boyer, 37–38.

88. Jackson, 159.

89. Corcoran, E1.

90. Oliver, *Songsters and Saints*, 189.

91. Ibid., 190–191.

92. Shaw, Malcolm. "Arizona Dranes and OKeh, 1926–1928," *Storyville* 27, 1970, 85–88.

93. Corcoran, E1.

94. Oliver, *Songsters and Saints*, 202–208.

95. Ibid., 208–209.

96. Lomax, John A. and Alan Lomax. *Our Singing Country* (New York: The Macmillan Company, 1941), 24. ("The Blood-Stained Banders," No. 744. Acc. on guitar and sung by Jimmie Strothers, Virginia State Prison Farms, 1936.)

97. Erlewine et al., 224.

98. *The Complete Blind Willie Johnson*, Columbia/Legacy CD C2K 52835, 1993. (Liner notes by Samuel Charters, 10.)

99. Erlewine et al., 224–225.

100. Roberts, John Storm. *Black Music of Two Worlds* (New York: Praeger Publishers, 1972), 171.

101. Charters, Samuel B. *The Country Blues* (New York: Rinehart & Company, Inc., 1959), 165.

102. Erlewine et al., 224.

103. Corcoran, Michael. "Blind Willie Johnson: He left a massive imprint on the blues, but little is known about him," *Austin American-Statesman*, 28 Sept. 2003, sec. K1.

104. Oliver, *Songsters and Saints*, 1–2.

105. Ibid., 280–281.

106. Boyer, 29.

107. Southern, 245.

108. Seroff, Doug. "Polk Miller and the old South Quartette," *78 Quarterly* 3, 1988, 34.

109. Lornell, 14–15.

110. Warner, 2.

111. Seroff, Doug. "On the Battlefield: Gospel Quartets in Jefferson County, Alabama," *Repercussions: A Celebration of African-American Music*, eds. Geoffrey Haydon and Dennis Marks (London; Century Publishing, 1985), 32.

112. Lornell, 14.

113. Seroff, "On the Battlefield," 34.

114. Turner, Patricia. *Dictionary of Afro-American Performers: 78 RPM and Cylinder Recordings of Opera, Choral Music and Song, c. 1900–1949* (New York: Garland Publishing, 1990), 172–173.

115. Ibid.

116. Tyler, Mary Ann L. "The Music of Charles Henry Pace and Its Relationship to the Afro-American Church Experience" (Ph.D. diss., University of Pittsburgh, 1980), 8.

117. Turner, 275–280.

118. Tyler, 153.

119. Ibid.

120. Reagon, Bernice Johnson, ed. *We'll Understand It Better By and By: Pioneering African American Gospel Composers.* Boyer, Horace Clarence. "Kenneth Morris: Composer and Dean of Black Gospel Music Publishers" (Washington, D.C.: Smithsonian Institution Press, 1992), 310.

121. "E.C.P." (probably Elsie Clews Parsons). "From Spiritual to Vaudeville," *Journal of American Folk-Lore* 35, 1922, 331.

122. Boyer, 30.

123. Rubman, Kerill Leslie. "From 'Jubilee' to 'Gospel' in Black Male Quartet Singing" (M.A. thesis, University of North Carolina, Chapel Hill, 1980), 32.

124. Ibid., 42–43.

125. Perkins, A. E. "Negro Spirituals from the Far South," *Journal of American Folk-Lore* 35, 1922, 224.

126. Seroff, "On the Battlefield," 35–36.

127. Lornell, 20.

128. Boyer, 31.

129. Dent, Cedric Carl. "The Harmonic Development of the Black Religious Quartet Singing Tradition" (Ph.D. diss., University of Maryland at College Park, 1997), 3.

130. Ibid., 14–15.

131. Buchanan, Samuel Carroll. "A Critical Analysis of Style in Four Black Jubilee Quartets in the United States" (Ph.D. diss., New York University, 1987), 14.

132. Ibid., 84–86.

133. *From Spirituals to Swing,* Columbia Record Album G31093, G S vol. 2. Produced by John Hammond, liner notes by Charles Edward Smith, 31.

134. Sterns, Michael. *The Story of Jazz* (New York: Oxford University Press, 1956), 138.

135. Buchanan, 87.

136. Dent, 41.

137. Ibid., 23.

138. Ibid., 25.

139. Ibid., 5.

140. Rubman, 43.

141. Ibid., 44.

142. Ibid.

143. Ibid.

144. Various artists. *Jubilee to Gospel: A Selection of Commercially Recorded Black Religious Music, 1921–1953,* Selected and annotated by William H. Tallmadge, John Edwards Memorial Foundation, JEMF-108. Biographical notes and related discography by Doug Seroff, booklet.

145. Lornell, 19–20.

146. Buchanan, 76.

147. Lornell, Kip. *Virginia's Blues, Country and Gospel Records, 1902–1943* (Lexington: University Press of Kentucky, 1989), 125–133.

148. Ibid., 68.

149. Lornell, *Happy in the Service of the Lord,* 21–22.

150. Seroff, *Repercussions,* 35.

151. McCallum, Brenda. "Songs of Work and Songs of Worship: Sanctifying Black Unionism in the Southern City of Steel," *New York Folklore* XIV 1–2, 1988, 12–14.

152. Ibid., 14.

153. Ibid., 15.

154. Ibid.

155. Ibid., 16.

156. Ibid., 17–18.

157. Ibid., 19.

158. Ibid.

159. Allen, Ray. "African-American Sacred Quartet Singing in New York City," *New York Folklore* XIV 3–4, 1988, 7.

160. Ibid.

161. Seroff, "On the Battlefield," 34.

162. Buchanan, 54–55.

163. Ray, 7.

164. Boyer, 45.

165. Lornell, *Happy in the Service of the Lord,* 36–37.

166. Ibid., 37–38.

167. Ibid., 39.

168. Ibid., 107–108.

169. Warner, 2–3.

170. Ibid., 3.

171. Shaw, Arnold. *Black Popular Music in America: From the Spirituals, Minstrels, and Ragtime to Soul, Disco, and Hip-Hop* (New York: Schirmer Books, 1986), 182–193.

172. Dent, 48.

173. Boyer, 44.

174. Warner, 35.

175. Heilbut, Anthony. *The Gospel Sound: Good News and Bad Times* (New York: Limelight Editions, 1997), 370.

176. "Orlandus Wilson," *Times (London)* 29 Jan. 1999, sec. 1F, 27.

Chapter 8

1. Lomax, John A. and Alan Lomax. *Our Singing Country* (New York: The Macmillan Company, 1941), 34.

2. McClain, William B. "Preface," *The Songs of Zion,* eds. J. Jefferson Cleveland and Verolga Nix (Nashville, Abingdon Press, 1981), x.

3. Dorsey, Thomas. "Gospel Music," *Reflections on Afro-American Music,* ed. Dominique-Rene De Lerma (Kent, OH: Kent State University Press, 1973), 191.

4. Floyd, Samuel A., Jr. *The Power of Black Music: Interpreting Its History from Africa to the United States* (New York: Oxford University Press, 1995), 59.

5. Boyer, Horace Clarence. *How Sweet the Sound: The Golden Age of Gospel* (Washington, D.C.: Elliott & Clark Publishing, 1995), 26.

6. Ibid., 27.

7. Floyd, 63.

8. Oliver, Paul, Max Harrison, and William Bolcom, eds. *The New Grove Gospel, Blues, and Jazz, with Spirituals and Ragtime* (New York: W.W. Norton & Company, 1986), 190.

9. Jones, Ralph H. *Charles Albert Tindley, Prince of Preachers* (Nashville: Abingdon Press, 1982), 15–141.

10. Harris, Michael W. *The Rise of the Gospel Blues: The Music of Thomas Andrew Dorsey and the Urban Church* (New York: Oxford University Press, 1992), 75.

11. Boyer, Horace Clarence. "Charles Albert Tindley: Progenitor of African American Music," *We'll Understand It Better By and By*, ed. Bernice Johnson Reagon (Washington, D.C.: Smithsonian Institution Press, 1992), 57.

12. Ibid.

13. Jones, 82–83.

14. Boyer, *How Sweet the Sound*, 45.

15. Boyer, "Charles Albert Tindley," 59.

16. Cleveland, J. Jefferson and Verolga Nix, eds. *Songs of Zion: Supplemental Resources 12.* (Nashville, TN: Abingdon Press, 1981), #41.

17. Ibid., #55.

18. Floyd, 127.

19. Ibid., 63.

20. Boyer, *How Sweet the Sound*, 57.

21. Floyd, 63.

22. Ibid., 127.

23. Heilbut, Anthony. *The Gospel Sound: Good News and Bad Times* (Reprint, New York: Limelight Editions, 1997), 23.

24. Cleveland, 1.

25. Patrick, Elizabeth. "Lucie (Lucy) Campbell Williams (1885–1962): Composer, Educator, Evangelist," *Notable Black American Women*, ed. Jessie Carney Smith (Detroit: Gale Research, Inc., 1992), 154.

26. George, Luvenia A. "Campbell, Lucie E. (1885–1963)," *Black Women in America: An Historical Encyclopedia*, ed. Darlene Clark (Brooklyn, NY: Carlson Publishing Inc., 1993), 217.

27. George, Luvenia A. "Lucie E. Campbell: Her Nurturing and Expansion of Gospel Music in the National Baptist Convention, U.S.A., Inc.," *We'll Understand It Better By and By*, ed. Bernice Johnson Reagon (Washington, D.C.: Smithsonian Institution Press, 1992), 113.

28. Ibid., 119.

29. Harris, 68–69.

30. Boyer, *How Sweet the Sound*, 42.

31. Ibid., 43.

32. Ibid.

33. Harris, 69.

34. Ibid.

35. Ibid., 69–70.

36. Harris, Michael W. "Conflict and Resolution in the Life of Thomas Andrew Dorsey," *We'll Understand It Better By and By*, ed. Bernice Johnson Reagon (Washington, D.C.: Smithsonian Institution Press, 1992), 166–167.

37. Ibid., 167.

38. Ibid., 168.

39. Harris, *The Rise of the Gospel Blues*, 19.

40. O'Neal, Jim and Amy O'Neal. "The *Living Blues* Interview: Georgia Tom Dorsey," *Living Blues* 20, 1974/1975, 17–19.

41. Harris, "Conflict and Resolution in the Life of Thomas Andrew Dorsey," 172–173.

42. Boyer, *How Sweet the Sound*, 59.

43. Floyd, 126–127.

44. Harris, *The Rise of the Gospel Blues*, 75.

45. Boyer, Horace Boyer. "Lucie E. Campbell: Composer for the National Baptist Convention," *We'll Understand It Better By and By*, ed. Bernice Johnson Reagon (Washington, D.C.: Smithsonian Institution Press, 1992), 106.

46. Boyer, "Charles Albert Tindley," *How Sweet the Sound*, 59.

47. Harris, *The Rise of the Gospel Blues*, 81.

48. Ibid., 88.

49. Oliver et al., 79.

50. O'Neal, 23.

51. Harris, *The Rise of the Gospel Blues*, 93–95.

52. Ibid., 96.

53. Ibid.

54. Tyler, Mary Ann L. "The Music of Charles Henry Pace and Its Relationship to the Afro-American Church Experience" (Ph.D. diss., University of Pittsburgh, 1980), 23.

55. Harris, *The Rise of the Gospel Blues*, 97.

56. Ibid.

57. Wilson, Olly. "The Heterogeneous Sound Ideal in African-American Music," *New Perspectives on Music: Essays in Honor of Eileen Southern*, ed. Josephine Wright (Michigan: Harmonie Park Press, 1992), 337.

58. Harris, Michael W. "Conflict and Resolution in the Life of Thomas Andrew Dorsey," 178.

59. West, Hollie I. "The Man Who Started the Gospel Business," *Washington Post*, 7 Dec. 1969, sec. H10.

60. Harris, "Conflict and Resolution in the Life of Thomas Andrew Dorsey," 179.

61. Ibid.

62. Harris, *The Rise of Gospel Blues*, 148.

63. Oliver et al., 79.

64. O'Neal, 24–27.

65. Harris, Michael W. "Conflict and Resolution in the Life of Thomas Andrew Dorsey," 180.

66. Ibid.

67. Harris, *The Rise of Gospel Blues*, 178.

68. Ricks, George Robinson. "Some Aspects of the Religious Music of the United States Negro: An Ethnomusicological Study with Special Emphasis on the Gospel Tradition" (Ph.D. diss., Northwestern University, 1960), 136–137.

69. Harris, *The Rise of Gospel Blues*, 191–196.

70. Ibid.

71. Ibid., 212.

72. Ibid., 213.

73. Ibid., 212–214.

74. Ibid., 228.

75. Ibid., 234–235.

76. Ibid., 238.

77. Ibid., 239.

78. Ibid., 242.

79. West, sec. H10.

80. Kalil, Timothy M. "Thomas A. Dorsey and the Development and Diffusion of Traditional Black Gospel Piano," *Perspectives on American Music, 1900–1950*, ed. Michael Saffle (New York: Garland Publishing, Inc., 2000), 172–177.

81. O'Neal, 29.

82. Hurt, James. "'Promised Land?' The Black Chicago Renaissance and After," *Illinois History Teacher* 7.2, 2000, 32–35.

83. For an excellent overview of Bronzeville, see Drake, St. Clair and Horace Cayton. *Black Metropolis: A Study of Negro Life in a Northern City* (New York: Harcourt, Brace & Co., 1945).

84. Jackson, Mahalia with Evan McLeod Wylie. *Movin' on Up* (New York: Hawthorn Books, 1966), 47.

85. Erlewine, Michael, Vladimir Bogdanov, Chris Woodstra, and Cub Koba, eds. *All Music Guide to the Blues*, 2nd ed. (San Francisco: Miller Freeman Books, 1999), 295–296.

86. Harris, *The Rise of Gospel Blues*, 255–256.

87. Ibid., 257.

88. Banks, Lacy J. "Gospel Music: A Shout of Black Joy," *Ebony* 27, 1972, 162.

89. Harris, *The Rise of Gospel Blues*, 257.

90. Jackson, Jerma A. "Testifying at the Cross: Thomas Andrew Dorsey, Sister Rosetta Tharpe, and the Politics of African-American Sacred and Secular Music" (Ph.D. diss., Rutgers, The State University of New Jersey, 1995), 223.

91. Young, Alan. *Woke Me Up This Morning: Black Gospel Singers and the Gospel Life* (Jackson, MS: University Press of Mississippi, 1997), xxvi–xxv.

92. Heilbut, 3.

93. Jackson, 226–227.

94. Work, John W. "Changing Patterns in Negro Folk Songs," *Journal of American Folk-Lore* LXII, 1949, 141.

95. Jackson, 229.

96. Neirenberg, George T. *Say Amen, Somebody*. Pacific Arts Video Records PAVR-547, 1980.

97. Heilbut, 10–11.

98. Reagon, Bernice Johnson. "Kenneth Morris: "I'll Be a Servant for the Lord," *We'll Understand It Better By and By*, ed. Bernice Johnson Reagon (Washington, D.C.: Smithsonian Institution Press, 1992), 330–332.

99. Heilbut, 10–11.

100. Boyer, Horace Clarence. "Kenneth Morris: Composer and Dean of Black Gospel Music Publishers," *We'll Understand It Better By and By*, ed. Bernice Johnson Reagon (Washington, D.C.: Smithsonian Institution Press, 1992), 311.

101. Ibid., 332.

102. Grattan, Virginia, ed. *American Women Songwriters: A Biographical Dictionary* (Westport, CT: Greenwood Press, 1993), 223–224.

103. Williams-Jones, Pearl. "Roberta Martin: Spirit of an Era," *We'll Understand It Better By and By*, ed. Bernice Johnson Reagon (Washington, D.C.: Smithsonian Institution Press, 1992), 255.

104. Ibid., 185–195.

105. No author listed. *Tribute: The Life of Dr. William Herbert Brewster* (Memphis: Brewster House of Sermon Songs, Christian Literature and Dramatic Arts, circa 1982), 14. (Courtesy of the Brewster House of Sermon Songs, Christian Literature and Dramatic Arts, 1185 East Trigg Avenue, Memphis, TN, 38106.)

106. Ibid., 15.

107. Reagon, Bernice Johnson. "William Herbert Brewster: Rememberings," *We'll Understand It Better By and By*, ed. Bernice Johnson Reagon (Washington, D.C.: Smithsonian Institution Press, 1992), 201.

108. Ibid., 212–213.

Chapter 9

1. Reich, Howard. "Present at the Creation: Remembering the early days of gospel music in Chicago," *Chicago Tribune* 27 May 1990, 14.

2. Ibid.

3. Baldwin, James. *The Fire Next Time* (New York: Dial Press, 1963), 47.

4. Kaatrud, Paul Gaarder. "Revivalism and the Popular Spiritual Song in Mid-Nineteenth Century America: 1830–1870" (M.A. thesis, University of Minnesota, 1977), 290.

5. Ibid., 289.

6. Harris, Michael W. *The Rise of the Gospel Blues: The Music of Thomas Andrew Dorsey in the Urban Church* (New York: Oxford University Press, 1992), 285.

7. Seroff, Doug. "On the Battlefield: Gospel Quartets in Jefferson County, Alabama," *Repercussions: A Celebration of African-American Music*, eds. Haydon, Geoffrey and Dennis Marks (London: Century Publishing, 1985), 37–38.

8. Ricks, George Robinson. *Some Aspects of Religious Music of the United States Negro: An Ethnomusicological Study with Special Emphasis on the Gospel Tradition* (New York: Arno Press, 1977), 141.

9. Ibid., 142.

10. Hinson, Glenn D. "When the Words Roll and the Fire Flows: Spirit, Style and Experience in African American Gospel Performance" (Ph.D. diss., University of Pennsylvania, 1989), 102–103.

11. O'Neal, Jim and Amy O'Neal. "The *Living Blues* Interview: Georgia Tom Dorsey," *Living Blues* 20, 1974–1975, 31.

12. Jackson, Jerma A. "Testifying at the Cross: Thomas Andrew Dorsey, Sister Rosetta Tharpe, and the Politics of African-American Sacred and Secular Music" (Ph.D. diss., Rutgers, the State University of New Jersey, 1995), 210–211.

13. Heilbut, Anthony. *The Gospel Sound: Good News and Bad Times*, 25th anniversary ed. (New York: Limelight Editions, 1997), 29.

14. Stearns, Marshall W. *The Story of Jazz* (New York: Oxford University Press, 1956), 135–136.

15. Johnson, Deborah Jean. "Arrangements and Performance of Spirituals and Gospel Songs from the Eighteenth Century to the Twentieth Century" (M.A. Thesis, California State University, Long Beach, 1980), 15.

16. Stearns, 102.

17. Raichelson, Richard M. "Black Religious Folksong: A Study in Generic and Social Change" (Ph.D. diss., University of Pennsylvania, 1975), 243–244.

18. Davis, Gerald L. *I Got the Word in Me and I Can Sing It, You Know: A Study of the Performed African-American Sermon.* (Philadelphia: University of Pennsylvania, 1985), from the epigraph.

19. O'Neal, 17.

20. Ibid., 17–18.

21. Duckett, Alfred. "On His 75th Anniversary: An Interview with Thomas A. Dorsey," *Black World* 23, July 1974, 8.

22. Jackson, 203–204.

23. MacDouglad, Duncan, Jr. "The Popular Music Industry," Radio Research, eds. Lazarsfeld, Paul F. and Frank N. Stanton (New York: Arno Press, 1941), 71.

24. Broughton, Viv. *Too Close to Heaven: The Illustrated History of Gospel Music* (London: Midnight Books, 1996), 71.

25. Lornell, Kip. *Happy in the Service of the Lord: Afro-American Gospel Quartets in Memphis* (Urbana: University of Chicago Press, 1988), 23.

26. Boyer, Horace. *How Sweet the Sound: The Golden Age of Gospel* (Washington, D.C.: Elliott & Clark Publishing, 1995), 44.

27. Warner, Jay. *The Billboard Book of American Singing Groups: A History 1940–1990* (New York: Billboard Books, 1992), 35.

28. Lornell, 23.

29. Ibid., 27.

30. Balliett, Whitney. "Profiles: Barney Josephson," *New Yorker,* 9 Oct. 1971, 54.

31. Beasley, Maurine H., Holly Schulman, and Henry R. Beasley. *The Eleanor Roosevelt Encyclopedia.* (Westport, CN.: Greenwood Press, 2001), 22–24.

32. No author listed. "Golden Gate in Washington," *Time,* 27 Jan. 1941, 50.

33. Warner, 35.

34. Ibid., 36.

35. Oliver, Paul, Max Harrison, and William Bolcom. *The New Grove Gospel, Blues, and Jazz, With Spirituals and Ragtime* (New York: W.W. Norton & Company, 1986), 202–203.

36. Boyer, 34.

37. Erlewine, Michael, Vladimir Bogdanov, Chris Woodstra, and Cub Koba, eds. *All Music Guide to the Blues,* 2nd ed (San Francisco: Miller Freeman Books, 1999), 122.

38. Salvo, Patrick and Barbara Salvo. "75 Years of Gospel Music," *SEPIA,* April 1974, 62.

39. Zolten, Jerry. *Great God A'mighty! The Dixie Hummingbirds: Celebrating the Rise of Soul Gospel Music* (Oxford, U.K.: Oxford University Press, 2003), 84–85.

40. Boyer, 118–119.

41. Zolten, 90–97.

42. Ibid., 101–102.

43. Ibid., 105–107.

44. Erlewine et al., 122.

45. Wolff, Daniel with S. R. Crain, Clifton White, and G. David Tenenbaum. *You Send Me: The Life and Times of Sam Cooke* (New York: William Morrow and Company, Inc. 1995), 41–42.

46. Boyer, 67–68.

47. Kalil, Timothy A. "Thomas A. Dorsey and the Development and Diffusion of Traditional Black Gospel Piano," *Perspectives on American Music, 1900–1950*, ed. Michael Saffle (New York: Garland Publishing, Inc., 2000), 184.

48. Jackson, Irene V. *Afro-American Religious Music: A Bibliography and Catalogue of Gospel Music* (Westport, CT: Greenwood Press, 1979), 140.

49. Heilbut, 10.

50. Boyer, 69–70.

51. Heilbut, 207.

52. Boyer, 70–72.

53. Heilbut, 284.

54. Boyer, 78.

55. Ibid., 78–79.

56. Erlewine et al., 25.

57. Kael, Pauline. "Saved!" *New Yorker*, 4 Apr. 1983, 125.

58. Nierenberg, George T. *Say Amen, Somebody*. Pacific Arts Video Records PAVR-547, 1980.

59. Kael, 125.

60. Erlewine et al., 406–407.

61. Heilbut, 198.

62. Smith, Jessie C., ed. *Notable Black American Women* (Detroit: Gale Research, 1992), Jarmon, Laura C. "Willie Mae Smith, Singer, Religious Leader," 1050.

63. Dargan, William Thomas and Kathy White Bullock. "Willie Mae Ford Smith of St. Louis: A Shaping Influence Upon Black Gospel Singing Style," *This Far By Faith: Readings in African-American Women's Religious Biography*, eds. Judith Weisenfeld and Richard Newman (New York: Routledge Press, 1996), 37.

64. Ibid., 38–41.

65. Heilbut, 196.

66. Dargan and Bullock, 48.

67. Heilbut, 62.

68. Ibid., 188.

69. Corrigan, Patricia and Martha Shirk. "Willie Mae Ford Smith; Gained Acclaim as Top Gospel Singer," *St. Louis Post-Dispatch*, 4 Feb. 1994, 04B.

70. Boyer, Horace Clarence. "Take My Hand, Precious Lord, Lead Me On," *We'll Understand It Better By and By*, ed. Bernice Johnson Reagon (Washington, D.C.: Smithsonian Institution Press, 1992), 145.

Chapter 10

1. Hinson, Glenn D. "When the Words Roll and the Fire Flows: Spirit, Style and Experience in African American Gospel Performance" (Ph.D. diss., University of Pennsylvania, 1989), 1.

2. Wright, Richard. *12 Million Black Voices* (Reprint, New York: Thunder's Mouth Press, 1988), 131–132 (Photography direction by Edwin Rosskam).

3. Jackson, Jerma A. "Testifying at the Cross: Thomas Andrew Dorsey, Sister Rosetta Tharpe, and the Politics of African-American Sacred and Secular Music" (Ph.D. diss., Rutgers, 1995), 264.

4. Heilbut, Anthony. *The Gospel Sound: Good News and Bad Times* (New York: Limelight Editions, 1997), 190–191.

5. Zolten, Jerry. *Great God A'mighty! The Dixie Hummingbirds: Celebrating the Rise of Soul Gospel Music* (Oxford: Oxford University Press, 2003), 69.

6. Hammond, John with Irving Townsend. *John Hammond on Record: An Autobiography* (New York: Ridge Press/Summit Books, 1977), 203.

7. Lewis, George D. "Native Sons . . . Music and Art," Illinois Writers Project: "Negro in Illinois" Papers, Box 49, 14, 4. Chicago Public Library.

8. Visser, Joop. *Sister Rosetta Tharpe: The Original Soul Sister*, CD Liner notes, Proper Records, Properbox 5, 11–13.

9. No author listed. "Singer Swings Same Songs in Church and Night Club," *Life*, 28 Apr. 1939, 37.

10. Young, Alan. *Woke Me Up This Morning: Black Gospel Singers and the Gospel Life* (Jackson: University Press of Mississippi, 1997), 107–108.

11. Ibid., 11.

12. Jackson, 268–9.

13. Visser, 14–17.

14. Ibid., 20.

15. Shuker, Roy. *Understanding Popular Music* (London: Routledge, 1994), 41.

16. Sterling, Christopher and John M. Kittross. *Stay Tuned: A History of American Broadcasting* (Mahwah, NJ: Lawrence Erlbaum Associates, 2002), 214.

17. Ibid.

18. Hajduk, John Charles. "Music Wars: Conflict and Accommodation in America's Culture Industry, 1940–1960" (Ph.D. diss., State University of New York at Buffalo, 1995), 221–231.

19. Ibid., 271.

20. Ibid., 271–273.

21. Ibid., 291–297.

22. Ryan, John. *The Production of Culture in the Music Industry: The ASCAP-BMI Controversy* (Lanham, MD: University Press of America, 1985), 65.

23. O'Neal , Jim and Amy O'Neal. "The *Living Blues* Interview: Georgia Tom Dorsey," *Living Blues* 20, 1974–1975, 29.

24. Hajduk, 301.

25. Visser, 21–22.

26. Ibid., 23–24.

27. Helibut, 193.

28. Zolten, 142.

29. Visser, 31–34.

30. Jackson, 176.

31. Boyer, Horace Clarence. *How Sweet the Sound: The Golden Age of Gospel* (Washington, D.C.: Elliott & Clark Publishing, 1995), 157–158.

32. Wolff, Daniel with S. R. Crain, Clifton White, and G. David Tenenbaum. *You Send Me: The Life and Times of Sam Cooke* (New York: William Morrow and Company, Inc. , 1995), 87.

33. No author listed. "20,000 Watch Wedding of Sister Rosetta Tharpe," *Ebony,* Oct. 1951, 27.

34. Boyer, 158.

35. No author listed. "Rosetta Tharpe Says—I've Never Been a Jazz Singer," *Melody Maker,* 18 Apr. 1959, n.p.

36. Helibut, 193–194.

37. Visser, 35.

38. George, Lynell. "The Gospel According to Sister Rosetta," *Los Angeles Times,* 19 Oct. 2003, pt. 5, 49.

39. Ward-Royster, Willa and Toni Rose. *How I Got Over: Clara Ward and the World-Famous Ward Singers* (Philadelphia: Temple University Press, 1997), 3–38.

40. Erlewine, Michael, Vladimir Bogdanov, Chris Woodstra, and Cub Koba, eds. *All Music Guide to the Blues,* 2nd ed. (San Francisco: Miller Freeman Books, 1999), 455.

41. Ward-Royster et al., 60–63.

42. Reagon, Bernice Johnson. "William Herbert Brewster: Rememberings," *We'll Understand It Better By and By,* ed. Bernice Johnson Reagon (Washington, D.C.: Smithsonian Institution Press, 1992), 209.

43. Heilbut, 99.

44. Ward-Royster et al., 67.

45. Ibid., 72–88.

46. Ibid., 97–98

47. Ibid., 98–99.

48. Heilbut, Anthony. "If I Fail, You Tell the World I Tried: William Herbert Brewster on Records," *We'll Understand It Better By and By,* ed. Bernice Johnson Reagon (Washington, D.C.: Smithsonian Institution Press, 1992), 233–234.

49. Ibid., 243–244.

50. No author listed. *Tribute: The Life of Dr. William Herbert Brewster* (Memphis: Brewster House of Sermon Songs, Christian Literature and Dramatic Arts,1982), 15.

51. Heilbut, "If I Fail, You Tell the World I Tried: William Herbert Brewster on Records," 242.

52. Ibid., 241.

53. Magness, Perre. "Brewster: A Father of Gospel Music," *Commercial Appeal,* 8 June 2000, CC2.

54. Wheeler, Maurice B. "Clara Mae Ward: Singer," *Notable Black American Women,* ed. Jessie Carney Smith (Detroit: Gale Research, Inc., 1991), 1204.

55. Ward-Royster et al., 110–111.

56. Ibid., 115–116.

57. Ibid., 117–118.

58. Titon, Jeff Todd. *Rev. C. L. Franklin: Give Me This Mountain: Life History and Selected Hymns* (Urbana, IL: University of Chicago Press, 1989), 1–24.

59. Ibid., 47–211.

60. Ibid., 215.

61. Cummings, Tony. *The Sound of Philadelphia* (London: A Methuen Paperback, 1975), 20.

62. Ward-Royster et al., 104–105.

63. Heilbut, Anthony, *The Gospel Sound*, 109.

64. Ward-Royster et al, 107.

65. Fox, Ted. *Showtime at the Apollo* (New York: Holt, Rinehart and Winston, 1983), 233.

66. Gehman, Richard. "God's Singing Messengers," *Coronet* 44:3, July 1958, 112.

67. Ibid.

68. No author listed. "Glamour Girl of Gospel Music: Clara Ward has dazzling $50,000 wardrobe, makes $250,000 a year," *Ebony*, Oct. 1957, 24.

69. Ward, Clara. "How a Visit to the Holy Land Changed My Life," *Color*, May 1956, 14.

70. Ward-Royster et al., 119–120.

71. "Glamour Girl of Gospel Music," 27.

72. Erlewine et al., 455–456.

73. Ward-Royster et al., 109.

74. Erlewine et al., 455.

75. Heilbut, 110–111.

76. Ward-Royster et al., 138–139.

77. Ibid., 165.

78. Ibid., 171.

79. Heilbut, 310–313.

80. Broughton, Viv. *Too Close to Heaven* (London: Midnight Books, 1996), 94.

81. No author listed. "Singing for Sinners," *Newsweek*, 2 Sept. 1957, 86.

82. Ellison, Ralph. "As the Spirit Moves Mahalia," *Saturday Review*, 27 Sept. 1958, 70.

83. Terkel, Studs. "A Profile of Mahalia," *Down Beat*, 11 Dec. 1958, 14.

84. Jones, Pearl Williams. "Mahalia Jackson: Singer," *Notable Black American Women*, ed. Jessie Carney Smith (Detroit: Gale Research, Inc., 1991), 557.

85. Terkel, 13–14.

86. Pleasants, Henry. *The Great American Popular Singers* (New York: Simon and Schuster, 1974), 200.

87. Goreau, Laurraine. *Just Mahalia, Baby* (Waco, Texas: Word Books, 1975), 45.

88. Jackson Mahalia with Evan McLeod Wylie *Movin' on Up* (New York: Hawthorn Books, 1966), 49.

89. Goreau, 53–54.

90. Jackson, 57.

91. Goreau, 55.

92. Ibid., 55–56.

93. Ibid., 56.

94. Jackson, 60.

95. Ibid., 63.

96. Ibid., 66.

97. Harris, Michael. *The Rise of the Gospel Blues: The Music of Thomas Andrew Dorsey in the Urban Church* (New York: Oxford University Press, 1992), 258.

98. Ibid.

99. Jackson, 66.

100. Pleasants, Henry. *The Great American Popular Singers* (New York: Simon and Schuster, 1974), 190.

101. Hinson, Glenn D. "When the Words Roll and the Fire Flows: Spirit, Style and Experience in African American Gospel Performance" (Ph.D. diss., University of Pennsylvania, 1989), 129.

102. Ibid., 2.

103. *Amadeus,* dir. Milos Forman, 158 minutes, Warner Brothers, 1984, DVD.

104. Burnim, Mellonee V. "The Black Gospel Music Tradition: A Complex of Ideology, Aesthetic, and Behavior," *More Than Dancing: Essays on Afro-American and African Music and Studies,* ed. Irene V. Jackson (Westport, CT: Greenwood Press, 1985), 156–157.

105. Goreau, 65.

106. Ibid., 61–66.

107. Ibid., 72–75.

108. Jackson, 80.

109. Goreau, 87–88.

110. Ibid., 91.

111. Pleasants, 63.

112. Goreau, 107–108.

113. Ibid., 109.

114. Ibid., 113–114.

115. Erlewine et al., 215.

116. Oliver, Paul, Max Harrison, and William Bolcom, eds. *The New Grove Gospel, Blues, and Jazz with Spirituals and Ragtime* (New York: W.W. Norton & Company, 1986), 209.

117. Mellers, Wilfrid. *Angels of the Night: Popular Female Singers of Our Time.* (Oxford, U.K.: Basil Blackwell, Ltd., 1986), 12.

118. Roberts, John Storm. *Black Music of Two Worlds* (New York: Praeger Publishers, 1972), 171–172.

119. Tallmadge, William T. "Dr. Watts and Mahalia Jackson—The Development, Decline and Survival of a Folk Style in America," *Enthnomusicology* 2, May 1961, 95–99.

120. Mellers, 13.

121. Erlewine et al., 215.

122. Pleasants, 209–210.

123. Oliver et al., 209.

124. Pleasants, 210.

125. Heilbut, 58.

126. Hentoff, Nat. "Mahalia Jackson," *Jazz Journal* 11:5, May 1958, 17.

127. Duke Ellington and His Orchestra, with Mahalia Jackson *Black, Brown and Beige,* Sony Records, 1958.

128. Mahalia Jackson, *Live at Newport,* Columbia Records, 1958.

129. Hunter, Ross, producer. *Imitation of Life,* 128 minutes. Universal Studios, 1959.

130. Erlewine et al., 215.

131. Hentoff, Nat. From an undated article in *The Reporter.* Recorded in Goreau, 17.

132. Hentoff, 231.

133. Goreau, 285–286.

134. Ibid., 290–302.

135. Ibid., 314–318.

136. Ibid., 347.

137. Ibid., 357–358.

138. Schwerin, Jules. *Got to Tell It: Mahalia Jackson, Queen of Gospel* (New York: Oxford University Press), 169.

139. Goreau, 363–364.

140. Jackson, 215.

141. Goreau, 609.

142. Schwerin, 179–184.

Chapter 11

1. Macon, Evelyn. Interview by Vivian Morris. "Negro Laundry Workers," *American Life Histories: Federal Writer's Project, 1936–1940.* Library of Congress, Washington, D.C., 10 Feb. 1939. The Archive of Folk Song, File 45–4.

2. Webb, Jacquie Gales, Lex Gillespie, and Sonja Williams, producers. Lou Rawls, host. "Black Radio . . . Telling It Like It Was: Sounding Black, Program #6." Radio Smithsonian Transcript (Washington, D.C.: Smithsonian Institution, 1996), 19.

3. George, Nelson. *The Death of Rhythm & Blues* (New York: Pantheon Books, 1988), 24.

4. Zolten, Jerry. *Great God A'mighty! The Dixie Hummingbirds: Celebrating the Rise of Soul Gospel Music* (Oxford, U.K.: Oxford University Press), 209.

5. George, 26.

6. Ibid., 27.

7. Price, Deborah Evans. "MCA Bows Peacock Imprint for Gospel Releases," *Billboard,* 3 Oct. 1998, 4.

8. Wolff, Daniel with S. R. Crain, Clifton White, and G. David Tenenbaum. *You Send Me: The Life and Times of Sam Cooke* (New York: William Morrow and Company, Inc., 1995), 74.

9. Ibid., 76.

10. Boyer, Horace. *How Sweet the Sound: The Golden Age of Gospel* (Washington, D.C.: Elliott & Clark Publishing, 1995), 89.

11. Milkowski, Bill. "Label Watch: Riches from the Savoy Vaults," *Jazztimes* 30, no.4 (2000): 89–90.

12. Wade, Dorothy and Justine Picardie. *Music Man: Ahmet Ertegun, Atlantic Records and the Triumph of Rock 'n' Roll* (New York: W.W. Norton & Company, 1990), 59.

13. George, 28–29.

14. Boyer, 53.

15. Ibid.

16. Webb, Jacquie Gales, Lex Gillespie, and Sonja Williams, producers. Lou Rawls, host. "Black Radio . . . Telling It Like It Was: Let's Have Church, Program #10" (Washington, D.C.: Smithsonian Institution, 1996), 4.

17. Lornell, Kip. *Happy in the Service of the Lord: Afro-American Gospel Quartets in Memphis* (Urbana, IL: University of Illinois Press, 1988), 50.

18. Ibid., 76–77.

19. Ibid., 96.

20. Ibid., 119.

21. Boyer, 168–169.

22. MacDonald, Fred, J. *Don't Touch That Dial!* (Chicago: Nelson-Hall Publishers, 1979), 366.

23. Schwerin, Jules. *Got to Tell It: Mahalia Jackson, Queen of Gospel* (New York: Oxford University Press, 1992), 109.

24. Ibid.

25. Carpenter, Bill. "The Shirley Caesar You've Never Met," *Rejoice!*, Oct./Nov. 1992, 4.

26. Heilbut, Anthony. *The Gospel Sound: Good News and Bad Times* (New York: Limelight Editions, 1997), 75.

27. Funk, Ray. "The Soul Stirrers: A look at the early years of one of the most influential black gospel quartets," *Rejoice!*, Winter 1987, 13.

28. Seroff, Doug. "On the Battlefield: Gospel Quartets in Jefferson County, Alabama," *Repercussions: A Celebration of African-American Music*, eds. Geoffrey Haydon and Dennis Marks (London: Century Publishing, 1985), 42.

29. Wolff et al., 25–45.

30. Seroff, 43.

31. Funk, 14.

32. Ibid.

33. Wolff et al., 46.

34. Seroff, 41.

35. Heilbut, 80–81.

36. Erlewine, Michael, Vladimir Bogdanov, Chris Woodstra, and Cub Koba, eds. *All Music Guide to the Blues,* 2nd ed. (San Francisco: Miller Freeman Books, 1999), 408.

37. Funk, 15.

38. Ibid., 16.

39. Wolff et al., 43.

40. Ibid., 22.

41. Boyer, Horace Clarence. "Gospel Blues: Origin and History," *New Perspectives on Music: Essays in Honor of Eileen Southern*, ed. Josephine Wright (Warren, MI: Harmonie Park Press, 1992), 135.

42. Erlewine et al., 409.

43. Funk, 16.

44. Wolff et al., 47–48.

45. Ibid., 19.

46. Ibid., 21.

47. Ibid., 24–26.

48. Ibid., 28.

49. Ibid., 32.

50. Ibid., 42.

51. Ibid., 44.

52. Ibid., 47.

53. Ibid., 47–48.

54. Ibid., 51–52.

55. Ibid., 54–56.

56. Ibid., 57–61.

57. Ibid., 65–67.

58. Funk, 17.

59. Wolff et al., 68.

60. Ibid., 81.

61. George, 79.

62. Ibid.

63. Funk, 18.

64. Fox, Ted. *Showtime at the Apollo* (New York: Holt, Rinehart and Winston, 1983), 236.

65. George, 70–71.

66. Wynn, Ron. "Rebert H. Harris: Doves, Sam Cooke, and Undiluted Gospel," *Rejoice!*, June/July 1991, 23.

67. Wolff et al., 179.

68. George, 81.

69. Funk, 20.

70. Ibid.

71. Ibid., 12.

72. George, 79.

73. Heilbut, 91–92.

74. No author listed. "Chicago gospel pioneer R. H. Harris dead at 84." In Associated Press, 6 Sept. 2000. LexisNexis.

75. Ibid.

76. Talevski, Nick. *The Unofficial Encyclopedia of the Rock and Roll Hall of Fame* (Westport, CT: Greenwood Press, 1998), 41.

77. No author listed. "46th Grammy Awards Nominations," *Daily Variety*, 5 Dec. 2003, 77.

78. Gart, Galen and Roy C. Ames, eds. *Duke/Peacock Records: An Illustrated History with Discography* (Milford, NH: Big Nickel Publications, 1990), 3–9. (With a chapter on Peacock's gospel music by Ray Funk.)

79. Ibid., 12–36.

80. Ibid., 61.

81. Funk, Ray, "Let's Go Out to the Programs: The Peacock Gospel Years," *Duke/Peacock Records: An Illustrated History with Discography*, eds. Galen Gart and Roy C. Ames (Milford, NH: Big Nickel Publications, 1990), 48.

82. Ibid., 37.

83. Wadey, Paul. "Percell Perkins: Only Sighted Member of the Five Blind Boys of Mississippi," *The Independent: London,* 24 Mar. 2003, 20.

84. Funk, "Let's Go Out to the Programs: The Peacock Gospel Years," 37.

85. Ibid.

86. Ibid., 38.

87. Erlewine et al., 142.

88. Heilbut, 47.

89. Wolff et al., 70.

90. Wadey, 20.

91. Erlewine et al., 142.

92. Wolff et al., 70.

93. Funk, "Let's Go Out to the Programs: The Peacock Gospel Years," 40.
94. Zolten, 221.
95. Gart, "Let's Go Out to the Programs: The Peacock Gospel Years," 41.
96. Ibid.
97. Zolten, 234–235.
98. Ibid., 236.
99. Heilbut, 37.
100. Boyer, 122–123.
101. Gart, "Let's Go Out to the Programs: The Peacock Gospel Years," 41.
102. Zolten, 257–258.
103. Ibid., 263–265.
104. Ibid., 267–268.
105. Ibid., 286–288.
106. Salvo, Patrick and Barbara Salvo. "45 Years of Gospel Music," *SEPIA*, April 1974, 62.
107. Ibid., 64.
108. Zolten, 318.
109. McGarvey, Seamus. "An Interview with Ira Tucker of the Dixie Hummingbirds," *Blues & Rhythm, The Gospel Truth*, June 1986, 14.
110. Zolten, 159.
111. Funk, "Let's Go Out to the Programs: The Peacock Gospel Years," 42–43.
112. Boyer, 204.
113. Erlewine et al., 394.
114. Zolten, 159–160.
115. Ibid., 245–246.
116. Ibid., 253.
117. Wolff et al., 110.
118. Zolten, 64.
119. Wolff et al., 110–111.
120. Ibid., 111.
121. Heilbut, 123–125.
122. Ibid., 127–130.
123. Ibid., 129.
124. Erlewine et al., 394.
125. Pareles, Jon. "At Gospel Festival, Music Inspired by Hope," *New York Times,* 11 Nov, 1988, C21.
126. Warner, Jay. *The Billboard Book of American Singing Groups: A History, 1940–1990* (New York: Billboard Books, 1992), 58.
127. Heilbut, 116–117.
128. Warner, 58.
129. Heilbut, 118.
130. Ibid., 119.
131. Ibid.
132. Zolten, 283–284.
133. Fox, 232.
134. Boyer, 175.

135. Erlewine et al., 419–420.

136. Pareles, 21.

137. Heilbut, 116.

138. Cohodas, Nadine. *Spinning Blues into Gold: The Chess Brothers and the Legendary Chess Records* (New York: St. Martin's Press, 2000), 271.

139. Hannusch, Jeff. "Lew Chudd," *Living Blues,* Sept./Oct. 1998, 51–52.

140. Collis, John. *The Story of Chess Records* (New York: Bloomsbury Publishing, 1998), 187.

141. Various artists. *The Specialty Story Box Set.* Specialty SPCD 4412.

142. Gart, 127.

Chapter 12

1. Ertegun, Ahmet. *What'd I Say: The Atlantic Story, 50 Years of Music* (New York: Welcome Rain Publishers, 2001), 193.

2. Carawan, Guy and Candie Carawan, eds. and compilers. *Sing for Freedom: The Story of the Civil Rights Movement Through Its Songs* (Bethlehem, PA: A Sing Out Publication, 1990), 97.

3. Shelton, Robert. *The Face of Folk Music* (New York: Citadel Press, 1968), 179.

4. Wolfe, Tom. *The Bonfire of the Vanities* (New York: Farrar, Straus, Giroux, 1987), 143.

5. Coleridge-Taylor, Samuel. *Twenty Four Negro Melodies Transcribed for the Piano by S. Coleridge-Taylor With a Preface by Booker T. Washington* (Boston: Oliver Ditson Company, 1905), ix.

6. Oster, Harry. "Easter Rock Revisited: A Study in Acculturation," *Louisiana Folklore Society 1* 3, 1958, 37–41.

7. Stearns, Marshall W. *The Story of Jazz* (New York: Oxford University Press, 1956), 137.

8. Raichelson, Richard M. "Black Religious Folksong: A Study in Generic and Social Change" (Ph.D. diss., University of Pennsylvania, 1975), 233.

9. Buchanan, Samuel Carroll. "A Critical Analysis of Style in Four Black Jubilee Quartets in the United States" (Ph.D. diss., New York University, 1987), 99–100.

10. Strachwitz, Chris. *Acapella Gospel Singing.* Folklyric Records, Number 9045, 1986. Liner notes.

11. Ibid.

12. Jackson, Joyce Marie. "The Performing Black Sacred Quartet: An Expression of Cultural Values and Aesthetics" (Ph.D. diss., Indiana University, 1988), 139.

13. Frazier, E. Franklin. *The Negro in the United States* (New York: MacMillin, 1957), 692–693.

14. Guralnick, Peter. *Sweet Soul Music: Rhythm and Blues and the Southern Dream of Freedom* (New York: Harper & Row Publishers, 1986). See also Garland, Phyl. *The Sound of Soul* (Chicago: Henry Regency Company, 1969). Starr, Larry. *American Popular Music: From Minstrelsy to MTV* (Oxford, U.K.: Oxford University Press, 2003). Neal, Mark Anthony. *What the Music Said: Black Popular Music, Black Public Culture* (New York: Routledge, 1999).

15. West, Cornel. *Prophetic Fragments* (Grand Rapids, MI: William B. Eerdmans, 1988), 178–179.

16. Neal, 38.

17. Garland, 199.

18. Guralnick, 335.

19. Black, Doris. "How Black Churches Became a School for Singing Stars," *SEPIA* 22, 1973, 80.

20. Garland, 198.

21. Ibid.

22. Guralnick, 348.

23. Young, Alan. *Woke Me Up This Morning: Black Gospel Singers and the Gospel Life* (Jackson: University of Mississippi Press, 1997), 194.

24. Black, 78.

25. Mellers, Wilfrid. *Angels of the Night: Popular Female Singers of Our Time* (Oxford, U.K.: Basil Blackwell, Ltd., 1986), 14–15.

26. Guralnick, 351.

27. Ibid., 352.

28. Collis, John. *The Story of Chess Records* (New York: Bloomsbury Publishing, 1998), 53.

29. Darden, Robert. "Gospel Lectern: Pops Staples 1st I AM solo album is a solid gospel set," *Billboard*, 16 Apr. 1966, 57.

30. Warner, Jay. *The Billboard Book of American Singing Groups: A History, 1940–1990* (New York: Billboard Books, 1992), 300.

31. Erlewine, Michael, Vladimir Bogdanov, Chris Woodstra, and Cub Koba, eds. *All Music Guide to the Blues,* 2nd ed. (San Francisco: Miller Freeman Books, 1999), 413.

32. Neal, 82–83.

33. Floyd, Samuel A. *The Power of Black Music: Interpreting Its History from Africa to America* (New York: Oxford University Press, 1995), 200–201.

34. Carawan, 6.

35. Webb, Jacquie Gales, Lex Gillespie, Sonja Williams, producers. Lou Rawls, host. "Black Radio . . . Telling It Like It Was: Civil Rights," Radio Smithsonian transcript, 1996, 6–8.

36. Haralambos, Michael. *Right On: From Blues to Soul in Black America* (New York: Drake Publishers, Inc., 1975), 139–140.

37. Spencer, Jon Michael. *Protest & Praise: Sacred Music of Black Religion* (Minneapolis: Fortress Press, 1990), 84.

38. Carawan, 15.

39. Warner, 300–301.

40. Berson, Misha. "Mavis Staples Makes a Joyful Noise in Tribute to Mahalia Jackson," *Seattle Times*, 28 Oct., 2003, E4.

41. Heilbut, Anthony. *The Gospel Sound: Good News and Bad Times* (New York: Limelight Editions, 1997), 339.

42. Dylan, Bob and Mavis Staples. "Gonna Change My Way of Thinking." *Gotta Serve Somebody: The Gospel Songs of Bob Dylan.* Various artists. Columbia CK 89015, 2003.

43. Werner, Craig. *A Change Is Gonna Come: Music, Race & the Soul of America* (New York: Plume/Penguin Group, 1998), 30.

44. Katz, Larry. "Pops Staples' Memorable Voice Brought Gospel to the Masses," *Boston Herald,* 21 Dec. 2000, 47.

45. Himes, Geoffrey. "Staple Singers' American Roots," *Washington Post*, 4 July 1997, Weekend: 14.

46. Heilbut, 161–162.

47. Ibid., 85.

48. Young, 112.

49. Erlewine et al., 96.

50. No author listed. "Dorothy Love Coates, Sing of Gospel Music, Dies at 74," *New York Times*, 12 Apr. 2002, B7.

51. Carpenter, Bill. "Obituaries: Dorothy Love Coates," *Goldmine*, 28 June 2002, 41.

52. Heilbut, 297–298.

53. Ibid., 165–169.

54. Coates, Dorothy Love. "The Hymn." *Soul of the Original Gospel Harmonettes/ Peace in the Valley*. Vee-Jay Records COL 7729, 1964.

55. Heilbut, 168.

56. Ibid., 160.

57. *New York Times*, B7.

58. Cammeron, Dwight, producer. *Still Holding On: The Music of Dorothy Love Coates and the Original Gospel Harmonettes* (University of Alabama Center for Public Television and Radio, 2000).

59. Jefferson, Margo. "Revisions: Spiritual Infuses the Mainstream, but Who Is Uplifted?" *New York Times*, 23 Jan. 2001, E2.

60. Werner, 95.

61. Dorothy Love Coates. "I Won't Let Go of My Faith." *Soul of the Original Gospel Harmonettes/Peace in the Valley*. Vee-Jay Records COL 7729, 1964.

62. Boyer, Horace Clarence. *How Sweet the Sound: The Golden Age of Gospel* (Washington, D.C.: Elliott & Clark Publishing, 1995), 215–218.

63. Collins, Lisa. "In the Spirit," *Billboard*, 5 Feb. 1994, 33.

64. Trescott, Jacqueline. "Praising the Lord and Albertina Walker; Upper Marlboro Salute Spotlights Pioneering Gospel Singer's Life and Lessons," *Washington Post*, 4 May 1998, Style D01.

65. Hoekstra, Dave. "Success Followed Caravans," *Chicago Sun-Times*, 12 June 1994, People Plus 7.

66. Boyer, 218–219.

67. Hoekstra, 7.

68. Heilbut, 131–135.

69. Ibid., 135–137.

70. Boyer, 220.

71. Heilbut, 142.

72. Trescott, D01.

73. Boyer, 222–223.

74. Heilbut, 325.

75. Emerson, Ken. "Inez Andrews Sings a Gospel Tribute," *New York Times*, 9 Mar. 1979, C1.

76. Shelby, Joyrice. "Queen of Gospel's Musical Message," *New York Daily News*, 19 Oct. 1997, Suburban 3.

77. Boyer, 223–224.

78. Shelby, 3.

79. Ibid.

80. Boyer, 225.

81. Darden, Robert. "Shirley Caesar, Singing Evangelist," *Rejoice!*, Summer 1990, 8.

82. Hoekstra, 7.

83. Erlewine et al., 77.

84. Darden, 9.

85. Caesar, Shirley. *Shirley Caesar, The Lady, the Melody, and the Word: The Inspirational Story of the First Lady of Gospel* (Nashville: Thomas Nelson Publishers, 1998), 73–74.

86. Trescott, Jacqueline. "What Is Caesar's Is Also God's; The Grammy Winner's at Home in the Theater, Pulpit or Choir Loft," *Washington Post*, 22 Feb. 1998, G01.

87. Caesar, 84–88.

88. Darden, 9.

89. Caesar, 88–91.

90. Darden, 9.

91. Ibid., 10.

92. Jones, Steve. "Gospel Great Shirley Caesar Emphasizes Holy Message in Her Music," *USA TODAY*, 12 Jan. 1998, Life 3D.

93. Caesar, 149–150.

94. Boyer, 222.

95. Caesar, 151–152.

96. Lamey, Mary. "Shirley Caesar Brings Her Gospel to Town," *Montreal Gazette*, 30 Oct. 1999, C5.

97. Trescott, G01.

98. Hoekstra, 7.

Chapter 13

1. Beardsley, John, William Arnett, Paul Arnett, Jane Livingston, and Alvia J. Wardlaw. *Gee's Bend: The Women and Their Quilts* (Atlanta, GA: Tinwood Books, 2002), 7.

2. Brown, Mick. "Pastor Cleveland, Superstar," *Manchester Guardian Weekly*, 11 Jan. 1981, 19.

3. Boyer, Horace Clarence. *How Sweet the Sound: The Golden Age of Gospel* (Washington, D.C.: Elliott & Clark Publishing, 1995), 226–227.

4. Heilbut, Anthony. *The Gospel Sound: Good News and Bad Times* (New York: Limelight Editions, 1997), 191.

5. Reagon, Bernice Johnson. "Conversations: Roberta Martin Singers Roundtable," *We'll Understand It Better By and By: Pioneering African American Gospel Composers*, eds. Williams-Jones, Pearl and Bernice Johnson Reagon (Washington, D.C.: Smithsonian Institution Press, 1992), 295.

6. Boyer, 227–228.

7. Heilbut, 154.

8. Erlewine, Michael, Vladimir Bogdanov, Chris Woodstra, and Cub Koba, eds. *All Music Guide to the Blues*, 2nd ed. (San Francisco: Miller Freeman Books, 1999), 51.

9. Ibid.

10. Fox, Ted. *Showtime at the Apollo* (New York: Holt, Rinehart and Winston, 1983), 232.

11. Ibid., 231.

12. James, Etta with David Ritz. *Rage to Survive: The Etta James Story* (Cambridge, MA: Da Capo Press, 1998), 76.

13. Heilbut, 145.

14. Himes, Geoffrey. "Gospel's Gold Is Back on Track," *Washington Post*, 27 Aug. 1993, Weekend N17.

15. Erlewine et al., 52.

16. Ibid., 31.

17. Cogan, Jim and William Clark. *Temples of Sound: Inside the Great Recording Studios* (San Francisco: Chronicle Books, 2003), 170–171.

18. Hammond, John with Irving Townsend. *John Hammond on Record: An Autobiography* (New York: Ridge Press/Summit Books, 1977), 359.

19. Heilbut, 229.

20. Trescott, Jacqueline. "As the Spirit Moves Him: 'Black Nativity' Producer Mike Malone's Light-Footed Gospel," *Washington Post*, 24 Dec. 1994, Style B1.

21. Heilbut, 229.

22. Valentine, Penny and Vicki Wickham. *Dancing With Demons: The Authorized Biography of Dusty Springfield* (New York: St. Martin's Press, 2000), 47–48.

23. Oliver, Paul, Max Harrison, and William Bolcom. *The New Grove Gospel, Blues, and Jazz, With Spirituals and Ragtime* (New York: W.W. Norton & Company, 1986), 219.

24. Boyer, 231–232.

25. Heilbut, 146–155.

26. Shephard, Richard F. "'But Never Jam Today' Follows Recipe," *New York Times*, 24 Apr. 1969, 40.

27. Heilbut, 155.

28. Gussow, Mel. "Stage: Back on Broadway, 'Your Arms Too Short'," *New York Times*, 3 June 1980, C 7.

29. Kroll, Jack. "Gospel Truth," *Newsweek*, 10 Jan. 1977, 66.

30. Burdine, Warren, Jr. "The Gospel Music and Its Place in the Black American Theatre (1998)," *A Sourcebook of African-American Performance: Plays, People, Movements*, ed. Annamarie Bean (London: Routledge Press, 1999), 194–195.

31. Heilbut, 311.

32. *Jubilee Showcase*, produced by Sid Ordower Enterprises. Various directors. 30 minutes. The Center for Black Music Research, 1964. Videocassette.

33. Erlewine et al., 51.

34. West, Cornel. "Black Strivings in a Twilight Civilization," *The Future of the Race*, Cornel West and Henry Louis Gates, Jr., eds. (New York: Vintage Books, 1997), 81.

35. Caggiano, Brenda. "Cleveland's True Gospel," *Washington Post*, 6 Aug. 1989, Limelight G3.

36. Ibid.

37. Shaw, Arnold. *Black Popular Music in America* (New York: Schirmer Books, 1986), 216.

38. Caggiano, G3.

39. Boyer, 247.

40. No author listed. "Gospel's James Cleveland dead at 59," *Toronto Star,* 11 Feb. 1991, Entertainment D8.

41. Boyer, 248.

42. Collis, John. *The Story of Chess Records* (London, Bloomsbury Press, 1998), 181.

43. Collins, Lisa. "James Cleveland Dead at 59; He was Dubbed 'King' of Gospel Music," *Billboard,* 23 Feb. 1991, 4.

44. DjeDje, Jacqueline Cogdell. "Gospel Music in the Los Angeles Black Community: A Historical Overview," *Black Music Research Journal* 9, no. 1, 1989, 69.

45. DjeDje, Jacqueline Cogdell. "The California Black Gospel Music Tradition: A Confluence of Musical Styles and Cultures," *California Soul: Music of African Americans in the West,* eds. Jacqueline DjeDje and Eddie S. Meadows (Berkeley, CA: University of California Press, 1998), 141–143.

46. Harrington, Richard. "Inspiring the Multitudes: The Rev. James Cleveland and His Gospel Legacy," *Washington Post,* 17 Feb. 1991, Sunday Show G1.

47. DjeDje, "The California Black Gospel Music Tradition," 158.

48. Collins, 4.

49. Brown, 19.

50. Young, Alan. *Woke Me Up This Morning: Black Gospel Singers and the Gospel Life* (Jackson, MS: University Press of Mississippi, 1997), xxix.

51. Boyer, 126–127.

52. Young, xxx–xxxi.

53. Shaw, Arnold. *Honkers and Shouters: The Golden Years of Rhythm and Blues* (New York: Collier Books, 1978), 356–357.

54. Harrington, G1.

55. Ibid.

56. Boyer, 248–249.

57. No author listed. "Gospel: Rev. James Cleveland's GMWA Mass Choir, *Standing in Need of a Blessing,*" *Billboard,* 13 May 2000, 27.

58. Harrington, G1.

59. Davis, Stephen. *Old Gods Almost Dead: The 40-Year Odyssey of the Rolling Stones* (New York: Broadway Books, 2002), 355.

60. Neal, Mark Anthony. *What the Music Said: Black Popular Music and Black Popular Culture* (New York: Routledge, 1999), 82.

61. Ibid., 83.

62. Rosenthal, Elizabeth. *His Songs: The Musical Journey of Elton John* (New York: Billboard Books, 2001), 131–133.

63. Heilbut, 216.

64. Collins, 4.

65. Boyer, 249.

66. Harrington, G1.

67. Heilbut, 350.

68. Hall, Carla. "Thousands Mourn Gospel Great James Cleveland; Singing Fills L.A. Auditorium as Friends and Admirers Pay Tribute to Minister, Musician," *Washington Post,* 17 Feb. 1991, A10.

69. Harrington, G1.

70. Cambell-Ingram, Sharon. "James Cleveland (1931–1991): A Tribute," *Rejoice!,* June/July 1991, 27.

71. Harrington, G1.

72. Warren, Gwendolin Sims. *Ev'ry Time I Feel the Spirit* (New York: Henry Holt and Company, 1997), 312–314.

73. Jones, Bobby with Lesley Sussman. *Touched By God: Black Gospel Greats Share Their Stories of Finding God* (New York: Pocket Books, 1998), 91.

74. DjeDje, "The California Black Gospel Music Tradition," 146.

75. Ibid., 152.

76. Romanowski, Patricia and Holly George-Warren, eds. *The New Rolling Stone Encyclopedia of Rock & Roll* (New York: Fireside, A Rolling Stone Press Book, 1995), 424–425.

77. Heilbut, 248.

78. Webb, Jacquie Gales, Lex Gillespie, Sonja Williams, producers. Lou Rawls, host. "Black Radio . . . Telling It Like It Was: Jack Cooper and Al Benson, Program #3," Radio Smithsonian transcript, 1996, 17–18.

79. Whitburn, Joel. *The Billboard Book of Top 40 Hits* (New York: Watson/Guptill Publishing, 2001), 296.

80. Jones, 95.

81. *It's Your Thing*. Directed by Mike Gargiulo. Produced by the Isley Brothers. 120 minutes. Medford Film, 1969. Videocassette.

82. Russell, Tom and Sylvia Tyson, eds. *And Then I Wrote: The Songwriter Speaks* (London: Arsenal Pulp Press, 1996), 21.

83. Romanowski, 425.

84. Jones, 90–91.

85. Ely, Gordon. "'Oh Happy Day'—Hawkins Has New Album, With Old Song," *Richmond Times-Dispatch,* 28 Feb. 1999, H-6.

86. http://www.lovecenter.org

87. Heilbut, 248.

88. Crouch, Andrae and Nina Ball. *Through It All* (Waco, TX: Word Books, 1974), 18–23.

89. Doreschuch, Bob. "Backstage with Andrae Crouch," *Contemporary Keyboard,* 1979, 6–14.

90. Burrell, Walter Rico. "The Gospel According to Andrae Crouch," *Ebony,* Sept. 1982, 60.

91. Crouch, 37–47.

92. Ibid., 47–49.

93. DjeDje, "The California Black Gospel Music Tradition," 166.

94. Gersztyn, Bob. "Andrae's Music Will Never Lose Its Power," *Door Magazine,* 1 Mar. 2004 (www.thedoormagazine.com/archives.html).

95. Crouch, 66–72.

96. Ibid., 95–97.

97. Cusic, Don. *The Sound of Light: A History of Gospel Music* (Bowling Green, OH: Bowling Green State University Popular Press, 1990), 126–129.

98. Kidula, Jean. "The Gospel of Andrae Crouch," *California Soul: Music of African Americans in the West*, eds. Jacqueline DjeDje and Eddie S. Meadows (Berkeley, CA: University of California Press, 1998), 299.

99. Broughton, Viv. *Too Close to Heaven: The Illustrated History of the Gospel Sound* (London: Midnight Books, 1996), 145.

100. Boyer, Horace Clarence. "A Comparative Analysis of Traditional and Contemporary Gospel Music," *More Than Dancing: Essays on Afro-American Music and Musicians*, ed. Irene V. Jackson (Westport, CN: Greenwood Press, 1985), 128.

101. Ibid.

102. Ibid., 127.

103. Hitchcock, H. Wiley and Stanley Sadie, eds. *The New Grove Dictionary of American Music, vol. 1* (London: Macmillan Press, 1986), 549.

104. Kidula, 313.

105. Ibid., 300.

106. Boyer, *More Than Dancing*, 128.

107. Cox, Donna McNeil. "Contemporary Trends in the Music Ministry of the Church of God in Christ," *Journal of Black Sacred Music*, Fall 1988, 23–28.

108. Boyer, *More Than Dancing*, 127.

109. Ricks, George Robinson. *Some Aspects of the Religious Music of the United States Negro: An Ethnomusicological Study with Special Emphasis on the Gospel Tradition* (New York: Arno Press, 1977), 398–399.

110. Ibid.

111. Floyd, Samuel A., Jr. *The Power of Black Music: Interpreting Its History from Africa to the United States.* (New York: Oxford University Press), 197.

112. Kidula, 308–309.

113. Baker, Paul. *Contemporary Christian Music: Where It Came From, What It Is, Where It's Going* (Westchester, IL: Crossway Books, 1985), 188.

114. Broughton, 150.

115. Collier, Aldore. "Gospel Star Andrae Crouch Takes Pulpit of Late Father's Church," *Jet* 88, no. 16, Oct. 1995, 32–33.

116. Crowe, Jerry. "Meet *Pastor* Andrae Crouch," *Los Angeles Times*, 21 Sept. 1995, F4.

117. Burrell, Walter. "The Gospel According to Andrae Crouch," *Ebony* 37, Sept. 1982, 57.

118. See their Web site at <http://www.newcmc.org>.

119. Gersztyn, http://www.thedoormagazine.com.

120. Crouch, 148.

121. Floyd, Samuel A., Jr. *The Power of Black Music*, 196.

122. Gersztyn, thedoormagazine.com.

Chapter 14

1. Walker, Alice. *The Way Forward Is With a Broken Heart* (Reprint, New York: Ballantine Books, 2001), 144.

2. Gregory, Neal and Janice Gregory. *When Elvis Died* (Washington, D.C.: Communications Press, Inc., 1980), 124.

3. Boyer, Horace Clarence. "A Comparative Analysis of Traditional and Contemporary Gospel Music," *More Than Dancing: Essays on Afro-American Music and Musicians*, ed. Irene V. Jackson (Westport, CN.: Greenwood Press, 1985), 136.

4. Boyer, Horace. "Gospel Blues: Origin and History," *New Perspectives on Music: Essays in Honor of Eileen Southern*, eds. Josephine Wright with Samuel A. Floyd, Jr. (Warren, MI: Harmonie Park Press, 1992), 144.

5. Iverem, Esther. "Mighty Clouds' Burst of Sound; The Gospel Truth: This Ageless Quartet Still Brings Sunshine to Fans' Hearts," *Washington Post*, 22 Apr. 1996, C01.

6. Broughton, Viv. *Too Close to Heaven: The Illustrated History of the Gospel Sound* (London: Midnight Books, 1996), 103–104.

7. Erlewine, Michael, Vladimir Bogdanov, Chris Woodstra, and Cub Koba, eds. *All Music Guide to the Blues*, 2nd ed. (San Francisco: Miller Freeman Books, 1999), 317.

8. Banks, Lacy J. "Gospel Music: A Shout of Black Joy," *Ebony* 27, 1972, 168.

9. Seigal, Buddy. "Mighty Joe; Singer's Joy: Leading the Mighty Clouds of Joy," *San Diego Union-Tribune*, 25 Jan. 2001, Night & Day 14.

10. Dyer, Ervin. "Forecast: Heavy Gospel; Mighty Clouds of Joy Will Mix It Up at Peabody Concert," *Pittsburgh Post-Gazette*, 30 Mar. 1997, Arts & Entertainment 9.

11. Iverem, C01.

12. Young, Bob. "Gospel Group Makes Mighty Joyful Noise Unto the Lord," *Boston Herald*, 28 Oct. 1997, Arts & Life 027.

13. Young, Alan. *Woke Me Up This Morning: Black Gospel Singers and the Gospel Life* (Jackson, MS: University Press of Mississippi, 1997), 63.

14. Heilbut, Anthony. *The Gospel Sound: Good News and Bad Times* (New York: Limelight Books, 1997), 129.

15. Young, Bob, 027.

16. Ibid.

17. Martin, William. *With God on Our Side: The Rise of the Religious Right in America*, 2nd ed. (New York: Broadway Books, 1997), 159.

18. Troutman, Roger. *The Saga Continues*. Warner Brothers, 1984. Warner Bros. compact disc.

19. Young, Bob, 027.

20. Dyer, 9.

21. Franklin, Aretha and others. *One Lord, One Faith, One Baptism*. Arista, 1987. ASCD 8497.

22. Seigal, 14.

23. Smith, Pepper. "From Happy Land to Clubland with the Five Blind Boys of Alabama," *Rejoice!* April/May 1992, 4.

24. Harrington, Richard. "Blind Boys' New 'Spirit,'" *Washington Post*, 12 Oct. 2001, Weekend T15.

25. Gill, Andy. "An Open Invitation to the Spirit," *The Independent (London)*, 28 May 1992, 14.

26. Collins, Lisa. "In the Spirit," *Billboard*, 16 Sept. 1995, 41.

27. Erlewine et al., 141–142.

28. Gersztyn, Bob. "The Blind Boys of Alabama: A Trip Down the Gospel Highway With Clarence Fountain," *TheDoorMagazine*, May/June 2003, 17.

29. Smith, 5.

30. Gill, 14.

31. Hamlin, Jesse. "What Blind Boys See in 'Gospel': Legendary Group Molded Play's Sanctified Sound," *San Francisco Chronicle*, 8 Nov. 1990, E1.

32. Ibid.

33. Burdine, Warren B. "The Gospel Musical and Its Place in the Black American Theatre (1998)," *A Sourcebook of African-American Performance: Plays, People, Movements*, ed. Annemarie Bean (London: Routledge, 1999), 197–198.

34. Hamlin, E1.

35. Floyd, Samuel A., Jr. *The Power of Black Music: Interpreting Its History from Africa to the United States* (New York: Oxford University Press, 1995), 199.

36. Harrington, T15.

37. Aiges, Scott. "Blind Boys and Real World Give Contemporary Voice to Old-Time Gospel," *Billboard*, 7 Apr. 2001, 99.

38. Ibid, 11.

39. Moon, Tom. "Six decades on, gospel group still knows how to find inspiration," *Rolling Stone*, 27 Sept. 2001, 70.

40. Orshoski, Wes. "Real World's Blind Boys: Despite Secular Forays, God's Work Still Job No. 1," *Billboard*, 12 Oct. 2002, 15.

41. Kemp, Mark. "Really really old gospel group makes magic," *Rolling Stone*, 19 Sept. 2002, 99.

42. Gersztyn, 18.

43. Aiges, 99.

44. Floyd, John. "Southern-Fried Soul," *Miami New Times*, 15 July 1999, Music 1.

45. Heilbut, 273.

46. Reynolds, R. J. "AVI Expands into Reissue Biz With Nashboro, Excello Titles," *Billboard*, 10 Dec. 1994, 18.

47. Price, Deborah Evans. "MCA Bows Peacock Imprint for Gospel Releases," *Billboard*, 3 Oct. 1998, 4.

48. http://www.Tyscot.com/about%us.html

49. Darden, Bob. "Dr. Scott sinks his teeth into the gospel music biz," *Billboard*, June 2, 1990, 52A.

50. http://www.airgospel.com/catalog.asp

51. Hulbert, Dan. "When economy tumbles, voices of hope rise toward heaven; if church is sanctuary, this Southern sound is rock of ages," *Atlanta Constitution*, 2 Aug. 1992, N1.

52. http://www.airgospel.com/catalog.asp

53. Blake, John. "Sing Praise: The road to glory runs through Atlanta," *Atlanta Constitution-Journal*, 21 Oct. 2002, 1C.

54. Ward, Ed. "The Lucky Label That Saved Soul," *New York Times*, 2 May 1999, Section 2, 17.

55. Collins, Lisa. "New Heights for Miss. Choir," *Billboard*, 23 Apr. 1994, 1.

56. Ibid.

57. McAdams, Janine. "Malaco Earns Fans Sans Fanfare; Has Been Steady R&B, Gospel Presence," *Billboard*, 2 May 1992, 20.

58. Heilbut, 336.

59. Smith, "The Mississippi Mass Choir: God Gets the Glory!" *Rejoice!* Dec. 1990/Jan. 1991, 13.

60. Collins, "New Heights for Miss. Choir," 1.

61. *Word 1951–1976, Twenty-five years on the growing edge of faith.* Word Records SPL—127/129. Booklet.

62. Carmichael, Ralph. *He's Everything to Me* (Waco: Word Books, 1986), 177.

63. Darden, Bob. "Williams' 'Every Moment' has proved a multiformat hit," *Billboard*, 16 Dec. 1989, 56.

64. Darden, Bob. "Command should put Word in contemporary spotlight," *Bill-board*, 2 Dec. 1989, 55.

65. Green, Al, with Davin Seay. *Take Me to the River* (New York: HarperEntertainment, Inc., 2000), 11–16.

66. Ibid., 188–189.

67. George, Nelson. *The Death of Rhythm & Blues.* (New York: Pantheon Books, 1988), xx.

68. Green, 179.

69. Ibid., 292–297.

70. Werner, Craig. *A Change Is Gonna Come: Music, Race & the Soul of America* (New York: Plume Book/Penguin Press, 199), 182.

71. Ibid., 182–183.

72. Ibid., 183.

73. Green, 333.

74. Ibid., 200.

75. Guralnick, Peter. *Last Train to Memphis: The Rise of Elvis Presley* (Boston: Little, Brown, 1994), 39.

76. Gregory, 120.

77. Ibid., 108.

78. Jones, Steve. "Together the Winans stand," *USA Today*, 26 Apr. 2002, 16D.

79. Winans, CeCe with Renita J. Weems. *On a Positive Note: Her Joyous Faith, Her Life in Music, and Her Everyday Blessings* (New York: Pocket Books, 1999), 34–38.

80. Harrington, Richard. "First Family of Gospel: The Winans, Raised to Sing the Lord's Praise—in Sweet Harmony," *Washington Post*, 5 Apr. 1992, G1.

81. Ibid., G5.

82. Ibid.

83. Jones, 16D.

84. Brock, Ollie. "The Winans: Musicians With a Message," *Rejoice!* Oct./Nov. 1991, 19–21.

85. Winans, 54–60.

86. Ibid., 84–100.

87. Ibid., 116.

88. Ibid., 151.

89. Ibid., 158–161.

90. McAdams, Janie and Lisa Collins. "Gospel Acts Getting Spirited Reception in R&B Arena," *Billboard*, 14 Dec. 1991, 1.

91. Darden, Bob. "On stage and on record, BeBe & CeCe's songs shine," *Billboard*, 16 July 1988, 44.

92. Jones, 16D.

93. Hulbert, N 1.

94. Darden, Bob. "Tramaine Hawkins, Sparrow: a match made in heaven," *Billboard*, 17 Sept. 1988, 67.

95. Harrington, G5.

Chapter 15

1. Wright, Richard. *Native Son* (New York: Harper & Row, 1940), 237–239.

2. Shaw, Arnold. *Honkers and Shouters: The Golden Years of Rhythm and Blues* (New York: Collier Books, 1978), 22.

3. Heilbut, Anthony. *The Gospel Sound: Good News and Bad Times* (New York: Limelight Editions, 1997), 248.

4. Darden, Bob. "Tramaine Hawkins, Sparrow: a match made in heaven," *Billboard*, 17 Sept. 1988, 67.

5. Jones, James T. IV. "Three pick paths off pop's track," *USA Today*, 4 Dec. 1990, 5D.

6. Collins, Lisa. "In the Spirit," *Billboard*, 10 Dec. 1994, 40.

7. No author listed. "Gospel Divas: Traditional and contemporary singers receive unprecedented recognition," *Ebony*, Apr. 1994, 82.

8. Jones, Bobby, Dr. *Touched by God: Black Gospel Greats Share Their Stories of Finding God* (New York: Pocket Books, 1998), 237–239.

9. Ibid., 241–242.

10. Millner, Denene. "Pal's Death was Kee to Salvation: Drug Dealer John Turned to Gospel After He Saw His Best Friend Gunned Down," *New York Daily News*, 9 June 1996, Spotlight, 35.

11. Jones, Bobby, 246.

12. Darden, Bob. "New Life's 'Wait on Him' is an overnight hit for Kee," *Billboard*, Feb. 24, 1990, 45.

13. Collins, Lisa. "In the Spirit," *Billboard*, 18 Sept. 1993, 34.

14. Collins, Lisa. "In the Spirit," *Billboard*, 7 Jan. 1995, 31.

15. Borzillo, Carrie. "John P. Kee & Choir 'Show Up' on Charts: Secular Promos Aid Gospel Success of Verity/Jive Artist," *Billboard*, 25 Feb. 1995, 23.

16. Millner, 35.

17. Jones, Bobby, 247–248.

18. Collins, Lisa. "John P. Kee Shows His 'Strength': His Fourth Set Gets Label's Biggest Gospel Campaign," *Billboard*, 27 Sept. 1997, 18–20.

19. Ibid., 20.

20. No author listed. "Spotlight: The New Life Community Choir Featuring John P. Kee," *Billboard*, 11 Nov. 2000, 29.

21. Jones, Bobby, 249.

22. Ibid., 248.

23. Ibid., 289.

24. Ibid., 291–292.

25. Darden, Bob. "Vickie Winans proves a vital part of gospel's 1st family," *Billboard*, 20 Aug. 1988, 56.

26. Jones, Bobby 292–295.

27. Smith, Edwin. "The Unveiling of Vickie Winans," *Rejoice!*, June/July 1992, 3.

28. McAdams, Janie and Lisa Collins. "Gospel Acts Getting Spirited Reception in R&B Arena," *Billboard*, 14 Dec. 1991, 1.

29. Smith, 3–4.

30. Kinnon, Joy Bennett. "Vickie Winans: At Home with the Gospel Star Who Lost 75 Pounds and Reenergized Her Career," *Ebony*, Aug. 2003, 140.

31. Ibid.

32. Collins, Lisa. "In the Spirit: Williams Wins Five Stellar Awards," *Billboard*, 24 Jan. 2004, 14.

33. Darden, Bob. "Forgiveness is the theme of Vickie Winans' next album," *Billboard*, 27 Aug. 1988, 55.

34. McClurkin, Donnie. *Eternal Victim/Eternal Victor* (Lanham, Maryland: Pneuma Life Publishing, 2001), 11–13.

35. Jeffers, Glenn. "How Donnie McClurkin Overcame Rape, Sexual Abuse and Leukemia Scare to Become a Gospel Music Star," *Ebony*, Aug. 2001, 110–112.

36. Ibid., 114.

37. Waldron, Clarence. "Donnie McClurkin Gospel Music's Hidden Treasure," *Jet*, 6 Jan. 2003, 59.

38. Collins, Lisa. "In the Spirit," *Billboard*, 6 Oct. 2001, 46.

39. Waldron, 59.

40. Ibid., 58.

41. Ibid.

42. Matthews, Kyle. "We Fall Down," BMG Songs, Inc. 1988 (ASCAP).

43. Jones, Bobby, 104–107.

44. Ibid.

45. Ibid., 108–111.

46. Himes, Geoffrey. "Yolanda Adams: Moving Mountains," *Washington Post*, 11 Feb. 2000, Weekend N08.

47. No author listed. "Yolanda Adams preaches new traditionalist word," *USA Today*, 6 Aug. 1992, Life 9D.

48. Jones, Bobby, 111.

49. Ibid.

50. Collins, Lisa. "In the Spirit," *Billboard*, 5 Feb. 1994, 33.

51. Collins, Lisa. "Tribute's Adams Has 'Stellar' Night: Gospel Business Honors Year's Top Acts," *Billboard*, 3 Dec. 1994, 11.

52. Himes, N08.

53. Bream, Jon. "Gospel According to Yolanda Adams is powerful," *Minneapolis Star Tribune*, 5 Mar. 2000, 1F.

54. Millner, Denene. "Adams Keeps the Faith & Has Crossover Smash," *New York Daily News*, 18 Oct. 2000, New York Now 48.

55. Ibid.

56. Vara, Richard. "Gospel on the go: Local Singer on 'Mountain High' with Grammy." *The Houston Chronicle*, 26 Feb. 2000, Religion 1.

57. Harrington, Richard. "Yolanda Adams: Reaching Beyond the Choir," *Washington Post*, 22 June 2001, Weekend T06.

58. Segal, David. "Spin Control: Candidate's Musical Tastes," *Washington Post*, 27 Jan. 2004, Style C01.

59. No author. "Super Bowl XXXVIII: Calendar of Events." *Houston Chronicle*, 30 Jan. 2004, Special Section 15.

60. Jones, Bobby, 117.

61. Himes, Geoffrey. "Yolanda Adams: Moving Mountains," *Washington Post*, 11 Feb. 2000, Weekend N08.

62. Franklin, Kirk and Jim Nelson Black. *Church Boy: Kirk Franklin, An Autobiography* (Nashville: Word Publishing, 1998), 26–29.

63. Ibid., 35–38.

64. Ibid., 63–64.

65. Ibid., 81.

66. Ibid., 82–83.

67. Ibid., 114–119.

68. Ibid., 127–128.

69. Ibid., 131–136.

70. Ibid., 142–144.

71. Ibid., 147–148.

72. Ibid., 149–153.

73. Neal, Mark Anthony. *What the Music Said: Black Popular Music and the Black Public Culture* (New York: Routledge, 1999), 171.

74. Joseph, Mark and Dave Mustaine. *Faith, God and Rock 'n' Roll* (London: Sanctuary Publishing, 2003), 192.

75. Collins, Lisa. "High-Powered Gospel Genre Energized by Both Traditional and Transitional," *Billboard*, 13 Aug. 1994, 33.

76. Borzillo, Carrie. "Franklin, Family Cross Lines: GospoCentric Act Multichart Success," *Billboard*, 25 Feb. 1995, 1, 23.

77. Ibid., 23.

78. Franklin, 165–166.

79. Millner, Denene. "Hallelujah! Gospel Goes Pop: In Its New Incarnation, God's Music Manifests a Righteous Beat—and You Can Dance to It," *New York Daily News*, 13 June 1996, New York Now 47.

80. Franklin, 167–169.

81. Franklin, 1–8.

82. Franklin, 185.

83. Light, Alan, ed. *The Vibe History of Hip Hop* (New York: Three Rivers Press, 1999), 214.

84. Neal, 171.

85. Michaels, Dave. "Medley of Funk, Hip-Hop—God's Property Seeks to Sway Gen-X to Jesus," *Dallas Morning News,* 9 Aug. 1997, Religion A10.

86. Ibid.

87. No author listed. "Hottest Gospel Artists: African-American artists take music to a higher level," *Ebony,* Aug., 1998, 74.

88. Soeder, John. "However the Spirit Moves Him: Kirk Franklin Combines Gospel and Hip-Hop to Deliver God's Message, To the Dismay of Some Old-School Devotees," *Seattle Times,* 11 Feb. 1999, G4.

89. Ibid.

90. Cooper, Carol. "With God on Our Side," *Village Voice,* Apr. 15, 2003, 65.

91. Flores, Raul A. "Salvation Through Song: Gospel Stars Pack Houses with Rousing Event," *San Antonio Express-News,* 7 Mar. 2003, Weekend 11H.

92. Soeder, G4.

93. Orlean, Susan. "Devotion Road: What is it like to sing for Jesus in American today? The life is almost the same as it was fifty years ago—when the Jackson Southernaires first hit the gospel highway," *New Yorker,* 17 Apr. 1995, 65–71.

94. Collins, Lisa. "Gospel Catalog: A Wealth of Reissued Oldies Testifies to the Market's Enduring Value," *Billboard,* 7 June 2003, 27.

95. Warren, Gwendolyn Sims. *Ev'ry Time I Feel the Spirit* (New York: Henry Holt and Company, 1998), 269.

96. Ibid., 271.

97. Boyer, Horace Clarence. "Roberta Martin: Inventor of Modern Gospel Music," *We'll Understand It Better By and By*, ed. Bernice Johnson Reagon (Washington, D.C.: Smithsonian Institution Press, 1992), 276.

98. Jones, Bobby, 228.

99. Humphrey, Mark A. "Holy Blues: The Gospel Tradition," *Nothing But the Blues: The Music and the Musicians*, ed. Lawrence Cohn (New York: Abbeville Press, 1993), 147.

100. Pareles, Jon. "At Gospel Festival, Music Inspired by Hope," *New York Times,* 11 Nov. 1988, C21.

101. Moyers, Bill. *Amazing Grace with Bill Moyers.* Directed by Elena Mannes. 88 minutes. Alexandria, VA: Public Affairs Television, Inc. PBS Video 1990.

102. *Fried Green Tomatoes.* Directed by Jon Avnet. 2 hours 10 minutes. Universal City, CA: MCA/Universal Pictures, 1992.

103. Marsalis, Wynton. *In This House/On This Morning.* Sony Records 1994.

104. Harrington, Richard. "Amazingly Graced: The Lord Was Kind to Marion Williams, And Did She Ever Return the Favor," *Washington Post,* 10 July 1994, G4.

105. Heilbut, Anthony. *The Gospel Sound: Good News and Bad Times* (New York: Limelight Editions, 1997), 222.

106. Mellers, Wilfred. *Angels of the Night: Popular Females Singers of Our Time.* (Oxford, U.K.: Basil Blackwell, Inc., 1986), 5.

107. Jeffers, Glenn. "Why Gospel Music Is So Hot," *Ebony,* July 2002, 114.

108. Ibid.

109. Collins, Lisa. "Gospel Catalog: A Wealth of Reissued Oldies Testifies to the Market's Enduring Value," *Billboard,* 7 June 2003, 27.

Index